Edited by **Michael N Huhns**
Microelectronics and Computer Technology Corporation
Austin, Texas

Distributed
Artificial Intelligence

Pitman, London

Morgan Kaufmann Publishers, Inc., Los Altos, California

PITMAN PUBLISHING
128 Long Acre, London WC2E 9AN

First published 1987

Available in the Western Hemisphere from
MORGAN KAUFMANN PUBLISHERS, INC.,
95 First Street, Los Altos, California 94022

ISSN 0268-7526

British Library Cataloguing in Publication Data
Distributed artificial intelligence.—
    (Research notes in artificial intelligence,
    ISSN 0268-7526)
    1. Artificial intelligence—Data
processing   2. Electronic data processing
—Distributed processing
    I. Huhns, Michael N.   II. Series
    006.3   Q336

ISBN 0-273-08778-9

Library of Congress Cataloging in Publication Data
Huhns, Michael N.
    Distributed artificial intelligence.

    (Research notes in artificial intelligence)
    Bibliography: p.
    Includes index.
    1. Artificial intelligence.   2. Electronic data
processing—Distributed processing.3. Problem
solving—Data processing.   I. Title.   II. Series:
Research notes in artificial intelligence (London,
England)
Q335.H77   1987   006.3   86-33259
ISBN 0-934613-38-9

Reproduced and printed by photolithography
in Great Britain by Biddles Ltd, Guildford

CONTENTS

Foreword

This monograph presents a collection of papers describing the current state of research in distributed artificial intelligence (DAI). DAI is concerned with the cooperative solution of problems by a decentralized group of agents. The agents may range from simple processing elements to complex entities exhibiting rational behavior. The problem solving is cooperative in that mutual sharing of information is necessary to allow the group as a whole to produce a solution. The group of agents is decentralized in that both control and data are logically and often geographically distributed. The papers describe architectures and languages for achieving cooperative problem solving in a distributed environment, and include several successful applications of distributed artificial intelligence in manufacturing, information retrieval, and distributed sensing.

Appropriateness of DAI

As the first available text on distributed artificial intelligence, this book is intended to fulfill several needs. For researchers, the research papers and descriptions of applications are representative of contemporary trends in distributed artificial intelligence, and should spur further research. For system developers, the applications delineate some of the possibilities for utilizing DAI. For students in artificial intelligence and related disciplines, this book may serve as the primary text for a course on DAI or as a supplementary text for a course in artificial intelligence. A preliminary version of the book has already been used successfully as a text for an industrial short course and for a graduate seminar on DAI. Finally, this book is intended as a reference for students and researchers in other disciplines, such as psychology, philosophy, robotics, and distributed computing, who wish to understand the issues of DAI.

There are five primary reasons why one would want to utilize and study DAI.

1. DAI can provide insights and understanding about interactions among humans, who organize themselves into various groups, committees, and societies in order to solve problems.

2. DAI can provide a means for interconnecting multiple expert systems that have different, but possibly overlapping expertise, thereby enabling the solution of problems whose domains are outside that of any one expert system.

3. DAI can potentially solve problems that are too large for a centralized system, because of resource limitations induced by a given level of technology. Limiting factors such as communication bandwidths, computing speed, and reliability result in classes of problems that can be solved only by a distributed system.

4. DAI can potentially provide a solution to a current limitation of knowledge engineering: the use of only one expert. If there are several experts, or several nonexperts that together have the ability of an expert, there is no established way to use them to engineer a successful system.

5. DAI is the most appropriate solution when the problem itself is inherently distributed, such as in distributed sensor nets and distributed information retrieval.

Distributed artificial intelligence also provides the next step beyond current expert systems. It suggests the following approach to their development: build a separate subsystem for each problem domain and based on the ability of each expert, and then make these subsystems cooperate. This approach potentially has the following additional advantages:

1. Modularity: The complexity of an expert system increases rapidly as the size of its knowledge base increases. Partitioning the system into N subsystems reduces the complexity by significantly more than a factor of N. The resultant system is easier to develop, test, and maintain.

2. Speed: The subsystems can operate in parallel.

3. Reliability: The system can continue to operate even if part of it fails.

4. Knowledge acquisition: It is easier to find experts in narrow domains. Also, many problem domains are already partitioned or hierarchical—why not take advantage of this?

5. Reusability: A small, independent expert system could be a part of *many* distributed expert systems—its expertise would not have to be reimplemented for each.

Research Directions in DAI

Current research in DAI can be characterized and understood in the context of the following paradigm: there is a collection of agents (logically-distinct processing elements) which are attempting to solve a problem. Although there are identifiable global states and goals of the problem-solving, each agent has only a partial and inexact view of these.[1] Each agent attempts to recognize, predict, and influence the global state such that its local view of the goals is satisfied. The methods it has available are to *compute* solutions to subproblems, which are in general interdependent, and to *communicate* results, tasks, goals, estimates of the problem-solving state, etc. Research is underway on all aspects of this paradigm and a cross-section of it—organized into the three parts Theoretical Issues, Architectures and Languages, and Applications and Examples—is presented in this book.

The first part, Theoretical Issues, addresses ways to develop 1) control abstractions that efficiently guide problem-solving, 2) communication abstractions that yield cooperation, and 3) description abstractions that result in effective organizational structure. In Chapter 1, Ginsberg describes principles of rationality by which agents solving interdependent subproblems can achieve their goals without communicating explicit control information among themselves. Another way in which an agent can achieve its goals is to influence a future global state by reorganizing and managing other agents: these then work to achieve the global state desired by the first. This is sometimes done by transmitting tasks, and possibly the knowledge needed to solve them, to the other agents. These organizational issues are addressed in the paper by Durfee *et al.* in Chapter 2; further, Chapter 3 presents a language for describing, forming, and controlling organizations of agents.

The second part of this book describes architectures for developing and testing DAI systems. Bisiani *et al.*, Gasser *et al.*, and Green have each constructed generic environments within which DAI systems can be developed (Chapters 4–6). These are medium-scale systems which could involve up to several hundred agents. By contrast, the system described by Shastri in Chapter 7 potentially could utilize the processing power of thousands of agents in a connectionist encoding of the inheritance and categorization features of semantic nets. In Chapter 8, Sridharan presents a way in which various algorithms can be executed efficiently and naturally on large collections of processors.

The applications described in the third part of the book, Chapters 9–11, comprise manufacturing, office automation, and man-machine interactions. In addition, the annotated bibliography in Chapter 12 should provide a useful guide to the remainder of the

---

[1]The global state may not be determinate if the distributed system is asynchronous.

field.

To enable individual research efforts (like those described in this book) to be related to the field as a whole, participants at the Sixth Workshop on DAI identified eight dimensions by which DAI systems could be classified.[2] A version of these dimensions and the attributes that define a spectrum of possible values for each dimension are shown in the following table:

Table 1: Dimensions for Categorizing DAI Systems

Dimension	Spectrum of Values
System Model	Individual .. . . Committee . . . . Society
Grain	Fine . . . . Medium . . . . Coarse
System Scale	Small . . . . Medium . . . . Large
Agent Dynamism	Fixed . . . . Programmable . . . Teachable . . . . Autodidactic
Agent Autonomy	Controlled .. . . Interdependent . . . . Independent
Agent Resources	Restricted .. . . Ample
Agent Interactions	Simple . . . . Complex
Result Formation	By Synthesis . . . . By Decomposition

In this table, *grain* is the level of decomposition of the problem, *system model* refers to the number of agents used to solve the problem, and *system scale* refers to the number of computing elements used to implement the agents. Some of the attributes apply to an entire DAI system, while the rest are used to characterize the individual agents in the system. Classifying the papers in this volume according to these dimensions yields the following results:

Table 2: Categorizing the DAI Systems in this Book

Dimension	Spectrum of Values						
System Model	7	1	11	2,3,4,5,6,9,10			
Grain	7		2,3,8,9			10,4,5,6,1,11	
System Scale	1	2,3,4,5,10		6,8,9,11			7
Agent Dynamism	8	7,11			1	2,9,10	
Agent Autonomy	8			2,3,11		1,7,9,10	
Agent Resources	7,10,11	2,3		1,9			
Agent Interactions	7	1,9,10				2,3,4,5,6,11	
Result Formation	2,3,6,7,9,11			1			10

The numbers in the table refer to chapters in this book where the DAI systems are described.

Not all dimensions are relevant to all systems. In particular, some chapters describe general-purpose architectures and languages for DAI that would be characterized by a

---

[2]N. S. Sridharan, "Report on the 1986 Workshop on Distributed Artificial Intelligence," to appear in *AI Magazine*, 1987.

range of possible attribute values for some of the dimensions. However, the table shows the broad coverage of DAI which this book presents.

Acknowledgements

I would like to thank Michael Genesereth and Matthew Ginsberg for organizing the Fifth Workshop on Distributed Artificial Intelligence, held at Sea Ranch, California in December 1985. The papers in this monograph were first presented there, and the format of this book is based on their collection and categorization of these papers. The papers themselves represent the contributions of some of the leading researchers in the field. I am grateful to Microelectronics and Computer Technology Corporation for providing the environment and support for artificial intelligence research which made this compilation possible. I would also like to thank Dr. N. S. Sridharan for encouraging and inspiring me to edit this monograph.

—*Michael N. Huhns*

Part I

Theoretical Issues

Chapter 1

Decision Procedures

Matthew L. Ginsberg

Abstract

Distributed artificial intelligence is the study of how a group of individual intelligent agents can combine to solve a difficult global problem; the usual approach is to split the original problem into simpler ones and to attack each of these independently. This paper discusses in very general terms the problems which arise if the subproblems are *not* independent, but instead interrelate in some way. We are led to a single assumption, which we call *common rationality*, that is provably optimal (in a formal sense) and which enables us to characterize precisely the communication needs of the participants in multiagent interactions. An example of a distributed computation using these ideas is presented.

1.1 Introduction

The thrust of research in distributed artificial intelligence (DAI) is the investigation of the possibility of solving a difficult problem by presenting each of a variety of machines with simpler parts of it.

The approach that has been taken has been to consider the problem of dividing the original problem: what subtasks should be pursued at any given time? To which available machine should a given subtask be assigned? The question of how the individual machines should go about solving their subproblems has been left to the non-distributed AI community (or perhaps to a recursive application of DAI techniques).

The assumption underlying this approach—that each of the agents involved in the solution of the subproblems can proceed independently of the others—has recently been called into question [2,3,6,7,10]. It has been realized that, in a world of limited resources,

3

it is inappropriate to dedicate a substantial fraction of those resources to each processor. The increasing attractiveness of parallel architectures in which processors share memory is an example of this: memory is a scarce resource.

Automated factories must inevitably encounter similar difficulties. Are the robots working in such factories to be given distinct bins of component parts, and nonoverlapping regions in which to work or to travel from one area of the factory to another? It seems unlikely.

My intention in this paper is to discuss these issues at a very basic (i.e., formal) level. I will be interested in situations where:

1. A global goal has been replaced by a variety of local ones, each pursued by an individual agent or process, and

2. The actions of the individual agents may interact, in that success or failure for one such agent may be partially or wholly contingent upon an action taken by another.

The first of these is a massive disclaimer. I will *not* be concerned with the usual problem of dividing the global goal, but will assume that this has already been done. My intention is merely to remove the constraint that the subproblems or subagents cannot interact; the problem of subdividing problems in the absence of this constraint is outside the intended scope of this paper.

The second remark above explicitly allows for "partial" success or failure—corresponding, for example, to the speed with which a given subgoal is achieved.

In the case where the agents do not interact, we will assume that each knows enough to evaluate the results of its possible actions. For agent i, this evaluation will be incorporated in a payoff function p which assigns to any alternative m the value of that course of action. Thus if M represents the set of all of i's possible courses of action, p is simply a function

$$p : M \longrightarrow \mathbb{R}. \tag{1.1}$$

That the range of p is $\mathbb{R}$ as opposed to $\{0, 1\}$ reflects our allowing for a varying degree of success or failure.

Determining the function p is a task that lies squarely within the province of non-distributed AI research. Given such a function, selecting the alternative m which maximizes $p(m)$ is straightforward.

In the absence of interaction, the problems of the individual agents would now be solved. If the success or failure of some agent depends on actions taken by another, however, this is not the case: the function p in Equation 1.1 will have as its domain the set of actions available to *all* of the agents, as opposed to a single one.

4

This sort of problem has been discussed extensively by game theorists. They do, however, generally make the assumption that the agents have common knowledge of each others' payoff functions. This need not be valid in an AI setting.

We will address this problem in due course; our basic view is that the fundamental role of communication between interacting intelligent agents is to establish an agreed payoff function as described in the last paragraph. Before turning to this, let us examine in an informal way some situations in which interaction is important.

The first is one which we will refer to as *coordination*. Suppose that two robots, one in Boston and the other in Palo Alto, decide to meet in Pittsburgh to build a widget. Now, building a widget is a complicated procedure unless you happen to have both a zazzyfrax and a borogove, although either in isolation is useless. Zazzyfraxen are available only in New York, and borogoves only in San Francisco; should the robots stop on their travels to acquire their respective components?

The answer is clearly that they should; note, however, that for either robot to do so involves a great many assumptions about the other robot. The Palo Alto robot needs not only to know about the availability of zazzyfraxen in New York—he must also assume that the Boston robot knows about the borogoves in San Francisco, *and* that the Boston robot knows the Palo Alto robot knows about the zazzyfraxen, and so on. Halpern and Moses [8] have described this sort of situation as *common knowledge*.

As we remarked earlier, common knowledge of this sort is presumed by the game theorists in their assumption of common knowledge of the payoff function. But even this is not enough to ensure coordination of the robots' actions: the Palo Alto robot must assume that the Boston robot is sensible enough to stop in New York, which implies that the Boston robot knows *he* is sensible enough to stop in San Francisco, and so on. So even common knowledge of the payoff function is not enough: some sort of common knowledge of the methods by which the robots select their actions is also required.

The game theorists deal with this last requirement by fiat, assuming [13] that any "rational" agents will coordinate their actions in such a situation. This seems unnecessarily *ad hoc*, and also appears to conflict with the philosophy that each agent strives to achieve a purely local goal.

Our robots somehow overcome these difficulties, starting a successful widget business in Pittsburgh. At some point, however, their zazzyfrax breaks, and they arrange with the New York factory to exchange five widgets for a replacement. Since the robots need the zazzyfrax as quickly as possible and the New York factory is equally anxious to get its widgets, it is decided that each group will ship their contribution to the exchange immediately, trusting the other to act similarly.

5

In the absence of legal sanctions, why should either agent ship the goods? The result of this, however, is for there to be no transaction—an outcome worse for *both* agents than if they had acted as agreed.

The problem is one of *cooperation*; the scenario we have presented is Hofstadter's [9] reformulation of the well-known *prisoner's dilemma*.

The game theorists have no answer in this case. Not only does the pursuit of a local goal offer no incentive for cooperation, it actively *discourages* it. The robots' business, having become too dependent on the zazzyfrax technology, goes bankrupt.

1.2 Solutions to Problems of Interaction

Our example may have been far-fetched, but the problems are real. The coordination problem has straightforward analogs in automated factories, as does the cooperation one: why should one robot or agent stop to arrange delivery of a part required by another when doing so does not further its own local ambitions?

A variety of solutions has been proposed. The one which has received the most attention in the AI literature [2,3,12] has been to ensure that the agent responsible for dividing the original problem into more manageable smaller ones does so in a way which ensures that the subtasks do not interact. We have already remarked that this may be overly constraining in many situations.

It has also been suggested that the agents communicate their intentions to one another. Rosenschein [15] has demonstrated, however, that there is no reason for independent agents to communicate honestly. Since a statement of the form, "I intend to do *x*," is virtually unprovable, the value of such communication is extremely limited. Indeed, it was the non-binding nature of communication that led to the downfall of the entreprenuerial robots of the last section. Rosenschein and Genesereth [14] have suggested remedying this by making the commitments binding, but it is not clear how this can be enforced.

The game theorists use different approaches. We have already remarked upon their adoption of a definition of rationality that considers coordinated action; it unfortunately does not seem possible to formalize this in a way that is clearly consistent with the "local utility maximization" that is generally assumed. The game theorists themselves have remarked upon this [11].

Cooperation is harder to come by than is coordination. The game theorists achieve it by assuming there is some facility for retribution; this amounts to assuming that the given interaction is only one of a series. Axelrod [1] has shown that cooperation can evolve under these assumptions.

6

Again, the view that an agent's actions should be governed by a concern for its future welfare is not in keeping with the idea that such an agent should act to maximize a purely local payoff. We have similar objections to schemes that include an *ad hoc* "altruism factor" in the payoff function.

1.3 Notation

In order to formalize a solution to these difficulties, we need first to formalize the problem. We begin by generalizing (1). There, for each agent i, we had a function

$$p_i : M_i \longrightarrow \mathbb{R},$$

where M_i is the (assumed finite) set of allowable "moves" for player i. In the interactive case, this generalizes to a function

$$p_i : \prod_{i \in P} M_i \longrightarrow \mathbb{R}, \tag{1.2}$$

where P is the set of all players involved in the interaction and p_i assigns to player i his "payoff" if a particular joint move is made by the players in P.

For $S \subset P$, we will denote $P - S$ by $\bar{S}$; we will also write simply i instead of $\{i\}$ where no confusion is possible. (Thus $\bar{i} = P - \{i\}$, for example.) We also write M_S for $\prod_{i \in S} M_i$, so that the individual payoff functions in Equation 1.2 become

$$p_i : M_P \longrightarrow \mathbb{R}.$$

The various p_i can be collected into a single *payoff function*

$$p : P \times M_P \longrightarrow \mathbb{R}. \tag{1.3}$$

We will identify a game or interaction g with the associated payoff function as in Equation 1.3.

We will denote by m_S an element of M_S; this is a collective move for the players in S. To $m_S \in M_S$ and $m_{\bar{S}} \in M_{\bar{S}}$ correspond an element $\vec{m}$ of M_P. The payoff function in Equation 1.3 can now be interpreted by noting that for $(i, \vec{m}) \in P \times M_P$, $p(i, \vec{m})$ is the payoff to player i if the joint move $\vec{m}$ is made. We can now see that a game is *noninteractive* if and only if it satisfies:

$$m_i = n_i \quad \Rightarrow \quad p(i, \vec{m}) = p(i, \vec{n});$$

in other words, the payoff to each player depends only on that player's action.

In cases where only two agents are interacting, we will use a matrix notation to represent the payoff function. Here is an example:

	C	D
A	3 1	2
B	2 5	0 1

The first player selects one of the two rows by choosing A or B; the second selects one of the columns by choosing C or D. The payoffs correspond to the numbers in the associated boxes: if move AC is selected, for example, the row player above would receive a payoff of 3 while the column player would receive 1. The single entry "2" in the AD position corresponds to an identical payoff of 2 for both players.

Here is the payoff function for a noninteractive game:

	C	D
A	3 5	3 1
B	1 5	1

Here is one requiring coordination:

	C	D
A	7	4
B	5	6

Games such as this, where one outcome (AC above) is preferred by all players to any other, are referred to as "no-conflict games" in the game theory literature [13].

Finally, here is the prisoner's dilemma. Each agent can "cooperate" (C) or "defect" (D):

	C	D
C	3 3	0 5
D	5 0	1

Independent of the other's action, each agent is better off defecting than cooperating. Unfortunately, the payoff resulting from mutual defection is worse for *both* agents than that corresponding to mutual cooperation.

1.4 Rationality

Game theory literature generally examines single games and considers what it means for specific moves in these games to be rational. "Rational" here is generally only defined informally, having to do with maximizing the player's return under some ill-defined assumptions.

It seems to me that, rather than the particular move being rational (or not), it is the *analysis leading to the move* which should be examined. So I will try to develop a framework that lets me discuss these analyses rather than simply the moves they select.

Let P be a fixed group of players. Given a game g, let us denote by g_i the moves for i which are legal in g. We also denote the (assumed finite) set of all games by G, and take G_i to be $\bigcup_{g \in G} g_i$, so that G_i is the collection of all moves for i which are legal in *some* game. We will assume throughout that any game obtained by permuting the players in some particular game $g \in G$ is also in G, so that $G_i = G_j$ for all i and j.

We now define a *decision procedure* for player i to be a function

$$D_i : G \longrightarrow G_i$$

such that $D_i(g) \in g_i$ for all $g \in G$. In other words, D_i assigns to each game a specific legal move for i in that game and therefore encodes the process whereby i selects his move. For a fixed group S of players, we denote $\prod_{i \in S} D_i$ by D_S. Thus

$$D_S(g) = \prod_{i \in S} D_i(g);$$

D_S is the "collective" decision procedure used by the players in S to select a joint move. For $S \subset S'$, we will denote by π_S the projection operator from $D_{S'}$ to D_S.

We turn next to the issue of comparing decision procedures among various players. When we say, "the other agents will behave as I do," for example, we mean not that the other players' behavior is identical to our own given the present circumstances, but that they would act similarly *were they to find themselves in our current situation*.

This notion depends on that of "permuting" the players in a game in order to examine that game from another player's point of view. In order to capture this idea, suppose that there are n players in P, and denote by S_n the group of permutations on an n-element set. Given a game with payoff function p, and a fixed permutation $\sigma \in S_n$, we can define a permuted game p_σ with payoff function given by

$$p_\sigma(\sigma(i), \sigma(\vec{m})) = p(i, \vec{m}).$$

Since we are identifying games and payoff functions, it follows from this that a permutation σ induces a mapping (also to be denoted σ) from games to games.

To get a feel for this, we might say that a decision procedure C_i is *unbiased* if $C_i(g) = C_i(\sigma(g))$ whenever $\sigma(i) = i$. In other words, a shuffling of the other players in the game does not affect i's choice of action; he is uniform in his treatment of them.

Slightly more generally, we might fix $S \subset P$ and assume that $\sigma C_S(g) = C_S(\sigma(g))$ whenever $\sigma(S) = S$. The implication of this is not only that the group S is unbiased toward the remaining players in $\bar{S}$, but also that the behaviors of the individuals within the group are identical in the above sense.

Suppose now that player i uses his decision procedure D_i to select a move m_i in a game g, and that p is the payoff function associated with this game. The other players in the game use their collective decision procedure $D_{\bar{i}}$ to select a move $m_{\bar{i}}$ and the resulting payoff to i is therefore

$$pay(i, D_P, g) = p(i, \vec{m}). \tag{1.4}$$

The function *pay* here gives the payoff to i in the game g if he uses the decision procedure D_i; note that the appearance of D_P in Equation 1.4 means that *pay* is a function of all of the D_j's, and not just D_i.

If we knew the expected distribution of games, we could amalgamate Equation 1.4 over all games to get the expected payoff corresponding to the decision procedure D_i generally. Although this is an extremely strong assumption, we will have use of it, so here goes: We need a *density function* ρ_i which assigns to each game $g \in G$ its likelihood of occurring; $\sum_{g \in G} \rho_i(g) = 1$. The expected payoff corresponding to D_i is now given by

$$pay(i, D_P) = \sum_{g \in G} \rho_i(g) pay(i, D_P, g). \tag{1.5}$$

Again, this has dependence on the decision procedures of the other players as well.

Under these strong assumptions, it is clear that rationality corresponds to maximizing Equation 1.5. The idea we want to capture is that a decision procedure is *irrational* if it results in a payoff that is provably suboptimal—recall, though, that the dependence of Equation 1.5 on $D_{\bar{i}}$ leads to a potential ambiguity in a definition such as that D_i is irrational if there exists another decision procedure C_i such that

$$pay(i, D_P) < pay(i, C_P). \tag{1.6}$$

We will resolve this ambiguity by quantifying over the $C_{\bar{i}}$ and $D_{\bar{i}}$ which appear implicitly in the above expression, but in doing so, want to capture the notion that our analysis should proceed, not by immediately selecting some decision procedure as rational, but by gradually eliminating decision procedures that are *irrational*. We will also assume the existence of some predicate $allowed(C_P, D_P)$; intuitively, $allowed(C_P, D_P)$ if C_P and D_P are decision procedures we would like to include in the quantification of Equation 1.6.

10

Given a collection D of joint decision procedures, and a player $i \in P$, we define a *global irrationality operator* for i, to be denoted I_i, taking $I_i(D)$ to be the set of all decision procedures D_i such that there exists a C_i in $\pi_i(D)$ such that, for all C_P and D_P with $allowed(C_P, D_P)$, if $\pi_i(D_P) = D_i$ and $\pi_i(C_P) = C_i$, then

$$pay(i, D_P) < pay(i, C_P). \tag{1.7}$$

Intuitively, if we have constrained the decision procedures of the players involved in such a way as to determine that the joint decision procedure should lie in D, the decision procedure D_i is irrational for i if there exists another decision procedure C_i which is better for any choice of decision procedures $C_{\bar{i}}$ and $D_{\bar{i}}$ allowed within D.

We now define a *global rationality operator* R by

$$R(D) \equiv D - \bigcup_{j \in P} \pi_j^{-1}[I_j(D)].$$

This is the collection of decision procedures which are left after removing all of those which are in the range of the various irrationality operators.

Lemma 1.1 *For any collection D of decision procedures, $\lim_{n \to \infty} R^n(D)$ exists.*

Proof. We have assumed that the collection of moves in any game and the collection of all games are both finite, so D is finite. Since $R(D') \subset D'$ for any collection D' of decision procedures, there must exist some integer n with $R^{n+1}(D) = R^n(D)$, and the conclusion follows. □

We now let $\mathbb{D}$ be the collection of all joint decision procedures for the players in P, and define a decision procedure to be *globally rational* if it is a member of $R^\infty(\mathbb{D})$ as above. A decision procedure D_i for player i will be globally rational if and only if it is in $\pi_i(R^\infty(\mathbb{D}))$; a single move m_i will be (globally) rational in a game g if there is a (globally) rational decision procedure D_i with $D_i(g) = m_i$.

In general, of course, the density function ρ_i will not be known; we will therefore need a notion of rationality depending only upon the local payoffs appearing in Equation 1.4. To this end, we repeat the construction above, defining a *uniform irrationality operator* I_i^u, with $I_i^u(D)$ being the set of all decision procedures D_i such that there exists a C_i in $\pi_i(D)$ such that, for all C_P and D_P with $allowed(C_P, D_P)$, if $\pi_i(D_P) = D_i$ and $\pi_i(C_P) = C_i$, then

$$pay(i, D_P, g) \leq pay(i, C_P, g) \tag{1.8}$$

for all games g, with the inequality being strict in at least one case. In other words, a decision procedure is uniformly irrational if there is another decision procedure which is

11

better in some specific game, and no worse in all others. We will occasionally refer to a uniformly rational decision procedure simply as *rational*.

Note that we do *not* call a decision procedure irrational merely because it does not achieve an optimal payoff in *every* game: it is only if a better payoff could be achieved in some game *without reducing the payoffs in other games* that the definition applies.

Lemma 1.2 *Any globally rational decision procedure is uniformly rational.*

Proof. For any allowed decision procedures C_P and D_P, summing Equation 1.8 over all games reproduces Equation 1.7, so that $I_i^u(D) \subset I_i(D)$ for all collections D of decision procedures. The conclusion follows. □

The results of the next section deal with conditions which must be satisfied by any uniformly rational decision procedure. The point of the lemma is that a globally rational decision procedure must meet these requirements as well.

The nature of the definitions of rationality depends, of course, on the *allowed* predicate. If, for example, we knew the decision procedures of the other players, we could restrict *allowed* to these decision procedures, so that our decision procedure could be easily determined by the definition of uniform rationality (Equation 1.8). Essentially, we would be moving with complete knowledge of the other players' choices of action.

In practice, of course, this will not be the case, and *allowed* will hold for a variety of decision procedures other than the ones the other players are actually using. This will lead to some freedom in our own (presumed rational) choice of decision procedure; our interest will be in determining the nature and amount of this freedom given a variety of (incomplete) assumptions regarding the decision procedures of the other players or agents.

At this point, we have made no such assumptions at all. The fact that *allowed* is a relation on *two* decision procedures, for example, allows us to consider situations where the decision procedures of the other agents are not independent of our own. In fact, the ability to drop this independence assumption is the pragmatic reason we are working not with the moves themselves, but with the analyses which lead to them. By working in this fashion, it is possible to assume that the agents have knowledge of each others' strategies without being led to the circular arguments that otherwise pervade this sort of analysis.

As an example, consider the following well-known "paradox": an alien approaches you with two envelopes, one marked "$\$$" and the other "$\not c$". The first envelope contains some number of dollars, and the other the same number of cents. The alien is prepared to give you the contents of either envelope.

The catch is that the alien, who is omniscient, is aware of the choice you will make. In an attempt to discourage greed on your part, he has decided to put one unit of currency in the envelopes if you will pick "$", but one thousand units if you will pick "¢". Bearing in mind that the alien has decided upon the contents of the envelopes *before* you pick one, which should you select? (If this example is insufficiently compelling for an AI audience, multiply all of the figures by a million.)

Here are the payoffs for this game; the alien's payoffs simply reflect his desire to teach you the desired lesson. (He can make all the money he needs in the stock market, anyway.)

	1000	1
$	0 1000.	1 1.
¢	1 10.	0 0.01

Since the payoff for $ is greater than that for ¢ for either of the alien's options, any of the conventional game-theoretic analyses will lead us to select the dollar envelope, and we will presumably receive only $1 as a result.

The decision procedure paradigm is flexible enough to handle this situation. If we are player 1 and the alien is player 2, we have that the only allowed D_2 is:

$$D_2(g) = \begin{cases} 1000, & \text{if } D_1(g) = ¢, \text{ and} \\ 1, & \text{if } D_1(g) = \$. \end{cases} \tag{1.9}$$

Inserting this into Equation 1.4 gives $pay(1, ¢, g) = 10$ and $pay(1, \$, g) = 1$, allowing us to conclude from Equation 1.8 that it is indeed irrational to pick $ in this game.

In no way have we avoided the paradox of the alien's omniscience; we have merely found a way to *describe* this omniscience in the decision procedure Equation 1.9. We will see in the next section that the "case analysis" argument which would have led us to select $ in the above game is valid if the decision procedures of the various players are independent.

It is a small step from the scenario we have described to one with a more serious difficulty. Suppose that player 1 in the above game, instead of being you or I, is another omniscient alien. The new alien, in an attempt to encourage the original one to be more cautious with its money, decides to select $ if the offering alien puts one thousand units of currency in the envelopes, and to select ¢ otherwise. What happens?

Here are the payoffs for the new game:

	1000	1
$	0 1	1 0
¢	1 0	0 1

The situation appears to be circular; in fact the descriptions of the two aliens are inconsistent. The decision procedure of the new alien is supposedly given by:

$$D_1(g) = \begin{cases} \text{¢}, & \text{if } D_2(g) = 1, \text{ and} \\ \text{\$}, & \text{if } D_2(g) = 1000. \end{cases}$$

This in in clear conflict with Equation 1.9, in that there are no allowed C_P or D_P for this game. (Is this example an argument for monotheism?)

The specific assumptions regarding the decision procedures of the other agents which will interest us are the following:

Common rationality: $allowed(C_P, D_P)$ implies $\sigma C_P(g) = C_P(\sigma(g))$ for all games $g \in G$ and $\sigma \in S_n$, and similarly for D_P. This assumption (which cannot be described in the conventional game-theoretic formalism) is particularly appropriate to an AI setting; it would be straightforward to equip potentially interacting agents with matching decision procedures. We will see in section 1.6 that it is in fact sufficient to equip the agents with only the common rationality *assumption* (theorem 1.8) and also that this is, at least in some sense, a good idea (theorem 1.9).

Independent rationality: $allowed(C_P, D_P)$ implies $C_{\bar{\imath}} = D_{\bar{\imath}}$. This amounts to agent i's assuming that his decision procedure does not influence the others. This assumption is generally made in the game theory literature, and is equivalent to assuming that the moves of the other players are fixed in advance (since their decision procedures are), although the exact nature of these moves remains unknown.

1.5   Uniform Rationality

In this section we investigate the consequences of our definitions of rationality. We will assume throughout that g is some fixed game with payoff function p.

Theorem 1.3 (Case analysis) *Assuming independent rationality, if for some moves c_i and d_i, for all rational $m_{\bar{\imath}}$,*

$$p(i, d_i \times m_{\bar{\imath}}) < p(i, c_i \times m_{\bar{\imath}}),$$

then d_i is not rational in g.

14

Proof. Suppose that $D_i(g) = d_i$, and let C_i be the decision procedure given by

$$C_i(g') = \begin{cases} D_i(g'), & \text{if } g' \neq g; \\ c_i, & \text{if } g' = g. \end{cases}$$

For any allowed $C_{\bar{\imath}}$ and $D_{\bar{\imath}}$, $C_{\bar{\imath}} = D_{\bar{\imath}}$; it follows that if we set $m_{\bar{\imath}} = C_{\bar{\imath}}(g) = D_{\bar{\imath}}(g)$,

$$pay(i, D_P, g) = p(i, d_i \times m_{\bar{\imath}}) < p(i, c_i \times m_{\bar{\imath}}) = pay(i, C_P, g),$$

while $pay(i, D_P, g') = pay(i, C_P, g')$ for $g' \neq g$, so that the decision procedure D_i is irrational.   □

It is an invalid application of this theorem that led us to choose \$ in the paradox of the last section. Of course, the formulation of the interaction there is such as to indicate clearly that the independent rationality assumption does *not* hold.

The dependence of the proof on the independent rationality assumption lies in part in the statement that $pay(i, D_P, g') = pay(i, C_P, g')$ for $g' \neq g$. In order to conclude this, we needed to know that the other agents would not change their actions in g' in response to our selecting the move c_i in g.

If this result allows us to conclude that there is a unique rational move in some game g, this is known as the *solution in the complete weak sense* in the game theory literature.

The consequences of case analysis are quite well known. Consider the example used to introduce our payoff matrix notation:

	C	D
A 3	1	2
B 2	5	1 0

Independent of the column player's choice, the row player will be better off if he makes move A, since his payoff will be 3 as opposed to 2 if the other player selects C, and 2 as opposed to 0 if D is chosen. Case analysis therefore implies that A is the only rational move for the row player in this game.

The column player can now reason that the row player can be counted on to make move A, and will therefore respond with D (receiving a payoff of 2 instead of 1).

The joint move AD is Pareto suboptimal, however, in that the column player would have benefitted, at no cost to the row player, if BC had been selected instead. The prisoner's dilemma is an extension of this idea:

	C	D
C	3 $\quad$ 0	0 $\quad$ 5
D	5 $\quad$ 0	0 $\quad$ 1

Case analysis leads each player to defect, leading to a result which is unfortunate for both of them.

The difficulty is a consequence of the fact that the agents are pursuing their goals too blindly: they are employing the independent rationality assumption in a situation where it is inadvisable to do so. In general, the consequences of theorem 1.3 will make the independent rationality assumption inconsistent with any cooperative or altruistic behavior.

Common rationality provides an answer:

Theorem 1.4 (Cooperation) *Assume common uniform rationality, and suppose that g has moves $\vec{c}$ and $\vec{d}$ such that $\vec{d}$ is Pareto suboptimal, with $\vec{c}$ being an improvement which is possible as the outcome of a common decision procedure for the players involved. Then $D_P(g) \neq \vec{d}$. In other words, the collective move $\vec{d}$ is avoided.*

Proof. Suppose that $D_P(g) = \vec{d}$, so that $D_i(g) = d_i$ for all players i. Now let G' be the set of all games obtained by permuting the players in P, and consider the decision procedure C_i obtained by modifying D_i so that the move $\vec{c}$ and its permuted versions are obtained for the games in G'. The hypotheses of the theorem will allow us to apply Equation 1.8 to conclude that D_i is irrational. □

If mutual defection is to everyone's disadvantage, then at least one player will cooperate. For an interaction such as the prisoner's dilemma which is symmetric (in that $p_\sigma = p$ for all σ), it follows that all of the players cooperate. This conclusion has an analog in the informal arguments of [4] and [9].

No-conflict games are handled as a special case of this result:

Corollary 1.5 (Coordination) *Assume common uniform rationality, and suppose that g has a move $\vec{c}$ such that for any $\vec{d} \neq \vec{c}$,*

$$p(j, \vec{c}) \geq p(j, \vec{d})$$

for all players j, with the inequality being strict for at least one j. Then $D_P(g) = \vec{c}$.

Proof. Apply theorem 1.4 to eliminate each of the alternatives. □

Returning to theorem 1.4 itself, note that it does *not* imply that all of the players cooperate; the possibility of one agent cooperating while the others defect (undoubtedly beneficial to the defectors and disastrous for the cooperator) is typical of the "altruism" allowed under the common rationality assumption. Consider the following non-result:

Non-theorem 1.6 (Restricted case analysis) *Suppose that there exist c_i and d_i such that, for all $c_{\bar{i}}$ and $d_{\bar{i}}$,*

$$p(i, \vec{d}) < p(i, \vec{c}).$$

Then d_i is irrational in g.

Proof? If $D_i(g) = d_i$, consider the decision procedure given by

$$C_i(g') = \begin{cases} D_i(g'), & \text{if } g' \neq g; \\ c_i, & \text{otherwise.} \end{cases}$$

This leads to $pay(i, C_P, g) > pay(i, D_P, g)$ independent of the nature of the *allowed* predicate. □

The problem is that we cannot show that

$$pay(i, C_P, g') \geq pay(i, D_P, g') \tag{1.10}$$

for $g' \neq g$. Independent rationality allows us to conclude this, of course; witness theorem 1.3. But under the common rationality assumption, if the "better" move c_i forces a reduced payoff for some other player, then Equation 1.10 will specifically *not* hold for some permutation of g. This of course does not mean that C_i is irrational; it merely means that C_i cannot be used to prove that D_i is.

Restricted case analysis is in fact independent of the assumption of common rationality, although it is consistent with it.

1.6   Global Rationality

In general, of course, any given game will have more than one Pareto optimal outcome, and it follows that theorem 1.4 cannot be used to identify a unique rational move in such a game. Under some circumstances, the stronger condition of global rationality can provide an answer to this. Before investigating this issue, however, consider the following symmetric game;

17

	A	B
A	0	1
B	1	0

Common rationality does very poorly here, resulting in a payoff of 0 for both players. The difficulty lies in the symmetry—if the payoffs are replaced by $1 + \epsilon$ and $1 - \epsilon$, this difficulty will be avoided. We therefore define a game g with payoff function p to be *uniformly disambiguated* (or simply *disambiguated*) if $p_\sigma \neq p$ for every nontrivial permutation σ of the players in g.

Recall that we apply the permutation σ to both the player *and* the move. Thus the following (symmetric) game is not uniformly disambiguated:

	A	B
A	0 1	2
B	2 1	0

while this game *is* uniformly disambiguated:

	A	B
C	0 1	2
D	2 1	0

To see that this last game is not symmetric, all we need do is note that the column player has a fundamental advantage in it.

Note also that, in the presence of the common rationality assumption $D_j = \sigma D_i \sigma^{-1}$, the payoff function Equation 1.4 has no unexpressed dependence on the decision procedures of the other players, since there is already an explicit dependence on D_i in $pay(i, D_P, g)$.

For a fixed game g, we define the *orbit* of g, denoted $o(g)$, to be the set of all games obtained by permuting the players in g. We also extend the payoff function to orbits, defining

$$\overline{pay}(i, D_P, g) = \sum_{g' \in o(g)} \rho_i(g') pay(i, D_P, g'). \tag{1.11}$$

A game g will be called *globally disambiguated* if $\overline{pay}(i, D_P, g) \neq \overline{pay}(i, C_P, g)$ whenever $D_i(g) \neq C_i(g)$. Note that, as a result of the appearance of ρ_i in Equation 1.11, this definition is dependent upon the values of the density function.

Theorem 1.7 *Assume common rationality. Then there is a unique globally rational move in any globally disambiguated game.*

Proof. We can assume without loss of generality that G, the set of all games, is equal to $o(g)$ for some single game g. Now $pay(i, D_P) = \overline{pay}(i, D_P, g)$. Let $\{C_i\}$ be the collection of all decision procedures which maximize this payoff; the global disambiguation ensures that the C_i's agree on g. $C_i(g)$ is therefore the unique globally rational move in g. □

This is in some sense a surprising result, since it does not require the players to have common knowledge of the payoff function (in that each agent knows that the other agents know that it knows the payoff function, etc.). Halpern and Moses refer to this situation, where everyone knows p, but without the further requirements of full common knowledge, as *E-knowledge*. In light of their result [8] that it is virtually impossible for a distributed system to achieve common knowledge, this is an important consideration.

Although theorem 1.7 implies that there is a unique globally rational decision procedure for the players involved, it does *not* imply that this decision procedure D_P need satisfy the common behavior assumption $\sigma(D(g)) = D(\sigma(g))$ for all σ and g. The reason for this is that different density functions may lead individual players to behave in distinct fashions. Suppose, however, that we say that the various agents' density function ρ_i *match* if $\rho_{\sigma(i)}\sigma = \rho_i$ for all $\sigma \in S_n$. We then have the following:

Theorem 1.8 *Suppose that each agent in a globally disambiguated interaction makes the assumption of common behavior, and that the density functions of the various agents match. Then the common behavior assumption will in fact be valid.*

Proof. Fix two players i and j in P, with $j = \sigma(i)$. We now have

$$
\begin{aligned}
pay(j, D_P, \sigma(g)) &= p_\sigma(\sigma(i), D_P(\sigma(g))) \\
&= p_\sigma(\sigma(i), \sigma(D_P(g))) \\
&= p(i, D_P(g)) \\
&= pay(i, D_P, g),
\end{aligned}
$$

from which we see that the global payoffs for the various players are identical. It follows that if a decision procedure C_i produces a universal improvement over D_i for player i, the permutation $\sigma C_i \sigma^{-1}$ will produce a universal improvement over the permuted version of D_i for j. Thus, if D_i is irrational for i, $\sigma D_i \sigma^{-1}$ will be irrational for j. In light of theorem 1.7, which states that each agent will have at most one globally rational decision procedure in this situation, the conclusion follows. □

In other words, we do not need to equip interacting agents with decision procedures which are in fact permutations of one another; if we provide them merely with the *assumption* of common behavior and with instructions to behave in a globally rational fashion, their decision procedures will match as a result.

If we are interested in situations where all of the agents *agree* about the likelihood of various interactions, then the density functions will match if and only if $\rho = \rho\sigma$ for all σ, so that the likelihood of a game is not changed by permuting it. In other words, equal density functions will match just in case each agent is as likely to find himself in any particular situation as is any other. The more general formulation amounts to the statement that the agents *believe* themselves to be equally likely to find themselves in specific interactions—for example, each might believe interactions unfavorable to him to be more likely than others. These differing density functions will still match if the amount of pessimism is uniform among the various agents.

Consider now a meta-game M in which a "move" for player i is the selection of a decision procedure D_i, so that a joint move is the selection of a joint decision procedure D_S. We define the payoffs in M by

$$p(i, D_P) = pay(i, D_P);$$

this is the payoff to i of selecting decision procedure D_i (if the other players select the decision procedure $D_{\bar{i}}$). The main result of this section is the following:

Theorem 1.9 *If all players have matching density functions, and all games in G are locally disambiguated, then any collective decision procedure D_P which obeys the common behavior assumption and is globally rational for the players in P will be Pareto optimal in the meta-game M.*

Proof. Again, we can assume without loss of generality that $G = o(g)$ for some fixed game g with payoff function p.

Under the assumption of common behavior, there will be a single move $\vec{c}$ which is made in g, with permutations of $\vec{c}$ being made in permutations of g. Now fix a player i; we will denote by C_i the decision procedure which generates the move $\vec{c}$.

The payoff to i of the decision procedure C_i is now given by

$$pay(i, C_P) = \sum_{g' \in G} \rho_i(g')pay(i, C_P, g')$$

$$= \sum_{\sigma \in S_n} \rho_i(\sigma) pay(i, C_P, \sigma(g))$$

$$= \sum_{\sigma} \rho_i(\sigma) p_\sigma(i, C_P(\sigma(g)))$$

$$= \sum_{\sigma} \rho_i(\sigma) p_\sigma(i, \sigma(\vec{c}))$$

$$= \sum_{\sigma} \rho_i(\sigma) p(\sigma^{-1}(i), \vec{c}).$$

The local disambiguation assumption guarantees that every move $\vec{c}$ is available as the outcome of a commonly rational decision procedure; C_i will therefore be globally rational just in case

$$\sum_{\sigma} \rho_i(\sigma) p(\sigma^{-1}(i), \vec{c}) \geq \sum_{\sigma} \rho_i(\sigma) p(\sigma^{-1}(i), \vec{d}) \qquad (1.12)$$

for all moves $\vec{d}$ in g.

If C_i were not Pareto optimal, there would be a collection of moves, one for each game in G (i.e., for each $\sigma \in S_n$), leading to better global payoffs for all of the players in g. If we denote these moves by $\vec{m}_\sigma$, the payoff to i will be

$$\sum_{\sigma \in S_n} \rho_i(\sigma) p_\sigma(i, \vec{m}_\sigma).$$

Meanwhile, the payoffs to another player $\sigma'(i)$ will be

$$\sum_{\sigma \in S_n} \rho_{\sigma'(i)}(\sigma) p_\sigma(\sigma'(i), \vec{m}_\sigma).$$

It follows that C_i will not be Pareto optimal only if

$$\sum_{\sigma} \rho_{\sigma'(i)}(\sigma) p_\sigma(\sigma'(i), \vec{m}_\sigma) \geq \sum_{\sigma''} \rho_i(\sigma'') p(\sigma''^{-1}(i), \vec{c})$$

for all σ', with the inequality being strict at least once. (The global payoff under common behavior does not change from player to player). This implies

$$\sum_{\sigma'} \sum_{\sigma} \rho_{\sigma'(i)}(\sigma) p_\sigma(\sigma'(i), \vec{m}_\sigma) > n! \sum_{\sigma''} \rho(\sigma'') p(\sigma''^{-1}(i), \vec{c}). \qquad (1.13)$$

The left hand side of Equation 1.13 can be easily rewritten as

$$\sum_{\sigma} \sum_{\sigma'} \rho_{\sigma'(i)}(\sigma) p_\sigma(\sigma'(i), \vec{m}_\sigma) = \sum_{\sigma} \sum_{\sigma'} \rho_i(\sigma'^{-1}\sigma) p(\sigma^{-1}\sigma'(i), \sigma^{-1}(\vec{m}_\sigma)).$$

If we write σ'' for $\sigma'^{-1}\sigma$ and $\vec{m}'_\sigma$ for $\sigma^{-1}(\vec{m}_\sigma)$, this is now

$$\sum_{\sigma} \sum_{\sigma'} \rho_{\sigma'(i)}(\sigma) p_\sigma(\sigma'(i), \vec{m}_\sigma) = \sum_{\sigma} \sum_{\sigma''} \rho_i(\sigma'') p(\sigma''^{-1}(i), \vec{m}'_\sigma)$$

$$\leq \sum_{\sigma} \sum_{\sigma''} \rho_i(\sigma'') p(\sigma''^{-1}(i), \vec{c})$$

$$= n! \sum_{\sigma''} \rho_i(\sigma'') p(\sigma''^{-1}(i), \vec{c}).$$

This is in conflict with Equation 1.13, and the proof is complete.   □

I cannot resist the temptation to rephrase this: if all men are indeed created equal, the Golden Rule is valid. Well, at least it's Pareto optimal.

1.7   Communication

We seem to have drifted rather far from the concerns of DAI. This is not the case, though; the point of this paper is the following:

Proposal. *Intelligent agents should be equipped with the common behavior assumption.*

There are a variety of reasons for this. The first is the Pareto optimality of common rationality, as in theorem 1.9. Provided that the agents being considered expect to encounter a similar distribution of interactive situations, there is *no* assumption or set of assumptions which will make them uniformly more effective problem solvers.

It can be argued that the assumption of matching density functions is an invalid one, and this is a fair criticism. In the presence of specific information regarding differences in the density functions of various agents, it is possible that more effective assumptions can be found. But in many cases, the strength of the local results in section 1.5 may be sufficient to ensure a satisfactory result if the common rationality assumption is adopted.

Additional advantages are a consequence of theorem 1.7. *Provided that interacting agents can agree on a globally disambiguated payoff function for a game g, they need communicate no further.* This is a consequence of the fact that this payoff function, in combination with the common behavior assumption, will be sufficient to determine the agents' actions.

There are a variety of advantages to restricting communication in this fashion. Firstly, it is possible to establish uniform protocols for the exchange of information regarding payoff matrices. In a ring, for example, the agents would broadcast their respective versions of the payoff function in turn; as soon as there was uniform agreement on a value, the interaction could proceed.

The reason that we are able to get by without *common* knowledge of the payoff function will be a bit clearer if we return to our widget example. Let us suppose that the Palo Alto robot broadcasts a payoff matrix indicating the advisability of stopping to pick up the various tools, and that the Boston robot confirms this. At this point, the situation is the following:

1. Both robots know that it is to their advantage to stop and acquire the tools, and

2. The Palo Alto robot knows that the Boston robot knows that this is the case.

22

It is *not* the case, though, that the Boston robot knows that the Palo Alto robot is aware of the advantages to be gained by acquiring the tools, since the Palo Alto robot has not yet acknowledged the Boston robot's message confirming the payoff function (nor will he); all that the Boston robot knows is that *when the Palo Alto robot receives the Boston robot's last message*, he will be aware of the values in the confirmed payoff matrix.

The effect of this is that the Boston robot does not know precisely *when* the Palo Alto robot will be prepared to start on his journey to Pittsburgh; all he knows is that when he arrives, he will have a borogove with him.

Let us return to more general considerations. In the presence of disagreement, for example, it will often be possible for one agent to *prove* its description of the payoff function to be correct. Such a proof might simply explain the situation in which that particular agent finds itself, or might instead provide a useful medium for agents to advise one another about possibly unforeseen consequences of their activities. If the Boston robot in our widget example had been unaware of the value of having a zazzyfrax and a borogove to help with the construction, the demonstration by the Palo Alto robot that there was mutual benefit to be had by stopping and picking up these tools would constitute advice of just this sort.

The fact that it is possible to demonstrate the accuracy of a payoff function will also alleviate problems arising from the fact that it may be to a particular agent's advantage to lie, as has been remarked by Rosenschein [15]. It is awkward to prevaricate in a situation where one can be required to vindicate one's claims! The only other solution which has been proposed to this, again by Rosenschein [14], is to have agents exchange binding promises, but it is not at all clear how the binding nature of these promises could be effected.

There is one point we have left unaddressed, and that involves the practical import of the disambiguation assumptions in the theorems of the last section. Fortunately, the following result should be fairly clear:

Theorem 1.10 *Every game is arbitrarily close to one which is locally and globally disambiguated.*   □

Note, however, that since in some cases the decision procedure produced by theorem 1.7 may vary discontinuously with respect to the payoff function for the game in question, it is possible for a group of intelligent agents to have difficulty agreeing on a perturbation that would disambiguate it. It does not appear that such difficulties can be addressed within the framework we have developed.

1.8 An Application

Let me end with an example that will hopefully make the practical import of these ideas a bit clearer. I will imagine a very simple environment which contains two processors and one peripheral which can be used by the processors to speed their computation. One of the processors is initially responsible for dividing a problem into two smaller ones; it then hands one of these subgoals off to the other machine. The peripheral might be, for example, a floating point accelerator (FPA).

The two processors (which I will call simply 1 and 2) must now decide whether or not to request access to the FPA; each processor has the option of making a request (R) or of making no request (N). In the interest of simplicity, I will assume that there is no facility for arbiting between conflicting requests: if both processors request the peripheral, both are denied access.

The payoffs to the two processors are related inversely to the amount of time that they will take to complete their respective tasks. I will assume, though, that the payoff to each processor is simply the amount of time taken for its computation, with the goal of the processors now being to *minimize* their payoffs.

Initially, then, each processor receives a task, and will determine what the advantage is of requesting access to the FPA. Let me assume that each processor makes this calculation for itself and transmits the results. If processor 1 (the "row" player) had payoffs of 6 (without the FPA) and 2 (with it), while processor 2 had payoffs of 4 and 1, the payoff matrix would look like this:

	R	N
R	6 4	2 4
N	6 1	6 4

$$(1.14)$$

Note first that this game is a version of the prisoner's dilemma. Since each processor is no worse off requesting access to the FPA than not, an application of case analysis will lead to the unfortunate choice $\{RR\}$.

Let us suppose for the moment that the density functions ρ_i are uniform over all games. An examination of Equation 1.12 now reveals that any commonly rational move will be one which maximizes the total payoff to all of the players involved. This leads to the joint move RN above; the processor which will benefit the most from the use of the FPA requests it. The effect of this is to minimize the total amount of time needed for the two processors to complete their computations (i.e., they use the fewest number of cycles).

Let us now allow the two processors to do a little more metalevel reasoning. They realize that if processor 1 does not request the FPA, but waits until the other processor is done with it before starting its own computation, it will actually complete its task in 3 units of time, as opposed to 6. The second processor can reason similarly, and the payoff matrix should therefore be replaced with this one:

	R	N
R	4 6	3 2
N	1 3	4 6

$$(1.15)$$

Common rationality now leads to the joint move NR; the second processor requests the FPA while the first waits for him to finish using it.

Other density functions can be used to produce different results. If, for example, it is desired to have the slowest processor complete its task in the shortest time possible, the density functions need merely be taken to be very sharply increasing functions of the time needed to complete the task without access to the FPA. If it is desired to have the *fastest* processor complete its task as quickly as possible (perhaps to begin consideration of another problem), the density functions should be very sharply *decreasing* functions of the time needed to complete the task *with* access to the FPA. An examination of Equation 1.12 will make both of these claims clear. Of course, all of these methods can be used just as easily with the revised payoff function (1.15) as with the earlier version (1.14).

Let me conclude by describing the advantages of the common rationality approach over a few other possibilities. The one that springs to mind most quickly is that of having the task-assigning machine determine which of the subprocessors should use the FPA. This will be reasonable in simple situations, but there may well be a substantial amount of analysis involved in arriving at the payoff functions appearing in (1.14), and this analysis can be usefully distributed between the other machines. It should not be argued, however, that this substantial analysis is a "waste of time"—Smith has pointed out [16] that meta-analysis will become increasingly important as machines tackle more and more difficult problems.

The attractiveness of common rationality is also not merely a consequence of the harsh penalty we have imposed if both processors request access to the FPA. Suppose that the FPA is merely assigned at random in such a case; (1.14) should now be replaced with:

	R	N
R	$2\frac{1}{2}$ 4	4 2
N	1 6	4 6

Individual rationality still forces the move $\{RR\}$; although this move is no longer Pareto-suboptimal (as it was earlier), there may nevertheless be many situations in which we want to avoid it.

A final possibility would be to have the processors agree on a payoff function and to then have one of them determine what action should be taken. The point of theorem 1.8, however, is that this is unnecessary: the various processors will coordinate their actions automatically, without needing to select a single machine to arbitrate their decisions.

Not only is this additional complication unnecessary, but there are many situations where it will be outright impossible—the interaction may be unexpected, or may be between agents with conflicting goals. There are a variety of examples in [5], although the state of research into the problems of interacting intelligent agents seems to preclude describing them quantitatively at this point.

1.9   Conclusion

The decision procedure paradigm is a new one in which to examine multiagent interactions: the results of this paper should be novel to both game-theoretic and AI audiences.

The advantage of this paradigm is that it makes it possible to avoid the usual assumption that the decision methods of the various agents are independent. This independence can be assumed, but it is only one of a variety of assumptions which can be made.

One of these, which we have referred to as common rationality, seems especially attractive. It enables us to understand coordinated action in terms of local utility maximization, and solves the prisoner's dilemma. We have also showed common rationality to be Pareto optimal among the collection of all possible assumptions which might be made by interacting agents about each other.

The common rationality assumption is also strong enough to limit the communication needed between such interacting agents. By allowing the agents to communicate information describing their situation instead of describing their proposed intentions, we can establish a uniform protocol for this communication while avoiding the difficulties that would otherwise be a consequence of potential agent dishonesty.

26

The difficulties with the common rationality approach appear to lie in two assumptions: that the interacting agents have matching density functions, and that any particular game not be locally or globally ambiguous. Only the first of these is likely to present a serious difficulty in practice, and future research will need to address interaction between agents with varying expectations about the situations in which they will find themselves.

Acknowledgements

The fact that I have occasionally chosen to disagree with the conclusions that Mike Genesereth and Jeff Rosenschein have drawn elsewhere is unrepresentative of the influence they have had on this work. Discussions with them have been invaluable to my development of any thoughts in this area; many of the ideas in this paper also appear in a paper authored jointly with them [5].

This research has been supported by the Office of Naval Research under grant number N00014-81-K-0004.

References

[1] R. Axelrod, *The Evolution of Cooperation*, Basic Books, Inc., New York, 1984.

[2] D. D. Corkill and V. R. Lesser, "The Use of Meta-Level Control for Coordination in a Distributed Problem Solving Network," *IJCAI-83*, Karlsruhe, West Germany, 1983, pp. 748–756.

[3] R. Davis, "A Model for Planning in a Multi-Agent Environment: Steps Toward Principles For Teamwork," Working Paper 217, MIT AI Lab, 1981.

[4] R. Davis and R. G. Smith, "Negotiation as a Metaphor for Distributed Problem Solving," *Artificial Intelligence*, vol. 20, 1983, pp. 63–109.

[5] M. R. Genesereth, M. L. Ginsberg, and J. S. Rosenschein, "Cooperation without Communication," 1985 DAI Workshop, Sea Ranch, California, 1985.

[6] M. Georgeff, "Communication and Interaction in Multi-agent Planning," *AAAI-83*, Washington, D.C., 1983, pp. 125–129.

[7] M. Georgeff, "A Theory of Action for Multi-agent Planning," *AAAI-84*, Austin, Texas, 1984, pp. 121–125.

[8] J. Halpern and Y. Moses, "Knowledge and Common Knowledge in a Distributed Environment," *Proceedings of the Third Annual ACM Conference on Principles of Distributed Computing*, Vancouver, British Columbia, Canada, 1984.

[9] D. R. Hofstadter, "Metamagical Themas—The Calculus of Cooperation Is Tested Through a Lottery," *Scientific American*, vol. 248, 1983, pp. 14–28.

[10] K. Konolige, "A First-Order Formalization of Knowledge and Action for a Multi-agent Planning System," Tech Note 232, SRI International, Menlo Park, California, 1980.

[11] R. D. Luce and H. Raiffa, *Games and Decisions, Introduction and Critical Survey*, John Wiley and Sons, New York, 1957.

[12] T. W. Malone, R. E. Fikes, and M. T. Howard, "Enterprise: A Market-Like Task Scheduler for Distributed Computing Environments," Working paper, Cognitive and Instructional Sciences Group, Xerox Palo Alto Research Center, 1983.

[13] A. Rapoport and M. Guyer, "A Taxonomy of 2 x 2 Games," *Yearbook of the Society for General Systems Research*, vol. XI, 1966, pp. 203–214.

[14] J. S. Rosenschein and M. R. Genesereth, "Deals Among Rational Agents," *IJCAI-85*, Los Angeles, California, 1985.

[15] J. S. Rosenschein, *Rational Interaction: Cooperation Among Intelligent Agents*, Ph.D. thesis, Stanford University, 1985.

[16] D. E. Smith, *Controlling Inference*, Ph.D. thesis, Stanford University, 1985.

Matthew L. Ginsberg
The Logic Group
Knowledge Systems Laboratory
Department of Computer Science
Stanford University
Stanford, California 94305

Chapter 2

Cooperation Through Communication in a Distributed Problem Solving Network

Edmund H. Durfee, Victor R. Lesser, and Daniel D. Corkill

Abstract

Self-interest can lead to cooperation. For example, communicating problem solvers whose individual goals (self-interests) are compatible might unwittingly cooperate as they pursue these goals separately, or they might intentionally cooperate to better achieve their individual goals. Our approach to distributed problem solving is to provide self-interested problem solving nodes with the ability to interact cooperatively when it is to their mutual advantage. In this paper, we outline techniques for coordinating nodes in distributed problem solving networks so that they work together coherently. Because exchanged information can influence a node's local decisions, we introduce mechanisms that increase network coherence by helping each cooperating node in a network to communicate more intelligently. We also describe mechanisms that enable each node to understand its current and likely future problem solving actions, and we provide experimental results indicating that the node can use these mechanisms to make better communication decisions, to improve its internal control decisions, and to increase network coherence by informing other nodes about its intentions.

2.1 Introduction

There is no mystery to why people cooperate. Cooperation occurs when each person believes that he or she will benefit more by cooperating than by acting in some other way. Similarly, groups of people will cooperate for their mutual benefit: businesses cooperate to increase profits, and nations cooperate in part to improve security (increase the survival probability of their people). In such situations, the cooperating *agents*, be they individuals or groups, only cooperate to improve their own self-interests. The prevalence of cooperation in human society, and in the world in general, indicates that there are many ways that selfish agents can interact for their mutual benefit.

Despite its prevalence, however, cooperation is still a poorly understood phenomenon. The advent of computers as agents in human environments has led to many interesting problems that stress issues in cooperation. For example, cooperation among humans is facilitated because people have an understanding of each other—each can predict the others' actions because they have so much in common (their humanity). Human-computer interactions are often fraught with frustration and misunderstanding because neither agent has an adequate view of why the other is behaving as it is [23]. Furthermore, computer-computer interactions have been similarly problematic because computers have primitive, if any, abilities to understand other computers. Unlike natural systems where such understanding evolved with the species, artificial systems must explicitly be given such understanding.

The research described in this paper is a step toward this end. The artificial systems studied use artificial intelligence techniques to solve problems. A network of these problem solvers perform *distributed problem solving* by cooperating as a team to solve a single problem. The principal focus of this research is on developing mechanisms that allow each problem solver to understand what other problem solvers are doing. With this understanding, the problem solvers can act as a more coherent team.

After we more fully introduce our view of cooperation in distributed problem solving networks, we provide an overview of distributed problem solving techniques and outline our experimental testbed for studying distributed problem solving. In the remainder of the paper are described mechanisms that improve cooperation by allowing each problem solver to better understand overall network problem solving. First we discuss how more intelligent decisions about the communication of partial solutions can enhance network coherence. These decisions are further improved through mechanisms that enable a problem solver to better understand its own past, present, and intended future actions, and these mechanisms are subsequently described. We then outline how the communication interface between problem solvers is augmented so that the problem solvers can not only exchange *domain-level* information about partial solutions, but also exchange *meta-level* information that is specifically intended to improve coordination between problem solving activities. Finally, we summarize our current ideas about distributed problem solving and describe the future directions of our research.

2.2   Cooperation

Since problem solvers can cooperate in many different ways, distributed problem solving provides a rich environment to study issues in cooperation among artificial systems. The actions of each problem solver depend on the desired outcomes of the interactions between problem solvers: the problem solvers base their actions and interactions on one or more goals of cooperation. The possible goals of cooperation include:

- To improve performance (form an overall solution faster) by working in parallel.

- To increase the variety of solutions by allowing agents to form local solutions without being overly influenced by other agents.

- To increase the confidence of a (sub)solution by having agents rederive (verify) each other's results, possibly using different problem solving expertise and data.

- To increase the probability that a solution will be found despite agent failures by assigning important tasks to multiple agents.

- To reduce the amount of unnecessary duplication of effort by letting agents recognize and avoid useless redundant activities.

- To improve the overall problem solving by permitting agents to exchange predictive information.

- To reduce communication by being more selective about what messages are exchanged.

- To improve the use of computing resources by allowing agents to exchange tasks to better balance the computational load.

- To improve the use of individual agent expertise by allowing agents to exchange tasks so that a task is performed by the most capable agent(s).

- To minimize the time agents must wait for results from each other by coordinating activity.

Because the problem solving agents cannot achieve all of these often conflicting goals simultaneously, they must cooperate differently depending on the particular problem solving situation. For example, if a solution must be found quickly, the agents should not spend time verifying each other's results or developing a wide variety of solutions. Because of the diversity in the forms that cooperation can take in a distributed problem solving system, distributed problem solving is an appropriate context in which to study issues in cooperation.

2.2.1 Self-Interested Problem Solvers

A distributed problem solving network can be viewed in two ways. When viewed as a single entity, the network is a system for decomposing a problem and assigning subproblems to its various subprocessors. Alternatively, the network can be viewed as a collection of independent problem solvers that can communicate. While the first view of distributed problem solving stresses intelligent *network control* (to decompose the problem and assign subproblems appropriately), the second view emphasizes intelligent *local control* of each individual problem solver (to decide which local tasks to pursue in order to best contribute to network performance).

We view a distributed problem solving network as a set of independent communicating agents, and thus our research has concentrated on developing problem solvers that have sophisticated local control. Each problem solver has the knowledge and intelligence needed to make its own decisions about subproblems to solve and about subproblem solutions to communicate. The emphasis of this work has therefore been on developing mechanisms that allow problem solvers to individually make decisions that contribute to achieving the goals of the overall network.

Since the individual problem solvers make local decisions about what actions to take, each problem solver essentially pursues activities that appear interesting from its local viewpoint. Each problem solver is thus *self-interested* because it attempts to maximize its local rewards (to achieve its local goals, to follow its local heuristics). Local viewpoints can vary from one problem solver to another, and the compatibility of the individual viewpoints determines whether problem solvers will cooperate, compete, or merely co-exist.

2.2.2 Cooperation Through Self-Interest

Cooperation can evolve in a population due to self-interest. For example, Dawkins has shown that genes, when viewed as self-interested agents, can cooperate to mutually improve their chances of reproducing [9]. Similarly, Axelrod has identified attributes of self-interested agents that successfully cooperate when confronted with the prisoner's dilemma [1]. A more extensive discussion about cooperation among various types of self-interested agents is presented elsewhere [10].

To cooperate, self-interested problem solvers must recognize that cooperation is in their self-interest. That is, they must have local knowledge that guides them into cooperating when cooperation is potentially to their mutual benefit. This knowledge can take many forms. For example, when problem solvers use goals to guide their decisions, cooperation can be promoted by allowing the problem solvers to share high-level goals. Since each self-interested problem solver is attempting to achieve the shared high-level goals, the problem solvers will tend to cooperate. Note, however, that if the agents have differing views on how to achieve these goals or different interpretations of these goals, then they may perform competitive actions. Examples of this phenomenon occur in human problem solving: just because the president and the congress share the goal of lowering the deficit, their different perspectives might lead them toward competing solutions.

Rosenschein and Genesereth misleadingly call agents that share goals *benevolent* agents [24]. Actually, these agents are completely self-interested since each performs actions only to satisfy its own local interpretations of these goals. Benevolence is neither assumed nor needed for the agents to cooperate.[1] What *is* necessary, however, is some degree of common knowledge: intentional cooperation among self-interested agents requires some amount of common knowledge so that agents can comprehend and anticipate each other's actions. The approach recommended by Rosenschein and Genesereth, for example, is to allow agents to share decision matrices rather than goals. But since both goals and decision matrices guide agents' decisions, these approaches are essentially the same—they use slightly different forms of common knowledge to lead self-interested nodes into cooperating.

Even if problem solvers want to cooperate due to their common knowledge, effec-

---

[1]Attributes such as benevolence, malevolence, and altruism are conferred on an agent by other agents when the other agents cannot otherwise rationalize the agent's decisions. For example, an intelligent agent may perceive a parent's self-sacrifice as being altruistic, when in fact the parent may have had no choice (its actions are genetically ingrained and it cannot even recognize alternative actions). Altruism is attributed to the parent because the intelligent agent views the decisions differently. Similarly, an agent that appears to be benevolent (or malevolent) will only seem that way because other agents assign different rewards to its decisions than it does itself.

tive cooperation in a distributed problem solving network can still be difficult to achieve because of the changing characteristics of the problem solving situation. The common knowledge inherent in shared high-level goals or decision matrices might not help agents make useful coordination decisions as problem solving progresses (if new subproblems appear at one or more problem solvers, new subproblem solutions are formed, problem solvers or communication links fail, etc.). The principal focus of this paper is to describe new mechanisms that improve the dynamic view that each problem solver has of network activity. With this improved view, each problem solver can make more intelligent decisions about what local actions will most contribute to network activity, and the entire network thus behaves more coherently.

2.3 Distributed Problem Solving

Achieving coherent cooperation in a distributed problem solving network is a difficult task [8,21]. In the type of distributed problem solving network studied in this paper, each agent is a semi-autonomous problem solving *node* that can communicate with other nodes. Nodes work together to solve a single problem by individually solving interacting subproblems and integrating their subproblem solutions into an overall solution. These networks are typically used in applications such as distributed sensor networks [22,25], distributed air traffic control [2], and distributed robot systems [15], where there is a natural spatial distribution of information but where each node has insufficient local information to completely and accurately solve its subproblems.

2.3.1 Approaches to Distributed Problem Solving

Three important approaches have been taken to improve coordination among cooperating nodes. These approaches, which are by no means mutually exclusive [26], are multi-agent planning, negotiation, and the functionally-accurate, cooperative approach. In the multi-agent planning approach, the nodes typically choose a node from among themselves (perhaps through negotiation) to solve their planning problem and send this node all pertinent information. The planning node forms a multi-agent plan that specifies the actions each node should take and the planning node distributes the plan among the nodes. Since the multi-agent plan is based on a global view of the problem, the important interactions between agents can be predicted and synchronized around [3,16]. If it can be effectively implemented, this form of multi-agent planning seems suitable in domains such as air traffic control where it is imperative that node interactions with dire consequences (such as vehicle collisions) are assured of being detected and avoided [2].

34

Unfortunately, achieving a global view of the problem might be time consuming and communication intensive, and the performance of the entire network depends on the planning node and would be compromised if that node fails. An alternative form of multi-agent planning is to provide each node with accurate models of the other nodes (for example, Corkill's MODEL nodes [3], Georgeff's process models [17], or Konolige's belief subsystems [18]) and allow the nodes to cooperatively form a multi-agent plan in a distributed fashion. Although this technique may reduce time requirements (the nodes can plan in parallel) and increase reliability, maintaining node models that accurately predict future actions (and interactions) may be impractical due to communication delays and bandwidth limitations. The multi-agent planning approach, where all of the future actions and interactions are fully predicted, may thus be infeasible in many realistic situations.

In most domains, fortunately, the consequences of unexpected node interactions are not dire: these interactions usually just degrade performance. In the negotiation approach [8], a node will decompose a problem task into some set of subtasks and will assign these subtasks to other nodes (for parallel execution) based on a bidding protocol [25]. Since nodes may have different capabilities, the bidding protocol allows a subtask to be assigned to the most appropriate available node (nodes that are already working on subtasks are not available to bid until they have finished their tasks). A node that is awarded one subtask may thus be unavailable to perform a subsequently formed subtask despite being the best node for that subtask. If the node had been able to predict that a more suitable subtask might soon be formed, the node would not have bid on the earlier subtask so that it would be available later. The inability of nodes to make such predictions can therefore cause incoherence in the problem solving network: the nodes could make a more coherent team and improve their overall performance if they could assign subtasks to nodes better.

In the *functionally-accurate, cooperative* (FA/C) approach to distributed problem solving [21], nodes cooperate by generating and exchanging tentative, partial solutions based on their limited local views of the network problem. By iteratively exchanging their potentially incomplete, inaccurate, and inconsistent partial solutions, the nodes eventually converge on an overall network solution. To cooperate coherently, the nodes would need to predict what partial solutions would be exchanged in the future and when, so that they could modify their problem solving activities to form compatible partial solutions. To make these predictions, each node needs to understand its own plans and the plans of the other nodes. Without this understanding, nodes may require much more time to converge on a solution since they may work at cross-purposes.

Prediction is therefore crucial for coherent cooperation. While multi-agent planning requires accurate predictions before it can form acceptable plans, the negotiation and

FA/C approaches can perform despite a lack of adequate predictions, but incoherence can degrade their performance. Better predictions in both of these approaches have been achieved through *organization*: by providing nodes with organizational information (the general capabilities and responsibilities of other nodes, the communication patterns between nodes), the nodes have a general understanding of each other and can therefore make better predictions. In the negotiation approach, this allows nodes to use focused addressing techniques in making better subtask to node assignments, while in the FA/C approach, it allows nodes to better decide which of their potential problem solving tasks is likely to improve network problem solving. However, an organization can only make limited improvements to coherence since it helps a node predict what other nodes are generally likely to do, but provides little help in predicting when important interactions are likely to take place.

The mechanisms described in this paper are a step toward providing nodes with the ability to predict their own actions and to predict the actions of other nodes based on exchanged information. Before describing these mechanisms in detail, we first provide an overview of the experimental domain and the testbed in which the mechanisms have been implemented.

2.3.2   The Distributed Vehicle Monitoring Testbed

A vehicle monitoring problem solver generates a dynamic map of vehicles moving through an area monitored by acoustic sensors. The vehicles' characteristic acoustic signals are detected at discrete time intervals, and these signals indicate the types of vehicles passing through the area and their approximate locations at each sensed time. An acoustic sensor's range and accuracy are limited, and the raw data it generates can be errorful, causing non-existent (ghost) vehicles to be "identified" and causing actual vehicles to be located incorrectly, misidentified, or missed completely. A vehicle monitoring node applies signal processing knowledge to correlate the data, attempting to recognize and eliminate incorrect noisy sensor data as it integrates the correct data into an answer map.

In a network of vehicle monitoring nodes, where each is responsible for a portion of the sensed area, the nodes develop partial maps in parallel and exchange these to converge on a complete map. Distributed problem solving is advantageous in this domain for various reasons. Since the nodes work in parallel, the time needed to generate an entire map is reduced. The nodes can be spatially distributed to reduce the distances that large quantities of raw sensory data must be transmitted, thereby lowering communication costs. Finally, the system is more robust since a node failure only disrupts the monitoring of a portion of the area. However, distributed vehicle monitoring must overcome the difficulties of coordination and cooperation common to distributed problem solving networks.

By simulating a network of vehicle monitoring nodes, the Distributed Vehicle Monitoring Testbed (DVMT) provides a framework where general approaches for distributed problem solving can be developed and evaluated [19,20]. By varying parameters in the DVMT that specify the accuracy and range of the acoustic sensors, the acoustic signals that are to be grouped together to form patterns of vehicles, the power and distribution of knowledge among the nodes in the network, and the node and communication topology, a wide variety of cooperative distributed problem solving situations can be modeled.

Each problem solving node has a Hearsay-II, blackboard-based architecture [14], with knowledge sources and blackboard levels of abstraction appropriate for vehicle monitoring. A *knowledge source* (KS) performs the basic problem solving tasks of extending and refining *hypotheses* (partial solutions), where each hypothesis tentatively indicates where a certain type of vehicle was at one or more discrete sensed times. The basic Hearsay-II architecture has been augmented to include more sophisticated local control and the capability of communicating hypotheses and goals among nodes [4,6]. In particular, a goal blackboard, a goal processing module, and communication knowledge sources have been added (Figure 2.1).

Goals are created on the goal blackboard to indicate a node's intention to refine and extend hypotheses on the data blackboard, and each goal is initially rated based on the confidence in the hypotheses that triggered its formation. Through goal processing, a node forms *knowledge source instantiations* (KSIs) that represent potential KS applications on specific hypotheses to satisfy certain goals. The scheduler ranks a KSI based both on the estimated beliefs of the hypotheses it may produce and on the ratings of the goals it is expected to satisfy. Appropriate goal processing to modify goal ratings can therefore alter KSI rankings to improve local control decisions. The network organizational structure, for example, is specified as a set of node *interest areas* that affect goal processing decisions: a node will increase the ratings of goals that fall within its areas of network responsibility while decreasing the ratings of other goals. Since goal ratings affect KSI rankings, the interest areas can influence node activity; but because there are other factors in ranking KSIs (such as the expected beliefs of the output hypotheses), a node still preserves a certain level of flexibility in its local control decisions. The organizational structure thus provides guidance without dictating local decisions, and can be used to control the amount of overlap and problem solving redundancy among nodes, the problem solving roles of the nodes (such as "integrator", "specialist", and "middle manager"), the authority relations between nodes (whether nodes are biased to prefer

37

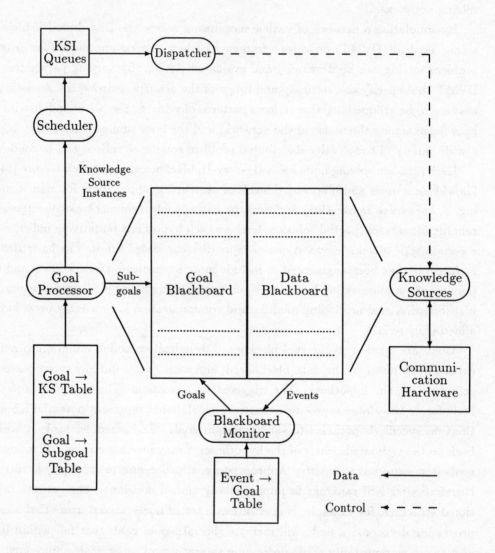

A KS forms hypotheses on the data blackboard, which in turn trigger the formation of goals on the goal blackboard. The goal processor forms KSIs to satisfy the goals, and the KSIs are scheduled. The dispatcher then invokes the KS for the best pending KSI and the cycle repeats.

Figure 2.1: DVMT Node Architecture.

work based on received data or on locally generated data), and the potential problem solving paths in the network [5].

Put simply, a node repeatedly performs a problem solving cycle: it executes a KS to post hypotheses on the blackboard, the new hypotheses trigger the creation of suitable goals for refining and extending them, the goal processing forms and rates KSIs to satisfy these goals, and the scheduler chooses the KSI to invoke next and triggers the appropriate KS to execute. Concurrently, a transmission processor and a reception processor each maintains a queue of communication KSIs (ranked by the rating of the information to be communicated and by the interest areas), and each executes KSs to transmit or receive messages [11]. The cyclic problem solving activity begins when signal hypotheses are posted based on sensor data, and a node then processes its most promising signal data to form tracks. Through goal processing, the goals to extend these tracks boost the importance of KSIs that may lead to the desired extensions. This form of problem solving is called *island-driven* because it uses islands of high belief to guide further processing. This problem solving is also *opportunistic* because nodes can react to highly-rated new data (perhaps received from another node) to form alternative islands of high belief. Finally, the cyclic problem solving activity terminates when one or more hypotheses matching a predefined solution is formed.[2]

2.4   Coherence and Communication

There are three major characteristics of the information communicated among nodes that affects coherence: relevance, timeliness and completeness. *Relevance* measures, for a given message, the amount of information that is consistent with the solution derived by the network. Irrelevant messages may distract the receiving node into wasting its processing resources on attempts to integrate inconsistent information, so higher relevance of communicated information can result in more global coherence (since this information stimulates work along the solution path). *Timeliness* measures the extent to which a transmitted message will influence the current activity of the receiving node. Since timeliness depends not only on the content of the message but also on the state of the nodes, a message's timeliness can vary as node activity progresses. If the transmitted information will have no effect on the node's current activity, there is no point in sending

---

[2]The solution is thus specified before problem solving begins, but a node cannot use this information to guide its processing. Without the availability of such an "oracle", termination of problem solving is much more difficult, requiring nodes to determine whether further problem solving is likely to improve upon a possible solution which it has already generated or will cause it to generate another potentially better solution. In effect, the termination decision depends on the criteria for deciding whether network goals have been satisfied [7].

it; however, if the transmitted information will distract the receiving node to work in a more promising area, or if the node needs the information to continue developing a promising partial solution, then it is important that the information be sent promptly. Finally, *completeness* of a message measures the fraction of a complete solution that the message represents. Completeness affects coherence by reducing the number of partially or fully redundant messages communicated between nodes—messages which negatively distract nodes into performing redundant activity. Furthermore, as the completeness of received messages increases, the number of ways that the messages can be combined with local partial results decreases due to their larger context. Finally, achieving completeness is important to minimize communication requirements in our loosely-coupled distributed system.

It is important to note that these three characteristics of communicated information are interdependent (as will be seen in empirical results to be presented later in the paper). For example, higher completeness leads to higher relevance but also a potential decrease in timeliness. Thus, communication policies often involve tradeoffs among the three characteristics.

These characteristics of communicated information are affected by both the local control in a node (which generates the potential information that can be transmitted), and the communication policy (which decides what information should be sent, to what nodes, and when). Increased global coherence could be achieved by improving only local node control, by improving only communication policies, or by a combination of both. In each of these cases, more intelligent decisions result if a node has a better understanding of what it has already done, what it is likely to do, and the activities and intentions of other nodes.

2.4.1 Implementing More Sophisticated Communication Policies

Our first approach to improving the basic communication policy of sending all candidate hypotheses (as defined in the node's organizational structure) was to develop a simple version of a *locally-complete* communication policy. This policy, originally developed by Lesser and Erman [22], required significant modification to handle the DVMT's more complex task processing structure.

The basic communication policy, which we call *send-all*, often results in a node transmitting a small or irrelevant hypothesis, even though the subsequent internal processing of the sending node will immediately improve upon this data. Because a node might produce a large number of these small hypotheses in the process of generating a more

40

complete hypothesis, the transmission of each of these less complete hypotheses would be deleterious in terms of minimizing channel usage and maximizing completeness. Furthermore, because these smaller hypotheses are transmitted immediately (before any activity to support or refute them is done), they are more likely to be irrelevant. Finally, these incomplete and incorrect hypotheses could distract the recipient node into working in inappropriate areas. If nothing else, the recipient node is likely to combine these smaller hypotheses together into a larger hypothesis—a redundant activity, since the sending node both generates and transmits this larger hypothesis as well.

The locally-complete communication policy is based on a node transmitting only those hypotheses which it can not improve upon. This policy minimizes the number of transmissions while maximizing the completeness and relevance of each message. The implementation of this policy in the testbed illustrates how the node's awareness of its activities (in this case future ones) is necessary for intelligent communication. To estimate whether a hypothesis is locally complete, the queue of pending local KSIs must be examined. If there exists a KSI to improve upon the hypothesis, either by increasing its length or belief, then the hypothesis is not yet locally complete. However, the existence of such a KSI does not necessarily mean that an improved hypothesis will be created. The rating of the KSI might be so low that it will never be executed. Furthermore, even if executed, the resulting hypothesis from the KSI might not be an improvement because the KSI might fall short of its intentions.

Thus, due to the uncertainty as to whether a more locally-complete hypothesis might ever be formed, such a policy will not be effective in terms of timeliness—a locally-incomplete hypothesis might be useful to another node, and we should not hold it back too long waiting for something better.

To partially rectify this problem, we introduce a time-out mechanism that heuristically balances the desire for completeness with that of timeliness. As in the less sophisticated send-all policy, any hypothesis that meets the criteria for communication stimulates the creation of a communication KSI to perform the transmission. However, we now associate with this transmission KSI an invocation delay. If the KSI is to transmit a locally-complete hypothesis, this delay is set to zero; otherwise the delay is set to a *user specified* value (we discuss this issue later). The delay acts as a timeout value—if sufficient time elapses without the creation of a more complete version of the hypothesis, the transmission KSI is invoked to transmit the locally-incomplete version. However, if the improved (but still possibly locally incomplete) hypothesis is created, a KSI to send it is generated (with a new invocation delay), and the KSI of the now inferior hypothesis is deleted from the pending transmission KSI queue.

By providing a node with a chance to improve upon a hypothesis before that hypothesis is transmitted, the locally-complete policy will reduce the number of small and irrelevant hypotheses transmitted while allowing the timely transmission of better hypotheses. This can result in improved network performance due to reduction of redundant work and distraction. However, because transmitted hypotheses are used both to focus activity in the receiving node and as data to be combined with the local hypotheses, delaying the transmission of some locally-incomplete hypotheses might adversely affect performance. What is needed is a policy which will send locally-incomplete hypotheses for predictive purposes as well as locally-complete hypotheses for integration.

The communication policy we have developed for this situation has been dubbed *first-and-last*. It is essentially the locally-complete policy with the added stipulation that if a hypothesis that is eligible for transmission does not incorporate any previously communicated hypotheses, then transmit it without delay. Hence, the first partial hypothesis will be transmitted for predictive information, and the last locally-complete version will be sent for integration information, but any intervening locally-incomplete versions will not be transmitted.

An equivalent set of communication policies was also implemented for goal communication. A goal is locally complete when the node has created as much context for it as it can. Stated another way, a goal is locally complete if the hypotheses that stimulated its creation are all locally complete. Furthermore, the first-and-last policy is considered to be very important for goals, because the primary purpose of a goal is to focus activity at the receiving node. As we investigate more complex environments, we expect the first-and-last policy to become increasingly important.

2.4.2 Experiments with the Communication Policies

We illustrate the communication policies using three vehicle monitoring environments (Figure 2.2). The *normal* environment consists of four nodes, each attached to a different sensor, where the sensors overlap slightly (Figure 2.2a). Data is sensed over eight time intervals. The acoustic sensors attach more credence to more strongly sensed (louder) signals than to weaker (fainter) signals; data from the vehicle track has strongly and weakly sensed regions. A moderately sensed "ghost" track, perhaps caused by echoes from the vehicle or by sensor errors, parallels the vehicle track. In the *overlap* environment (Figure 2.2b), the overlap between the sensor regions is increased over the normal environment. Since each node has a more global view, the potential for finding the solution rapidly is increased. However, because there is more overlap, there is also more potential for redundant problem solving. Finally, the *twice-data* environment (Figure 2.2c) is similar to the normal environment, except that there are fifteen time intervals, forming additional data points between each of those in the normal environment. Because this effectively doubles the number of locally-incomplete hypotheses a node will produce, the locally-complete and first-and-last policies should be even more effective on this environment. To simplify our experiments, *all* of the data was available at the start of the problem solving. The invocation delay used by the locally-complete and the first-and-last policies was ten time units, which is usually sufficient to allow a more locally-complete version of a hypothesis to be formed.

The experimental results provide evidence supporting our expectations (Table 2.1). In all cases, the number of hypotheses transmitted under the locally-complete policy is less than the number transmitted by the send-all policy, with the first-and-last policy falling between. The improved performance in the locally-complete policy can be attributed to a reduction in distracting, irrelevant, and incomplete information passed between the nodes. The first-and-last policy is less effective because it communicates more of this detrimental information: the degradation of problem solving based on this information outweighs the minor improvements in problem solving afforded by the earlier exchange of predictive information.[3]

The degree to which these policies affect performance depends on the environment. In the normal environment, many of the additional communicated hypotheses do not affect the recipient nodes: either the received hypothesis does not trigger activity to improve upon it or else the triggered activity coincides with the actions the node was already taking. In the overlap environment, however, each node has data from a larger portion of the sensed area. Because a node is more likely to have data to combine with a received hypothesis, the small number of additional messages permitted by some policies cause the nodes to waste more time on unnecessary activities. In the twice-data environment, the abundance of data means that any received hypothesis that does trigger activity will trigger substantial amounts of activity. The first-and-last policy sends the small hypotheses that the locally-complete policy withholds, and these hypotheses degrade performance by stimulating large amounts of unimportant work. Although the send-all policy sends many more hypotheses than the first-and-last policy, further performance degradation is modest: most of the additional (larger) transmitted hypotheses only trigger the same activities as earlier (smaller) hypotheses. These communication policies have been used in numerous other environments, including ten to fifteen node simulations, with similar results.

---

[3]The mechanisms we introduce later in this paper help a node avoid negative distraction and the first-and-last policy does improve performance in some (larger) environments (see Table 3, the twice-data environment).

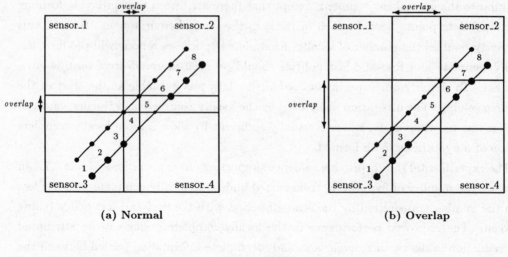

(a) Normal

(b) Overlap

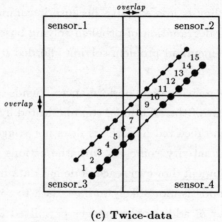

(c) Twice-data

Three experimental environments are illustrated. The normal environment (a) has eight data points on both the ghost track (upper) and the vehicle track (lower). The overlap environment (b) has the same data but more sensor overlap. The twice-data environment (c) has the same overlap as (a) but twice as much data. The size of a data point indicates how strongly it is sensed.

Figure 2.2: Sensor and Data Configurations for Three Environments.

Environment	Communication Policy	Solution Time	Total Transmitted Hyps
Normal	Send-all	49	25
	Loc-comp	45	10
	F-and-L	49	20
Overlap	Send-all	52	16
	Loc-comp	39	11
	F-and-L	46	13
Twice-data	Send-all	107	74
	Loc-comp	70	17
	F-and-L	99	29

Legend

Environment:	The simulated environment
Solution Time:	Earliest time at which a solution was found
Total Transmitted Hyps:	The total number of hypotheses transmitted

Optimal solution time for the normal environment is 23 regardless of the communication policy and assuming that the nodes perform the most appropriate actions at all times.

Table 2.1: A Summary of Communication Performance.

2.5 Planning for Problem Solving

The user specified invocation delay for locally-incomplete hypotheses is inflexible to specific problem solving situations that nodes may encounter. Instead, we would like a node to determine an appropriate delay for transmitting a locally-incomplete hypothesis (or goal) based on predictions about its future activities. Such predictions are infeasible in the basic problem solving architecture, which represents future activities simply as a priority queue of KSIs. Because both local activity and received information can stimulate the creation of new, highly-rated KSIs, estimating the future activity of a node (or even just attempting to estimate when a particular KSI will be invoked) is a complex and highly uncertain task. A node with a better perspective on its past, present, and potential future activities can make better communication decisions. Such a node can also make improved decisions about its local problem solving actions and can better understand how its activities fit into its organizational responsibilities.

Although the priority queue of pending KSIs allows for rampant opportunism in a node, nodes often methodically perform sequences of related actions. For example, given a highly rated hypothesis, a node typically executes a sequence of KSIs that drive up low level data to extend the hypothesis. However, the entire sequence of KSIs is never on the queue at once. We have therefore developed a structure, called a *plan*, to explicitly represent a KSI sequence.

2.5.1 Blackboards, Plans, and Node Activities

Each *plan* represents a desire to achieve a high-level goal by performing a sequence of activities. To identify plans, the node needs to recognize these high-level goals. Inferring high-level goals based on pending KSIs is an inappropriate strategy; it is like attempting to guess a chess opponent's strategy by observing isolated moves. Furthermore, the hypothesis and goal blackboards provide information at too detailed a level to infer these high-level goals. What is required is a structure similar to the blackboards that groups related hypotheses and goals together. We have developed a preliminary version of this structure which we call the *abstracted blackboard*, a structure reminiscent of the focus-of-control database first used in the Hearsay-II speech understanding system [14]. Our implementation of the abstracted blackboard is incomplete because it does not adequately incorporate the information from the goal blackboard. However, for the type of processing done in the DVMT, hypothesis abstraction is usually effective.

Related hypotheses are grouped together on the abstracted blackboard based on their blackboard level, their time, and their region characteristics. This clustering allows us to differentiate between areas of the solution space. In our preliminary implementation, the abstracted blackboard takes the form of a two-dimensional array, with level and time indices. When a hypothesis is created, it is incorporated into this structure by stepping through the sensed times of the hypothesis, and modifying the appropriate level-time entry in the abstracted blackboard. Each level-time entry contains some number of regions, and if the location associated with the sensed time can be included in one of these regions (perhaps by enlarging the region within certain bounds), the hypothesis is associated with that region. Otherwise, a new region is formed for the hypothesis.

Each level-time-region of the abstracted blackboard is summarized into a set of values that are derived from the associated hypotheses. These values include the maximum belief of the hypotheses in the level-time-region, the number of highly believed hypotheses, the number of KSIs stimulated by these hypotheses that have yet to be invoked, the total number of hypotheses in the level-time-region and how many uninvoked KSIs are associated with them, and an indication as to the other level-time-regions that share at least one of the hypotheses. This information allows the *situation recognizer* to develop a higher level view of the problem solving. For example, low maximum belief indicates the problem solving approach in that area should be reevaluated, a large number of equally rated hypotheses could imply that there is uncertainty that should be resolved, and a large number of pending KSIs indicates the need for making an informed and judicious choice as to which action to take next. Based on this higher-level view, we can begin to form higher level goals. A goal might be to merge hypotheses in adjacent clusters, to improve the belief of an established hypothesis, or to extend a highly believed hypothesis into a new region.

The detection of these goals, and the subsequent generation and ranking of their respective plans, is in itself a complex problem solving task. Our current implementation is a first pass toward this end, in which we only consider very simple but important plans. Given the abstracted blackboard, our planner scans down it, looking for regions of high belief. Having found such a *stimulus region*, the planner determines whether there is any indication that the data in this region can be improved (this is done by determining whether any corresponding lower level regions have higher belief than the upper level regions), and if so indicated, a plan is formed to achieve this improvement. Otherwise, a plan is generated to extend this highly rated region, either by merging a hypothesis in this region with a hypothesis in an adjacent cluster on the same level (if any), or by driving lower level data in an adjacent area up to a level at which it can be incorporated. If none of these plans can be formed, then a plan to synthesize the hypotheses in this highly rated region up to a higher blackboard level may be formed.

Plans in our current implementation are not yet fully developed, because a plan should not only involve the specification of an eventual goal, but also of a sequence of actions needed to achieve this goal. Our implementation currently does not represent the entire sequence, but only the next potential step(s) in achieving the desired result. To this end, a queue of KSIs is associated with a plan, comprising the current set of potential tasks that are related to the plan. These are found through the hypotheses in the associated regions of the abstracted blackboard. The queue of KSIs is priority rated—the next activity carried out by a plan is always the highest rated KSI. In turn, the node maintains a queue of plans, ordered based on their respective ratings. Currently, a plan rating is based on a number of factors, including the belief of its stimulus region, the level of its stimulus region, the ratings of its KSIs, and whether the stimulus region represents hypotheses generated locally or it represents received hypotheses (to reason more fully about potentially distracting information received from outside). Therefore, in choosing its next activity, a node will invoke the highest rated KSI in the highest rated plan.

We have therefore made important modifications to the control structure of a node (Figure 2.3). In a KSI-based node (a node without plans), the highest rated KSI is always invoked next. The rating of the KSI is based on the ratings of the goals it is intended to satisfy and the anticipated beliefs of the hypotheses it will produce. In a plan-based node, the primary factor in determining the next activity is choosing the top plan. As the figure indicates, the creation and ranking of plans requires the planner to integrate the influences of the long-term strategy of the organizational structure, the medium-term higher-level view of the current situation, and the short-term KSI input indicating actions that can be achieved immediately. Hence, KSI ratings only affect the choice of the next plan to a small extent, being more important in the choice of specific activity once the plan is chosen.

It is important to recognize that our use of plans has not changed the basic opportunistic problem solving strategy of the node. Because we are working on the best plan at any given time, we are being opportunistic on the plan level instead of the KSI level. Unlike KSIs, however, plans can be interrupted or aborted if something more promising comes along. Therefore, a node using plans need not be any less opportunistic than a node without plans. If an area outside the current plan looks most promising, a plan to work in this area will be formed with a higher rating. This plan will supplant the current plan at the top of the plan queue, and our attention will turn to invoking the activities of this better plan. Note that we have essentially interrupted one plan to work on a better one—once the better plan is fulfilled (or aborted), we can return to the interrupted activities. Finally, by representing sets of tasks as plans, we can make more informed decisions about switching to new tasks. For example, without plans, a promising new KSI can distract the node, despite that node being nearly done with an important sequence of tasks. When plans are introduced, a node can reason about the time invested in a particular area, and about whether it really should leave this area for another.

2.5.2   Experiments with Plan-based Nodes

To illustrate the effectiveness of plan-based problem solving, we present data from three environments in Table 2.2. The first environment consisted of a single node receiving data from all four sensors shown in Figure 2.2a. When the node based its activities simply on the KSI queue, solution generation took significantly longer than if the node used plans. This is due to the role that plans play in focusing the problem solving activity toward extending areas of high certainty, even into regions of lowly rated data. The second environment has four nodes, each receiving the information from a different sensor in Figure 2.2a. Again, the plan-based control works much better. Furthermore, the importance of using predictive information from other nodes is illustrated. When we incorporate only internally generated hypotheses into the abstracted blackboard, the problem solving is less efficient than if all hypotheses (internally generated and received) are abstracted. Finally, the third environment is identical to the second except that the

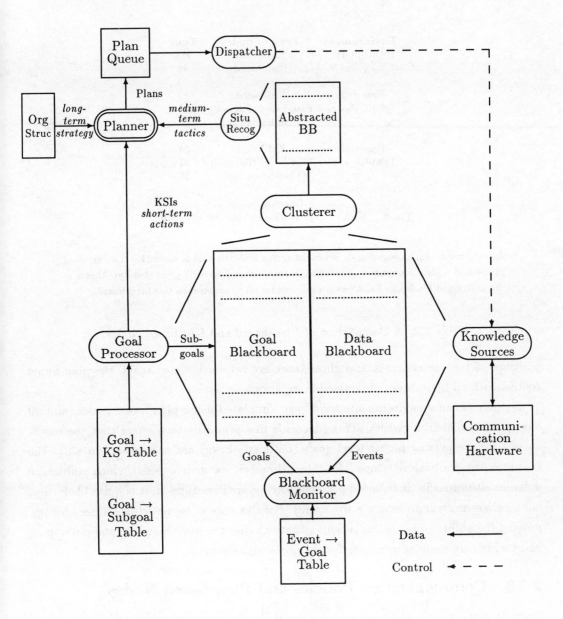

The planner integrates information about the KSIs, problem solving situations, and organizational structure to form plans. The dispatcher invokes the KS for the best KSI of the best plan. Any new hypotheses that the KS forms trigger changes to the goal and abstracted blackboards, generating new information for the planner. The cycle then repeats.

Figure 2.3: The Modified Problem Solving Architecture of a Node.

Environment	Type of nodes	Time
One-node	KSI-based	213
	Plan-based	58
Four-node	KSI-based	49
(ghost above)	Plan-based (internal)	39
	Plan-based (all)	36
Four-node	KSI-based	34
(ghost below)	Plan-based (internal)	31
	Plan-based (all)	26

Legend

Time: Earliest time at which a solution was found

A comparison of plan-based node networks versus KSI-based node networks. Two types of plan-based node are presented, one which includes only internally generated hypotheses in the abstracted blackboard and one which includes all hypotheses in this blackboard.

Table 2.2: A Comparison of Plan-based and KSI-based Nodes.

positions of the vehicle track and ghost track are reversed. Once again, the plan-based control with all hypotheses abstracted is superior.

Numerous other environments have been simulated using plan-based nodes, and all have produced similar results. This success is due primarily to the fact that the mechanisms for recognizing higher level goals (outlined above) are appropriate in all of the environments we have developed to date. However, as environments which emphasize different situations in distributed problem solving are investigated, it is quite likely that our mechanisms will no longer prove useful. For this reason, we anticipate a need for improving the ability to recognize various situations that the node may face and developing plans which are more appropriate for the particular situation.

2.5.3   Communication Policies and Plan-based Nodes

Because plans represent sequences of activities, our communication policies based on locally-complete hypotheses become that much simpler. Currently, we have eliminated associating a delay with a transmission KSI. Instead, in deciding whether to invoke a transmission KSI, we merely compare the transmittable hypothesis with the current plan. If that plan does not involve the hypothesis, we assume that the hypothesis will not be improved upon in the near future and thus invoke the transmission KSI without delay. On the other hand, if the plan represents an intention to improve upon the hypothesis, then we do not invoke the transmission KSI (but it remains on the queue). If the plan completes successfully, then a transmission KSI for the improved hypothesis is formed and the original transmission KSI is removed. If the plan is aborted or unsuccessful (fails to create a better hypothesis), or if the plan is interrupted by a plan not involving the hypothesis, then the original transmission KSI is invoked. As our understanding of problem solving activities increases, and our representations of plans improves, we may further embellish upon this implementation so that it can reason about the tradeoffs involved in waiting if the plan to improve the hypothesis is "near" the top of the plan queue. Note that this problem is similar to the problem of making estimations about when a KSI will be invoked in a KSI-based node. However, because the effects of plans are more predictable than those of KSIs, it may be feasible to make projections as to when a particular plan is likely to be at the top of the queue.

The first-and-last policy is again very similar to the locally-complete policy outlined above, except we communicate the first piece of a hypothesis even if it is being improved upon by the current plan. The results of running these policies using plan-based nodes on the three environments in Figure 2.2 are summarized in Table 2.3. In the normal environment, the locally-complete policy is slightly worse than the others because nodes retain locally-incomplete hypotheses that could be used by their neighbors. We therefore see the timeliness drawbacks in a locally-complete policy. In the overlap environment, the locally-complete policy works slightly better in terms of solution time. The first-and-last policy focuses the nodes on redundant activities, and so, the solution takes longer to generate, but fewer hypotheses are communicated due to the duplication among nodes. Finally, the twice-data environment indicates that the predictive qualities of the first-and-last policy can be slightly advantageous in terms of solution time at the cost of requiring more communication than the locally-complete policy.

Comparing Table 2.3 with Table 2.1, we recognize that increasing the sophistication of the node dramatically improves the speed at which the network finds the solution, regardless of the communication policy. Furthermore, because nodes have an enhanced understanding of their local processing, they are less easily distracted by received information, so that the communication policy has much less effect on the rate of solution generation, even though it still has a significant effect on the number of hypotheses transmitted. However, despite the improvement, the problem solving is still far from optimal as reported in Table 2.1. Even with increased local sophistication of the nodes, the node network falls prey to redundant and unnecessary activity because a node has a very limited view of the activities at other nodes.

Environment	Communication Policy	Solution Time	Total Transmitted Hyps
Normal	Send-all	36	15
	Loc-comp	39	13
	F-and-L	38	15
Overlap	Send-all	38	25
	Loc-comp	36	21
	F-and-L	39	14
Twice-data	Send-all	51	51
	Loc-comp	50	19
	F-and-L	48	21

Legend

Environment:	The simulated environment
Solution Time:	Earliest time at which a solution was found
Total Transmitted Hyps:	The total number of hypotheses transmitted

Table 2.3: Communication Performance with Plan-based Nodes.

2.6 Increasing Network Coherence

We have seen how the performance of the node network can be improved by allowing the individual nodes to reason more fully as to the appropriate activities to perform, based on their local state. We now briefly describe the implications of allowing nodes to communicate this state information to let their neighbors make even more sophisticated decisions about local activities. For example, if two nodes have overlapping sensed areas, each might reason about the other's past, present, and future actions in the overlapping area when deciding whether to work there itself.

By transmitting the abstracted blackboards (or portions thereof), nodes can reason about the *past* activities of their neighbors. Furthermore, if a node knows the current plan of its neighbor, it can reason about the *present* actions of its neighbor. Reasoning about the *future* actions of a node, however, is a complex problem. This reasoning involves considering not only the current plans in the node's queue and making estimations about their durations and effects, but also what further information the node may receive (from another node or from its sensor) that could affect its activities. A plan may have associated with it some estimations as to its duration and probability of completion, or even more specific information about how its execution could be affected by received information [10].

Our current implementation assumes that a node can make completely accurate short-term predictions about future activity based solely on the plan queue. We simulate this best-case scenario by allowing a node access to the abstracted blackboard and plan queue

Environment	Type of nodes	Time
Four-node	Plan-based + mlc (internal)	27
(ghost above)	Plan-based + mlc (all)	26
Four-node	Plan-based + mlc (internal)	28
(ghost below)	Plan-based + mlc (all)	26

Legend

Time:	Earliest time at which a solution was found
mlc:	Meta-level Communication

Effects of meta-level communication on network problem solving. Two types of plan-based node are presented, one which includes only internally generated hypotheses in the abstracted blackboard and one which includes all hypotheses in this blackboard. Both types of nodes can both send and receive meta-level information.

Table 2.4: Performance of Plan-based Node Networks with Meta-level Communication.

of another node. We have yet to develop more realistic scenarios where nodes must transmit this *meta-level* information as they transmit hypotheses, and must therefore reason about relevance, timeliness, and completeness.

Meta-level information helps nodes to achieve their goals of cooperation. For example, a node may use meta-level information to avoid redundancy. In developing a plan, a node can determine if the plan represents redundantly deriving information that another node has either generated (present in the abstracted blackboard) or is in the process of generating (the top plan). By avoiding redundant activity, improvements in solution generation rate can result because less highly rated but potentially useful activities will be invoked earlier (rather than redundant invocation of highly rated activities). Comparing Table 2.4 with Table 2.2, we recognize that meta-level information allows us to come very close to the optimal solution time without reduction of belief. (Note that the one-node environment will be unchanged because there is no communication, and that the meta-level information is not used in KSI-based nodes, and so, will not affect them.)

2.6.1 Communication Policies and Meta-level Communication

The communication policies for plan-based nodes previously outlined can be modified to exploit the additional knowledge provided by the meta-level communication. In determining whether to send a hypothesis to its neighbor, a node can use the meta-level information to estimate the effects of the hypothesis on that neighbor. The node can reason about the utility of the hypothesis in terms of stimulating activity, avoiding redundancy, or generating the solution. Indeed, in an environment where messages may be lost or garbled, communication of meta-level information can allow nodes to recognize when to retransmit a hypothesis because the anticipated effects of that hypothesis were not seen. In the future, separate communication policies may be obviated since nodes might be capable of accurately predicting the effects of sending a potential message rather than relying on an unadaptive communication policy to make communication decisions.

In the current implementation, the locally-complete policy takes the position that it is important to communicate a hypothesis if the hypothesis is locally complete, if the hypothesis provides information that the receiving node will otherwise redundantly derive, or if improvement of the hypothesis will not affect its anticipated utility. The first-and-last policy is the same as the locally-complete except that the first piece of the hypothesis will be sent for predictive purposes. The effects of these policies are summarized in Table 2.5. We first note that the policy does not affect the time at which the solution is generated—nodes have such complete views of the network activities that information is communicated in a timely fashion and will not cause distraction. Therefore, our communication policies really only affect the number of hypotheses communicated, and in all cases the locally-complete policy sends the least and send-all the most. Secondly, we note that solution generation in the overlap environment requires no more time than in the normal environment. This is an indication of how the exchange of meta-level information can be used to direct nodes away from redundant processing. Finally, it is interesting that the meta-level communication does not significantly reduce the number of hypotheses transmitted (compare Tables 2.3 and 2.5). There are two reasons for this. First, because the nodes avoid redundancy, a number of different hypotheses are created and transmitted earlier in the experiment. Second, because the nodes are so well coordinated, they tend to generate and exchange the complete solution at the same time.

2.7 Conclusions and Future Research

Self-interest can lead to cooperation if two conditions are met. First, there must be potential benefits for cooperation in the agents' environment. In many cases, such an environment is purposely designed (a decision matrix is built, high-level goals are shared), while at other times cooperation is potentially advantageous by chance (such as in genetic evolution). The second feature is that agents must exist that can achieve these potential benefits. Once again, they can be intentionally designed (like computer software) or created by chance (gene combinations and mutations).

For natural or artificial self-interested agents to *intentionally* cooperate for their mu-

Environment	Communication Policy	Solution Time	Total Transmitted Hyps
Normal	Send-all	26	15
	Loc-comp	26	12
	F-and-L	26	13
Overlap	Send-all	26	16
	Loc-comp	26	13
	F-and-L	26	14
Twice-data	Send-all	41	27
	Loc-comp	41	16
	F-and-L	41	19

Legend

Environment:	The simulated environment
Solution Time:	Earliest time at which a solution was found
Total Transmitted Hyps:	The total number of hypotheses transmitted

Table 2.5: Communication Performance with Plan-based Nodes, Meta-level Communication.

tual benefit, they must have some common knowledge so that they can anticipate each other's actions and plan cooperative interactions. Cooperating problem solvers, for example, can share high-level goals to improve the chances that they will cooperate effectively. To further improve the coherence of cooperation, the problem solvers can communicate information that increases each other's awareness of network activities.

The focus of this paper has been on describing mechanisms that allow problem solving nodes to make intelligent use of communication resources to improve network coherence in the distributed vehicle monitoring testbed. By introducing simple communication policies into the nodes, we recognized the effects of communication decisions on network coherence. Communication decisions were improved by providing nodes with the ability to achieve a high-level view of their activities and to use this view when determining what information to send and when planning their future problem solving actions. Finally, coherence was further improved by allowing nodes to communicate meta-level information based on their high-level views and plans. Through these mechanisms, nodes improved each other's awareness of network activities without incurring excessive communication and computation overhead.[4] Since the nodes have more knowledge in common, the efficacy of their cooperation can be dramatically increased.

Our future research plans are to concentrate on the strong connection between distributed planning and distributed problem solving: effective distributed problem solving requires that agents plan their actions and interactions rather than making isolated and

---

[4]Evaluations of the costs of these mechanisms are discussed elsewhere [13].

short-sighted decisions. To plan their actions and interactions, agents must have so-phisticated planners that can: interleave planning and execution, monitor and revise inappropriate plans, make temporal predictions about when actions and events may oc-cur, and use models of other agents to develop plans that will allow the agent to interact favorably with other agents. This last requirement involves using and improving the communication mechanisms that we have described in this paper. Currently, to create this planner we are improving the representation of the state of a node, enhancing the mechanisms to recognize problem solving situations, and extending the plan structures to incorporate more information [10,12]. Our preliminary experiments indicate that these developments should significantly improve the performance of distributed problem solv-ing networks, and may also be useful in blackboard-based problem solving systems in general.

Acknowledgements

This research was sponsored, in part, by the National Science Foundation under Grant MCS–8306327, by the National Science Foundation under Support and Maintenance Grant DCR-8318776, by the National Science Foundation under CER Grant DCR-8500332, and by the Defense Advanced Research Projects Agency (DOD), monitored by the Office of Naval Research under Contract NR049–041.

References

[1] Robert Axelrod, *The Evolution of Cooperation*, Basic Books, 1984.

[2] Stephanie Cammarata, David McArthur, and Randall Steeb, "Strategies of Cooper-ation in Distributed Problem Solving," *Proceedings of the Eighth International Joint Conference on Artificial Intelligence*, pp. 767–770, August 1983.

[3] Daniel D. Corkill, "Hierarchical Planning in a Distributed Environment," *Proceed-ings of the Sixth International Joint Conference on Artificial Intelligence*, pp. 168–175, August 1979.

[4] Daniel D. Corkill and Victor R. Lesser, *A Goal-Directed Hearsay-II Architecture: Unifying data and goal directed control*, Technical Report 81-15, Department of Com-puter and Information Science, University of Massachusetts, Amherst, Massachusetts 01003, June 1981.

[5] Daniel D. Corkill and Victor R. Lesser, "The Use of Meta-level Control for Co-ordination in a Distributed Problem Solving Network," *Proceedings of the Eighth International Joint Conference on Artificial Intelligence*, pp. 748–756, August 1983.

[6] Daniel D. Corkill, Victor R. Lesser, and Eva Hudlicka, "Unifying Data-Directed and Goal-Directed Control: An example and experiments," *Proceedings of the Second National Conference on Artificial Intelligence*, pp. 143–147, August 1982.

56

[7] Daniel David Corkill, *A Framework for Organizational Self-Design in Distributed Problem Solving Networks*, PhD thesis, University of Massachusetts, Amherst, Massachusetts 01003, February 1983, (Available as Technical Report 82-33, Department of Computer and Information Science, University of Massachusetts, Amherst, Massachusetts 01003, December 1982).

[8] Randall Davis and Reid G. Smith, "Negotiation as a Metaphor for Distributed Problem Solving," *Artificial Intelligence*, vol. 20, pp. 63–109, 1983.

[9] Richard Dawkins, *The Selfish Gene*, Oxford University Press, 1976.

[10] Edmund H. Durfee, *An Approach to Cooperation: Planning and Communication in a Distributed Problem Solving Network*, Technical Report 86-09, Department of Computer and Information Science, University of Massachusetts, Amherst, Massachusetts 01003, March 1986.

[11] Edmund H. Durfee, Daniel D. Corkill, and Victor R. Lesser, "Distributing a Distributed Problem Solving Network Simulator," *Proceedings of the Fifth Real-Time Systems Symposium*, pp. 237–246, December 1984.

[12] Edmund H. Durfee and Victor R. Lesser, "Incremental Planning to Control a Blackboard-Based Problem Solver," *Proceedings of the Fifth National Conference on Artificial Intelligence*, pp. 58–64, August 1986.

[13] Edmund H. Durfee, Victor R. Lesser, and Daniel D. Corkill, *Coherent Cooperation Among Communicating Problem Solvers*, Technical Report 85-15, Department of Computer and Information Science, University of Massachusetts, Amherst, Massachusetts 01003, April 1985, (Also to appear *IEEE Transactions on Computers*).

[14] Lee D. Erman, Frederick Hayes-Roth, Victor R. Lesser, and D. Raj Reddy, "The Hearsay-II Speech Understanding System: Integrating Knowledge to Resolve Uncertainty," *Computing Surveys*, vol. 12, no. 2, pp. 213–253, June 1980.

[15] Michael Fehling and Lee Erman, "Report on the Third Annual Workshop on Distributed Artificial Intelligence," *SIGART Newsletter*, vol. 84, pp. 3–12, April 1983.

[16] Michael Georgeff, "Communication and Interaction in Multi-agent Planning," *Proceedings of the Eighth International Joint Conference on Artificial Intelligence*, pp. 125–129, August 1983.

[17] Michael Georgeff, "A Theory of Action for Multiagent Planning," *Proceedings of the Fourth National Conference on Artificial Intelligence*, pp. 121–125, August 1984.

[18] Kurt Konolige, "A Deductive Model of Belief," *Proceedings of the Eighth International Joint Conference on Artificial Intelligence*, pp. 377–381, August 1984.

[19] Victor Lesser, Daniel Corkill, Jasmina Pavlin, Larry Lefkowitz, Eva Hudlicka, Richard Brooks, and Scott Reed, "A High-Level Simulation Testbed for Cooperative Distributed Problem Solving," *Proceedings of the Third International Conference on Distributed Computer Systems*, pp. 341–349, October 1982.

[20] Victor R. Lesser and Daniel D. Corkill, "The Distributed Vehicle Monitoring Testbed: A tool for investigating distributed problem solving networks," *AI Magazine*, vol. 4, no. 3, pp. 15–33, Fall 1983.

[21] Victor R. Lesser and Daniel D. Corkill, "Functionally-Accurate, Cooperative Distributed Systems," *IEEE Transactions on Systems, Man, and Cybernetics*, vol. SMC-11, no. 1, pp. 81–96, January 1981.

[22] Victor R. Lesser and Lee D. Erman, "Distributed Interpretation: A Model and Experiment," *IEEE Transactions on Computers*, vol. C-29, no. 12, pp. 1144–1163, December 1980.

[23] Horst Oberquelle, Ingbert Kupka, and Susanne Maass, "A View of Human-Machine Communication and Co-operation," *International Journal of Man-Machine Studies*, vol. 19, pp. 309–333, 1983.

[24] Jeffrey S. Rosenschein and Michael R. Genesereth, "Deals Among Rational Agents," *Proceedings of the Ninth International Joint Conference on Artificial Intelligence*, pp. 91–99, August 1985.

[25] Reid G. Smith, "The Contract-Net Protocol: High-Level Communication and Control in a Distributed Problem Solver," *IEEE Transactions on Computers*, vol. C-29, no. 12, pp. 1104–1113, December 1980.

[26] Reid G. Smith and Randall Davis, "Frameworks for Cooperation in Distributed Problem Solving," *IEEE Transactions on Systems, Man, and Cybernetics*, vol. SMC-11, no. 1, pp. 61–70, January 1981.

Edmund H. Durfee, Victor R. Lesser and Daniel D. Corkill
Department of Computer and Information Science
University of Massachusetts
Amherst, MA 01003

Chapter 3

Instantiating Descriptions of Organizational Structures

H. Edward Pattison, Daniel D. Corkill and Victor R. Lesser

Abstract

Instantiating and maintaining large distributed processing networks requires an explicit description of the system's organizational structure. Such a description identifies the system's functional components, their responsibilities and resource requirements, and the relations among them. Existing languages with features for describing organizational structure are inadequate for this task because they cannot describe the complex domain-specific relations found in many organizations. EFIGE is a language for specifying such relations. EFIGE aids the instantiation of these relations by allowing them to be constrained from the perspective of their members, and by allowing preferences to be expressed among instances of them. This chapter describes EFIGE and shows how relations with complex constraints may be implemented.

3.1 Introduction

The need to describe large and complex process structures—in order to instantiate them on specific processor configurations and to provide information to the operating system for resource allocation decisions and communication routing—has been recognized by a number of researchers, and they have developed languages for this purpose. These languages include DPL-82 [1], HISDL [2], ODL [3], PCL [4], PRONET [5], and TASK [6]. However, these languages are very weak in their ability to specify the complex processing structures necessary for the next generation of network architectures and distributed applications. This is especially true for applications with closely interacting tasks implemented on networks which are heterogeneous compositions of databases, effectors, sensors, and processors with various processing speeds and memory sizes. For example, the specification of the processing structure of a distributed processing network that performs signal interpretation requires a complex, domain-specific, communication relation between interpreting nodes and sensing nodes. This communication relation requires each interpreting node to communicate only with the smallest group of sensing nodes that can provide it with information about the region for which it is responsible. At the same time, each sensing node is required to communicate with a limited number of integrating nodes in order to minimize the time it must allocate for communication.

The specification of such complex process structures involves identifying functional components (such as interpreting and sensing nodes), their responsibilities (providing interpretations of the signals detected in a particular region) and resource requirements (processor speed and memory size, knowledge about interpreting signals, etc.), and the relations among them (communication and authority). Together, this information is a specification of the system's *organizational structure*. We see specification of organizational structure as not just parameter substitution and macro expansion, but rather a problem of *organizational planning* under conflicting instantiation constraints. These constraints arrive from the need to specify complex relations among the components of an organization. Relations include communication relations, authority relations that specify the importance given to directives from other nodes, and proximity relations that specify spatial positioning among objects. All of these relations may be complicated by interacting constraints. This was true of the communication relation between sensing and interpreting nodes given above, and is true of other relations as well. For example, a producer of a product whose value decreases with time may require that it be located near the consumer using the product or that both be located near nodes of a reliable transportation network.

Existing languages have implemented a few specific relations but their approach is limited. A communication relation, for instance, is described by explicitly stating that process X is to communicate with process Y. If the processes may be replicated, this statement becomes X_i communicates with Y_i, where i identifies a specific copy of each process. This form of description is not general enough. If Y_3, for example, is lost due to node failure, X_3 might as well be lost. Any information it was to have received from Y_3 will not be forthcoming and it will be idle; the production of any information it was to have sent Y_3 will consume system resources in vain. Since the description specifies only that X_3 is to communicate with Y_3, there is no way to find a substitute and one cannot be created because the characteristics of Y_3 that made communication with X_3 important are unknown.

Both the ability to specify more complex relations and to allow network designers to specify domain specific relations (such as the communication relation given above) are needed. Instead of requiring designers to specify communication relations as point-to-point connections, they should be asked to supply the criteria by which such pairings can be determined. The criteria that a member of one domain of a relation uses to recognize an acceptable member from another domain are called *constraints*. Constraints *specify* a relation because they indicate which pairings of a member of one domain with the members of another are permissible. More precisely, a relation defines a subset of the ordered pairs (in general, n-tuples) that is the Cartesian cross-product of each domain of the relation, where each constraint in the relation is a predicate that selects some of the pairings as more significant than others. We will more loosely describe constaints as defining a new, more restricted relation, by *refining* the definition of a more general relation.

In this chapter we describe a language, called EFIGE (pronounced "effigy"), for specifying the complex relations needed to describe a distributed problem solving system's organizational structure. We also describe an interpreter for EFIGE, that is able to instantiate a particular organization by combining a description (in EFIGE) of a generic *class* of organizational structures and a set of instantiation constraints that specify the particular instantiation. The introduction of relations defined with constraints to organization descriptions significantly enhances the description as a symbolic representation of the organization. It allows the description of organizational *classes*, as opposed to descriptions of specific instances of some class. Constraints, however, complicate organization instantiation. To instantiate a relation, solutions must be found that satisfy each of the constraints in the relation. This requires searching large spaces of possible solutions in an attempt to find values that will simultaneously satisfy all of the constraints. As an interim approach, we have adapted an algorithm from the Artificial Intelligence literature that is used to eliminate inconsistent assignments of values to constraints [7]. This approach is limited, however, because it tries to choose solutions that satisfy one constraint without first performing some analysis that will insure that the solution will be acceptable to the remaining constraints. The use of a more sophisticated approach awaits further research.

In the next section we present an example of an organizational structure, then discuss how it might be described in an organizational description language. Section 3.3 introduces the description language EFIGE and indicates how structures are described within this language. Section 3.4 describes how descriptions are instantiated, and Section 3.5 discusses the current status of this work and its relation to ongoing research.

3.2 An Example

In this section, a *hierarchical* organizational structure for distributed signal interpretation is presented. We use this organization as an example with which to identify organizational features requiring description.

In our scenario for distributed signal interpretation, different kinds of signals are emitted by various vehicles as they move through a region. The system's task is to create a history of vehicular activity within the region based on the signals it detects. One processor organizational structure for performing signal interpretation is the *hierarchical* organization. It has three types of components: *sensing nodes*, which perform signal detection and classification; *synthesizing nodes*, which make local interpretations of the signal information they receive from the sensing nodes; and *integrating nodes*, which combine interpretations received from other nodes to create interpretations over larger portions of the sensed region. Figure 3.1 illustrates an instance of the hierarchical organizational structure that has one integrating node, four synthesizing nodes, and four sensing nodes. The figure also shows the lines of communication between the nodes, although the directionality of these communication links and the information transmitted is not the same between all pairs of nodes. Finally, the figure indicates the overlapping regions scanned by each sensor. Figure 3.2 shows another instance of the hierarchical organizational structure. It has five integrating nodes, sixteen synthesizing nodes, and sixteen sensing nodes.

Figures 3.1 and 3.2 show two *instances* of the same organizational *class*. The goal of this work is to develop a way of describing organizational classes, as opposed to describing specific organizations that are instantiations of some class. The key features of any organizational class are the different types of components (in the distributed signal interpretation application, sensing, synthesizing, and integrating nodes) and the relations between them (communication between sensing and synthesizing nodes, synthesizing and integrating nodes, and low-level and high-level integrating nodes[1]). Each type of component has its own particular set of responsibilities to carry out (signal detection, interpretation, integration) and a set of requirements for resources to be utilized in meeting its responsibilities (processing hardware, knowledge about signal interpretation, etc.). The

---

[1]This last relation is not instantiated in Figure 3.1 because there is only one integrating node.

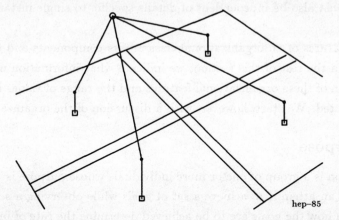

hep–85

Figure 3.1: An instance of the hierarchical organizational structure with one integrating node (circle), four synthesizing node (dots), and four sensing nodes (squares).

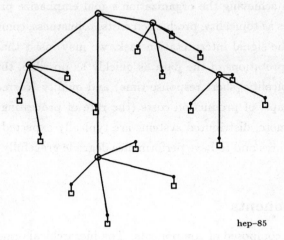

hep–85

Figure 3.2: The hierarchical organizational structure with five integrating nodes, sixteen synthesizing nodes, and sixteen sensing nodes.

63

relations between component types are independent of the numbers of components that may be instantiated for each type or on what processor they may execute—synthesizing nodes must always receive signal information from sensing nodes. For that reason, their descriptions must also be independent of details specific to single instances of the organization.

The key features of an organizational class are its components and the relations between them. In the rest of this section, we indicate what information must be included in a description of these organizational features and the range of values that will have to be accommodated. We start, however, with a discussion of the organization's *purpose*.

3.2.1   Purpose

An organization is a group of one or more individuals whose purpose is to perform some set of tasks in an attempt to achieve a set of goals while observing a set of constraints. Constraints on how the goals are to be achieved determine the rate of processing needed and, in turn, affect the size and complexity of the organization. For example, the goal of the hierarchical organization is to create a high-level history of vehicular activity over a region. The tasks required to achieve the goal include the detection and classification of acoustic signals generated by the vehicles, the weighing of evidence for the presence of a particular type of vehicle based on the signal types detected, and determining the paths of vehicles through the region and recording them.

Constraints on achieving the organization's goal emphasize processing tradeoffs between such features as topicality, production costs, robustness, completeness, and quality. For example, in the signal interpretation task, we may insist that the system produce highly rated interpretations of the data as quickly as possible, thus emphasizing maximal values for topicality (short response time) and quality (correct interpretations), at the expense, perhaps, of production costs (the rate of processing needed to derive the answer). Furthermore, distributed systems are typically expected to be robust; able to adjust to node failures and to have performance degrade gracefully as error in the system increases.

3.2.2   Components

Organizations are composed of components. The hierarchical organization, for instance, has three components: sensing, synthesizing, and integrating nodes. What these components have in common are sets of *responsibilities* and *resources* to be used in meeting them.

Responsibilities

Components perform tasks. These include: a subset of the tasks necessary for accomplishing the organization's purpose; management tasks incurred as organizational overhead; and—especially in human systems—tasks that counter, or do not contribute towards, the organization's purpose but are, for idiosyncratic reasons, important to the component. One way of specifying responsibilities is by assigning components subregions of the problem-solving space defined by the organizational task. For the signal interpretation task, the dimensions of the problem-solving space might be the physical region monitored by the system, problem-solving events (such as the detection of a signal of a certain type, the decision that a group of signals were produced by a particular type of vehicle, etc.), abstraction levels (signals of different types, groups of signals, vehicle types, patterns of vehicles), and time. Out of all of the tasks that an organization for signal interpretation needs to perform to meet its goals, sensing nodes perform only the signal detection task. Other components are responsible for performing the remaining tasks.

Resources

Components possess certain resources with which they are expected to perform their tasks, thus the resources required by a component will depend on the roles it plays in the organization. We describe three "flavors" of resources: software resources (knowledge), hardware resources (tools), and other components (consultants). Access to a component resource is access to another set of software and hardware resources and another list of component contacts.

Knowledge. We also describe three types of knowledge: **algorithms**, **data bases**, and **expertise**. Algorithms specify how to process data, data bases are repositories of information, and expertise refers to the type of heuristic knowledge characteristic of expert systems. The problem-solvers located at each node may incorporate any or all of these forms of knowledge. Algorithms and expertise, for example, tell a node how to interpret signal data as evidence for the presence of vehicles and how to track those vehicles. Some knowledge may be meta-level knowledge used to determine when it is appropriate to apply domain-specific knowledge.

Tools. In addition to knowledge about how to perform a task, a worker may require particular implements with which to execute the task. These can be effectors (a robot arm or the hammer or wrench that the arm may wield during a particular process) or sensors (the devices that a sensing node uses to detect signals). Use of a tool requires that the worker have additional knowledge: how to use it.

Consultants and Subcontractors. If unexpected problems arise that are outside the range of expertise of a component, it is useful to know of someone who does have the expertise. Given this information, the component could ask for problem solving advice or contract the problem's solution to the expert. Similarly, a component might find it useful to know who can use its data, who can provide it with missing data, or who is available to share its processing load. Smith has investigated a method of distributed problem solving, called the contract-net approach, in which a node, given a problem that it cannot solve alone, contracts for the solution of the problem or of its subproblems [8]. This method does not rely on knowing in advance who is capable of solving the problems or subproblems, since they can be broadcast to the network, but this information is used if available. This is known as *focused addressing*. We can imagine a scenario in the signal interpretation task in which a sensing node begins sending a synthesizing node information about signals of a type for which the node has no knowledge. If the synthesizing node knows, however, of another node that does have the knowledge, it could ask for help. If not, it could broadcast a request for the knowledge it needs.

Individual Characteristics

There may be information about a component that is not directly related to its responsibilities or resource requirements. For instance, it may be necessary to have some abstract description of how the component will function, especially if the organization's performance is to be evaluated before instantiation. The level of detail will vary with the application, but can include estimates of the average reliability of the component's outputs, mean time to failure, rates at which inputs can be processed, or even a state transition model that simulates how the component will behave. Pavlin, for example, presents a way of modeling the behavior of an entire distributed problem solving organization [9].

3.2.3   Relations Between Components

Components in an organization do not exist, nor do they function, independently of one another. Components interact. Commands, information, and subassemblies (including partial solutions) are passed between them, and they may work cooperatively at performing operations on some object. These interactions are expressed as relations between the components involved.

66

Relations between components can be arbitrarily complex. It will seldom be the case that only a single relation will exist between only two components. In general, a conjunction of relations between groups of components will be required. These groups may, in turn, be formed from other relations.

Communication

The most important relation between two or more components is who talks to whom. This is the relation shown most prominently in Figures 3.1 and 3.2, where each internode line represents an instance of a communication relation. The communication relation is used to identify a component's sources of a particularly valuable resource, *information*, and to identify the consumers of the information it produces.

Equally important are the details of what is exchanged during communication. The need to associate a message structure with a communication relation complicates its instantiation. It requires that objects satisfying the relation must, additionally, satisfy the constraint that their message structures be compatible. That is, if one object expects to send messages consisting of certain information in a specific format, the other object in the relation (assuming the binary case) must be prepared to receive that information in the same format.

Finally, it may be necessary to associate a specific communication strategy with a communication relation. Durfee, Lesser, and Corkill have investigated the effects of several communication strategies on the global behavior of a distributed problem solving network [10].

Authority

Authority is a relation that indicates how much emphasis should be given to messages from different sources or, possibly, to different messages from the same source. If the message has authority, the component may allow it to have greater impact on its activities. In the five-node organization, the integrating node may be given the authority to direct synthesizing nodes to look for evidence of vehicles in regions it designates. Upon reception of such a message, a synthesizing node might cease whatever processing it had chosen to do (based on the local information available to it) and take up the requested work.

How much attention should be paid to an authority? The component may realize that the environment has changed and the authority's instructions are no longer appropriate. Should they be followed, ignored, or disputed? A synthesizing node may have very strong evidence that a vehicle's path lies in a certain direction when it receives a directive from the integrating node to look elsewhere. The node must decide if it is more important to continue processing the strong data or to follow the integrator's instructions. In fact, it may be desirable to have individual variation between nodes, weighting some synthesizing nodes with greater bias toward the integrating node's authority than others. Nodes with little bias towards authority are called self-directing or *skeptical*. Reed and Lesser have discussed the importance of self-direction in the members of honey bee colonies [11]. Corkill discusses the use of skeptical nodes in distributed problem solving organizations performing signal interpretation [12].

In general, organizational relations can be described on two levels, at a (relatively) global level outlining the relation and its participants, and at the local level, where details and individual variance are elaborated.

Location, Proximity, et cetera

Many other important relations may exist between the components of an organization. For instance, if one component is a producer of a product whose value decreases with time, the component using that product may need to be located nearby, or they may both need to be placed near terminals of a reliable transportation network. Sales offices for a manufacturer may need to be located across the country, instead of all in one city. Sensing nodes in the organizations for signal interpretation need to be distributed across the entire region. Synthesizing nodes need to communicate with a sensing node (more generally, group of sensing nodes) that scans the nodes' region of responsibility.

3.2.4   Composite Components

Organizations are often composed of suborganizations. In order to simplify descriptions of such organizations, the suborganizations are treated as single components and the interactions among these components are detailed; then the components are "enlarged" to reveal the suborganization they represent. While these *composite* components do not have physical counterparts in the actual organization, they serve two purposes: they help make descriptions of organizations understandable, and they group physical components that perform the same organizational function. For these reasons, an organizational description language should provide the ability to logically "package" an organization as a single component of another organization. Furthermore, the language should treat individual and composite components the same. If one description knows as little as necessary about another, it will be easier to make modifications.

Composite components allow recursive descriptions of organizations. If there are enough nodes (twenty-one, for instance), the hierarchical organization (Figure 3.2) is instantiated as an integrating node with hierarchical organizations as its components. Each of these hierarchical suborganizations is again instantiated with its share of the original nodes. When the number of nodes becomes small enough, the organization is instantiated as a single integrating node with synthesizing nodes under it. If the number of nodes is small enough to start with, of course, no composite components need to be created. The synthesizing nodes are created right away. This is the case for five nodes, for example.

3.3 Describing Organizational Structures with EFIGE

This section introduces EFIGE, a language for describing organizational structures. Descriptions of organizations in EFIGE are hierarchical. That is, they are composed of either individual or composite structures, and a composite structure's components may be individual or composite. Figures 3.3 and 3.4 show part of the description of the hierarchical organization presented in Figures 3.1 and 3.2. Descriptions have global names, parameters that may have default values, and local variables. Components are given local names, are conditionally instantiated, may be replicated, and information—in the form of values for parameters—may be partitioned among them. Parameterized descriptions and conditional instantiation of components allow descriptions to be defined recursively. This is the case with the hierarchical organization.

Figure 3.5 shows part of the description of an individual component. Fields are provided for specifying the individual's duties within the organization, listing the resources the individual will require to meet its duties, and for additional information about the individual that may be accumulated during instantiation or may provide information to be used to estimate the individual's processing characteristics. Values for these fields are necessarily application dependent.

3.3.1 Relations

The hierarchical approach we have presented for describing organizations is similar to the specification framework of other languages. What gives our approach additional representative power is the introduction of relations and constraints into this hierarchical descriptive framework.

EFIGE allows relations of any kind to be established between components and allows additional information to be associated with the relation. For instance, almost all languages for describing organizational structures give their individual and composite struc-

```
;; All descriptions are given names.

(NAME hierarchical

;; A 'composite' description has components.

TYPE composite

;; Descriptions are parameterized.  The user can specify that a
;; parameter be bound to a different value than its default.

PARAMETERS
  ((number-of-integrating-nodes  :DEFAULT 5)
   (region                       ...  ))

;; The LOCAL-VALUES field is used to compute and assign values to
;; local variables.

LOCAL-VALUES
  ((number-of-synthesizers  ...  )
   (number-of-hierarchies   ...  ))

;; The COMPONENTS field lists the components of a composite
;; organization.

COMPONENTS

  ;; Components are given local names.

  ((COMPONENT-NAME synthesizers

    ;; Components are described by other organizational descriptions.
    ;; A description called 'synthesizing-node' is used to describe this
    ;; component.  It could be used to describe other components, as well.
    ;; 'Synthesizing-node' has a parameter, 'region', which will be set to
    ;; the value of 'worker-region' (defined in the COPIES field).
```

Figure 3.3: Part of the Description of the Hierarchical Organization

```
DESCRIPTION (synthesizing-node ((region worker-region)))

;; The organization that describes a component may be instantiated
;; more than once, depending on the value in the COPIES field.
;; 'Synthesizing-node' is to be instantiated 'one-less-node' times.
;; 'One-less-node' is a local variable defined in the LOCAL-VALUES
;; field.

COPIES (one-less-node

        ;; The VARY clause of the COPIES field is a construct for
        ;; declaring variables and assigning them a sequence of values
        ;; 'Worker-region' will be assigned a different value for each
        ;; instantiation of 'synthesizing-node'; consequently, each
        ;; instantiation will have a different value for its 'region'
        ;; parameter.

        (VARY
          (worker-region  ... )))

;; Components are only instantiated if their PRECONDITION predicate
;; function evaluates to true.  This component is to be instantiated
;; only if 'number-of-nodes' is within the range 3-5, inclusive.

PRECONDITION (within-subrange? number-of-nodes 3 5))

;; A second component.

(COMPONENT-NAME subhierarchy

  ;; The component, 'subhierarchy', is described by the description,
  ;; 'hierarchical', thus this component is recursive.

DESCRIPTION  (hierarchical  ... )
COPIES        (number-of-hierarchies
                 (VARY  ... ))
PRECONDITION (> number-of-nodes 5))
 ... )
... )
```

Figure 3.4: More of the Description of the Hierarchical Organization

```
;;; This description is of an individual structure, it has no components :::

(NAME synthesizing-node
 TYPE individual

 ;; Descriptions of individuals have PARAMETERS and LOCAL-VALUES fields,
 ;; but we'll ignore them here.


      ...


 ;; The tasks that an individual are to perform are specified in the
 ;; RESPONSIBILITIES field.  For our application, responsibilities are
 ;; specified as regions of the problem-solving space and rated by
 ;; importance.  'Sl-sensor-regions' is bound to a description of a
 ;; problem-solving region in the LOCAL-VALUES field.

 RESPONSIBILITIES
   ((PROCESS-AREA (sl-sensor-regions)
     IMPORTANCE       ...  )
        ...       )

 ;; The resources the individual needs to perform the tasks for which it is
 ;; responsible are given in the RESOURCES field.  One resource required by
 ;; our application is knowledge about specific tasks.

 RESOURCES
   (KNOWLEDGE-SOURCES
     ((KS-NAMES (determine-communication-kss ?this-description)
       GOODNESS       ...  )
        ...   ))

 ;; The CHARACTERISTICS field contains information that will vary
 ;; between individuals--even though they belong to the same component of
 ;; the organization--or information that can be used to simulate the
 ;; individual's behavior.

 CHARACTERISTICS
   (LOCATION   ...  )
    ...  )
```

Figure 3.5: Part of the Description of an Individual

tures *ports* and allow the composite structures to specify *communication links* among the ports of their components and between ports belonging to the composite structure and its component ports. But a communication link is only one kind of relation and ports are just devices for associating message structures, directionality, and other information with the relation. These concepts have been generalized in EFIGE.

There are three parts to the description of a relation and each part appears within the description of a different structure. The *declaration* of a relation between components appears in a composite structure (Figure 3.6). A declaration simply specifies that a relation exists between one, or more, components. Either type of component (individual or composite) can participate in a relation, but it is more likely that a composite structure will *forward* membership in the relation to some of its own components instead (Figure 3.7). Forwarding may occur again if the component to which membership in a relation is forwarded is another composite structure. Finally, the relation is *refined* within the structures that are to actually participate in it (Figure 3.8). This is where the constraints are specified and it is here, also, that any additional information is associated with it.

It should be noted that one relation may depend on the instantiation of another. For example, an integrating node may wish to communicate only with synthesizing nodes that receive information from sensing nodes with particular characteristics. This requires that the `sensor-synthesizer` communication relation be instantiated before the `integrator-synthesizer` relation. Because EFIGE is currently unable to recognize such situations, relations must indicate the order in which they are to be evaluated, relative to all of the other relations in the organization. This also helps the user avoid making circular references in constraints. The evaluation order of a relation is specified with its declaration.

A `RELATIONS` field is part of both composite and individual structure descriptions. It contains a list of parts of relations, although only refinement parts can appear in descriptions of individuals. Figure 3.6 shows the declaration part of a relation in EFIGE. The `RELATION-NAME` field gives the relation a local name; the `RELATION-TYPE` field indicates the type of relation expression. (The value `new` is used to indicate the declaration part of a relation, `forward` indicates the forwarding part, and `refine` the refinement part.) These two fields appear in all parts of the description of a relation. The integer expression in the `EVALUATION-ORDER` field is used to establish a partial order among `new` relations. The relations will be sorted in increasing order by their values for this field.

The `RELATE` field declares a relation between components by listing them as members of the *domains* of the relation. An *n*-ary relation has *n* domains. Each domain is provided with a name; component names, paired with the name of one of their relation

```
RELATIONS

  ;; Entries in the RELATIONS field are given names.

  ((RELATION-NAME sensor-synthesizer

    ;; Entries of type 'new' are used to declare the existence of a
    ;; relation between components of an organization.

    RELATION-TYPE new

    ;; This new relation is to be among the first implemented.

    EVALUATION-ORDER 1

    ;; This relation has two domains.  The first is given the name,
    ;; 'sensor', and consists of the structures instantiated for the
    ;; component, 'sensor-array'.  Within those structures, more
    ;; information about the relation is contained in an entry in
    ;; their RELATIONS field with the name, 'to-synthesizer'.
    ;; Similarly, the second domain is named, 'synth', and its
    ;; members are the structures instantiated for the 'synthesizer'
    ;; component.  These structures contain an entry in their
    ;; RELATIONS field with the name, 'to-sensor', that also
    ;; contains more information about the relation.

    RELATE ((sensor sensor-array$to-synthesizer)
            (synth  synthesizers$to-sensor)))
    ...
)
```

Figure 3.6: Example of the Declaration of a Relation

```
(RELATION-NAME middle-integrator

  ;; Composite structures may have entries in their RELATIONS field
  ;; with type, 'forward'.  These pass the composite structure's
  ;; membership in a relation on to one (or more) of the structure's
  ;; components.

  RELATION-TYPE     forward

  ;; The structures instantiated for the 'integrator' component will
  ;; become members in the relation in place of the composite structure.
  ;; The entry in their RELATIONS field with the name, 'upper-exchange',
  ;; will contain more information about the relation.

  FORWARD           (integrators$upper-exchange))
```

Figure 3.7: Forwarding a Relation

parts, are listed after it. All copies of the component will be included in the domain. The relation parts in the components must either refine the relation or forward it. The relation sensor-synthesizer in Figure 3.6 has two domains named sensor and synth. The members of the sensor domain are all of the copies of the structure instantiated for the component sensor-array. Similarly, the members of the synth domain are the structures instantiated for the synthesizers component. Within these structures, there must be an entry in their respective RELATIONS fields named to-synthesizer and to-sensor, respectively.

Figure 3.7 shows an example of the forwarding of a relation. In effect, forwarding a relation results in the replacement of the reference to a composite structure in the original relation with the list of the composite structure's components. Thus the structures instantiated for integrators will receive membership in the relation instead of the structure which includes middle-integrator.

A refine expression is embedded in the structure that will participate in the relation. It contains constraints for refining the relation and additional data that is to be associated with the relation. Constraints are discussed below. Figure 3.8 gives an example of relation refinement. The relation part to-sensor appears in the individual structure synthesizing-node which was instantiated as the synthesizers component of the composite structure hierarchical (Figures 3.3 and 3.4). It refines the relation sensor-synthesizer, which referred to it in Figure 3.6. Since this is (implicitly) a communication relation, to-sensor includes information that is to be associated with

75

the relation (such as the direction messages are to travel in the relation, their format, communication strategies, etc.).

3.3.2 Constraints

EFIGE allows each member of a relation to make local refinements to the relation's domains using a combination of restriction, group, and preference constraints. A relation, R, defines a set of n-tuples, $(x_1 \ldots x_n)$, that is the Cartesian product of n (not necessarily distinct) sets, $X_1 \times \ldots \times X_n$ (the domains of the relation). The number of n-tuples is equal to the product of the cardinality of each set. EFIGE uses restriction, group, and preference constraints to reduce the size of each of these sets and, hence, the size of R. They are described in this section.

Restriction

Restriction constraints are applied to the members of a set to identify those members for which the constraint evaluates to **true**. In other words, the constraint acts as a characteristic function, identifying a new set among the members of the old. EFIGE allows such a function to be provided for all of the domains of a relation:

$$(P_i X_i), i = 1 \ldots n$$

where

(FX) denotes the set $\{x | (x \in X) \wedge (Fx)\}$,

X_i is the i-th domain of R,

P_i is a predicate over X_i: the constraint. In effect, the relation becomes:

$$R = \prod_{i=1}^{n} (P_i X_i)$$

where $\prod_{i=1}^{n} X_i$ is used to indicate the Cartesian product, $X_1 \times \ldots \times X_n$.

Restriction constraints are used to identify those members in the other domains of a relation that are acceptable to the current member of the current domain as partners in the relation. The TASK language uses restriction constraints to direct assignment of resources [6]. These are limited to specification of proximity relations between processes and sets of physical resources identified by their attributes (features of the Cm* hardware). A TASK constraint, for example, might specify that a process must execute on a processor

76

```
(RELATION-NAME to-sensor

  ;; Each of the ultimate members of a relation (after all forwarding of
  ;; membership) has an entry of type 'refine' for that relation.
  ;; The 'refine' entry may provide each member with fields for the
  ;; description of additional information needed by the relation and may
  ;; reduce the size of the relation by allowing each member to reject
  ;; some of the tuples in which it was included when the relation was
  ;; originally defined (with a 'new' relation entry in the description
  ;; of some composite structure).

  RELATION-TYPE refine

  ;; The CONSTRAINTS field contains the constraints with which tuples
  ;; in the relation are selected and/or rejected (see Figure 9).

  CONSTRAINT
    ...

  ;; The ADDITIONAL-DATA field is used to add information to a
  ;; structure's description that is needed for the relation.  A
  ;; communication relation, for example, needs to know the direction
  ;; in which messages will travel, the type of message, and a
  ;; description of its format.

  ADDITIONAL-DATA
    ((communication
      ((DIRECTION   receive
        NATURE      (hyp)
        DISPATCHES ... ))
      ... ) ... )
    ... )
```

Figure 3.8: Relation Refinement

with a large local memory. Artificial Intelligence programs that perform planning tasks also use restriction constraints. For example MOLGEN, when planning experiments in molecular genetics, generates a constraint restricting the choice of a bacterium to one that resists an antibiotic [13].

Group

Group constraints are applied to a single set to create a set of sets. Each set in the new set is a subset of the original and, for each, the constraint evaluates to true. Thus the constraint is a characteristic function with a domain that is the power-set of the original set. As with restriction constraints, EFIGE allows a group constraint to be specified for each domain of a relation:

$$(Q_i \, \mathcal{P}(X_i)), i = 1 \ldots n$$

where

$\mathcal{P}(X)$ denotes the power-set of X,

Q_i is a predicate over $\mathcal{P}(X_i)$.

The group constraint, Q_i, identifies a set of sets: each subset, or group, is acceptable as the i-th domain of the relation. Thus alternate relations are possible, one for each combination of groups from each domain:

$$R = \prod [\bigvee [\prod_{i=1}^{n} (Q_i \, \mathcal{P}(X_i))]] \tag{3.1}$$

where $\bigvee X$ is used to indicate that alternative selections can be made from X and $\prod X$ denotes the Cartesian product of an indeterminate number of sets, the members of X.

Group constraints identify groups of objects that together satisfy some property that their individual members cannot (unless the size of a group is one). For instance, a relation in an organization that performs distributed signal interpretation may specify that sensing nodes are to communicate with synthesizing nodes. Each synthesizing node may use a group constraint to refine the relation by requiring that it communicate only with groups of sensing nodes that together can provide information about the entire region for which it is responsible. ADABTPL, a language for describing databases, employs both group constraints and restriction constraints [14].

Preference

Preference constraints implicitly define a partial order over a set by selecting one object from it. If this object is then removed, a second may be chosen, and so on. The i-th object in the ordering over a set X, where S is the preference constraint, is $(S\ V_i)$, for $1 \le i \le |X|$, where

$$V_i = V_{i-1} - \{(S\ V_{i-1})\}$$

$$V_1 = X$$

$$V_{|X|+1} = \phi.$$

Preference constraints may be used by any member of a relation to refine any domain:

$$(S_i^k\ X_i), i = 1 \ldots n, k \in \{1 \ldots |X_i|\}$$

where $(S^k X) \equiv (SV_k)$. Using preference constraints alone reduces the relation to a single tuple:

$$R = ((S_1^{k_1}\ X_1) \ldots (S_n^{k_n}\ X_n)), k_i \in \{1 \ldots |X_i|\}$$

During instantiation, preference constraints are employed to choose between the apparently equal options generated by a group constraint. For instance, the group constraint refining the communication relation between sensing and synthesizing nodes may identify two groups of sensing nodes that will be acceptable to a synthesizing node. A preference constraint is used to choose between them. The smaller group may be chosen in order to reduce communication overhead.

Composition

Composition provides a means for functional composition. Thus the domain of one constraint may be a set that has been defined by another constraint and the domains of a relation may be refined by many constraints. For instance:

$$R = \prod_{i=1}^{n} (S_i^{k_i}\ (Q_i\ \mathcal{P}(P_i\ X_i))), k_i \in \{1 \ldots |X_i|\} \tag{3.2}$$

where

S_i is a preference constraint,

Q_i is a group constraint,

P_i is a restriction constraint,

X_i is the i-th domain of R.

Note the differences between Equations 3.1 and 3.2. Preference constraints identify a single group from the list of groups produced by each group constraint, with the result that a single relation is selected from among the myriad possibilities.

EFIGE allows each member of a relation to refine (further specify) the relation using restriction, group, and preference constraints that are composed with each other in that order. The resulting constraint is evaluated for each member in its local context; thus the results may vary from member to member, even though the same constraint is applied. In any case, the solution to the overall relation then becomes (approximately) the union of the results of applying each of its members' local refinements:

$$R = \bigcup_{j=1}^{m} [\prod_{i=1}^{n} (S_{ij}^{k_j} (Q_{ij} \, \mathcal{P}(P_{ij} \, X_{ij})))]$$

where

$m = \sum_{i=1}^{n} |X_i|$ (i.e. j varies over all of the members of the relation),

$k_j \in \{1 \ldots |(Q_{ij} \, \mathcal{P}(P_{ij} \, X_{ij}))|\}$,

$X_{ij} = X_i - \{j\}$,

F_{ij} is member j's constraint on domain i.

Actually, the union operator is too simple for combining the local refinements to a relation. This is because the tuples in the desired relation must be *consistent* with one another. If, for example, the constraints for a member j of a binary relation select a tuple (jl), then the constraints for l should include that tuple in their selection as well. If this is not the case, it may be that the two members can be made consistent by using their second choices for tuples (choosing different values for k_j). Section 3.4 presents an algorithm for evaluating constraints and combining them in such a way that they are consistent.

Figures 3.9 and 3.10 show an example of the constraints a synthesizing node might use to refine a communication relation with sensing nodes. The PARTNERS field lists the names of the domains in the relation, omitting the name of the domain to which the synthesizing node belongs. The names in this list must match those given when the relation was declared (except for the name of the domain in which this constraint is a member). A restriction, group, and preference constraint must be provided for each of the domains listed. Thus the RESTRICTIONS, GROUPS, and PREFERENCES fields each contain a list of ordered pairs: the name of the domain followed by the constraint that will be applied to it. The restriction constraint is applied first to all of the members of a domain.

In Figures 3.9 and 3.10, the remaining contraints insure that the information associated with the relation (in the ADDITIONAL-DATA field, see Figure 3.8) is compatible and that the sensing node detects signals in at least part of the region for which the synthesizing node is responsible. Since this is a communication relation, compatibility means that there must be at least one sender and at least one receiver in the relation and that the proposed topics for discussion overlap. The group constraint is applied to those members that satisfied the restriction constraint. In this example, it will form groups of sensing nodes that together detect signals over the specified region. The preference constraint is applied to the groups to select one of them. In this case, it will choose the smallest group.

3.3.3 The Procedural/Declarative Interface

Figures 3.9 and 3.10 illustrate that much of the information in a description written in EFIGE is procedural. That is, functions provide details about how an organization is to be instantiated. This information is inherently application dependent; users of the language will need to develop libraries of the functions useful for each application. For instance, in Figure 3.9, the function, sensors-that-cover-region, returns groups of sensing nodes that, together, are able to detect signals from every part of a rectangular region. This function will not be of use in most applications. The declarative part of EFIGE, the component fields, provide a framework for organizing the procedural information and a method for applying it. Appendix B describes other functions needed to describe organizations for our distributed signal interpretation application.

3.4 Instantiating a Description

Instantiating an organization involves performing parameter substitution, testing component preconditions to find out which are to be instantiated, instantiating each component the specified number of times with the indicated parameter settings, and implementing relations between components. Implementing a relation requires finding solutions to each of the constraints associated with the relation. Finding these solutions is difficult because the solutions may interact. For example, the constraints refining a communication relation between synthesizing nodes and sensing nodes may choose the same sensing node for each of three synthesizing nodes. The sensing node's constraint's, however, may restrict it to communicating with any two of the synthesizing nodes, but not all three, in order to limit the amount of time it must allocate to communication. One of the synthesizing nodes will have to choose a different sensing node, which may affect the choices of other

CONSTRAINT

  ;; The PARTNERS field lists the other domains of the relation (other
  ;; than the one to which the owner of this constraint belongs). A
  ;; constraint of each type is provided for each of the domains.

(PARTNERS (sensor)

 ;; The RESTRICTIONS field predicates act as filters, rejecting
 ;; members of the other domains that do not meet their criteria.

RESTRICTIONS

  ;; The predicate 'compatable-communication?' examines the
  ;; descriptions in the ADDITIONAL-DATA fields of this relation
  ;; (see Figure 8) and each member of the 'sensor' domain for
  ;; consistency (e.g., since the DIRECTIONS field in this relation
  ;; is 'receive', the other must be 'send').

  ((sensor (and (compatable-communication?
              ?this-relation ?partner-relation)

  ;; This predicate determines if the area scanned by each sensing
  ;; node includes the area specified by region. The symbol
  ;; '?partner-structure' will be bound to each sensing node's
  ;; structure description. In contrast, the symbol
  ;; '?partner-relation', above, is bound to the relation entry in
  ;; each structure description that is used to refine the relation
  ;; between sensing and synthesizing nodes.

        (sensor-scans-part-of-region?
         region ?partner-structure))))

  ;; The functions in the GROUPS field select groups of tuples in
  ;; which the members of the given domain are, together, able to
  ;; satisfy some predicate. The function,
  ;; 'sensors-that-cover-region', returns a list of those groups of
  ;; non-redundant sensors that together are able to scan the area
  ;; given by 'region'. The symbol, '?candidate-structures', is
  ;; bound to a list of the the descriptions of those structures
  ;; that passed the restriction constraints.

Figure 3.9: Constraints

82

```
GROUPS ((sensor (sensors-that-cover-region
                 region ?candidate-structures)))

;; The functions in the PREFERENCE field return one of the
;; groups of tuples formed by the group constraints.  The
;; function, 'select-smallest-set' finds the group with the
;; least number of members.

PREFERENCE ((sensor (select-smallest-set ?groups))))
```

Figure 3.10: Constraints (continued)

nodes. In this section, we first present the algorithm for finding solutions to constraints, then briefly describe how the `hierarchical` organization is instantiated.

3.4.1 The Constraint Solution Algorithm

The algorithm we use for finding solutions to the interacting constraints associated with a relation first applies each member's preference and group constraints, then chooses a member with the smallest number of groups. Thus a synthesizing node whose group constraint produced only one solution will be processed before any node with two or more groups to chose from. This strategy minimizes branching in the search tree, which is important because we have no global knowledge to apply when choosing a branch. Instead we use local knowledge. The member's preference constraint is used to select one of its groups, if there is more than one. The selected group is a *local* solution. Local solutions are then used to build the global solution. The local solution lists the sensing nodes with which this synthesizing node will communicate, the global solution contains all of the sensing-synthesizing node pairings.

The groups of the other members of the relation that do not yet have a local solution must be made *consistent* with the solution just chosen. For the other members' groups to be consistent with the solution they must either:

1. contain the name of the member just processed, if the solution contains their name;

2. not contain the name of the member just processed, if the solution does not contain their name.

Inconsistent groups are deleted and the unprocessed member that now has the smallest group is selected for processing. Thus the choice of a local solution may prune the search tree and affect the order in which nodes in the tree are visited.

83

If any of the other members has all of its groups deleted, a new group must be chosen for the local solution, the effects of making the other members consistent with the old solution undone, and they must be made consistent with the new solution instead. If all of a member's groups are tried as local solutions without success, chronological backtracking is employed. The search is returned to the last member processed, its local solution is discarded, its consistency effects undone, and so on. If the search ends up back at the first member tried and tries all of its groups unsuccessfully, no global solution exists and the relation cannot be implemented.

The complete algorithm is included in Appendix A.

3.4.2 Instantiation of the Hierarchical Organization

Figure 3.11 shows how instantiation of each composite description leads to instantiation of individual components and the implementation of relations between them. The `hierarchical` organization was instantiated with the `number-of-nodes` parameter set to twenty-one and the `number-of-sensors` parameter set to sixteen. When the upper `hierarchical` structure was instantiated, the preconditions of only two of its components evaluated to true: the `integrators` component and the `subhierarchies` component. One copy of the `integrators`, and four of the `subhierarchies`, were instantiated. The `integrator-integrator` relation is implemented because, at this point, it is actually an `integrator-subhierarchies` relation. In the `subhierarchies`, membership in the relation is forwarded to their `integrators` components.

Each of the `subhierarchies` components is another `hierarchical` organization. This time, however, in each of them the precondition for the `subhierarchies` component evaluates to false and the recursion stops. The other components' preconditions evaluate to true and, for each of the new `hierarchical` organizations, one `integrators`, four `synthesizers`, and four `sensor-array` components are instantiated. In each organization, an `integrator-synthesizer` relation and a `synthesizer-sensor` relation is implemented.

3.5 Status and Ongoing Research

This section describes the current status of EFIGE followed by a discussion of improving the organization instantiation process and a discussion on using organization descriptions to automate the configuration process. These activities are steps toward an eventual goal of *organizational self-design*, where the organization is able to reconfigure modify itself in response to changes in its operating requirements and environment.

84

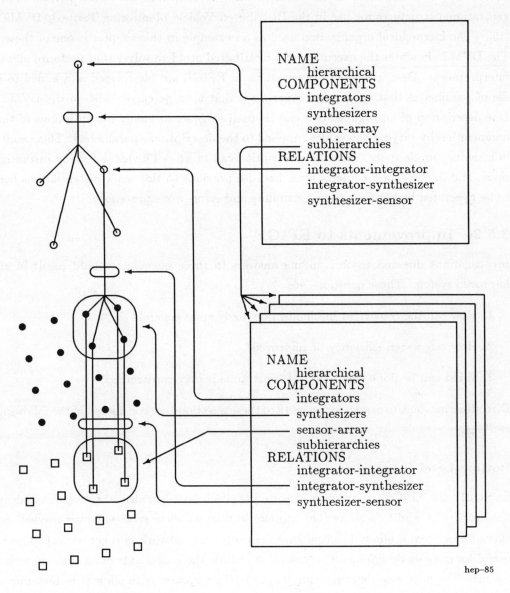

NAME
    hierarchical
COMPONENTS
    integrators
    synthesizers
    sensor-array
    subhierarchies
RELATIONS
    integrator-integrator
    integrator-synthesizer
    synthesizer-sensor

NAME
    hierarchical
COMPONENTS
    integrators
    synthesizers
    sensor-array
    subhierarchies
RELATIONS
    integrator-integrator
    integrator-synthesizer
    synthesizer-sensor

hep-85

Figure 3.11: Instantiation of the hierarchical organizational structure with sixteen sensors, sixteen synthesizing nodes, and five integrating nodes, requires five instantiations of the hierarchical composite description as well.

3.5.1 Status

EFIGE has been implemented in Common Lisp. Descriptions have been written of organizational structures for use in the Distributed Vehicle Monitoring Testbed (DVMT) [15]. (The hierarchical organization used as an example in this chapter is one of these.) The DVMT simulates the execution of a distributed problem solver that performs signal interpretation. Descriptions of organizations in EFIGE are interpreted and added to a file of parameters that specify the experiment that is to be carried out on the DVMT. One description of an organization can be used to generate many instantiations of the organization by varying the values supplied to the description's parameters. This results in a savings in file space, since one description can be stored instead of many instantiations, and in the experimenter's time, because previous to this work instantiations had to be generated by hand—a time-consuming and error-prone procedure.

3.5.2 Improvements to EFIGE

Investigations directed toward finding answers to three questions should result in an improved system. These questions are:

1. How can the constraint mechanism be made more general?

2. How can search efficiency be improved?

3. What can be done when a set of constraints is over-constrained?

Directions in which to search for answers to these questions are considered in the following sections.

Bottom-Level Constraints

Currently, the EFIGE interpreter is free to physically locate nodes wherever dictated by the description and to assume that communication channels exist wherever needed. In effect, the system is allowed to configure the processing network as is convenient. This is useful for initially designing an organization outside the constraints of an existing architecture. The next step for enhancing the EFIGE interpreter is to allow it to instantiate the "best" organization of a specified class, given a particular network architecture. This involves specifying *bottom-level* constraints representing the particular network architecture and incorporating those fixed constraints into the instantiation of an organization. Bottom-level constraints specify that the instantiated organization include components

86

with given values for some or all of their attributes or that particular relations be implemented. Such constraints could specify an entire processing network, making it the job of the interpreter to instantiate, as best as possible, an organization's functional components and their relations over a physical network that provides less than optimal support. For example, if bottom-level constraints specify that there are only a dozen processing nodes but the instantiated organization needs thirty-seven, the interpreter will have to assign multiple organizational nodes to the same processor.

Constraint Propagation

Because of the combinatorics, it may be unreasonable to apply restriction or group constraints to all of the members of a domain. For instance, the number of ways n synthesizing nodes can communicate with s sensing nodes, where any given synthesizing node may be assigned from zero to s of the sensing nodes, is 2^{ns}. The present algorithm attempts to avoid examining all of the objects of this set by eliminating subsets of objects on the basis of local information. Thus, if the restriction constraint for synthesizing node A selects sensing node P, P is checked to see if its restriction constraint selected A. If not, P is eliminated as a candidate for A. This eliminates from further consideration all of those configurations in which P and A are paired, thus cutting the search space in half. Unfortunately, evaluation of A's restriction constraint requires applying it to all of the sensing nodes in the domain and this is repeated for all of the synthesizing and sensing nodes in the relation.

Another approach to improving efficiency is constraint propagation [13]. In this method a description of the partner required by a member in a relation is gradually built up as constraints are evaluated. Constraint propagation, it is hoped, would allow the accretion of a more specific constraint that would identify, after only one pass say, the sensing nodes that both require and are required by a synthesizing node. Propagation of restriction constraints has been performed in systems such as MOLGEN [13]. Propagation of the more complex constraints used in EFIGE, however, is a problem that remains to be investigated.

Constraint Utility

When a set of constraints proves to be over-constrained, it would be useful to be able to intelligently modify them so that a solution can be obtained or to determine which ones must be satisfied and which ones can be safely ignored or relaxed. This requires knowledge about the purpose of the constraint (based on the organizational goals), so that judgments about its importance can be made, and it requires the ability to locate the conflict, to determine which constraints to modify. This may not always be possible. Fox assigns constraints *utility* ratings which can then be used to determine the usefulness of a given constraint's satisfaction, or lack of satisfaction, in a situation [16]. The least useful constraints are less likely to adversely affect results if they are not met. Utility ratings are also used during backtracking to find decision points where it is most likely that the wrong choice was made. A new choice is sought for and made at these points and the search is restarted.

Optimal Solutions

Group and restriction constraints provide binary valued ratings of choices: either an element of a set is accepted or it is rejected. Preference constraints order choices but provide no information about their relative worth. An assignment of relative worth to choices might allow more intelligent decisions to be made: several choices could turn out to be equivalent, or one choice may emerge as much more preferable than all others. The problem is, given the relative worth of local choices, how can they be optimized globally?

3.5.3 Organizational Self-Design

The long-term goal of this research is organizational self-design. An organization with this ability will perform the following tasks:

1. monitor the organizational structure's effectiveness in directing organizational activities,

2. identify new organizational structures appropriate to a new situation,

3. select the best among them,

4. implement the new structure over the network while preserving the network's problem solving activities.

This work's contribution toward organizational self-design is a language that provides for low-level, symbolic representations of organizational structures, but much work remains.

Organization Design

A slightly simpler problem is that of organization design. Organization design is the problem of choosing the best organization class—from a set of class descriptions—given knowledge about the organization's purpose (goal, task, and constraints on the goal) and

88

the environment in which the organization is to operate. In fact, there are two problems: determining which organizations satisfy the constraints and then deciding which is "best". These correspond to steps 2 and 3 of the organizational self-design task.

Repairing Broken Organizations

Another simplification of the organizational self-design task is the problem of reconfiguration. Reconfiguration is needed to repair a "broken" instance of an organization (for example, one in which a component has failed), given its organization class description and environment information. This includes the problem of fault detection/diagnosis (roughly step 1), but the emphasis is then placed on recovering lost functionality without adopting a new organizational structure (eliminating steps 2 and 3, simplifying step 4). This is still a difficult problem; more fundamental problems underlie both it and the problems of organizational design and self-design. The sections below discuss some of these more fundamental problems. They also adopt a further simplification by considering static organizations (an organization capable of self-design is, by definition, dynamic).

Task Description

The purpose of an organization is to perform some task. A description of that task is essential for organizational self-design, and may be useful during instantiation as well. It is required for organization design in order to assign components their tasks, which will include parts of the organization's task. Fox states that tasks can be described by listing inputs, outputs, the transformations inputs undergo to become outputs, and the state transitions the processor goes through during task execution [3]. Is this information adequate for describing tasks? What is a suitable notation for representing this information? Pavlin, for instance, uses a Petri-net inspired approach to model the behavior of distributed problem solving organizations, this method might be adapted to describe tasks as well [9].

Organizational Goals

The goals of an organization are its desired performance abilities. Examples of organizational goals include: meet a minimum production rate, do not expend more than can be recovered by a maximum per unit cost, products must meet minimum standards of quality and reliability, the organization must function at a minimum rate of efficiency, and so on. How can these organizational goals be formulated and evaluated? Assessing the ability of an organization to meet a set of goals may require simulating the organization and observing its behavior as it processes its tasks. How is this to be done?

Environment Model

The design of an organization that is able to meet its organizational goals requires information about the environment in which it will function. The environment is the ultimate source of the organization's inputs and the destination of its products. The model needs to include knowledge about the rate at which its inputs will arrive and the variability of that rate, the characteristics of its inputs and their variability, interactions or correlations between inputs, the effects of outputs on inputs, and the degree to which it is ignorant of any of these things. The model is a prediction of what the environment will be like when the organization is functioning within it. How can this knowledge be represented?

Integration of Knowledge.   How can the knowledge about the organization's task, its goals, and its environment be combined and used effectively when making choices during instantiation?

3.5.4   Summary

We have suggested that descriptions of organizational structure are important for the instantiation and maintenance of distributed systems over large heterogeneous networks. Current languages for describing organizational structure do not allow descriptions of arbitrary relations and are incapable of describing higher-order relations. We have identified three types of constraints (restriction, group, and preference) and have used them to describe and instantiate arbitrary and complex organizational relations. We have provided an algorithm for finding solutions to interacting constraints employed in descriptions of relations. Finally, we have tested these techniques by incorporating them in an organizational instantiation language, called EFIGE, and its interpreter.

Appendix A: The Complete Constraint Solution Algorithm

begin

Order relations with RELATION-TYPE "new" by EVALUATION-ORDER.

for

    each relation with RELATION-TYPE "new"

do

    Determine the members of each domain of the relation.

    for

        all members in the relation

    do

        Apply appropriate RESTRICTION constraint to members of each domain
            to form CANDIDATES set.

    end-for.

    for

        all members in the relation

    do

        Make CANDIDATE sets mutually consistent.

    end-for.

    if

        any member is left with an empty CANDIDATES set

    then

        Indicate **over-constrained**.

    else

        for

            all members in the relation

        do

            Apply appropriate GROUP constraint to each domain's CANDIDATES
                sets to form GROUP sets for each domain.

        end-for.

    end-if

Set PROCESSED stack to **empty**.

Set UNSOLVED list to list of all members in the relation.

repeat

    while

        (not **over-constrained**) and (UNSOLVED list not **empty**)

    do

        Set CURRENT-MEMBER to member in UNSOLVED list with smallest
            product of the number of GROUP sets for each domain.

        Set REJECTED list of CURRENT-MEMBER to **empty**.

        repeat

            if

                GROUP set for any domain of CURRENT-MEMBER is **empty**

            then

                Add members in REJECTED list to GROUP set.

                Set REJECTED list to **empty**.

                if

                    PROCESSED stack is **empty**

                then

                    Indicate **over-constrained**.

                else

                    Set CURRENT-MEMBER to top of PROCESSED stack.

                    Pop top of PROCESSED stack.

                end-if

            else

                Use PREFERENCE constraints to select a group for each
                    domain from GROUP sets of CURRENT-MEMBER.

                Set SOLUTION of CURRENT-MEMBER to selected groups.

                Delete selected groups from GROUP sets of CURRENT-MEMBER.

                Make GROUP sets of members in UNSOLVED list consistent
                    with SOLUTION of CURRENT-MEMBER.

                if

                    no member in UNSOLVED list left with an **empty** GROUP set

                then

                    Delete CURRENT-MEMBER from UNSOLVED list.

                    Add CURRENT-MEMBER to PROCESSED list.

                    Indicate **local-success**.

```
                    end-if
            end-if


        if
                (not over-constrained) and (not local-success)
        then
                    Undo consistency changes to members in UNSOLVED list.
                    Add SOLUTION of CURRENT-MEMBER to REJECTED list
                        of CURRENT-MEMBER.
            end-if
        until (local-success) or (over-constrained).
    end-while
    if
        (additional-solutions-requested) and (not over-constrained)
    then
        for
            all members in the relation
        do
            Save SOLUTION of member.
        end-for.
        Set CURRENT-MEMBER to top of PROCESSED stack.
        Pop top of PROCESSED stack.
        Add SOLUTION of CURRENT-MEMBER to REJECTED list
            of CURRENT-MEMBER.
    end-if
    until (no additional-solutions-requested) or (over-constrained).
end-for
end
```

Appendix B: Domain Specific Functions

This appendix describes some functions needed for the description of organizations in the DVMT. A few of these have been seen in the examples throughout this report.

The simplest class of functions tests, collects, or summarizes the contents of particular fields in a given description. For example, one function in this class tests if a node's knowledge sources include a particular set of knowledge sources, and another determines if a sensor is capable of detecting vehicular activity in some portion of a given region. Other examples examine a subfield of the CHARACTERISTICS field in a sensor description to see if it includes a given list of values, compare the rating of a sensor's accuracy at classifying and locating signals with a given value, test to see if an organization has interest-areas that intersect with a supplied list of interest-areas, list the classes of signals a sensor detects, and determine the communication knowledge sources an individual will need based on its communication activity.

Another function class tests for the presence of a relation between fields in multiple descriptions or summarizes data from multiple descriptions. The example in Section 3.2 includes a function from this class which finds all of the combinations of sensors (from a list of sensors) that will, between them, scan all of a given region. Other functions from this class check that the distance between two locations does not exceed a given value, order individual organizations by their distance from a given location and return a list of the n closest organizations, and return a region that encloses all of the regions scanned by a list of sensors.

A number of functions were written to perform operations on *regions*, two-dimensional rectangular areas specified by the coordinates of their lower-left and upper-right corners. (Technically, a region is just one dimension of an interest-area and it is only a matter of convenience that they are all rectangles in the DVMT.) Some of these functions

- compute a minimum enclosing rectangle

- accept a list of rectangles and return the rectangle that is overlapped by all of them

- accept two overlapping rectangles, break up the area of the first rectangle that is not overlapped by the second into smaller rectangles (at most, three are required), and return them in a list

- fill a rectangle with overlapping rectangles (this is used by a composite structure to assign regions to its components).

A final function, with arguments an integer, a maximum divisor, and a minimum quotient, returns a list of no more than maximum divisor integers, all of them at least as large as the minimum quotient, such that they all add up to the original number. This function is used to distribute employees to subhierarchies (in the example of Section 3.3), where managers do not want to manage more than some number of subhierarchies (maximum divisor) and a minimum number of employees are required to make up a hierarchy (minimum quotient).

Acknowledgements

This research was sponsored, in part, by the National Science Foundation under grants MCS-8306327 and DCR-8500332, and by the Defense Advanced Research Projects Agency (DOD), monitored by the Office of Naval Research under Contract NR049-041.

References

[1] Lars Warren Ericson, "DPL-82: A Language for Distributed Processing," *Proceedings of the 3rd International Conference on Distributed Computing Systems*, pp. 526–531, Miami/Ft. Lauderdale, Florida, October 1982.

[2] Willie Y-P. Lim. "HISDL—A Structure Description Language," *Communications of the ACM*, vol. 25, no. 11, pp. 823–830, November 1982.

[3] Mark S. Fox, *Organization Structuring: Designing large complex software*, Technical Report 79-155, Computer Science Department, Carnegie-Mellon University, Pittsburgh, Pennsylvania, December 1979.

[4] Victor R. Lesser, Daniel Serrain, and Jeff Bonar, "PCL: A process-oriented job control language," *Proceedings of the First International Conference on Distributed Computing Systems*, pp. 315–329, 1979.

[5] Richard J. LeBlanc and Arthur B. Maccabe, "The Design of a Programming Language Based on Connectivity Networks," *Proceedings of the 3rd International Conference on Distributed Computing Systems*, pp. 532–541, Miami/Ft. Lauderdale, Florida, October 1982.

[6] Anita K. Jones and Karsten Schwans, "TASK Forces: Distributed software for solving problems of substantial size," *4th International Conference on Software Engineering*, pp. 315–330, Munich, Germany, September 1979.

[7] David Waltz, "Understanding Line Drawings of Scenes with Shadows," in Patrick Winston, editor, *The Psychology of Computer Vision*, pp. 19–91, McGraw-Hill, 1975.

[8] Reid G. Smith, "The Contract Net Protocol: High-Level Communication and Control in a Distributed Problem Solver," *IEEE Transactions on Computers*, vol. C-29,, no. 12, pp. 1104–1113, December 1980.

[9] Jasmina Pavlin, "Predicting the Performance of Distributed Knowledge-Based Systems: A Modeling Approach," *Proceedings of the National Conference on Artificial Intelligence*, pp. 314–319, Washington, D.C., August 1983.

[10] Edmund H. Durfee, Victor R. Lesser, and Daniel D. Corkill, "Coherent Cooperation Among Communicating Problem Solvers," *IEEE Transactions on Computers*, 1987. (Accepted for publication. Also published as Technical Report 85-15, Department of Computer and Information Science, University of Massachusetts, Amherst, Massachusetts 01003, April 1985).

[11] Scott Reed and Victor R. Lesser, *Divison of Labor in Honey Bees and Distributed Focus of Attention*, Technical Report 80-17, Department of Computer and Information Science, University of Massachusetts, Amherst, Massachusetts 01003, September 1980.

[12] Daniel D. Corkill, *A Framework for Organizational Self-Design in Distributed Problem Solving Networks*, Ph.D. Thesis, University of Massachusetts, February 1983. (Also published as Technical Report 82-33, Department of Computer and Information Science, University of Massachusetts, Amherst, Massachusetts 01003, December 1982.).

[13] Mark Stefik, "Planning with Constraints (MOLGEN: Part 1)," *Artificial Intelligence*, vol. 16, pp. 111–140, 1981.

[14] David Stemple and Tim Sheard, "Specification and Verification of Abstract Database Types," *Proceedings of the 3rd ACM SIGACT-SIGMOD Symposium on Principles of Database Systems*, pp. 248–257, Waterloo, Ontario, Academic Press 1984.

[15] Victor R. Lesser and Daniel D. Corkill, "The Distributed Vehicle Monitoring Testbed: A tool for investigating distributed problem solving networks," *AI Magazine*, vol. 4, no. 3, pp. 15–33, Fall 1983.

[16] Mark S. Fox, *Constraint-Directed Search: A Case Study of Job-Shop Scheduling*, Ph.D. Thesis, Carnegie-Mellon University, 1983, (Also published as Technical Report CMU-CS-83-161, Computer Science Department, Carnegie-Mellon University, Pittsburgh, Pennsylvania 15213).

H. Edward Pattison, Daniel D. Corkill and Victor R. Lesser
Department of Computer and Information Science
University of Massachusetts
Amherst, MA 01003

Part II

Architectures and Languages

Chapter 4

The Architecture of the Agora Environment

R. Bisiani, F. Alleva, A. Forin, R. Lerner, and M. Bauer

Abstract

Agora is an environment that supports the construction of large, evolutionary programs that manipulate complex data structures, e.g., problem solving systems. **Agora** can be customized to support the computational model that is most suitable for a given application. **Agora** has been designed explicitly to support multiple languages and highly parallel computations by means of memory caching and pattern directed invocation. Systems built with **Agora** can be executed on a variety of general purpose multiprocessor architectures.

4.1 Introduction

The design and implementation of systems comprising both AI and "numeric" components on a multiprocessor is not a simple task. State-of-the-art AI environments solve some, but not all, the problems raised by such a task. These environments provide multiple programming models but fall short of supporting "non-AI" languages and multiprocessing. Some programming environments provide abstractions tailored to the incremental design and implementation of large systems (e.g., LOOPS [4], STROBE [9]) but have little support for parallelism. Other environments support general purpose parallel processing (e.g., QLAMBDA [7], Multilisp [6], LINDA [3]) but do not tackle incremental design (Linda) or non-shared memory computer architectures (QLAMBDA,

99

Multilisp). Some of these environments are also based on Lisp and are therefore most suitable (although not necessarily limited) to shared memory architectures.

This paper describes an environment, called **Agora** that specifically addresses the problem of supporting the design and implementation of heterogeneous systems on multiprocessors. **Agora** supports heterogeneous systems by providing a *parallel virtual machine* that is independent of any language, allows a number of different programming models and can be efficiently mapped into a number of different computer architectures. Rapid evolution is supported by providing *incremental programming* capabilities similar to those found in Lisp environments. Programs that run on the parallel virtual machine can be added to the environment and share the same data with programs that were designed independently. These characteristics make it possible to provide an unlimited set of *custom environments* that are tailored to the needs of a user, including environments in which parallel processing has been *hidden* from the end user. Finally, parallelism is strongly encouraged since systems are always specified as parallel computations even if they will be run on a single processor. **Agora** is not alone in developing this type of system. ABE [1] and AF [2] are two environments with goals similar to **Agora**'s.

Agora is not an "environment in search of an application" but is "driven" by the requirements posed by the design and implementation of the CMU[1] distributed speech recognition system [10]. During the past year, we designed and implemented an initial version of **Agora** and successfully used it to build two prototype speech-recognition systems. Our experience with this initial version of **Agora** convinced us that, when building parallel systems, the effort invested in obtaining a quality software environment pays off many-fold in productivity. **Agora** has reduced the time to assemble a complex parallel system and run it on a multiprocessor from more than six man-months to about one man-month. The main reason for this lies in the fact that the details of communication and control have been taken care of by **Agora**. Application research, however, calls for still greater improvement. Significant progress in evaluating parallel task decompositions, in CMU's continuous speech project, for example, will ultimately require a single person to assemble and run a complete system within one day.

This paper is an introduction to the architecture of **Agora** and a description of the experience of using **Agora** to build a large speech recognition system. The current structure of **Agora** is the outcome of the experience acquired with two designs and implementations carried out during 1985.

---

[1]Carnegie Mellon University

4.2 Agora's Architecture

Agora's structure can be explained by using a layered model (see Figure 4.1).

- *The bottom layer* is a network of heterogeneous processors: single processors, shared memory multiprocessors, loosely-connected multiprocessors and custom hardware accelerators. The Mach operating system provides the basic software to execute computations on all of these machines and **Agora** provides tools to distribute computations, as Mach abstractions, among the machines[2].

- *The Mach layer* provides three major abstractions: message passing, shared memory and threads. *Message passing* is the main communication mechanism: all **Agora** implementations can run on machines that provide message passing as the only communication mechanism. *Shared memory* (when available in the underlying computer system) is used to improve performance. *Threads* (computations that share their address space with other processes) are used to support the fast creation of new computations (a useful but not always vital characteristic).

- *The parallel virtual machine layer* represents the "assembly language level" of **Agora**. Computations are expressed (currently in **C** or Common Lisp) as independent procedures that exchange data by using **Agora**'s primitives and are activated by means of a pattern matching mechanism on data from other procedures. It is in this layer that the most suitable Mach primitives are selected, the code is compiled and linked, tasks assigned to machines, etc. Computations expressed at this level are machine independent. Although systems can be fully described at this level, the virtual machine level is best used through *frameworks* rather than programmed directly.

- *The framework layer* is the level at which most of the application researchers program. A framework is like a specialized environment built to interact with the user in familiar terms, translating them into the *parallel virtual machine* abstractions. The description, assembly, debugging and running of an application are all performed through its associated framework(s). This structure encourages the distinction between an *application engineer* and *researchers*. The structure of an application is designed into a set of frameworks by an application engineer. Researchers then use the frameworks to build and test the actual system. In many respects **Agora** frameworks are similar to ABE's frameworks, see [1].

---

[2]Mach is a Unix-compatible (TM) operating system that runs on multiprocessors, see [5].

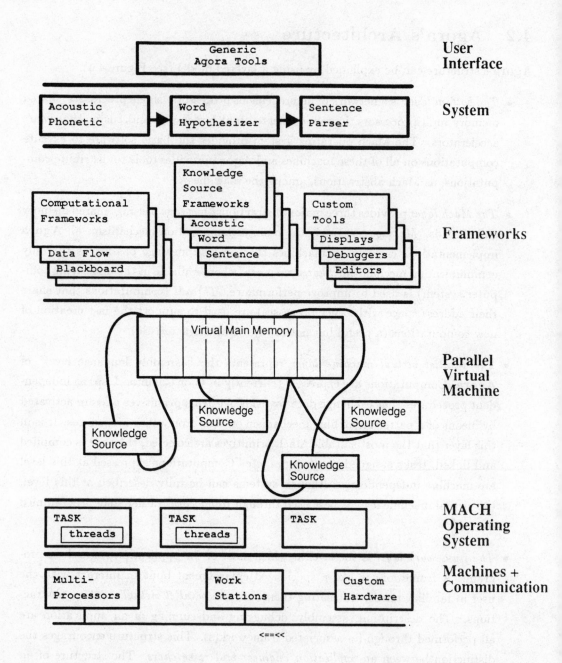

Figure 4.1: Layered Model of **Agora** and its Interfaces

102

4.3 The Agora Virtual Machine

The **Agora** virtual machine has been designed with two goals in mind: first, to be able to efficiently execute different programming models, and second, to avoid restricting the possible implementations to specific computer architectures. **Agora** represents data as sets of homogeneous *elements*. Each set of elements is stored in a global structure called a *clique*. A clique has a unique name and a type designation. **Agora** encourages the user to split a computation into separate components, called Knowledge Sources (KS), that execute concurrently, exchange data through cliques, and are activated when certain patterns of elements are generated. A clique can be accessed by any KS provided that it knows the name of the clique. Cliques are shared among KSs by first having some KS **create** the clique with some name and having the other KSs execute a **share** on it. In a speech recognition system, for example, an element could be a phoneme, word, sentence, etc.; a clique could contain a lattice of phonemes generated by a KS and a KS could be the routine that scores phonetic hypotheses.

4.3.1 Element Cliques

An Element Clique (EC) is a set of Elements, each of the same type. Element types are described within the KS code using the syntax of the language that is used to program the KSs, possibly with some additional information. The type definitions are interpreted by **Agora** and additional information is stripped from the source code by a preprocessor (built into the framework) before the code is handed to the compiler or interpreter. This means that users need not learn a special type definition language. This is in contrast with other language-independent data transport mechanisms, like the mechanism described in [8], that use a separate language to define the data. The additional information in the type declarations can contain information for scheduling and debugging purposes (e.g., the expected number of accesses per second, the legal values that elements can assume, display procedures, etc.).

KSs access elements in an EC through *capabilities*. Capabilities are manipulated using **Agora** functions and can be used to "copy" from an EC into the address space of a KS and vice versa (with shared memory, often no real copy will be necessary). There are two modes of access: *Read-only* and *Add-element*. Although anyone can read from an EC, KSs can only add elements if they have a capability to the EC with Add-Element access. In any event, once added, elements cannot be modified or deleted. Knowledge Sources can, however, signal that they are no longer interested in a given Element Clique, allowing some garbage collection.

4.3.2 Knowlege Sources

Each KS contains one or more functions. KS functions are completely independent and need only be able to deal with the types of elements they use. KSs are started by calling the **Agora** primitive `new_ks`. Unlike many parallel programming environments, KSs may be started at *any* time, allowing the system to tailor its computing resources to the dynamic needs of the running system.

When a KS is started, a pattern is specified for each KS function which, when satisfied, activates the function. Activation patterns are expressed in terms of *arrival events* and the values of the data stored in the elements. An arrival event is generated whenever an element has entered a clique. For example, one can specify a pattern that is matched every time a new element enters the clique or a pattern that only matches if a field in the element has a specific value. More than one clique can be mentioned in the same pattern but no variables are permitted in the pattern (i.e., there is no binding). It is also possible to specify if an element must be considered consumed by a successful match or if it can be used by other patterns. This can be very useful to demultiplex the contents of a clique into different KSs or to guarantee mutual exclusion when needed.

4.3.3 Agora Language Primitives

KS functions are written in any of the supported languages extended with the **Agora** library for that language. This library provides all of the **Agora** primitives, expressed in a way that is compatible with the language used. The **Agora** primitives are similar to the typical functions that an operating system would provide: start new processes (create new KS's in **Agora**), manipulate files (create, share and copy cliques) and schedule processes (e.g., change the amount of computation allocated to a KS).

The structure of a typical KS consists of the EC type definitions, a declaration of the KS's name and parameters, and the KS functions (entry points):

```
<EC type defns.>

KS foo(parameters);
{
    <global declarations>
    entry point triggered at creation time:
    {
        <code>
        ......
```

104

```
      creation of new and shared element streams;
      ......
      <code>
}
entry point triggered by a pattern:
{
      ......
      <code>
      ......
}
<more entry points>
}
```

In this description, `<code>` can contain any statement in the language that is being used and calls to any of the following **Agora** functions:

new_KS (name, inst., patterns, params.) → **KS** starts a KS; specifies how many instantiations to start, when the KS should be activated, and capabilities to be passed to the KS upon activation. The KS instantiation(s) remains active and can be reactivated an unlimited number of times. The user can explicitly allow or disallow **Agora** to use the same address space when a KS is built more than once.

create (ECname, ECtype, Access) → **capability** creates an *element clique* with the specified global name and global type. It also specifies the legal operations on the EC.

share (ECname, Access) → **capability** binds a local capability with a previously created EC and specifies the operations that will be performed on the EC (read, read/add) by the local KS. The operations specified must be consistent with the attributes of the element clique specified in the corresponding create().

get_activation ( ) → **capability** returns a capability to the element(s) that caused an activation (satisfied the activation pattern). If elements from more than one clique are involved successive calls to *activation* will return all the capabilities.

get (capability) → **local variable** copies the elements specified by the capability into the KS address space.

add (p, capability) adds the data to the element stream pointed to by the capability.

terminate (KS) terminates all the active instances of the KS effectively canceling the effect of new_KS. Can be used by a KS on itself (and its siblings).

update (KS, patterns) changes the activation patterns for a KS.

regulate (KS, new_power) controls the resource allocation.

4.3.4   The Mapping into the Mach Layer

KSs in the *parallel virtual machine* are mapped into Mach primitives. In this mapping a KS can be clustered with other KSs that can benefit from sharing computer resources. For example, a cluster could contain KSs that access the same clique or KSs that should be scheduled (i.e. executed) together. Mach provides two processing primitives, tasks and threads. A task is a normal process, while threads are light weight processes running in the same address space. Although clusters could be implemented as Mach tasks, with each KS implemented as a thread, sharing the address space between unrelated tasks can be very dangerous. Clusters containing multiple instances of the *same* KS, however, can be very effectively and simply, implemented as Mach threads. Heterogeneous clusters can be implemented as multiple processes which communicate either by shared memory or messages.

Currently, the composition of clusters must be fully specified by the user, but **Agora** maintains information on which KSs are runnable and on how much of the cluster computation power each KS should be receiving. The computation power associated with a KS can be controlled by any KS in a cluster by using **Agora** primitives.

In summary, the **Agora** virtual machine provides mechanisms to statically and dynamically control multiprocessing: KSs can be clustered in different ways and executed on different processor configurations and clusters can be used to dynamically control the allocation of processors. One should note that this opens up the possibility of implementing focus-of-attention policies within a system, but the responsibility of designing the control procedures remains with the user.

4.4   Frameworks

The framework level is the primary interface for describing, building and executing an application. Different applications require different computational models and a different style of interaction with the user. A framework provides an environment which is tailored to the requirements of the system or components for which it is used. It consists of a set of customized tools, unified into a single environment. This allows the tools to

106

work together and benefit through sharing of the knowledge of the task. To facilitate this sharing, **Agora** provides a simple frame language, CFrames, which implements a semantic net knowledge base which can be shared among the tools in a framework.

4.4.1   Typical Framework Tools

A tool, in a framework, is some program which the user can invoke from within the framework. It is either an external program (e.g., a C compiler or Screen editor) or another application created through **Agora**. All frameworks must contain some minimum set of tools. These tools must provide:

Task description: Some mechanism through which a user describes a system. This includes both defining the structure of the system, if not fixed by the framework, and providing the user-supplied code.

Preprocessors: Once the user has provided the necessary user-supplied code, the preprocessor translates that into parallel virtual machine primitives. This may include combining the user-supplied code with code defined within the framework to implement the desired programming model.

Multiprocess running and debugging: A user interface which allows the user to startup and run the system on a variety of real machines. More advanced frameworks will provide multiprocess debugging aids which continuously trace memory activity in a nonobtrusive way, perform controlled replay of a particular sequence of KS activations, start a number of EC and language debuggers, etc.

EC Display: Some mechanism should be provided to allow the user to view the data contained in the ECs of a running system. In primitive frameworks, the user can ask to see a particular element in some EC. More advanced frameworks may provide customized interactive displays.

EC Management: At a minimum, there must be some way to read elements from a file into ECs and vice versa. For better interaction, an element editor could be provided which allows the user to interactively view elements in ECs and add new elements to ECs.

Performance monitoring: The framework should provide the user with some idea of what is happening during a run of the system.

Of course, there can be a wide range of sophistication in these tools, ranging from a standard screen editor, the C compiler, Make, and some way to execute the resulting programs, to structured or graphical editors, graphical debuggers, and fancy displays of the contents of ECs, etc. Since tools are no different from user systems it is easy to continually program additional tools and integrate them with the basic system.

4.4.2 CFrames: The Knowledge Base

Agora provides a simple frame language (called CFrames) that is patterned after the SRL language [11]. CFrames lets users and programs store and access knowledge in the form of a semantic net. The semantic net is stored as Element Cliques and therefore can be shared by different tools, even tools running on different machines.

CFrames provides a simple but effective set of primitives. They allow the tools in a framework to manipulate a network of schemas (frames) which contain slots with values. The slots represent either attributes of the frame, or relations. In the latter case, the slot's values identify other frames, which forms the network. The initial implementation provides for inheritance of slots through *IS-A* relations among frames.

The network for a framework, managed by CFrames, is intended to be shared among a (possibly changing) set of tools. For this reason it is designed to be very flexible and is implemented using Element Cliques. Each tool in the framework can **share** the ECs which contain the network and then invoke CFrames primitives to find information in the network or add information, possibly adding slots and nodes to the network as it needs.

4.4.3 Designing and Using Frameworks

The framework structure encourages the distinction between an *application engineer* and *researchers*. The computational model and style of interaction of an application is designed into a set of frameworks by an application engineer. Researchers then use the frameworks to build and test the actual system.

Application Engineers first program one or more frameworks which implement the programming environments that an application requires. Typically, an application engineer takes an existing framework and adds new tools or replaces existing tools to create a new framework. A first level framework would provide a standard text editor, a compiler/linker, and some interface which allows a user to run an application. To implement a data-flow framework, for example, the application engineer would add the parallel virtual machine code to implement data-flow and remote-procedure-call communication mechanisms and a preprocessor tool to merge this code with the user-supplied code. A new, structured graphical editor could be supplied which would let a user define the data-flow structure of a system in terms of data-flow graphs and invoke the standard text editor

108

to fill in the boxes with code. A more specialized framework could "fix" the data-flow structure, providing the user with a number of "slots" each of which is to be filled in by the user (possibly from some library of routines). In any case, once the user has supplied all of the necessary code, the framework translates the user-supplied code into the proper parallel virtual machine abstractions.

Once a set of frameworks has been generated, *researchers* can then create a system by using the tools in a framework to fill in the necessary user-code and data. Since the framework hides the details of constructing a parallel system, the researcher need only be familiar with the user-specified code. In the speech system, for example, the word hypothesizer is described by using a framework that embodies the asynchronous control necessary to run the word hypothesizer in parallel and code to display the data processed: leaving the actual hypothesization code for the user to supply. A user of this framework need only be familiar with the word hypothesization algorithms and the language in which they are written in order to be able to experiment with different algorithms.

In many cases, the researcher will fill in the "slots" of a framework with other frameworks rather than actual code. This allows systems to be built out of separate modules. Furthermore, each of the submodules is itself a system which can be independently built and tested. In the speech system example, a complete word hypothesizer framework can be supplied to the *speech system* framework when the entire system is to be run. Whenever frameworks are merged into another framework the tools from all the original frameworks are made available in the combined framework.

4.4.4 Framework Summary

Frameworks provide an environment for users to construct their systems. An application engineer designs frameworks to hide the complexities of dealing directly with the parallel virtual machine, leaving the researchers to deal only with the details of their work. For the application engineers, **Agora** provides a semantic network knowledge base which can be shared by the tools in a framework. The structure of frameworks also makes it easy to refine the framework tools and add new tools. This encourages moving progressively more of the complexities of parallel programming from the user to the framework tools.

4.5 Example System Built with Agora

We will illustrate how **Agora** can be used by describing the design of the CMU speech recognition system, ANGEL [10]. ANGEL uses more computation than a single processor could provide (more than 1,000 MIPS), is programmed in two languages (the system currently comprises more than 100,000 lines of **C** and CommonLisp code), uses many different styles of computation, and is in continuous evolution since more than 15 researchers are working on it. Figure 4.2 shows the top level organization of the system. Arrows indicate transfer of both data and control. At the top level most of the components communicate using a data-flow paradigm, with the exception of the **Sentence Parser** and **Word Verifier** which use a remote-procedure-call paradigm. In the figure, two of the components, the **Acoustic Phonetic** and **Word Hypothesizer** components, contain a sketch of the structure of their subcomponents. The acoustic phonetic component, for example, uses both data-flow (the horizontal lines) and blackboard paradigms (the circle connected to the center KSs). It is important to note that Figure 4.2 shows the *current* structure and that part of the work being done on the system concerns expanding the number of modules and evaluating new ways of interconnecting them.

Frameworks are used to provide each component with the environment that is best suited to its development. At the top level there is a framework that provides a graphic editor to program data-flow and remote-procedure-call computations. Each subcomponent of the top level framework is developed using its own framework. We will use the **word hypothesizer** subcomponent as an example.

The word hypothesizer generates word hypotheses by applying a beam search algorithm at selected times in the utterance. The inputs of the search are the phonetic hypotheses and the vocabulary. The times are indicated by a marker, called *anchor*, that is computed elsewhere. The word hypothesizer must be able to receive anchors and phonemes in any order and perform a search around each anchor after having checked that all the acoustic-phonetic hypotheses within Δ time units from the anchor are available. Phonetic hypotheses arrive at unpredictable times and in any order.

The word hypothesizer requires two functions: *the matching function* (**match()**) that hypothesizes words from phonemes and *the condition function* (**enough_phonemes()**) that checks if there are enough phonemes within some time interval from the anchor. The editor provided by the word-hypothesizer framework lets a researcher specify these two functions and binds them with the parallel virtual machine level description. This combination is then compiled to provide the parallel implementation. The framework also contains a display function that can be altered by a user.

This fragment of code describes the KS-level implementation of the word hypothesizer framework:

```
/************** Element Clique Type Definitions **************/
Element-Type anchor {
    AnchorTime : integer;
```

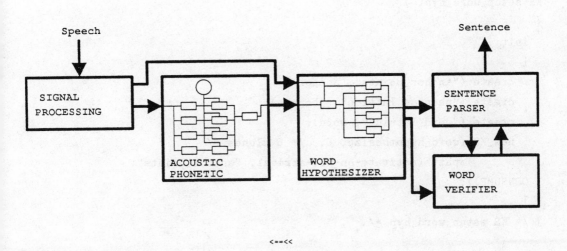

Figure 4.2: Structure of the ANGEL Speech Recognition System: Top-level and Internal Structure of the Acoustic-phonetic and Word-hypothesizer Modules

```
}
Element-Type phoneme {
    BeginTime, EndTime : integer;
    .....
}
Element-Type word {
    .....
}



/********************* Configuration KS *********************/
KS setup_word_hyp( )
{
  init:
  {
    create ("anchor_points", anchor);
    create ("phoneme_lattice", phoneme);
    create ("word_lattice", word);
    new_KS (word_hypothesize, 6,  /* 6 clones */
            patt (activate-on-new-arrival, "anchor_points",
  CONSUME));
  }
} /* KS setup_word_hyp */



/************************ Scheduler KS ************************/
KS word_hypothesize ( )
{
  CAP phons, words;
  init: /* Shares the necessary ECs to gain access to them*/
  {
    phons = share ("phoneme_lattice", Read);
    words = share ("word_lattice", Add);
  }
  entry: /* Activated by the arrival of an anchor */
  {
```

```
    CAP anch;
    word matched_word;
    anch := get_activation ( );
 /* checks time of last element in the phons clique */
    if condition (anch$->$AnchorTime,
 get_last_element(phons)$->$EndTime)
    {
       match (anch$->$AnchorTime, &matched_word);
       add_element (words, matched_word);
    }
    else
       new_KS (wait, 1, /* one instantiation */
               patt (activate-on-new-arrival, "phoneme_lattice"),
               anch$->$AnchorTime)
   }
} /* KS word_hypothesize */


/*************************** Wait KS **************************/
KS wait (anchor)
int anchor;
{
   CAP words;
   init:
   {
      words = share ("word_lattice", Add);
   }
   entry: /* Activated by the arrival of phoneme elements */
   {
      word *matched_word;
      if condition (anchor, get_activation( )$->$EndTime) then
      {
match (anchor, &matched_word);
         add_element (words, matched_word);
terminate (self());
      }
```

113

```
    }
} /* KS wait */



/*********************** Match Function **********************/
match (time_reference, matched_word)
int time_reference;
word *matched_word;
{
   ...
} /* match */



/******************** Condition Function ********************/
condition (t1, t2)
int t1, t2;
{
   ...
} /* condition */


/***********************************************************/
```

Please note that the use of **Agora**'s constructs, and not the syntax, is important.

At the beginning, the setup_word_hyp KS is started which starts six word_hypothesize KSs. Then, whenever some outside KS generates an anchor and places it on the anchor_points EC, the *entry* function of one of the word_hypothesize KSs is activated. Only one of the six KSs are activated since the pattern was set to *consume* the element which satisfies the pattern, thus making it unavailable for the other five word_hypothesize patterns. The activated function then checks to see if there are enough phonemes on the phoneme_lattice EC to run the match routine. If there are enough, it runs match, adds the matched word to the word_lattice EC and waits for another activation. If there are not enough phonemes, it starts a wait KS. This KS is activated whenever a phoneme element arrives on the phoneme_lattice EC. If, with the arriving phoneme, there are enough phonemes to do the match, the match is performed, the word is added to the word_lattice EC and the KS terminates. Figure 4.3 shows a pictorial description of the KSs and memory layout.

There are a number of ways in which the Word_Hypothesizer framework can map the

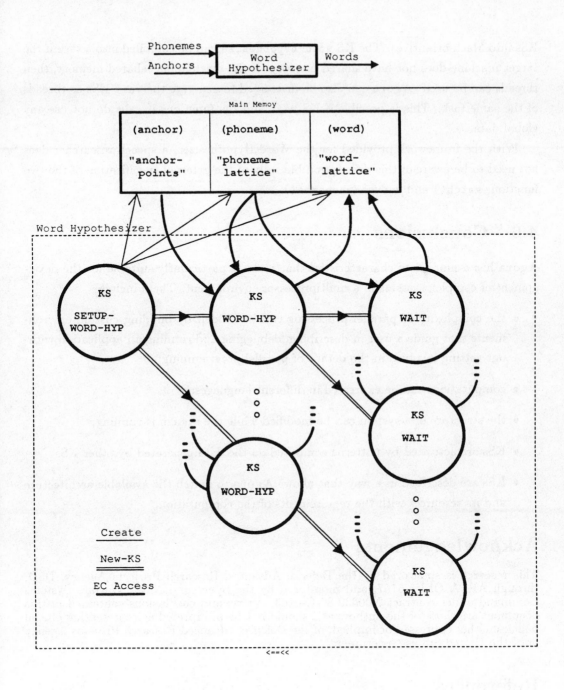

Figure 4.3: The Organization of the KS Level of the Word-Hypothesizer

KSs into Mach primitives. The KS `word-hypothesize` can be compiled into a task if the target machine does not have shared memory. If the machine has shared memory, then threads can be used. **Agora** can also be instructed to generate the `wait` KSs as threads of the same task. This is possible if KS `wait` and the functions it calls do not use any global data.

With the framework provided for the Word-Hypothesizer, a speech researcher does not need to be aware of this description but only of the external specification of the two functions `match()` and `enough-phonemes()`.

4.6   Conclusions

Agora has a number of characteristics that make it particularly suitable for the development of complex systems in a multiprocessor environment. These include:

- the complexity of parallel processing can be hidden by building custom environments that guide a user in describing, debugging and running an application without getting involved in the details of parallel programming;

- computations can be expressed in different languages;

- the structure of a system can be modified while the system is running;

- KSs are activated by patterns computed on the data generated by other KSs;

- KSs are described in a way that allows **Agora** to match the available architecture and its resources with the requirements of the computation.

Acknowledgements

This research is sponsored by the Defense Advanced Research Projects Agency, DoD, through ARPA Order 5167, and monitored by the Space and Naval Warfare Systems Command under contract N00039-85-C-0163. Views and conclusions contained in this document are those of the authors and should not be interpreted as representing official policies, either expressed or implied, of the Defense Advanced Research Projects Agency or of the United States Government.

References

[1] L. Erman, et al., "ABE: Architectural Overview," *Proceedings of the 1985 Distributed Artificial Intelligence Workshop*, Sea Ranch, California, December 1985.

[2] P. E. Green, "AF: A Framework for Real-time Distributed Cooperative Problem Solving," *Proceedings of the 1985 Distributed Artificial Intelligence Workshop*, Sea Ranch, California, December 1985.

[3] N. Carriero and D. Gelernter, "The S/Net's Linda Kernel," *Proceedings of the Tenth ACM Symposium on Operating Systems Principles*, December 1985.

[4] D. G. Bobrow and M. J. Stefik, "A Virtual Machine for Experiments in Knowledge Representation," Xerox Palo Alto Research Center TR, April 1982.

[5] R. Baron, R. Rashid, E. Siegel, A. Tevanian, and M. Young, "Mach-1: An Operating System Environment for Large Scale Multiprocessor Applications," *IEEE Software (Special Issue)*, July 1985.

[6] H. Halstead, "Multilisp: A Language for Concurrent Symbolic Computation," *ACM Trans. on Programming Languages and Systems*, vol. 7, no. 4, October 1985, pp. 501-538.

[7] R. P. Gabriel and J. McCarthy, "Queue-based Multiprocessing Lisp," *ACM Symp. Lisp and Functional Programming*, August 1984.

[8] A. D. Birrel and B. J. Nelson, "Implementing Remote Procedure Calls," *IEEE Trans. Computer Systems*, vol. 2, no. 1, February 1984, pp. 39-59.

[9] R. G. Smith, "Strobe: Support for Structured Object Knowledge Representation," *Proceedings of the Eighth International Joint Conference on Artificial Intelligence*, August 1983.

[10] R. Bisiani and D. A. Adams, "The CMU Distributed Speech Recognition System," *Eleventh DARPA Strategic Systems Symposium*, Naval Postgraduate School, Monterey, CA, October 1986.

[11] M. S. Fox and J. McDermott, "The Role of Databases in Knowledge-Based Systems," Robotics Institute TR, Carnegie-Mellon University, 1986.

R. Bisiani, F. Alleva, A. Forin, R. Lerner and M. Bauer
Department of Computer Science
Carnegie-Mellon University
Pittsburgh, PA 15213

Chapter 5

MACE: A Flexible Testbed for Distributed AI Research

Les Gasser, Carl Braganza and Nava Herman

Abstract

Parallelism in AI problem-solving applications can be exploited at many different levels: in hardware, in the implementation language (e.g., a production system language), in a problem-solving paradigm, or directly in the application. MACE (Multi-Agent Computing Environment) is an instrumented testbed for building a wide range of experimental Distributed Artificial Intelligence systems at different levels of granularity. MACE computational units (called "agents") run in parallel, and communicate via messages. They provide optional facilities for knowledge representation (world knowledge, models of other agents, their goals and plans, their roles and capabilities, etc.) and reasoning capabilities. The MACE environment maps agents onto processors, handles inter-agent communication, and provides:

- A language for describing agents,

- Tracing and instrumentation,

- A facility for remote demons,

- A collection of system-agents which construct user-agents from descriptions, monitor execution, handle errors, and interface to a user.

We have used MACE to model lower-level parallelism (a distributed system of production rules without global database or inference engine, where each rule is an agent) and to build higher-level distributed problem-solving architectures (domain-independent distributed blackboard and contract-net schemes). MACE is implemented on a 16-node INTEL SYM-1 large-memory hypercube and in a LISP machine environment.

5.1   Introduction

5.1.1   MACE Goals

Distributed Artificial Intelligence (DAI) is a subfield of AI concerned with the problems of describing and constructing multiple "intelligent" systems which interact. MACE (for Multi-Agent Computing Environment) is a language, programming environment, and testbed for DAI systems [8,9,10,17,20,27,35]. Other experimental testbeds have been built for DAI research (e.g., [18,21,30]), but these have generally encompassed only a single problem-solving architecture or domain (e.g., air-traffic control or distributed sensor nets; rule-based, blackboard, or contract-net architectures, etc.). In MACE we have built on these experiences to construct a testbed which will be useful for experimenting with a variety of architectures and problem-solving paradigms, at varying levels of granularity. The goal of MACE is to support experimentation with different styles of distributed AI systems, at different levels of complexity.

An experimental system built in MACE is a collection of *agents* which run in parallel and interact in organized ways. The dominant metaphor of MACE is that of a DAI system as an organization of problem-solvers. MACE supplies the basic constructs for describing features of agents which allow for reasoning about their organization (see below). At a high level, a programmer can describe the role and authority structure of agents, their goals, plans, skills, etc. A cluster of agents can be viewed abstractly as a unit, so agents can reason about other parts of the system as organizations with which they interact. In this way, MACE provides a basis for research into comparative organizational forms for problem-solving.

But not all MACE agents need to be complex; we would also like to experiment with DAI systems which don't require large-grain agents or knowledge of organization. The MACE organizational paradigm suffices to model very simple agents (such as a collection of individual production rules built as agents, which interact in highly structured ways). It can be used to describe collections of medium-granularity agents which interact more opportunistically (such as a blackboard system with multiple knowledge sources). It would be useful for describing large and complex collections of high granularity agents (such as a collection of higher-level problem-solvers with changing organizational structures).

Versions of MACE are now running on an Intel SYM-1 concurrent processor ("hypercube") and on TI Explorer LISP machines. Our emphasis is on experimentation with DAI techniques, not on efficient execution of MACE agent communities. MACE is an attempt to provide the tools for prototyping experimental systems which run in real parallel environments, but not for production-quality delivery systems.

This chapter describes the philosophy of MACE, the high-level constructs of MACE, and many of the functions which implement those high-level constructs.

5.1.2   General Description of MACE

A programming system should reflect the concepts and structures of the problems it is designed to express. The dominant metaphor of MACE is a collection of intelligent, semi-autonomous agents interacting in organized ways. In Wegner's terms [33], MACE is a *distributed, object-oriented system*. The MACE system is a collection of components, including:

- A collection of **agents**: Agents are the basic computational units of the MACE system. MACE agents are inherently "social" in nature: they know about some other agents in their environment, and expect to draw upon and coordinate with the expertise of others they know about. Thus they may need to know the identity and location of their acquaintances, something about their capabilities, etc. MACE agents represent this information in the form of "models of other agents in the world." In addition, agents may be organized into sub-units or coalitions which act in response to particular problems. In this sense they respond as organized groups or composites. The MACE Agent Description Language includes facilities for describing organized clusters of agents.

- A community of **system agents**: The pre-defined system agents provide MACE command interpretation, a standard user interface, the agent-builder cluster, error handling, tracing, execution monitoring, etc. Specific MACE agents serve as interactive tools for building MACE programs. Such tools include agents to build and edit the behaviors and structure of other agents, as well as to change the parameters of the execution environment or simulation.

- A collection of **facilities** which all agents may use: These include a pattern matcher, a simulator, several standard agent engines, handlers for standard errors, and standard messages understood by all agents. The MACE testbed is instrumented to allow for measurements of the characteristics of problem-solvers during experimental runs. Message traffic, queue and database sizes, work done by an agent (in

121

terms of elapsed real time or number of invocations), and load on a processor node are common measurements. We expect distributed AI systems constructed from collections of agents to be very complex [22,25,26]. In addition, we would like to have the control provided by repeatable tests, especially for development purposes. For this reason the MACE system includes a parameterized simulator. Agents communities can be developed on the simulator and moved to MACE on parallel hardware. MACE incorporates extensive pattern-matching facilities for interpreting messages, for pattern-directed invocation of asynchronous events (e.g., demons and other event-monitors), and for associative database access within agents.

- **A description database**: Agent descriptions are maintained in a description database by a system-agent cluster which constructs new descriptions, verifies descriptions, and constructs executable agents from descriptions.

- A collection of **kernels**: MACE kernels collectively handle communication and message routing, perform I/O to terminals, files, or other devices, map agents onto processors, and schedule agents for execution.

5.1.3 Related Work

The conceptual roots of MACE as a programming system are closest to ROSS, ACTORS, and LISP FLAVORS [14,21,34]. In such languages, the high level encapsulation units for computation are abstract data-types sometimes called *objects* [31]. Objects incorporate local variables and procedures, and interact by "sending messages" to one another. However, existing implementations of similar object-oriented languages are inherently sequential. Messages are really procedure calls, often implemented using constructs such as **funcall** or **apply**; the sending object must wait until the receiving object has processed a message before resuming. If the receipt of a message triggers more messages, there may be a depth-first activation pattern before the original sender can continue. While the metaphor of object-oriented systems suggests parallelism, most such languages actually are sequential in nature. The good reasons for this are the ease of implementation, lack of need for synchronization, and the fact that objects retain an interpretation context for return results automatically (see, e.g. ROSS [21].). However, parallel execution of objects is lost.

As an inherently parallel system, MACE presents some execution-time differences from existing object-oriented systems. In MACE, agents exhibit truly parallel execution, and we face the problems of synchronization and retaining interpretation contexts. Explicit synchronization can be performed using mailbox-level synchronization primitives;

since all communication is via messages, a programmer can create synchronization behaviors for an agent easily [28]. Retaining interpretation contexts is more difficult, but can be achieved by tagging messages with *computation identifiers* linked to *partial result frames* in the originating agent. The partial result frame contains enough information to continue the computation once the partial result (i.e. the work of another agent) is achieved. At a higher level, this concept can be expanded to maintaining *plans* for a computation. Outgoing and incoming messages are linked to *plan points*, which are tagged with instantiated variables as they are completed [16]. MACE provides a framework for storing an agent's plans, which can be used for this purpose.

There has been a tradition of experimental research and simulation in Distributed AI, which has provided a strong motivation for MACE. In early 1980's Smith and Davis reported on the Contract Net (CNET) system [5,30]. CNET used a bidding-contracting task allocation scheme to divide labor in a problem-solving task. The Contract Net was implemented as a simulation in LISP.

More recently, Lesser and Corkill at UMASS have constructed a testbed for distributed problem-solving research in a distributed sensor net domain, called the Distributed Vehicle Monitoring Testbed (DVMT) [18]. The DVMT is a collection of very complex problem-solving nodes each resembling a HEARSAY-II blackboard system, which cooperate to interpret signals from a sensor array. The nodes communicate by sending messages to one another. The DVMT is a large simulation system built in LISP. The DVMT simulator incorporates a language called EFIGE for describing the organizational communication structure among nodes and the problem-solving roles each node will play [24].

Rand researchers have constructed simulations of distributed problem solving in air traffic control and remotely-piloted vehicle domains, using the ROSS rule-based object-oriented simulation system [21]. ROSS is a flexible simulation system but its execution is sequential, not parallel.

Hewitt and his associates have introduced a highly concurrent programming system for DAI research based upon the ACTORS model. Actors are independent objects which communicate via messages and which have three activities: they can change state, send messages, and create new actors. The ACTORS work introduced the idea of **acquaintances** as other actors known in the environment. MACE has expanded upon this notion by allowing agents to incorporate detailed models of the behavior and capabilities of its acquaintances, and by allowing agents to reason about the actions of their acquaintances. Hewitt et al. have also constructed a simulator for their low-grain parallel ACTORS system [19].

Other single-paradigm domain-independent problem-solving frameworks and description systems have been built. These include the blackboard systems BB1 [13], and GBB [2], and the Stanford Knowledge Systems Laboratory ensemble which includes AGE, CAGE, POLIGON, etc. [23].

These systems have shown the utility of experimentation and simulation in DAI in single paradigms and for single domains. The thrust of MACE is to supply a distributed testbed for systems with varying architectures and granularity.

5.2   What is a MACE Agent?

MACE agents are self-contained, active *objects* which communicate with one another through messages. Agents exist in an *environment*, and have three aspects: They *contain knowledge*, they *sense their environment*, and they *take actions*.

Agents contain some knowledge and a means to manipulate that knowledge. Agents have *attributes*, which are properties of agents that can be referenced by the agent. The attributes are the repositories of the agent's knowledge. Attributes are not directly visible to any other agent, but the contents of attributes may be sent in messages to other agents, as a way of transferring knowledge. Attributes may have the full power of an associative, deductive database, incorporating pattern-directed retrieval and inferencing. (E.g., the attribute *acquaintances* is such a database).·

The environment of an agent comprises the MACE system, other agents, and the world outside MACE. Agents have two ways of sensing their environment. First, agents sense other agents and the outside world by receiving messages. Agents receive messages because other agents (including users or external processes) have sent them via the MACE kernel communication handlers and/or intermediary *interface agents*. Second, events in the kernel environment and internal to the agents themselves (e.g., alarm timers) can be sensed directly by the agent via its engine-shell (see below).

The active part of an agent is called its *engine*. Each agent's engine defines the agent's activities and how it interprets messages. The engine manipulates the knowledge stored by the agent's attributes in response to messages received by the agent. An agent's engine is its only active part. Agents can take 3 kinds of action:

- They can change their internal state by manipulating their attributes;

- They can send messages to other agents (by calling upon kernel communication handlers);

- They can send *monitoring requests* to the MACE kernel to monitor kernel-level events (e.g., timers), events elsewhere in the system, and their own internal state changes.

Only the last two types of action are visible outside the agent.

To carry out these actions, agents may contain locally-defined functions, which also cannot be referenced from outside the agent. These functions are a type of procedural knowledge which may be called upon by the agent's engine as it runs. Since these functions may give an agent specific skills, they may be sent in messages as a way of transferring skills to other agents.

Every agent has a *name* and a *class*. Agents are described by their *class*. There may be many *instances* of agents of the same class, but they will have unique names within that class. Uniqueness is determined by the combination of *name* and *class*.

5.3 What Agents Know

While the agent description framework is general, MACE provides facilities for representing particular kinds of knowledge. Frameworks for organizational and interactional knowledge are the primary higher-level knowledge structures built into MACE. Knowledge for organization and interaction is built into an agent attribute called its **acquaintances**. The acquaintances attribute provides an environmental model by representing explicit models of other agents in the world. This attribute is an associative database within an agent.

Agents may also have specialized local knowledge, represented in user-defined attributes. For example, some of our existing agents with rule interpreters for engines have a specialized **memory** attribute which stores is the production systems' working memory, and a specialized **behaviors** attribute which stores the procedural rules for operating on that memory.

5.3.1 Models of Other Agents in the World

Every agent has its own *model of the world*. This model encompasses knowledge of itself, other agents, their *roles*, their *skills*, their *addresses*, etc. This knowledge creates within the agent an image of its environment which it can interact with and change as its knowledge grows. Every agent holds its world model in an attribute called *acquaintances*. The agents it models are referred to as its acquaintances. Every agent's world model has representations of other agents in terms of the following qualifiers:

name The name of the agent being modeled.

class The name of the modeled agent's class.

address The location of the modeled agent. This address is used in communicating with the agent.

roles The *relationship(s)* the modeled agent bears to this agent, or a named role it plays. Currently, the role has several predefined values:

self The model is of the agent itself.

creator The model is of the agent's creator.

org-member The model is of a member of the organization which this agent manages (see below).

my-org-manager The model is of the top-level manager of the organization of which this agent is a part (see below).

co-worker The model is of a member of the organization of which this agent is also a part (see below).

This list of values may include additional user-declared roles.

skills Skills are what this agent knows to be the capabilities of the modeled agent. Skills are defined by *skill descriptors* which are pairs consisting of a set of patterns which match goals the skill will achieve, and a set of alternative methods for achieving the goals. The format of methods is left to the programmer (and they depend upon the engine used), but there are generally two types of methods: *Explicit procedures* can be invoked by the agent's engine. Their structure thus depends directly on the agent's engine definition. *Agent references* are the names of known agents which can possibly achieve the goals. Thus agents can do things by calling on other agents. Agent references are specified with an agent description and a message to be sent to that agent. One of our standard engines employs the descriptor USE to define explicit procedures, and REF to describe agent references. (See the CNET example below).

goals Goals are what this agent understands the modeled agent wants to achieve. Goals are represented by patterns which match programmer-specified descriptions of agent goals. Knowing about the goals of another agent is useful for mixed-initiative task allocation [5] and for reasoning about communication [3,29]. For task allocation, a *goal-association database* (agent attribute) can be used to associate an agent's skills with the goals of another agent which they will help to achieve. The modeler

126

agent can then reason about which acquaintances might provide a consumer for its services. For example, for *greedy robot* distributed task allocation in a multi-robot system [1] a robot task allocator must decide where to request more work. Acquaintance goals indicate where a greedy robot can market its production capabilities.

plans Plans are an agent's view of the way the modeled agent will achieve its goals. Plans are represented by a partially ordered collection of goals or skills, interspersed with *plan points*. Plan points are partial contexts from which the agent can resume computations when others have fulfilled their commitments to do some work [16].

5.3.2 Getting Acquainted

There must be a way for an agent to get to know about other agents. The MACE system provides two ways of instantiating an agent with the knowledge of other agents *built-in*. It also provides a system agent called the *directory* agent, which can furnish addresses of other agents in the system upon request.

An agent is instantiated with a model of its *creator* i.e. the agent or source which is responsible for its instantiation. The model contains only the name, class, address and role of the creator.

Each agent also carries a model of itself. This model can be set up in the class description of the agent, using the *plans, goals* and *skills* statements of the Agent Description Language (see Sec. 5.7.1). The name, class and address of the agent are provided by the MACE system; its role is set to *self*.

The user may specify some acquaintances which will be known at instantiation. These will be added to the default values for the acquaintance attribute in the class description of the agent. When the agent is instantiated, all its acquaintances' addresses will be present. This implies that the agent will not be instantiated until all its acquaintances exist. The roles of *self* and *creator* are reserved at instantiation.

There are means to *dynamically* alter an agent's concept of the world. The agent can add new acquaintances with the function add-acquaintance, as in

    (add-acquaintance CNODE-9 CNODE [role CNODE-MANAGER]))

which would make the agent whose name and class is (CNODE-9 CNODE) and whose role with respect to the invoking agent is CNODE-MANAGER, an acquaintance. Unwanted acquaintances can be removed with delete-acquaintance. In addition, the value of the individual qualifiers associated with an acquaintance can be modified with change-qualifier, a function that replaces the previous value of the qualifier with the newly specified one, or add-to-qualifier, a function which will add information to a qualifier:

(add-to-qualifier CNODE-9 CNODE [role POTENTIAL-NQ-CONTRACTOR])

would change CNODE-9's role, adding POTENTIAL-NQ-CONTRACTOR to CNODE-MANAGER.

At any time, an agent can query the *directory agent* for the addresses of other agents in the system. (See Sec. 5.9.3) The agent could then ask the other agents for pertinent information to fill up its model of these agents.

The MACE system provides *selectors* to query the agent's world model database according to specified criteria. Selectors are pattern-directed associative retrieval functions. Acquaintance selections can be made on the basis of name, class, role, skills, goals, plans and in combinations of these. They provide the agent with the ability to abbreviate references to acquaintances in a meaningful way, and to reason about work organization at run-time. A database selector is specified by the character '@', followed by a list containing name of the selector and a sequence of patterns to be extracted from the specified acquaintance qualifier. To be extracted, a qualifier must have entries which satisfy all of the patterns specified in the query. The selector will return the matching items, or nil, if there is no match. Depending on the type of query, a single item, (i.e. an address, a plan, a role, etc.), or a list of items may be returned. For example, the selector

@(goals-of *agent class*)

returns the goal list of the acquaintance whose name and class matches (*agent class*), while the query

@(roles CNODE-MANAGER ORG-MEMBER)

returns a list of addresses of acquaintances known to fill both the roles *CNODE-MANAGER* and *ORG-MEMBER*.

5.4   How Agents Sense Their World

Agents sense their world by receiving messages and by being forcibly notified of internal and system-level events. Most sensing is passive sensing in the form of receiving messages from the outside world. Some sensing is active sensing in the form of requests for notification of events.

The MACE system delivers messages addressed to an agent in the agent's *incoming-messages* queue. Messages are generally queued in the order in which they arrive, but message receipt may be prioritized. Before receiving at least one message, an agent is dormant. When a message arrives for an agent, the agent is activated.

128

The message received by the agent contains the address of the sender of the message. The agent can use this address to reply to the sender, if it so wishes. This information is provided by the MACE system; the sender does not have to include its address as part of the message.

Messages received by an agent will always be in the format:

(source-address message-content)

The source address is the address that is stored in the address part of the source agent's model of itself unless explicitly coerced to be some other address (see Sec. 5.5.1). The message content is the actual message sent to the agent. It is a LISP list. Beyond this, the MACE system puts no restraints on the form or content of the message. It is up to the agent to interpret and respond to the messages it receives using its own particular engine.

5.4.1   Monitoring Events: Demons, Event-Monitors and Synchronization

Two kinds of events can be monitored by agents in MACE:

- Events which are effects of some agent's visible actions. Such events include sending or receiving specific messages, agent status changes, and the actual creation or destruction of agents (e.g., placing an agent into a *new* state or deleting it from the directory). These events are monitored by *demons*. Demons are mappings from event descriptions to messages. A demon is always active. When an agent requests a demon to monitor a particular type of event, the demon waits until an event matching the description occurs, and then issues a specified message informing the agent of the event.

- Events which are the result of kernel actions or state-changes in the agent doing the monitoring. (No agent can directly monitor state-changes internal to another agent.) These events are monitored by *imps*. Imps are predicates on internal attributes or certain predefined kernel events (e.g., alarms, pattern-triggers). Imps are very powerful; they can invoke any LISP function within the agent. Imps are used for automatic interpretation of signals or error states, and for synchronization (e.g., for moving from a wait state to a running state when an alarm triggers.) They are evaluated after each execution cycle.

The engine shell provides a special imp which is a rudimentary alarm service within the event monitoring framework. The MACE engine-shell also provides an imp called a *pattern-trigger* which maps a message template to a procedure. When a message which matches a pattern trigger arrives at an agent, the procedure executes without the agent being activated. Pattern-triggers and demons together provide easy tracing facilities, and simple ways to implement guarded ports as in OIL [4]. Pattern-triggers are also sometimes more useful than engine-interpreted messages because their overhead can be ignored in experimental measurements of agent activations.

5.5   How Agents Act: Engines

MACE agents take actions when the kernel evaluates a function called the *engine* of the agent. An agent's engine is the only executable part of the agent, apart from its initialization code and the action parts of any imps. The engine and its associated attributes (e.g., a set of production rules which it references) provide the procedural knowledge incorporated in an agent.

The engine has many duties, including the responsibilities of handling all communication, error handling, acquiring and disseminating of knowledge about its environment, etc. What the engine does is the only outward manifestation of the agent's activities. It is the engine's responsibility to deactivate the agent when it has completed its current activities. The MACE system provides the function deactivate-me, which returns the agent to a dormant or waiting state where it will remain until it gets a new message. At that time it will be scheduled for execution once again. Unless it deactivates itself, an agent's engine is evaluated on every scheduling cycle. Specialized agents which poll external world states can be designed to be always active. The MACE system provides several simple engines which can be used when building agents: two are simple production system interpreters, and a third is a basic user-interface engine.

Before executing an agent's engine, the MACE system wraps it in an *engine shell*. The engine shell is a part of the MACE kernel which provides standard error handling facilities, protects the MACE system from engine errors, prioritizes messages, and handles standard messages which all agents understand (e.g., certain debugging and examination messages) The engine shell serves as a link between the agent and the MACE system. One of the primary functions of the engine shell is to trap irrecoverable errors caused by the agent's engine. The engine shell monitors an agent's activities and is involved in the tracing and profiling of an agent's execution. It performs all the necessary initialization for the agent, getting the addresses of its initial acquaintances, and executing its *init-code*.

Finally, the engine shell can prioritize messages in a partial order specified in a template provided by the agent. This is useful in prioritizing interactions among specific agents, and for prioritizing demon-activated messages.

5.5.1 Sending Messages

Agents communicate by sending messages. Messages can be addressed to individual agents, to groups of agents, or to all agents of a particular class. Messages can be addressed to agents on MACE systems on other machines, as long as a communication path exists.

Every agent in the MACE system has a unique address. This address is comprised of the agent's name, its class, the node on which it resides, and the machine on which the agent is running. This information is coded as a list, as follows:

(agent-name agent-class node machine)

The MACE system places this address in the acquaintance with the *self* role of the agent, allowing an agent to look up its own address. At instantiation the *acquaintances* attribute has the addresses of the creator of the agent, and the other agents which were defined to be its initial acquaintances. The agent can query the directory agent for addresses of other agents. (See Sec. 5.9.3)

There are three basic ways an agent can communicate with other agents. It can send a message to an individual agent, to a group of agents, or to all agents of a particular class. All messages will contain the address of the sender (as is stored in the agent's model of itself). The action of

(send-to-agent '(CNODE-1 CNODE 1 ORPHEUS) '(DIRECTED-AWARD ...))

is to send the message "(DIRECTED-AWARD ...)" to the agent whose name and class is CNODE-1 CNODE, and which is located on processor node 1 on a machine called OR-PHEUS. A message can be made to appear to have originated from a different agent if a return-address is explicitly provided. The message received by (CNODE-1 CNODE 1 OR-PHEUS) after

(send-to-agent '(CNODE-1 CNODE 1 ORPHEUS) '(START)
'(USER-1 USER 1 CSEVAX))

will appear to have come from (USER-1 USER 1 CSEVAX), irrespective of who had actually sent it. In addition there is an option which causes messages that are sent to non-existing agents to be returned to the sender; the default is to discard the message.

In addition to the function send-to-agent, there are functions that send messages to all agents which are instances of a particular class (that the directory agent knows about), and to all agents in a particular *group* (called, appropriately, send-to-class and send-to-group, respectively). Groups may be set up by individual agents to collectively address a number of agents. These groups names are specific to each agent, and cannot be shared across agents. Functions such as make-group, delete-group, add-to-group and remove-from-group are provided to create and manipulate groups.

5.5.2   Issuing Monitor Requests

MACE agents can act to invoke a demon by supplying event descriptions and notification messages to the demon. In the case of demons which monitor specific messages, message template patterns are supplied. Demons are invoked by

(demon *event-description notification-message*)

where *event-description* identifies the demon, and *notification-message* is the message to be sent to the invoking agent on the occurrence of the event.

Imps provide number of useful features to agents which help reduce the complexity of their engines. Powerful pattern triggered behavior can be created with the function pattern-trigger which accepts a pattern template to match incoming messages against, and an action which will be carried out when the message matches. Pattern variables can be used, and matching is done by a unification pattern matcher; bindings of the pattern variables can be used in the action specification. For example, our *allocation* agent (which maps and creates agents on nodes, on request from other agents) has initialization code:

(pattern-trigger '((KERNEL SYS ?n ORPH-SYS) (AGENT ?addr CREATED))
'(reply-to-pending-allocation-request ?n ?addr))

which causes its internal function reply-to-pending-allocation-request to be invoked whenever it gets a message from a MACE kernel saying that the kernel has created an agent (in response to an earlier request from the allocation agent). This imp has additional options that provide the ability to discard the incoming message, change the agent's state on occurrence of the message (i.e. wake it up if it was inactive), and to perform this match repeatedly.

The allocation agent also uses an *alarm* imp that periodically polls all the MACE kernels that it knows off, requesting load data, so that it can update its internal tables. The alarm imp is similar to the pattern-trigger imp, except that a time period (in seconds)

132

is specified instead of a pattern-template. The action is carried out after a specified time has elapsed since the invocation of the imp. The code looks like:

(set-alarm PERIOD '(send-to-group KERNELS '(RETURN-LOAD-FACTOR)))

The same options are provided for this imp too, except that here there is no message involved. Both imps return a request number that can be used to disable their actions.

5.6   Organizations

To save resources and attention when they act collectively, agents must organize their activities. Organizing conserves resources by providing a basis for expectations of how others will behave. We view an organization as a structure of expectations and commitments about behavior. The actions of organizational participants are patterned, often governed by routines, and based on expectations of others. An organization only really exists indirectly in the commitments and expectations of its members. In MACE, the term *organization* refers to the abstraction which allows agents to treat a collection of activities as being part of a known concerted effort or a known role. In this sense, a *role* is an accepted shorthand for a set of expectations. An organization is an abstract object about which agents can reason, and to which they can ascribe expectations and commitments. The abstraction can be simplified by naming the role of the organization, in the same way they may abstract their knowledge of the skills, goals, plans, etc. of other agents by naming their roles.

This view of organizations contrasts with the view presented by Pattison et al. in this volume [24]. From their perspective, an organization is a system of constraints on behavior; our view is that an organization is a set of commitments and expectations held by its members, and not only imposed structurally from outside. This allows us to model *negotiated order* properties of multi-agent systems more accurately [6,7,12,15,32].

MACE represents an organization as an abstract shell and a communication agent called a *manager*. The communication agent is named for the organization, and its primary organizational function is to disseminate messages which have been sent to the organization to the appropriate members of the organization. This abstract shell of an organization is represented as the world model of the manager agent. Each organizational member is represented in the world model with an *org-member* role entry. Thus the organization abstraction is the set of all acquaintances who are org-members. This set can be extracted using the @roles selector.

The manager of a MACE organization is primarily a bright secretary. The manager's engine maps most incoming messages to addresses of agents which handle them. The basic work of the manager, then, is *task allocation* for work arriving from outside the organization. Unlike most other agents, the manager's effect on a message may be invisible; when it arrives at its destination within the organization, the source of the message is most often the original sender.

Organization members can send messages to anyone they choose, without going through the manager. But they may also send a message which is representative of the organization, not themselves (like a form letter on organization letterhead). In this case the message is routed through the manager where the source address is converted to the name of the organization.

Organizations may be instantiated with staff members, or empty. The organization is a shell only, and if it has not been initialized with staff, it must issue staffing commands at the time it is initialized, to build member agents, to "hire" existing agents as members, etc. "Hiring" means establishing a mapping from messages received by the organization to agents which will handle the messages.

5.7   Describing Agents: The ADL and Description Database

MACE provides a language called the *MACE Agent Description Language* or *ADL* for describing agents. MACE differentiates the description of an agent from its executable form. Agent descriptions are stored in a database which is used by an agent cluster which constructs both new executable agents and new descriptions. New descriptions of agents are built using queries and assertions into the description database. The ADL is a procedural language for describing the database operations necessary to construct a new agent description.

We would often like to make or describe MACE agents which are have attributes in common with other MACE agents (e.g., engines, local functions, behavioral rules, etc.) Hierarchical classification and attribute inheritance are the schemes commonly used for related descriptions in object-oriented languages. In MACE, we often want to selectively import some but not all attributes of related agent-descriptions. Moreover, a distributed-memory parallel environment presents difficulties for inheritance-based schemes at execution time. In a distributed-memory parallel environment inheritance can be handled by sending messages to inherit superclass attributes. This introduces several problems with inheritance:

- <u>Speed</u>: If message delay is significant, if inherited attributes reside several levels away, or if the amount of data to be transmitted in an inheritance message is large, the overhead for inheritance may be great.

- Reliability: If the superclass object disappears or the machine upon which it resides is disabled, the subclass object cannot inherit attributes.

- Reference Problems: If objects are arbitrarily spread across machines, knowing the exact whereabouts of parents or children several levels away depends upon totally consistent address tables at the moment of inheritance.

- Conceptual Problems Conceptually, classification is a different problem than execution. Classification of agents and attributes ought to be done as they are specified, but not necessarily as they are executed.

Inheritance and classification schemes are important for knowledge representation and there are important research issues which center around how to implement inheritance in a distributed environment[1]. For the moment, however, we consider execution-time inheritance unworkable for MACE. Each executable MACE agent is a self-contained object which inherits nothing from other agents at run time. Descriptions of MACE agents involve inheritance, primarily for establishing default values for agent attributes. Any run-time attribute changes must be handled explicitly by updating agents.

The MACE *Agent Description Language* uses *class descriptions* to describe agents. Class descriptions have unique *class-names*, or may be unnamed. Named class descriptions are stored by the MACE system for future reference, either for building executable agents of the named class, or for serving as a template on which to draw to describe new classes. The MACE system provides a method for describing new agents from existing class descriptions. Unnamed class descriptions, however, cannot be referenced later.

Attributes are properties of agents which contain the agent's knowledge. They are only accessible to the agent to which they belong, and not to any other agent. Certain attributes are pre-defined by the MACE system. These attributes will always be present in an executable agent, and never appear in a class description. They may be referenced by the agent.

- The attribute *incoming-messages* has been defined to contain all the messages received by the agent. The messages are put there by the MACE system in the order

---

[1] For example, we are currently pursuing another line of thought which treats inheritance as a distributed database problem. Inheritance is only a problem when attributes change - otherwise inherited attributes can be compiled into distributed agents with the only cost being duplicate copies of information. Changes in inherited attributes can be announced via message. The system must have ways, then, of dealing with anomalies caused by action taken before an inheritance-change message is received. The associated costs benefits, and mechanisms are open research questions at the moment.

in which they are received, and it is the agent's responsibility to remove them. (see Section 5.5)

- The *status* attribute is used by the MACE system to reflect the current status of the agent. The attribute takes fixed values: *running, inactive, waiting, stopped*. The status attribute is visible and monitorable by other agents with demons.

Certain other attributes always appear in executable agents, but may be defined by a MACE programmer:

- The agent's *acquaintances* attribute will always appear, but may be defined by the programmer. This attribute at minimum contains the agent's model of itself and its creator.

- The agent's *processor* attribute defines the (logical) processor on which the agent will be loaded. If left unset by the programmer, the MACE kernel will load the agent and assign this attribute.

Besides these attributes, the user may define any attribute he wants, along with its initial values. The initial values will be set at instantiation.

5.7.1 Agent Description Language

The Agent Description Language, or ADL for short, is a language for describing agents, (i.e. *class descriptions*), either in terms of new or of pre-defined class descriptions. A new class may be defined by *importing* features of other *named* classes. Such features could be the *engine* or the *attributes*, of existing class descriptions, or even a complete class description itself. Some of the imported features may be *deleted* if not required. Additional features may be specified if so desired. The ADL also provides the facility to specify initialization procedures for the agent. This code is executed upon the instantiation of an agent, in the processor environment where the agent has been loaded.

A class description is composed of an optional class-name and a description body. The name is any acceptable LISP symbol. The class name, if specified, must be unique. If named, the new class description will be saved for future use. (See Section 5.9.3.)

Class descriptions can be built up from other existing class descriptions by using the *copy-of* statement. The new class will then be an identical copy of the class specified in the copy-of statement, including all default values and initialization code, which can be modified with the *delete, new* or *import* statements. Optionally, the user can describe a new class without copying an existing class. The copy-of statement, if used, can only occur once and must be the first statement of the description body.

The *import* statement provides a means to selectively pick desirable features of other class descriptions. Whatever initialization values were associated with the feature in the other class description, will be in effect in the new class description. Importable features are *engine*, *attributes*, and *functions*.

The *new* statement defines a new feature for the agent. The feature can be an attribute or part of an attribute (as in the case of the *plans*, *roles*, *goals* and *skills* statements), a function, or an engine. A feature may take an optional initial value, or, in the case of a function, must have a function definition which must be a valid LISP function. The *plans*, *roles*, *goals*, and *skills* statements specify agent qualifiers. The features specified by the *import* and *new* statements take precedence over the same features if described earlier in the description.

An initial value for any attribute may be specified. The initial value can be any LISP s-expression that can serve as an argument to the LISP function eval. The *plans*, *roles*, *goals* and *skills* statements and the attribute *acquaintances* take special initial values.

To remove features from the class description, the *delete* statement has to be used. This is useful in removing unwanted features when using a copy of another class description. It is not an error to delete a non-existent feature.

The description can contain arbitrary LISP code that will be executed when an agent of this class is instantiated. This code is placed in the *init-code* statement. The code forms no part of the agent, and cannot be referenced within the agent. However, it may refer to functions defined within the agent. Refer to Section 8 for an example of the ADL code for describing some CNET agents.

5.7.2   Accessing Attributes and Functions

Attributes are bound to their values and may referenced in the same way as any LISP variable, with one exception. If the attribute was not previously assigned a value by a programmer or by the MACE system, it will always have been bound to nil. The function set-attribute-value is used to assign values to the attributes. Local functions, accessible only within the agent, are used like any other LISP functions. However, they can only be defined with the NEW-DEFUN clause of the Agent Definition Language, as they may be inheritable.

5.8 An Example: the Contract Net in MACE

As one of several proof-of-concept studies for MACE, we implemented a general version of Reid Smith's Contract Net (CNET) problem-solver [5,30] in MACE, and applied it (as did Smith) to the N-Queens problem [35]. In this implementation, each CNET node is composed of an organization of four MACE agents, including a communication manager, a contract manager, a task processor, and a knowledge base. Each of the 4 agents comprising one CNET node may be mapped onto any MACE processor, depending on decisions of the allocator. Our CNET N-Queens experiment includes a manager agent called NQ which creates and initializes CNET agents and monitors the experimental runs. NQ issues building and allocation requests, and responds to requests from users via the MACE user-interface and command-interpreter agents. Using MACE on our 16-node Intel Hypercube we have run experiments using either four or six CNET nodes to solve problems of allocating 4 or 6 queens. Running a 6-Node by 6-Queen experiment requires 28 MACE agents, including 24 for the CNET, one NQ experiment manager, a user-interface, a monitor, and a MACE command interpreter. All of these agents execute concurrently.

Tables 1 and 2 present a selection of code from the MACE 6.0 description language to illustrate its use for describing some agents from our reimplementation of the Contract Net. These fragments illustrate the following points:

- Pattern descriptors.

- The use of pattern triggers.

- The use of acquaintances and acquaintance attribute retrieval.

- The use of organizations.

- Reasoning about allocation of work using models of other agents.

- Description and instantiation of individual classes and of organizations.

- The use of REF and USE skill descriptors.

5.9 An Environment for Building and Experimenting with Agents

We are working toward constructing MACE DAI systems which appear to be *organizations which solve problems.* Programming such a system means creating and managing

Table 5.1: Partial **Node Manager** Definition in **MACE**

; **Node Manager** is an organization with 3 members:

```
((name CNODE-1)
 (import ENGINE from CNET-DEF)
 (acquaintances
  (CNODE-1
   [roles (SELF CNODE-MANAGER)]
   [goals ((TASK-ANNOUNCEMENT $)
           (ANNOUNCE-TASK $)
           (ANNOUNCED-AWARD $)
           (DIRECTED-AWARD $)
           (ACCEPTANCE $)
           (REFUSAL $)
           (FINAL-REPORT $)
           (INFORMATION $)...)]
   [skills ([(DIRECTED-AWARD $spec)
             (use (send-to-agent
                   @(roles CONTRACT-MANAGER ORG-MEMBER)
                   '(DIRECTED-AWARD $spec)))]
           [(ANNOUNCE-TASK $task-spec)
            (ref (acquaintance with
                  [roles (CNODE-MANAGER POTENTIAL-NQ-CONTRACTOR)]
                  [goals (TASK-ANNOUNCEMENT $)])
             (by-sending '(TASK-ANNOUNCEMENT $task-spec)))]...)] ...)

  (CNODE-2 [roles (CNODE-MANAGER POTENTIAL-NQ-CONTRACTOR)]
           [goals ((TASK-ANNOUNCEMENT $)...)] ... )
  (CNODE-3 [roles (CNODE-MANAGER POTENTIAL-NQ-CONTRACTOR)...])

  (CONTRACT-MGR-1
   [roles (ORG-MEMBER CONTRACT-MANAGER)]
   [goals ((TASK-ANNOUNCEMENT $)
           (ANNOUNCED-AWARD $)
           (ELIGIBILITY-REPORT $)
           (DIRECTED-AWARD $)
           (ANNOUNCE-TASKS $)...)]...)

  (KBASE-MGR-1 [roles (KBASE-MANAGER ORG-MEMBER)])
  (TASK-MGR-1 [roles (TASK-MANAGER ORG-MEMBER)]) ) )
```

Table 5.2: Partial **Contract Manager** Definition in **MACE**

```
((name CONTRACT-MGR-1)
 (import ENGINE from CNET-DEF)
 (acquaintances
  (CONTRACT-MGR-1
   [roles (SELF)]
   [goals ((TASK-ANNOUNCEMENT $)
           (ANNOUNCED-AWARD $)
           (ELIGIBILITY-REPORT $)
           (DIRECTED-AWARD $)
           (ANNOUNCE-TASKS $)...)]
   [skills ([(TASK-ANNOUNCEMENT ?contract ?eligibility-spec)
             (ref (acquaintance with
                        [roles KBASE-MANAGER CO-WORKER])
                (by-sending
                   '(CHECK-ELIGIBILITY ?contract
                        ?eligibility 'task-announcement)))]
           [(ANNOUNCED-AWARD ?contract ?sender ?task-spec)
             (use [(ADD-CONTRACT ?contract)
                   (ref (acquaintance with
                        [roles TASK-MANAGER CO-WORKER])
                      (by-sending
                       '(EXECUTE-TASK ?contract
                         ?sender ?task-spec)))])])] ...)

  (CNODE-1 [roles (CNODE-MANAGER MY-ORG-MANAGER)])
  (KBASE-MGR-1 [roles (KBASE-MANAGER CO-WORKER)])
  (TASK-MGR-1 [roles (TASK-MANAGER CO-WORKER)]))

 (new   RANKED-TASK-LIST)
 (new   AWARDED-CONTRACT-LIST)
 (new   RESULT)
 (new   STRATEGY smallest-first)

 (new-defun STORE-BID-IF-ELIGIBLE (REPORT)...))
 (new-defun ACCEPT-OR-REFUSE-DIRECTED-AWARD ...))

 (init-code
      (pattern-trigger '(ELIGIBILITY-REPORT ?report)
       (cond ((TASK-ANNOUNCEMENT ?report)
              (STORE-BID-IF-ELIGIBLE ?report))
             (t (ACCEPT-OR-REFUSE-DIRECTED-AWARD ?report))))))
```

an organization of problem-solvers of varying complexity and power. The programmer of such a system should develop some of the specifications and technologies for solving the organization's problems, much as the founders of a human organization begin with some initial product ideas and (perhaps innovative) ways of producing them. In this task, the programmer should have the help of a group of specialists who are experts in the known techniques - information management, quality control, domain knowledge for particular applications, etc.

Specialized system agents should take on themselves much of the burden of actual system construction and operations - the programmer's task should be to establish initial forms, directions and policy. Thus eventually programmers should become managers of interdependent processes, rather than specifiers and builders of entire systems in detail. They specify staffing requirements with *job descriptions* - high-level descriptions of the special and general requirements of agents, described in terms of *roles, goals,* or *skills.* Some agents come with basic skills in their domain of expertise. For example, a *Quality Control* agent might have some general knowledge about testing techniques, statistical quality control, error-discovery procedures, etc. The quality-control agent should be able to accommodate new goals by learning new procedures, or by forming alliances with other agents who can achieve those goals (E.g., hiring or building new associates).

Programmers direct and organize agents by specifying their relationships to one another and by issuing *policies* and *goals* - high level directives and constraints on behavior. Agents carry out and interpret the policies and goals in the light of their own local circumstances. In this way, agents are problem-solvers, and systems are adaptive without explicit detailed control by a central actor or overseer.

Many organizations have similar components (sub-units). Programming should begin with a set of existing agents. One set of starting agents might be:

- *Garbage collectors* which clean up space and recover "used" agents;

- *Fault-control specialists* which handle errors and recognize anomalies;

- *Quality control specialists* which verify procedures or agent descriptions;

- *Organization specialists* which establish structures of communication, roles, authority, etc.

- *Personnel specialists* which associate existing agents with appropriate goals, and which order the construction of new agents;

- *Communications specialists* which display information to users and interact with them, which manage global address directories, etc.

141

- *Domain specialists* which handle particular parts of particular domain-related problems.

We already have incorporated simple versions of some of these agents (domain, communication and personnel specialists) into MACE.

5.9.1 Building Agents

The MACE system provides a *Class Description Database* of stored class descriptions which can be used in the creation of new class descriptions. Class descriptions are created and modified by issuing *design specifications* to the MACE system's *builder* agent, which is responsible for accepting commands to add, delete and modify class descriptions into or from the class database. Design specifications are messages, and they may be issued by any MACE agent. Typically they are issued by the user via a user-interface agent tied to the builder agent.

For example, when the *builder* receives a message

    (design-spec ((NAME CNODE) ...))

it describes and installs into the class database the class called *CNODE*. Other messages including delete-class and modify-class are provided to manipulate the class database. These messages have an option whereby the result status is sent as a message to the invoking agent.

Agent class-descriptions are not executable. From class descriptions, executable instance agents must be created. The builder agent also accepts *construction orders*, which are messages which cause it to construct agents, given their class description. The class descriptions can be given directly, or a reference can be made to a named, class description stored in the class-database. For example

    (construct CNODE-7 CNODE)

creates an instance of the agent class *CNODE*, called *CNODE-7*. The builder agent uses the allocation agent mentioned earlier to map the agent to a node.

At any time after instantiation any user-created agent can be destroyed, by itself or by any other agent. There is no restriction on who kills whom; a valid address suffices. To kill (CNODE-7 CNODE 1 ORPHEUS) any agent (including the agent in question) can call the kernel function:

    (kill-agent (CNODE-7 CNODE 1 ORPHEUS))

The agent's status is maintained by the MACE system in the *status* attribute. The status attribute can take any one of the following values: *new, inactive, active, waiting* and *stopped*. These values have meaning to the engine shell, which is an extension of the MACE system into the agent.

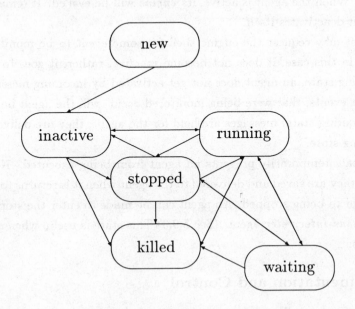

Figure 5.1: Agents' State Diagram

When an agent is first created it is mapped onto a (logical) processor by the Mace kernel, its status is set to *new*, and the engine shell starts initializing it. If the agent has been defined with pre-defined acquaintances, their addresses must be filled in by the engine-shell before the agent is free to send messages to them. At creation time, the pre-defined acquaintances may not yet exist. The agent's status remains as *new* until all its pre-defined acquaintances have also been created. The agent's engine is not activated during this period. When the addresses of all its acquaintances have been found, the engine shell will eval the *init-code* of the agent, if any, and change the status to *inactive*.

If the pre-defined acquaintances do not exist, the agent will never become active. One of the reasons for this status value is to be able to resolve circular acquaintance dependencies without a deadlock. By introducing the *new* state, the instantiation of agents no longer depends upon the existence of their acquaintances; only the actual

143

activation of the agent does so. The instantiation of agents only depends upon the builder agent. This provides an elegant solution to the problem of agents 'waking up' knowing the addresses of their acquaintances.

The agent remains in the *inactive* state until it receives a message. Its status then changes to *active*. When the agent is active, its *engine* will be eval'ed. It remains in the active state until it deactivates itself.

An active agent may request the engine shell for some event to be monitored, and then block itself. In this case, it does not become *inactive*, rather, it goes to a *waiting* state. In the waiting state, an agent does not get activated by incoming messages; only when the event, or events, that were being monitored occur, will the agent be activated once more. In a waiting state, messages are held for the agent; they are delivered when it leaves the waiting state.

The *stopped* state temporarily prevents an agent from being executed. None of its messages are lost; they are saved and delivered to the agent when it is returns to whatever state it was in prior to being stopped. An agent can be made to enter the stopped state through the *command-interpreter* agent. (See 5.9.3) This state is useful when debugging and tracing agents.

5.9.2 Instrumentation and Control

MACE is instrumented to allow for measurements of the characteristics of its agents during experimental runs. Message traffic, queue and database sizes, work done by an agent (in terms of amount of real time the agent is active, or number of agent evaluations), and load on a processor node (in terms of number of agents or total scheduler cycle time) are common measurements. Load factors are used by the allocator agent in determining where to load new agents. Instrumentation is carried out through the system's uses of the basic demon and imp mechanisms of MACE. Trace and instrumentation agents issue demon and imp requests, and collect and analyze the results.

The MACE simulator gives an added measure of control for debugging and repeatable experiments. While the standard (un-simulated) MACE executions involve random execution and message delivery delays, the simulator's behavior is deterministic. The simulator will model arbitrary logical processor speeds and interconnection topologies. It will also simulate errors in the communications and processing in the network, and agent breakdowns, with a specified probability rate. Like the un-simulated MACE system, the simulator will gather execution-time behavioral statistics, including message routing and traffic loads, agent and processor breakdowns, timing and synchronization information, and behavioral trace information for behavioral interpretation.

5.9.3 System Agents and Tools: The Predefined Community

The MACE system has several predefined system agents which work with a user to display information and interpret commands. This community includes:

- **User-Interfaces** A collection of *user-interface* agents control all terminal I/O. They are responsible for all communication to and from terminal-like output devices. Agents can request input or send output to a terminal or graphics device through these agents. When an agent requests input from a user, it send a message to the user-interface agent which, prompts the user. The input is sent to the requesting agent in a message. For example, this is the way the command-interpreter agent gets commands from a user. Multiple input requests from different agents can be explicitly serialized by synchronization with the user-interface, or agents can open different I/O windows for simultaneous communication.

- **Monitor**: Agents can send communications which are intended for transmission outside the MACE system, and which require no responses, to *monitor* agents. Monitor agents open trace and log files, display trace and error information on user-interface windows, and selectively filter instrumentation information for experimental tests.

- **Command-Interpreter**: System-related requests or queries can be directed to the *command-interpreter*. In addition, this agent serves as a link between the user and the user-defined agents; the user can communicate with all other agents through this agent. The command-interpreter accepts a number of commands from the user, including queries about system status, requests to monitor agent activities by tracing their actions, and requests to schedule agents on the system. Messages to the command interpreter may come from any MACE agent; typically they are issued by a user via a user-interface agent.

- **Builder**: The *builder* agent accepts agent design or construction orders. Given a design specification for an agent, it adds it to the class database it maintains. A construction order results in the creation of a new agent of a specified class (that may exist in its class database, or may be specified directly in the order using the ADL). In either case the requesting agent can be notified of the result of its request via a message.

- **Directory**: The *directory* agent maintains the address list of all the agents in the MACE system. Any agent in the system can query the directory agent for the address of other agents in the system. The directory agent provides a means for agents to get additional information about their environment, and to expand their model of the world.

During typical MACE experiments we have run, the user is communicating through the user-interface to the command interpreter agent, while an experiment manager agent is creating agents and making agent allocation requests, domain-related agents are solving the domain-related problems, and monitor agents are collecting and displaying data on the experiment.

5.10   Experiences and Conclusions

We have validated MACE by building several communities of interacting agents, based on existing Distributed AI paradigms. We have found MACE to be useful in coping with the diverse requirements and specifications of various problem solving domains.

Our re-implementation of the Contract Net has been described above. In addition, we have built three distributed production systems, based on the rule-agents concept - a dataflow-like approach to production systems [11]. Under this approach, each rule is an agent, and there is no global database or inference engine. Rules fire in parallel and send tokens to other rule-agents. Rule-agents themselves may query a user via the system user-interface and monitor agents for messages (i.e. data) which are not produced by other rules.

We have also built a simple distributed blackboard system, which implements a parallel arithmetic calculator. In the distributed blackboard, knowledge sources and blackboard levels are MACE agents. Different knowledge sources reduce subexpressions, perform simple arithmetic operations, and synthesize results [9].

Other experimental systems built using MACE to date include a system for simple visual scene analysis using schemas [17], a prototype multiple-agent diagnosis system [10], and a distributed planner for two cooperating robots [20].

Based on our experiences building these systems, we believe that several features of MACE have proven their worth or feasibility:

- *The creation of multi-grain systems.* We used MACE to build distributed systems of different granularity, ranging from the large grained contract net, a medium grained distributed blackboard, to the small grained rule agents. The description language of MACE is powerful enough to capture all of these; it permits the description of agents of varied complexities through the same language, providing the ability to use stepwise refinement in the construction of large and complex systems. Within a system, there are no constraints on all agents having the same level of granularity.

- *The construction of Multi-Mode sytems.* In MACE the user can control the interpretation of messages by providing specific engines to implement problem-specific syntax or message passing paradigms. This flexibility has been demonstrated in the implementation of MACE system agents which interpret messages using different syntactic structures by using different engines.

- *Abbreviated references.* Acquaintance selectors provide the agent with the ability to abbreviate references in a meaningful way that does not detract from the problem at hand. Reasoning about the division of work can be done at a high level without having to know about how the mapping between agents and their individual skills is performed. This bore fruit in the idea of high level organizations, permitting reference to a group of agents with shared goals, as a single entity. Organizations, used successfully in the implementation of the distributed blackboard and CNET, were proved to be a simple and effective solution to tasks which require the complex distribution of effort among a group of related agents.

- *Control through simulation.* The MACE system has been implemented in a simulated as well as in an actual parallel environment. The simulator, by its sequential nature, provides an alternative, easier to grasp, environment for the less experienced MACE programmer to familiarize himself with the MACE system and MACE programming. The initial versions of both the distributed blackboard and the contract net were developed in the simulated environment and then ported to the parallel implementation of MACE.

- *Debugging tools.* One of the goals of the MACE system is to provide an environment conducive to the development of distributed systems. We found the tracing and instrumentation features to be invaluable while debugging and testing the various modules which were developed. The most useful, at that time, was the ability of the tracing system to maintain a temporal link across concurrently executing (on separate processors), yet highly interdependent agents.

- *Description database.* MACE provides a database containing the description and specification of existing agent classes. The agent description language permits selective retrieval of these descriptions in the specification of new agent classes. Programmers using MACE tend to remake agents by example rather than explicitly coding a new one every time.

- *Inter-machine flexibility.* The flexibility of MACE is demonstrated by the fact that MACE recognizes and is able to communicate with MACE systems on other machines, as well as support a multi-user environment. Communication with other machines is provided by different drivers that are invoked by the use of a specific machine name in the destination address of a message. The advantage of this system is that the machines themselves may be *virtual machines* and thus communications can be tailored to practically any interface. This approach was used to extend, with minimal effort, the linkage of the tracing of the contract-net to an external graphic display. (This was used at a demonstration of the CNET running on MACE at the 1986 AAAI conference.) Extending MACE to a multi-user system merely called for a new user-interface agent for each user.

- *Multiple user interfaces.* We have built MACE experiments which included simultaneous line-oriented, window-based, and color graphic user-interfaces, each controlled by different agents, and running on different processors. This flexibility and multiplicity provides many compelling possibilities for research into multi-modality human-machine interaction.

Despite our successful use of MACE, we have found difficulties with certain aspects. We have also discovered several pressing research needs. These are being addressed for future versions of MACE.

- *Understanding DAI system execution.* Perhaps the most salient research issue to emerge from our MACE experiments is the pressing need for display and analytic techniques for understanding and debugging the parallel execution of heterogeneous DAI systems. Concurrency, problem-domain uncertainty, and non-determinism in execution together conspire to make it very difficult to comprehend the activity in a distributed intelligent system. Debugging and control become extremely difficult. While our tracing and display systems were very helpful, we urgently need graphic displays of system activity linked to intelligent model-based tools which help a developer reason about expected and observed behavior. We expect to apply the fruits of our research on multi-agent diagnosis here.

- *Inflexible mapping to nodes.* MACE provides no dynamic transfer of agents from one processing node another. Once an agent has been instantiated, it is impossible to reinstantiate it on another node or machine while maintaining local state. Though we have devised an dynamic load-balancing algorithm [27] and implemented the load measurements it needs, dynamic load balancing is currently impossible. This restriction will be removed in the next version of MACE.

- *Isolating basic operations for standard engines.* What are the high-level primitives for expressing computations in distributed AI systems? We would like to incrementally increase the expressive power of MACE by providing a better set of standard engines which incorporate actions which we have found repeatedly useful. These include asynchronous context maintainance using result-frames, and a language structure for expressing prospective reasoning primitives using *plan points*. We have found that much of the agent activity in the systems we have built involves combining asynchronously-arriving information from several sources with fairly limited computation (usually data extraction and insertion). We call this *form-filling*. MACE should have form-filling primitives.

- *Speed.* We have been only marginally concerned with speed of execution; our focus has been on parallel problem-solving architectures. Still, speed has emerged as a growing concern. Our experiments have been carried out using MACE on TI Explorer LISP machines and a 16-node Intel Hyprecube running Gold Hill Computers' CCLISP. All MACE code on both machines is compiled Common LISP. In the 6-node, 6-Queens CNET experiments, parallel MACE on the Hypercube gave us a 7-fold speedup (real time) over the MACE simulator on the Explorer. This comparison does not account for the added parallel simulation overhead on the Explorer, and so is of limited utility. Still, we need much greater speed per processor in a parallel architecture to provide adequate performance.

- *Adherence to Common LISP.* To insure the portability of MACE, we adhered to the use of only standard Common LISP. However, Common LISP does not provide any standard error trapping mechanism. We experienced the inconvenience of restarting the entire system due to some agent having an error in its code. We decided to compromise on the portability of MACE and use the error trapping facility provided by our Common LISP environment. However, we see this more as a reflection on Common LISP than on MACE.

With new generations of more powerful parallel hardware, distributed AI will become more possible and more attractive. We believe MACE will provide a useful step toward productive experimental DAI research.

Acknowledgements

We are grateful to Janet Coates, Eric Ho, Lunze Liu, Matt Staker, and Dit-An Yeung for their help building and documenting the experimental application systems and/or earlier versions of MACE. We are also grateful to Gary Doney and Fernando Tenorio for helpful comments on earlier drafts. We thank the Intel Corporation and Prof. Kai Hwang for their support. Part of this research was funded under Lawrence Livermore Laboratory contract number 86-5987.

References

[1] G. Bekey and L. Gasser, "Task Allocation Among Multiple Robots," presented at 1987 JPL Conference on Space Telerobotics, Pasadena, CA, January 20-22, 1987.

[2] D. D. Corkill, K. Q. Gallagher, and K. E. Murray, "GBB: A Generic Blackboard Development System," *Proceedings AAAI-86*, 1986.

[3] P. Cohen and H. Levesque, "Speech Acts and Rationality," *Proc. 23rd Meeting or the Association for Computational Linguistics*, Chicago, 1985.

[4] S. Cohen, J. Conery, A. Davis, and S. Robinson, *OIL PRogramming Language Reference Manual*, Technical Report, Schlumberger Palo Alto Research, 1985.

[5] R. Davis and R.G. Smith, "Negotiation as a Metaphor for Distributed Problem-Solving," *Artificial Intelligence* vol. 20, pp. 63-109, 1983.

[6] L. Gasser, "The Integration of Computing and Routine Work," *ACM Transactions on Office Information Systems*, vol. 4, no. 3, pp. 205-225, July, 1986.

[7] L. Gasser, "Negotiated Order: Concerted Action in Multi-Agent Systems," DAI Group Research Note 3, Distributed AI Group, Dept. of Computer Science, USC, 1986.

[8] L. Gasser, C. Braganza, and N. Herman, "MACE: Experimental DAI Research on the Intel Hypercube," in *Proceedings of the Second Conference on Hypercube Multiprocessors*, Knoxville, TN, September, 1986.

[9] L. Gasser, C. Braganza, and N. Herman, "Implementing Distributed AI Systems Using MACE," *Proc. IEEE Third Conference on AI Applications*, February, 1987.

[10] L. Gasser, M. Staker, and E. Ho, "A Prototype Multi-Agent Diagnosis System," DAI Group Research Note 19, USC Distributed AI Group, Dept. of Computer Science, USC, 1986.

[11] L. Gasser and M.F. Tenorio, "Rule-Agents: A Distributed, Object-Oriented Approach to Production Systems Using MACE," DAI Group Research Note 4, Distributed AI Group, Dept. of Computer Science, USC, 1986.

[12] E.M. Gerson and S.L. Star, "Analyzing Due Process in the Workplace," *ACM Transactions on Office Information Systems*, 4, no. 3, pp. 257-270, July, 1986.

[13] B. Hayes-Roth, "A Blackboard Architecture for Control," *Artificial Intelligence*, vol. 26, no. 2, pp. 251-321, March 1985.

[14] C. Hewitt, "Viewing Control Structures as Patterns of Passing Messages," *Artificial Intelligence*, pp. 323-364, 1977.

[15] C. Hewitt, "Offices are Open Systems," *ACM Transactions on Office Information Systems*, vol. 4, no. 3, pp. 271-287, July, 1986.

[16] R. Hill and L. Gasser, "Notes on Prospective Reasoning in Multi-Agent Systems," DAI Group Research Note 22, USC Distributed AI Group, Dept. of Computer Science, USC, 1986.

[17] E. Ho, E. Kiralay, and V. Natarajan, "Schema-Based Recognition of Environments," DAI Group Research Note 24, USC Distributed AI Group, Dept. of Computer Science, USC, 1986.

[18] V. R. Lesser and D. D. Corkill, "The Distributed Vehicle Monitoring Testbed: A Tool for Investigating Distributed Problem Solving Networks," *AI Magazine*, pp. 15-33, 1983.

[19] H. Lieberman, "An Object-Oriented Simulator for the Apiary," *Proc. 1980 Lisp Conference*, 1980.

[20] L. Liu, "A Distributed Planner for Two Cooperating Robots," DAI Group Research Note 21, USC Distributed AI Group, Dept. of Computer Science, USC, 1986.

[21] D. McArthur and P. Klahr, *The ROSS Language Manual*, Rand, 1982.

[22] S. Narain, D. McArthur and P. Klahr, "Large-Scale System Development in Several LISP Environments," in *Proceedings IJCAI-83*, pp. 859-861, International Joint Conference on Artificial Intelligence, 1983.

[23] H. P. Nii, "CAGE and POLIGON: Two Frameworks for Blackboard-based Concurrent Problem Solving," Report No. KSL 86-41, Knowledge Systems Laboratory, Computer Science Department, Stanford University, Stanford, CA, April 1986.

[24] E.H. Pattison, D.D. Corkhill, and V.R. Lesser. "Instantiating Descriptions of Organizational Structures," Technical Report 85-45, Computer Science Department, UMASS, Amherst, MA, November, 1985.

[25] J. Pavlin, "Predicting the Performance of Distributed Knowledge-Based Systems: A Modeling Approach," in *Proceedings AAAI-83*, pp. 314-319, American Association for Artificial Intelligence, 1983.

[26] J. Pavlin and D. D. Corkill, "Selective Abstraction of AI System Activity," in *Proceedings AAAI-84*, pp. 264-268, American Association for Artificial Intelligence, 1984.

[27] D. Persinger, "A Distributed Load Balancing Algorithm for MACE," DAI Group Research Note 23, USC Distributed AI Group, Dept. of Computer Science, USC, 1986.

[28] J. Peterson and A. Silberschatz, *Operating System Principles*, Addison-Wesley, 1983.

[29] R. Schank and K.M.Colby, *Scripts, Plans Goals, and Understanding*, Lawrence Erlbaum, 1977.

[30] R. G. Smith, *A Framework for Distributed Problem Solving*, UMI Research Press, Ann Arbor, Michigan, 1981.

[31] M. Stefik and D. Bobrow, "Object-Oriented Programming: Themes and Variations," *AI Magazine*, 6(4), Winter, 1986.

[32] A. Strauss, *Negotiations*, San Francisco: Jossy-Bass, 1978.

[33] P. Wegner, "Language Paradigms for Programming in the Large," Working Paper, Dept. of Computer Science, Brown University, 1985.

[34] D. Weinreb, D. Moon, and R. Stallman, *LISP Machine Manual*, Massachusetts Institute of Technology, 1983.

[35] D. Yeung, "Using CNET on the iPSC," DAI Group Research Note 20, USC Distributed AI Group, Dept. of Computer Science, USC, 1986.

Les Gasser, Carl Braganza and Nava Herman
Distributed Artificial Intelligence Group
Computer Science Department
University of Southern California
Los Angeles, CA 90089-0782

Chapter 6

AF: A Framework for Real-Time Distributed Cooperative Problem Solving

Peter E. Green

Abstract

This paper describes a software framework that supports the implementation of real-time artificial intelligence programs on multiple interconnected computers that may be geographically distributed. The framework, called AF for Activation Framework, is based on the paradigm of expert objects communicating by messages in the manner of a community of experts. One of the principal features of AF is the use of message priority levels as the basis for distributed scheduling and focus-of-attention mechanisms.

This paper traces the evolution of AF from HEARSAY II, through the Distributed Sensor Networks (DSN) testbed, to current work on real-time systems in the area of robotics. The DSN testbed used a distributed HEARSAY II approach to acoustically track low flying aircraft in real-time and provided valuable insight as to the issues that a real-time distributed AI system must address. This paper describes these issues and shows how AF addresses most of them.

Finally this paper describes the status of current work. It describes in some detail a framework written in the C language which is being applied to robotic systems. It also briefly describes a Lisp framework which is under development and current work on the development of a VLSI activation cell processor which will implement the AF paradigm in an architecture that is similar to that of a data flow computer.

6.1   Introduction

AF stands for Activation Framework. The genealogy of this method is shown in Figure 6.1. Major ideas were drawn from the HEARSAY II project [1] and the Distributed Sensor Networks (DSN) project [2], with inputs from the Vehicle Tracking Simulator project in the area of combining goal and data directed execution [3]. Another major source of ideas was from neural network modeling [4] and the concept of activation networks [5]. The concept of activation, drawn from this work, is used as the basis for making scheduling decisions and for supplying the metrics to make decisions with incomplete data. Many of the ideas for AF are based on real-time operating system concepts. Ideas were drawn from the Frame theories of Minsky [6], Winograd, Bobrow, and Collins [7], and the implementation of the PATREC program [8] which was part of the MDX project [9]. Ideas were also drawn from Hewitt's Actor model [10] and the Contract Net paradigm [11]. Activation Framework Objects have similarities to objects used in Smalltalk [12], LOOPS [13], and Lisp Flavors [14].

The original HEARSAY II program had a Blackboard data structure in which all hypotheses were kept, as shown in Figure 6.2a. Knowledge Source (KS) procedures were activated by a scheduler to put new hypotheses on the Blackboard, update the validity levels of existing hypotheses, and to remove hypotheses from the blackboard. This system was devised to understand connected speech in real time. It was unable to do this because (a) there was not enough processing power with a mainframe computer to handle even simple cases of connected speech, (b) HEARSAY II had problems focusing its resources on those actions most likely to lead to the desired goals, and (c) HEARSAY II did not effectively limit the combinatorial increase in possible interpretations of the speech data as more data arrived.

Experiments with a distributed version of HEARSAY II [15] paved the way for the Distributed Sensor Networks (DSN) project [16] which developed a testbed [17] to acoustically track low flying aircraft. The DSN testbed was a distributed AI system of six geographically distributed nodes with each node containing three processors that were used for data interpretation and message communications. DSN used a distributed HEARSAY II approach, as shown in Figure 6.2b, with separate Blackboards in each processor. It used a sequential layer-by-layer Knowledge Source procedure scheduling mechanism combined with a strict hypothesis pruning mechanism to achieve real-time operation [18]. Access to remote Blackboards was by means of messages sent to guardian processes in each processor.

DSN was successful in that it was a distributed AI system that ran in real-time. It was,

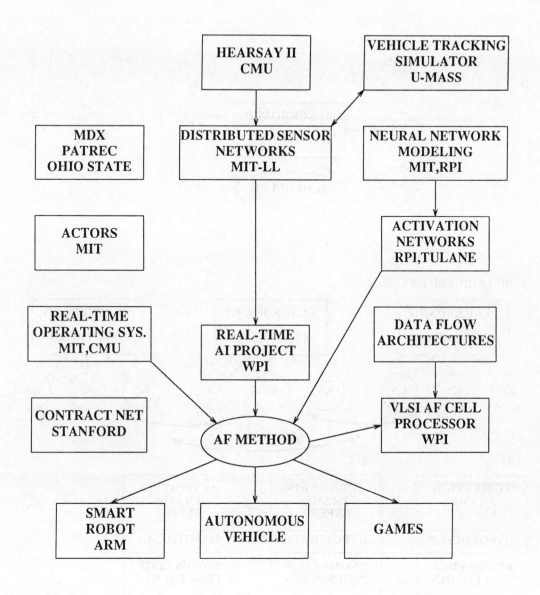

Figure 6.1: Genealogy of the AF Method

a) HEARSAY II

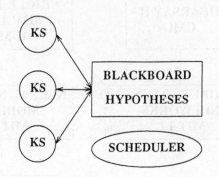

b) DISTRIBUTED HEARSAY

c) AF

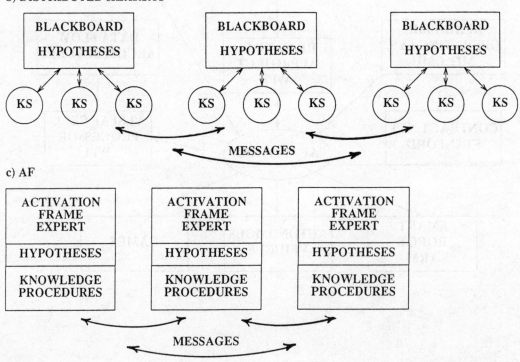

Figure 6.2: From HEARSAY to AF

however, structurally tailored to the specific application. Knowledge Sources interacted through the local Blackboards and there was no way of testing them separately before integration. Also the scheduling was statically determined and had no flexibility. This project was important in the issues it raised about the requirements for a real-time distributed AI system, not all of which DSN addressed successfully.

The principal issues identified were:

Resource Limitations The system must be able to work within limited computer execution cycles, memory, and communication bandwidth, and also with limited access to external equipment or human operators.

Concurrency The system must be able to handle events that occur at random times and in parallel with the actions of data acquisition and decision making.

Uncertainty about Future Events The system must be able to reason about events which may or may not occur and to make decisions based on the prediction of future outcomes of those decisions.

Reasoning about Time The sequence in which events occur and their relative timing is important. The system must be able to time-tag events and to plan actions with a knowledge of how long they will take.

Control Focus It is important to focus the actions of the system on the most critical actions first and to be able to do this without incurring a large overhead in doing so.

Timeliness The system must be able to make timely decisions with incomplete data. This is one of the most critical issues, as often it will be impossible to acquire and evaluate all possible data before a decision has to be made.

Modularity The expert modules that make up an expert system should be able to be developed by separate teams that are knowledgeable in the particular domain of the expert module. These modules should be separately testable and obey good software engineering practices in terms of data hiding and freedom from interaction side effects.

Distributability When an expert module is written, it should not be necessary to know on which processor in a distributed system it is to be run.

Two major problems with a distributed HEARSAY organization are that it lacks modularity and does not have an efficient way to trigger the execution of the Knowledge

157

Source procedures (KSs). All the KSs and Hypotheses in a processor interact through a common Blackboard structure which makes it difficult to develop KSs independently in a modular fashion. This also makes it difficult to control subtle interactions through the common Blackboard data structure. In a general HEARSAY scheme, the scheduler searches the Blackboard for hypotheses that require processing and then schedules the appropriate KSs to carry out the processing. This search is performed for each KS to process each hypothesis and results in a high overhead which is detrimental to real-time performance. The HEARSAY scheduling mechanism can also result in an unfocussed ordering of the execution of the KSs as KSs are triggered by the order in which the Blackboard is searched rather than the KS execution being ordered by a consideration of the current problem state and goals. Corkill [3] showed that the focus-of-attention performance of HEARSAY could be improved by the addition of a goal directed KS scheduling mechanism, but this adds further to the processing resources required for KS scheduling. A search for a simpler alternative solution to these problems led to the evolution of the AF organization, which shown in Figure 6.2c.

In the AF organization, hypotheses and procedural code for a local knowledge domain are integrated into an Activation Framework Object (AFO). These AFOs form a community of experts which communicate by means of message exchange. Each AFO can be thought of as being similar to a miniature HEARSAY II system with its local Blackboard and a limited set of KS procedures. Each AFO is self contained and its external interface is defined by the formats of the messages it sends and receives. It can be written and tested independently by a team that is expert in the AFO's local knowledge domain. A system consisting of many AFOs can be distributed over a number of processors with the scheduling of the AFOs being a function of the message traffic.

One of the key features of AF is the use of activation for decision making as illustrated by the example of Figure 6.3. In Figure 6.3a there are some rules for deducing the type of an animal from some observations. It should be noted that, in this case, all the observations must be available in order to make a decision. Alternately we can add together the positive and negative evidence indicated by each observation to obtain an activation level for each possible interpretation as shown in Figure 6.3b. These weighted evidence levels are akin to the certainty measures of MYCIN [19] and are represented graphically in bar-graph form in Figure 6.3c. As observations are made, the activation levels of the hypotheses for a particular end results are adjusted to reflect the weight of the evidence. At any time a choice can be made, for example to stay and see the zebra or to run from the tiger, based on the activation levels which reflect the evidence available to date. Also the difference between activation levels gives a measure of the uncertainty of the choice and could be used to plan which observations to perform next to reduce the uncertainty.

Our initial design had only one hypothesis contained in each Activation Framework Object and the system used the activation level of that hypothesis as the criterion for which AFO to execute next. It quickly became obvious that such a structure would result in too much fragmentation with too much message traffic. As a result multiple hypotheses are now embodied within an AFO. Each hypothesis has a name, a data structure, and an activation level which specifies the belief in its truth (positive activation levels) or falseness (negative activation levels). The AFO is itself given an activation level corresponding to the notion of this being evidence for the hypothesis that this AFO should be processed.

The final concept was drawn from the field of real-time operating systems and also from some observations on DSN. This was that the message traffic can be used to control the scheduling of the AFOs. If an AFO has no input messages then it need not be executed. Where there is a choice, those AFOs with many messages or higher priority messages should be run first. This led to the concept of having a sending AFO place an activation level (or priority) on each message and to use this to drive the scheduling of the system as described in the next section.

6.2 Activation Framework Objects, Messages, and Frameworks

An Activation Framework Object (AFO) is an expert in a limited domain area. Each AFO contains hypotheses about the state of that part of the problem environment in which it is an expert and procedural knowledge as to how to manipulate the hypotheses. AFOs have the ability to exchange information with other AFOs by means of messages. The message passing mechanism allows messages to be sent

Automatically If the AFO is given, or deduces, some new piece of information, it will inform those AFOs that it knows can use this information.

On Demand One AFO can ask another about the current value of a hypothesis, or can ask for the AFO to evaluate some data it is sent, or data that it needs to acquire to respond to the request.

Suggestively In this mode, one AFO sends a message to another that results in a change in the activation level of the evidence for or against some hypotheses that is in the domain of the second AFO.

a) Formal Logic

IF X HAS HAIR: X-> MAMMAL
IF X EATS MEAT AND IS MAMMAL: X-> CARNIVORE
IF X HAS STRIPES AND IS CARNIVORE X-> TIGER

b) Activation

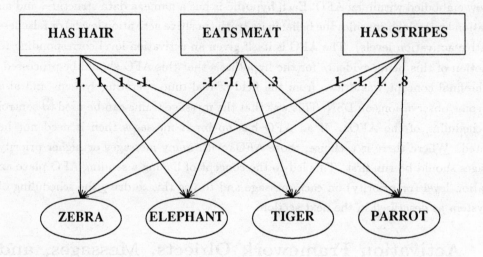

c) Bar Graph of Activation Levels

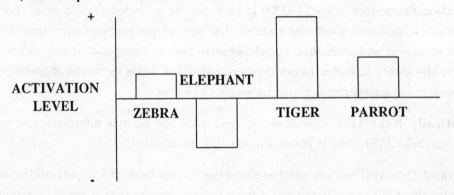

Figure 6.3: Formal Logic versus Activation

160

Automatic sending of information can be considered to correspond to forward chaining in a conventional expert system and on-demand sending of information to correspond to backward chaining. The suggestive mode is used to allow real-time decision making with incomplete data and its function in accumulating evidence for or against hypotheses has parallels in the confidence factors of MYCIN, the hypothesis supports of HEARSAY II, and other evidential support systems such as those described by Prade. [20] These modes of action are illustrated in Figure 6.4.

The structure of an AFO is shown in Figure 6.5. It has a name which is global and known to all other AFOs which need to communicate with it. It contains hypotheses, which can be singular entities or complex data structures. Each hypothesis is named and these names can be used by other AFOs to request the values of the hypotheses from their guardian AFO. Each AFO contains procedures which are triggered by incoming messages to act on local hypotheses and/or to send out other messages. In addition, each AFO may have space for local private data not directly accessible by other AFOs.

Messages are sent to an AFO by name, so that the sending AFO does not need to know the location of the recipient in a distributed system. Messages are placed on the receiving AFO's input queue in time and activation level order, with those messages having the highest activation level being at the front of the queue. The oldest messages are placed closer to the front of the queue than the most recent. Under most circumstances, this is the order in which an AFO takes and processes messages from its input queue. It can, however, follow local domain-specific rules by searching its input queue before selecting one or more message to be processed.

Generally an AFO will take one message from its input queue, process that message, and return control to the AFO scheduler so as to ensure a fair allocation of processing resources to all AFOs. AFOs, in general, will not wait on external events or messages being received. Rather, the procedure appropriate to the received message will be executed and then control returned immediately. The messages generated as a result of executing the procedure are placed on an output queue which is a no-wait operation. These messages are then delivered when the AFO scheduler regains control.

The format of a message object is shown in Figure 6.6. Each message contains a TO name which is the global name of the AFO to which it is to be delivered. It also contains the FROM name which is the name of the sending AFO so that a reply can be sent if needed. Each message is given an activation level by its sending AFO which is an indication of the level of importance attached to the message. Each message is given a message type, has an ASCII data body, and is tagged with the time it is sent.

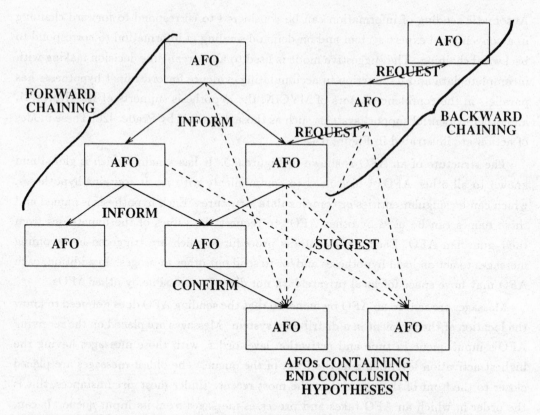

EARLY INFORMATION MAY BE PROVIDED BY SUGGESTION WHICH CAN BE
USED TO MAKE DECISIONS IN TIME CRITICAL SITUATIONS

Figure 6.4: Flow of Control in AF

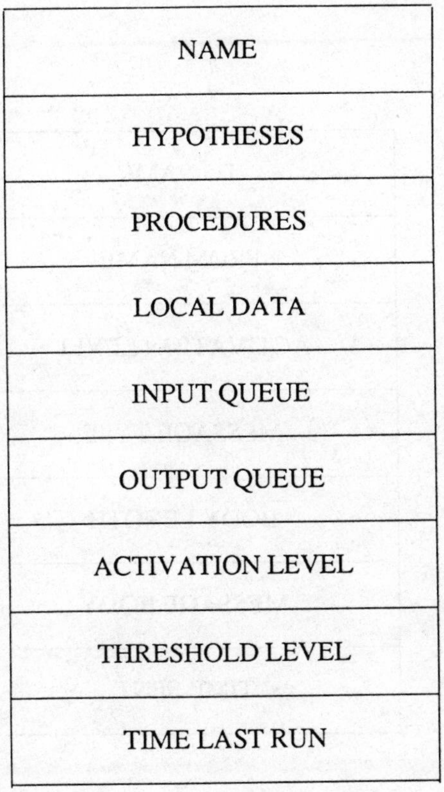

Figure 6.5: An Activation Framework Object

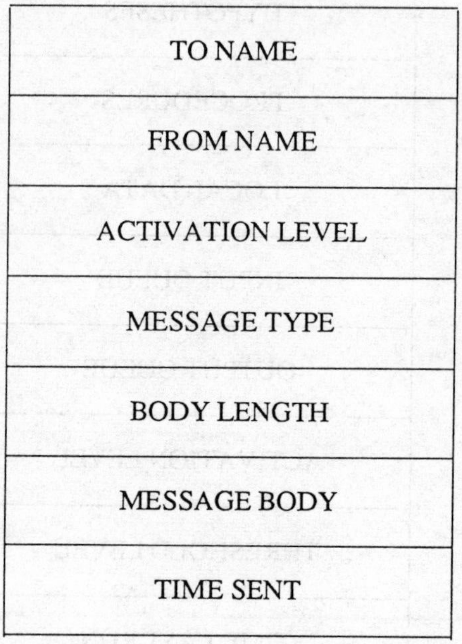

```
┌─────────────────────────────┐
│                             │
│         TO NAME             │
│                             │
├─────────────────────────────┤
│                             │
│        FROM NAME            │
│                             │
├─────────────────────────────┤
│                             │
│      ACTIVATION LEVEL       │
│                             │
├─────────────────────────────┤
│                             │
│       MESSAGE TYPE          │
│                             │
├─────────────────────────────┤
│                             │
│       BODY LENGTH           │
│                             │
├─────────────────────────────┤
│                             │
│       MESSAGE BODY          │
│                             │
├─────────────────────────────┤
│                             │
│        TIME SENT            │
│                             │
└─────────────────────────────┘
```

Figure 6.6: AF Message Object

The activation level of an AFO is the sum of the activations of the messages on their input queues. AFOs are scheduled if their activation level exceeds their threshold and the one with the highest activation is run first. When a message is taken off its input queue, the activation level of an AFO is reduced by the activation level of the message processed. The threshold level is used to preclude the execution of the AFO until enough messages have accumulated.

This use of activation levels to control the scheduling of processes is based on the observation that the processes to run in DSN were the ones with the highest message traffic. The mechanism used in AF gives priority to the running of AFOs with high priority messages on their input queue. It also gives priority to those AFOs which have accumulated a large number of low priority messages on their input queues. There is no global control of scheduling and no need to search a Blackboard data structure, as in HEARSAY II, to find which procedure to execute next. This mechanism is efficient as the activation level of the AFO is updated whenever a message is delivered and the scheduler simply has to run that AFO which has the highest activation level.

There could be a problem if AFOs which have just a few low activation messages on their input queues are never be run. In practice, this is not a problem provided that there are enough processor cycles for all AFOs to process all messages required by the overall problem state. These messages may wait a long time before being processed but will ultimately be processed when all higher priority messages on other AFOs have been processed. All messages are tagged with the time at which they are sent and all AFOs are tagged with the time at which they were last run. This information could be used to modify the scheduling algorithm to limit the amount of time the processing of an AFO is deferred, although at present this is not done.

The message type is a number that is unique to the receiving AFO. It need not be globally unique, only unambiguous to the recipient. As the development of the AF method progresses we are finding some messages that are common to nearly all AFOs such as give me the current value of some named hypothesis. Our current approach is to reserve some message types for generic messages such as the example just given and then to use others for application specific messages. As we find the same message format recurring in different applications we are replacing these application specific occurrences with generic message types.

The message body is an ASCII string. Internal to an AFO a hypothesis is a data structure that may contain numeric and string data. It may even be a list of objects. After much discussion of how we could uniformly represent this diversity of object structures in a message body we decided upon the ASCII string as a common denominator.

This implies that a hypothesis object must be encoded in an ASCII string when it is sent between AFOs and decoded when it is received. This means that both sending and receiving AFOs must use a mutually agreed message body format but do not need to use the same internal representation for the hypothesis data. The ASCII format is advantageous in that an entire message can be encoded in ASCII and sent over serial data links if needed. In this form messages can also be written on a logging file and printed out as a trace of systems activity.

AFOs are attached to Frameworks which are responsible for scheduling their attached AFOs and delivering messages local to the AFOs attached to the Framework, as shown in Figure 6.7. The Framework is also responsible for delivering messages to other Frameworks where appropriate. This message delivery is accomplished using the host O/S system message passing mechanism and each Framework has a routing procedure that translates the symbolic TO name to a system level identity for message delivery. The framework and its attached AFOs form a process which is scheduled by the host's O/S scheduler. The Framework scheduler will continue to schedule and execute AFOs until there are no more AFOs with activation levels above their threshold. At this point the Framework process will sleep until another message arrives for one of the AFOs to process. This mechanism relies on the operating system's pre-emptive scheduling mechanism to ensure fairness of the allocation of CPU cycles between the various Frameworks.

In some cases, it is necessary for an AFO to wait for input, such as from a user terminal or other equipment. In this case a single AFO is attached to the Framework and is allowed to wait for input, relying on the underlying mechanisms of the host operating system to allow other Frameworks to run their AFOs. This mechanism makes for a nice uniformity of representation but does raise the issue of what is an expert object. Our original concept was that of a community of expert objects cooperating by means of messages. We soon had to address the issue of whether an AFO that simply takes input from a user is an expert object or simply a procedure. One argument is that such an AFO is a simple dialogue expert. A counter argument is that it looks just like a user input procedure in implementation. For the present we have concluded that they are all objects and that *expertise is in the eye of the beholder*.

Frameworks and their associated AFOs can be written in a number of languages. So far one has been written in Lisp and one in the C language that supports AFOs written in both C and Fortran 77. ADA appears to be a good candidate language for writing a Framework but unextended PASCAL does not, due to its lack of support for separately compiled functions and access to system level facilities. There would also appear to be no reason why a Framework could not be written as an inference engine interpreting rules

166

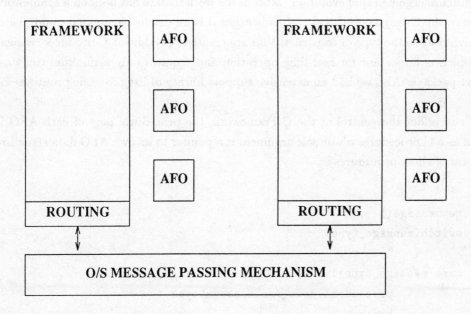

Figure 6.7: AFOs Attached to Frameworks

in response to arriving messages. The implementation for an expert AFO can be chosen to be appropriate to the problem domain. An inference network based expert might advantageously be written in Lisp whereas an expert that performed matrix arithmetic in, for example, a Kalman filter might best be written in Fortran 77. We are also planning to develop a language in which to express the AF paradigm. This language will have its features based on the common constructs in the programs we are developing to use AF.

6.3   Current Status

AF is still undergoing rapid evolution. Most of the work to date has been on a Framework written in the C language. C was chosen because it is an extensible language and places few barriers as to the type of constructs that are created. In addition C produces efficient code which is important for real-time operation and requires only a minimal run-time support package. Also we had an extensive support library of list processing routines for C.

To run under the control of the C Framework, the procedural part of each AFO is written as a C procedure, whose sole argument is a pointer to its own AFO data structure The form of these procedures is

```
getmessage()
switch(message_type)
        {
case message_type_1:
            procedural code for message type 1
            break;
case message_type_2:
            procedural code for message type 2
            break;
        }
    return;
```

Each section of procedural code must be atomic. That is, it cannot wait for an external event such as the arrival of a message. One or more messages can be sent within each procedural section. However, any action that would transfer control to the host O/S, such as I/O or a sleep, is not permitted unless the AFO is the only one attached to

168

the Framework. Where a request-response type action is to be carried out, the request is written as one section of procedural code and the response to the return message is written as another. In this way there is no need for an AFO to wait for a reply message, which in a distributed system may never come. The AFO can retain information about what messages have been sent and what replies are outstanding in its local data area, but it so far has been possible to write most AFOs in a form where they do not use hidden sequence information. AFOs written in this way are simpler in form and do not have the burden of handling lost messages.

The AFO procedures are linked to a list of AFO data structures which are declared in the main program. At present, a different main program has to be written for each instance of the Framework in order to declare and name all the AFOs. It is planned, however, to automatically generate this main program from a definition of the AFOs through a preprocessor to the C compiler.

The C Framework performs the following actions:

```
Find the AFO with the highest activation level
     if none then sleep
Execute AFO procedure
Take messages from its output queue and deliver them
     updating AFO activations upon delivery
Repeat sequence
```

Message delivery takes place by looking up the TO name for each message in a table of AFO names and addresses that is built from the list of AFOs when the Framework starts executing. The actions of the AFOs are started either by the arrival of external messages or by initiating an AFO with an activation level above its threshold.

This Framework has been tested using some simple games and has been found to run successfully. As an example of how a game can be implemented in this paradigm, a Tic-Tac-Toe game using five expert AFOs is shown in Figure 6.8. The first is a user input and display expert that also keeps the current state of the game board. This expert takes in a user specified move and then chooses a move in response. In choosing its move, this expert can send the current state of the game board to four other experts which perform the following functions:

Find a winning 3-in-a-row move

Find a move to stop the opponent from winning

Find good general attacking moves

Find good general defensive moves

In the cases of the good attacking and defending moves, the possible moves are ranked as to how good they are. The user input and display expert sends out requests to the four experts and chooses a suitable move based on their reply. The computer then displays the chosen move and takes in the next user move until the game is completed. Each expert is implemented as one AFO.

In its two dimensional form Tic-Tac-Toe is not very interesting except to test the Framework. In its three dimensional form, however, it does demonstrate some interesting possibilities of the AF method. One of the problems of games is future uncertainty, a property they share with real-time systems. In real-time systems the uncertainty comes from not knowing whether certain events will occur. In games the uncertainty comes from not knowing your opponent's moves. In both cases it is possible to predict the outcome of a particular move or choice by simulation. Inevitably the simulated scenario calls for another choice which will lead to alternate scenarios to be simulated. This leads to rapid growth of the ... if I do this and then he does this and I do that ... type of reasoning chain. One of the nice properties of AF is its ability to handle this type of reasoning cleanly.

In the case of Tic-Tac-Toe an expert that wishes to evaluate a possible move can postulate the state of the game board after the move and send it to an expert that predicts the opponents move. This latter expert carries out its actions by inverting the game board (0=X,X=0) and sending this inverted game state to the four move experts to choose possible moves. This situation can recurse through several iterations until one or more winning or losing moves are found. At this point, the message replies are "unwound" until the original requester is able to obtain an evaluation of the possible outcomes of the moves. We have found similar decision situations to exist in a number of problems such as smart robot arm that chooses the order in which to place items from a conveyer belt into bins and an autonomous vehicle navigator that must decide which way to proceed in a maze.

As the C Framework is evolving we are building in debugging aids. Two of the most useful are a log file of all message traffic and AFOs executed and an on-screen status display. This display shows the most recent messages delivered and the currently running AFO. At present we have only one Framework executing at a time, but we plan to use multiple windows on a terminal to display the status of concurrently executing Frameworks. The message traffic display is an excellent debugging aid and allows a

170

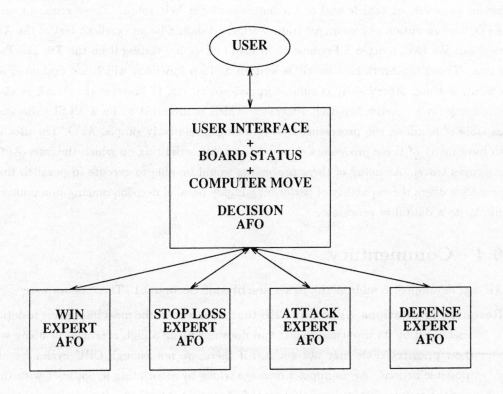

Figure 6.8: Tic-Tac-Toe Game Organization

171

good understanding of what is going on inside the Framework. As the AFOs become more complex, a simple message display may not be enough. It would, however, be simple to add an explanation field to each message to allow an AFO to explain (for human consumption) why it is sending the message. This would give AF an explanation capability which has proved to be beneficial in many expert systems.

Currently we are starting to apply the C Framework to the problem of the navigator for an autonomous vehicle and to the smart conveyer belt robot. These require many AFOs and execution of concurrent frameworks and should be an excellent test of the AF method. We have written a Framework in Lisp and we are testing it on the Tic-Tac-Toe game. This Framework has its AFOs written as Lisp functions which are evaluated at execution time, otherwise it is similar in concept to the C Framework. Work is also underway on an Activation Cell Processor which is intended to be a VLSI processor capable of handling the processing load of a single, relatively simple, AFO. The idea is to have many of these processors connected to a bit serial ring on which the inter-AFO messages travel. As many of these processors would be able to execute in parallel, this processor offers the capability of performing highly parallel decision making in a manner similar to a data flow processor.

6.4   Commentary

AF was developed to address the issues described in Section 6.1. These issues were:

Resource Limitations AF focuses CPU time resources on the most important task (as measured by its input messages) and does not incur a high overhead in doing so. Low priority AFOs may not get run if there are not enough CPU cycles for all possible actions. AF minimizes message traffic by associating hypotheses with the activation frame procedures that most frequently access them. It makes no attempt to conserve memory although there is a list management subsystem that is part of the C Framework which allows the effective management of lists of hypothesis objects.

Concurrency AF allows concurrent execution of Frameworks.

Reasoning about Uncertainty AF supports this by providing a mechanism for exploring alternative plans using messages to contain hypothesised scenarios which can be simulated and used as a basis for further decisions.

Reasoning about Time While not directly supported by AF, all hypotheses are tagged as to the time they were last updated, all messages are time tagged, and all AFOs

172

are tagged as to when they were last run. This facilitates reasoning about time.

Control Focus AF handles this by the transfer of the message activation levels to the frame object. This appears to be efficient and effective based on our limited experience to date.

Timeliness AF supports the need to make timely decisions with incomplete data by using the suggestion mode of operation on the evidential activation levels of the hypotheses.

Modularity AFOs are extremely modular, separately testable (using a Framework with the only other AFOs being for test input and output), and can be developed independently by a team with knowledge about its limited domain. The use of messages limits interactive side effects and internal hypothesis structure can be hidden from another ARO that calls upon the first for hypothesis values.

Distributability AFOs can be written without regard as to which machine they will be executed upon. They are restricted to run attached to a Framework which supports the language in which the AFO is written.

In conclusion, the AF method appears to meet the criteria we established as being desirable for this class of system. Much work remains to be done in developing the tools for constructing and debugging systems that use AF. There is also an even larger body of work to be done in applying AF and refining this method based on the lessons we learn.

Acknowledgements

This is to acknowledge the contributions of my graduate students Steffan Wyss, Weigeng Shi, and Yanlin Zhang who have done all the programming for AF and contributed many good ideas. This is also to acknowledge the contribution of Dave Brown and Lee Becker (fellow members of the Artificial Intelligence Research Group at Worcester Polytechnic Institute) in discussing AF, reviewing this paper, and making many useful suggestions.

References

[1] L. Erman, F. Hayes-Roth, V. R. Lesser, and R. D. Reddy, "The HEARSAY-II speech understanding system: Integrating knowledge to resolve uncertainty," *ACM Computing Surveys*, Vol. 12, pp. 213-253, 1980.

[2] P. E. Green, "Distributed Acoustic Surveillance and Tracking," *Proc. Distributed Sensor Networks Workshop*, pp. 117-141, M.I.T. Lincoln Laboratory, Lexington, MA, January 6, 1982.

173

[3] D. D. Corkill, "A Framework for Organizational Self-Design in Distributed Problem Solving Networks," COINS Technical Report 82-33, U. Mass. Computer and Information Science, Amherst, MA, February 1983.

[4] J. A. Feldman and D. H. Ballard, "Computing with Connections," Report TR72, Computer Science Department, University of Rochester, Rochester, NY, April 1981.

[5] L. A. Becker and M. V. Doran, "PLENs: A Modification of the Structure of Activation Networks for Control," Internal Report, Cognitive Modeling Group, Department of Computer Science, Tulane University, New Orleans, LA.

[6] M. Minsky, "A Framework for Representing Knowledge," in *The Psychology of Computer Vision*, ed. P. Winston, McGraw-Hill, New York, NY, 1975.

[7] T. Winograd, "Frame Declarations and the Declarative/Procedural Controversy," in *Representation and Understanding: Studies in Cognitive Science*, ed. D. G. Bobrow and A. Collins, pp. 185-210, Academic Press, New York, NY, 1975.

[8] S. Mittal and B. Chandrasekaran, "Patrec: A Knowledge-Directed Database for a Diagnostic Expert System," *IEEE Computer*, vol. 17, no. 9, pp. 51-58, September 1984.

[9] F. Gomez and B. Chandrasekaran, "Knowledge Organization and Distribution for Medical Diagnosis," *IEEE Trans. on Systems, Man, and Cybernetics*, vol. SMC-11, no. 1, pp. 34-42, January 1981.

[10] C. E. Hewitt, "Viewing Control Structures as Patterns of Passing Messages," *Artificial Intelligence*, vol. 20, no. 3, pp. 323-364, June 1977.

[11] R. Davis and R. Smith, "Negotiation as a Metaphor for Distributed Problem Solving," *Artificial Intelligence*, vol. 20, no. 1, pp. 63-109, January 1983.

[12] The Xerox Learning Research Group, "The Smalltalk-80 System," *Byte Magazine*, vol. 6, no. 8, pp. 36-48, August 1981.

[13] D. G. Bobrow and M. Stefik, *The LOOPS Manual*, Xerox PARC, Palo Alto, CA, December 1983.

[14] D. Weinreb and D. Moon, "Flavors: Message Passing in the Lisp Machine," A.I. Memo No. 602, MIT AI Laboratory, Cambridge, MA, November 1980.

[15] V. R. Lesser and L. D. Erman, "An Experiment in Distributed Interpretation," *IEEE Trans. on Computers*, vol. 29, no. 12, pp. 1144-1163, December 1980.

[16] J. R. Delaney, R. T. Lacoss and P. E. Green, "Distributed Estimation in the MIT/LL DSN Testbed," *Proc. American Control Conference*, pp. 305-311, San Francisco, CA, June 22, 1983.

[17] P. E. Green, "DSN Test-Bed Tour and Demonstration," *Proc. Distributed Sensor Nets Workshop*, pp. 163-174, M.I.T. Lincoln Laboratory, Lexington, MA, January 6, 1982.

[18] P. E. Green, "Resource Control in a Real Time Target Tracking Process," *Proc. Fifteenth Asilomar Conference on Circuits, Systems, and Computers*, pp. 424-428, Pacific Grove, CA, November 9, 1981.

[19] B. G. Buchanan and E. H. Shortliffe, *Rule-Based Expert Systems*, Addison Wesley, Reading, MA, 1984.

[20] H. Prade, "A Computational Approach to Approximate and Plausible Reasoning with Applications to Expert Systems," *IEEE Trans. on Pattern Analysis and Machine Intelligence*, vol. 7, no. 3, pp. 260-283, May 1985.

Peter E. Green
Artificial Intelligence Research Group
Worcester Polytechnic Institute
Worcester, MA 01609

Chapter 7

A Connectionist Encoding of Semantic Networks

Lokendra Shastri

Abstract

This paper presents a highly distributed solution to the problem of representing and reasoning with conceptual information. It describes how knowledge about concepts, their properties, and the hierarchical relationship between concepts (e.g., the IS-A relation) can be encoded as an *interpreter-free* massively parallel network of simple processing elements such that:

- the network can solve an interesting class of inheritance and categorization problems extremely fast—in time proportional to the depth of the conceptual hierarchy, and

- the network computes the solutions to the above problems in accordance with a formally justifiable theory of *evidential reasoning* that offers a principled way of handling *exceptions* and resolving *conflicting information* during inheritance, and finding *best matches* based on *partial information* during categorization.

The connectionist solution described here is distributed in the extreme sense of the word. It is realized as a network of a large number of very simple processing elements (nodes) that operate *without the intervention of a central controller*; the data as well as the mechanisms for accessing the data (i.e., the interpreter) are distributed across the network. A query is posed to the network by activating appropriate nodes in the network. Thereafter, all the nodes compute in parallel—each node updates its level of activity based on the activity of its neighbors, and communicates this level to its neighbors. At the end of a specified interval, the answer is available as the levels of activation of a relevant set of nodes.

7.1 Introduction

This paper describes a highly distributed solution to the problem of representing and reasoning with conceptual information based on the use of an *interpreter-free* massively parallel network of simple processing elements. After processing a query, answers from the network are available as the levels of activation of a relevant set of its nodes. This form of processing is similar to *spreading activation* and has been used to model memory processes in Cognitive Science and Artificial Intelligence [13,1][1]. In all these cases, however, spreading activation has been used to model rather diffuse and "approximate" effects such as semantic priming and associative recall, or to perform very underconstrained and inexact search in semantic memory. In contrast, the connectionist encoding described here uses spreading activation to draw very precise and well specified inferences. This precision and specificity is achieved by controlling the spread of activation. Furthermore, a salient feature of the network design is that this control is achieved not by a central controller, but by "control nodes" distributed throughout the network.

7.1.1 Motivation

Inheritance is the form of reasoning that leads an agent to infer ("by inheritance") properties of a concept based on the properties of its ancestors. For example, if we know that "Birds fly" and that "Tweety is a bird", we would want to infer that "Tweety flies".

Categorization is the dual of inheritance. Unlike inheritance which seeks some property value of a given concept, categorization seeks a concept that has some specified property values. In other words, given a *partial description* consisting of a set of property values, categorization amounts to finding a concept that best matches this description.

The stance taken in this work is that inheritance and categorization are important forms of *limited inference* [4,11]. It can be argued that these two complementary forms of reasoning lie at the core of intelligence, and act as precursors to more complex and specialized reasoning processes. This becomes apparent if one views inheritance and categorization in their extended sense: inheritance amounts to inferring properties of an entity "x" given that "x is an instance of concept/class C", and categorization amounts to finding a concept "C" on the basis of a partial description of "x", such that "x is an

---

[1]Marker passing [5] is a discrete variant of spreading activation and is discussed later in this section.

instance of C". In fact, categorization is a very general form of pattern matching; one in which target patterns (concepts) are organized in a hierarchy, and where the complete specification of a target pattern not only includes its local attributes (properties) but also the attributes it inherits from its ancestors.

Besides being important forms of limited inference, inheritance and categorization are also interesting for another reason: human agents perform these operations effortlessly and extremely fast—often in a few hundred milliseconds. This is specially significant given that human beings operate with a vast knowledge-base. In view of the above, it becomes important that we provide a *computational account* of how inheritance and categorization may be performed with such effectiveness, for if we build intelligent systems we should expect them to perform similar tasks in time scales that are comparable to those required by human agents[2]. The work described in this paper addresses this problem and provides such a computational account. It demonstrates that an interesting class of inheritance and categorization problems can be solved effectively by the proposed connectionist network.

In addition to offering computational effectiveness, the connectionist network computes solutions to the inheritance and categorization problems in accordance with a theory of evidential reasoning. The evidential formulation handles exceptions, as well as conflicting information in multiple inheritance situations in a semantically consistent manner, and thereby improves upon existing formalisms proposed to characterize inheritance. Furthermore, the same formulation offers a principled treatment of categorization. This paper is primarily about the connectionist realization of the evidential solution and a detailed discussion of the evidential formulation is beyond the scope of this paper. Nevertheless, a brief sketch of the argument in favor of an evidential approach is included below.

It is well understood that a simple characterization of inheritance is confounded by two aspects of world knowledge

Exceptions: There is a preponderence of situations where one may want to associate a property with a class, although—strictly speaking, the property may not hold for all members of the class. For example, we would like to associate the property of flying with birds in spite of the fact that Ostriches and Penguins do not fly.

Conflicting information: Often there exist several alternate but equally useful hierarchical organizations of concepts in a domain. This leads to situations wherein a concept may have multiple ancestors. The presence of multiple ancestors may

---

[2]The concern for computational effectiveness should not be shrugged off as merely a matter of *implementation detail,* efficiency, or programming tricks.

lead to ambiguity because some of the ancestors of a concept may have conflicting information attached to them. For example, an agent may hold the following beliefs simultaneously and may have to decide whether Dick is a pacifist or a non-pacifist:

```
Quakers tend to be pacifists.              - R1
Republicans tend to be non-pacifists.      - R2
Dick is a Quaker.
Dick is a Republican.
```

Nonevidential formulations such as the proposal of Etherington and Reiter based on Default Logic [3], or the formulation of Touretzky [16] handle exceptions reasonably well, but they do not handle conflicting information adequately. These proposals deal with conflicting information either by making arbitrary choices or by refraining from making a choice.

Default Logic makes the implicit assumption that all the default rules have the same "significance" or "import". From this it follows that if two or more rules have conflicting consequences then either the use of one rule should preclude the use of the other rules, or no conclusions should be drawn based on these rule. Etherington and Reiter's system would handle the Quaker example by arbitrarily choosing between one of two possible *extensions* and responding with an answer that lies in the chosen extension. The choice of extension would depend upon which of the two default rule R1, or R2 is selected first by the inference procedure. In either case the inference drawn would depend on *only one* of the two rules and in turn on an *ad hoc* order of rule application. Our intuitions, however, suggest that both R1 and R2 are relevant in drawing conclusions about Dick and both must affect the final conclusion. In general, *the final conclusion should reflect the combined effect of all the relevant information.*

Touretzky's formalism is also limited in its ability to deal with conflicting information. His principle of inferential distance ordering states that: if A inherits P from B, and ¬P from C, then "if A has an inheritance path via B to C and not vice verse, then conclude P; if A has an inheritance path via C to B and not vice versa then conclude ¬P; otherwise report an ambiguity [16]." The principle of inferential distance ordering however, does not solve the problem of combining conflicting information from disparate sources. It essentially treats all rules at the same inferential distance as having the same import and consequently, when faced with situations such as the Quaker example, Touretzky's system is forced to report an ambiguity.

Making an arbitrary choice, or refraining from making a choice need not be the only way of handling conflicting information. It is often the case that all rules do not have

180

the same import, for example, the agent may believe that the tendency of Quakers to be pacifists outweighs the tendency of Republicans to be nonpacifists. In this case it may be appropriate for it to infer that Dick is probably a pacifist. Such situations however, can be analyzed only if we employ a richer representation that allows us to represent the relative import of rules and provide a way of computing the combined effect of such rules. The need for combining relevant information to draw a conclusion becomes more apparent if we consider the following: suppose we add to the agent's beliefs that "Dick took part in antiwar demonstrations". Now it seems *even more* appropriate than before to infer that Dick is probably a pacifist.

One possibility is to consider statements such as R1 and R2 to be evidential assertions and to associate a numeric quantity with them to indicate their evidential import. Thus, "Quakers tend to be pacifists" may be interpreted to mean "the fact that 'x is a pacifist' lends evidence α to the fact that 'x is a pacifist' ". If one could assign meanings to numbers such as α and specify a formal calculus for computing the combined effect of assertions such as R1 and R2, then one would be able to handle situations such as the Quaker example satisfactorily.

The evidential framework we use derives from the principle of maximum entropy. Its details, its relation to bayes' rule and the Dempster-Shafer rule, and its merits are discussed in [15]; a brief version that deals primarily with inheritance appears in [14]. Based on this framework, the connectionist network described in this paper can encode knowledge specified in a representation language similar to semantic networks, but one that admits evidential assertions about concepts and their properties (such as "Quakers tend to be pacifists"). The computations performed by these networks are in accordance with the evidential formulation that specifies how such evidential information may be used in a semantically consistent manner during inheritance and categorization. Inheritance and categorization are posed as problem whose answers involve choosing the *most likely* alternative from among a set of alternatives - the computation of likelihood being carried out with respect to the knowledge encoded in the conceptual hierarchy. This reformulation provides a principled way of handling *exceptions* and resolving *conflicting information* during inheritance, and finding *best matches* based on *partial information* during categorization.

7.1.2   Relation to Other Parallel Implementations

The first attempt at a highly parallel encoding of conceptual hierarchies was undertaken by Fahlman [5]. His proposal for the NETL system consisted of a central computer connected to a large number of node and link elements, each of which was a hardware element. The nodes could pass a small number of messages called *markers* along the links under the control of the central computer. This operation of *marker-passing* was used to perform inheritance and categorization.

NETL's marker passing system had major limitations which have been discussed by Fahlman as well as others [6,7,3,2]. The answers provided by the network were sensitive to race conditions, especially in the presence of exceptions and multiple hierarchies. There were even more serious problems with the semantics (or the lack of it) of the IS-A links, given the existence of CANCEL links[3]. Another limitation of the marker passing approach was that each marker could only be either ON or OFF. This all-or-none nature of markers made the system incapable of supporting evidential reasoning. For example, categorization amounted to finding all concepts that had *all* the specified set of properties, and there was no notion of a "best match" or a "partial match" [7].

Recent work on Bayesian networks [12] deals with evidential reasoning in a parallel network, but the networks do not possess sufficient built-in control and structure to handle the kinds of inheritance and categorization tasks discussed in this paper. Furthermore, Pearl's results apply only to singly-connected networks (networks in which there is only one underlying path between any pair of nodes). More complex networks have to be *conditioned* to render them singly-connected. The solutions suggested in this paper apply to networks with multiple hierarchies where inheritance can be performed with respect to concepts having multiple parents [14] (Cf. the Quaker example).

Section 7.2 below briefly describes the representation language for specifying the conceptual structure, Section 7.3 describes the connectionist encoding to perform inheritance and categorization, and Section 7.4 presents some examples.

7.2 A Restricted Language for Representing Conceptual Knowledge

The representation langauge may be viewed as an extension of inheritance hierarchies to include relative frequency information specifying how instances of some concepts are distributed with respect to some property values. A summary description of the language follows. The agent's knowledge consists of the quintuple:

$$\Theta = \langle \mathcal{C}, \Phi, \#, \delta, \ll \rangle,$$

---

[3]Touretzky [16] has resolved some of these problems, but as mentioned above, his formulation does not handle multiple inheritance adequately, nor does it address the issue of categorization. See [15] for elaboration.

where $\mathcal{C}$ is the set of *concepts*, Φ is the set of *properties*, $\#$ is a mapping from $\mathcal{C}$ to the integers I, δ (the *distribution* function) is a partial mapping from $\mathcal{C} \times \Phi$ to the power set of $\mathcal{C} \times I$, and $\ll$ is a partial ordering defined on $\mathcal{C}$.

For each $C \in \mathcal{C}$, if C is a Token (instance) then $\#C = 1$, and if C is a Type (generic concept) then $\#C =$ the number of instances of C *observed by the agent*. By extension $\#C[P,V] =$ the number of instances of C that are observed by the agent to have the value V for property P. For example, $\#$APPLE[has-color, RED] equals the number of red apples observed by the agent. Finally, $\#C[P_1, V_1][P_2, V_2] \ldots [P_n, V_n] =$ the number of instances of C, observed to have the value V_1 for property P_1, value V_2 for property P_2, ..., and value V_n for property P_n.

The distribution function $\delta(C, P)$, specifies how instances of C are distributed with respect to the values of property P. Recall that a concept may have several values for the same property and hence, if C is a Type, then $\delta(C, P)$, corresponds to the summary information abstracted in C based on the instances of C. Using the $\#$ function, $\delta(C, P)$ may be expressed in terms of $\#[C, P]$'s. Thus, δ(APPLE, has-color) may be expressed as: $\{\#$APPLE[has-color, RED] $= 60, \#$APPLE[has-color, GREEN] $= 40\}$. Note that δ is only a partial mapping; an agent may not know $\delta(C, P)$ for may concepts–property pairs. In general, for a given C and P, an agent knows $\delta(C, P)$ only if this information may prove useful in making inferences about C.

A salient feature of the language is that either a concept is an instance of (subtype of) another concept or it is not, and the $\ll$ relation specifies this unequivocally. Exceptions only apply to property values. This goes a long way in assigning a clean semantics to the representation language.

In terms of the above notation, the inheritance and categorization problems may be restated as follows:

Inheritance

> **Given:** A concept C, a property P, and a set of property values, $V_{SET} = \{V_1, V_2, \ldots, V_n\}$,
>
> **Find:** $V* \in V_{SET}$, such that among members of V_{SET}, $V*$ is the *most likely value* of property P for concept C. In other words, find $V* \in V_{SET}$ such that, for any $V_i \in V_{SET}$, the best estimate of $\#C[P, V*] \geq$ the best estimate of $\#C[P, V_i]$'s.

For example, the inheritance problem where $C =$ APPLE, $P =$ has-color, $V_{SET} = \{$RED, BLUE, GREEN$\}$, may be paraphrased as:

"Is the color of an apple more likely to be red, green or blue?"

Categorization

> **Given:** a set of concepts, $C_{SET} = \{C_1, C_2, \ldots, C_n\}$, and an appropriate description consisting of a set of property value pairs, i.e., a $DISCR = \{[P_1, V_1], [P_2, V_2], \ldots, [P_m, V_m]\}$.
>
> **Find:** $C* \in C_{SET}$ such that *relative* to the concepts specified in C_{SET}, $C*$ is the *most likely* concept described by $DISCR$.

If $C_{SET} = \{\text{APPLE, GRAPE}\}$, $DISCR = \{[\text{has-color, RED}], [\text{has-taste, SWEET}]\}$ then the categorization may be paraphrased as follows:

"It is red in color and sweet in taste, is it more likely to be an apple or a grape?"

The solutions to these two problems are based on the principle of maximum entropy [10] and are described in [15]. A discussion of the solution is beyond the scope of this paper. The next section outlines the massively parallel (connectionist) encoding of the solution.

7.3 Connectionist Encoding

A connectionist network [8] consists of a large number of nodes connected via links. The nodes are computational entities defined by:

{q}: a small number (2 or 3) of states

p: a real-valued potential in the range [0,1],

v: an output value also in the range [0,1],

i: a vector of inputs $i_1, i_2, \ldots, i_n$,

together with functions P, V and Q that define the values of potential, state and output at time $t+1$, based on the values of potential, state and inputs at time t. A node does not treat all its inputs uniformly. Nodes receive inputs via *weighted* links. Each incident link provides an input whose magnitude equals the output of the node at the source of the link times the weight on the link. A node may have multiple input *sites*, and incoming links are connected to specific sites. Each site has an associated *site functions*. These functions carry out local computations based on the inputs incident at the site, and it is the result of this computation that is processed by the functions P, V and Q.

Connectionist networks offer a natural computational model for encoding evidential formalisms because of the natural correspondence between nodes and hypotheses, activation and evidential support, and potential functions and evidence combination rules.

184

However, in order to solve the inheritance and categorization problems, the network must perform very specific computations, and this requires that the network control the spreading of activation. Furthermore, the network must do so *without the intervention of a central controller*: once a query is posed to the network, the network should function autonomously. This requires that local control mechanisms be encoded at each node be a simple processing element. This design involves introducing explicit "control nodes"— namely, binder nodes and relay nodes, that mediate the spread of activation and provide *foci* for controlling it.

Another key issue is that of convergence; it must be established that a network eventually converges to a solution state. It has been proved that the networks described below converge, provided that the knowledge encoded in these networks satisfies certain constraints. In essence, these constraints require that appropriate subnetworks do not have cycles. (Note that the network as a whole may have cycles in it.) These constraints are not very restrictive. For instance, the solution applies to conceptual organizations where the Type structure defined over Tokens (instances) consists of *several* distinct taxonomies. In such an organization, each Token may have several parents, and hence, multiple inheritance is possible. Some other constraints are as follows: (i) values of a property and the concepts that the property applies to should belong to distinct ontological Types, for instance, values of property has-taste (SWEET-SOUR, ...), and property has-color (RED, BLUE, ...) are not subconcepts or superconcepts of things that these properties apply to; (ii) values of a property should be distinct from values of other properties, thus RED and SWEET should not be subconcepts or superconcepts of one another. It is argued in [15] that these constraints do not impose any unnatural (counterintuitive) restrictions on the conceptual structures that can be dealt with in parallel by the connectionist encoding.

Before describing the encoding in detail, we consider as an example Figure 7.1 which shows a network that encodes:

"Dick is a Quaker and a Republican"

"Most Quakers have pacifist beliefs", and

"Most Republicans have nonpacifist beliefs"

It is assumed that one of the properties attached to persons is "has-belief", some of whose values are "pacifist" and "nonpacifist". The figure only shows about half the connections. In particular, the connections from property values to concepts have been suppressed for better readability. The likelihoods of being pacifists and nonpacifists for Quakers and Republicans are encoded as weights of appropriate links (cf. Section 7.3.1).

To illustrate how queries are posed, the question of Dick's beliefs on pacifism (or lack of them) will be posed to the network. This is done by activating the nodes DICK,

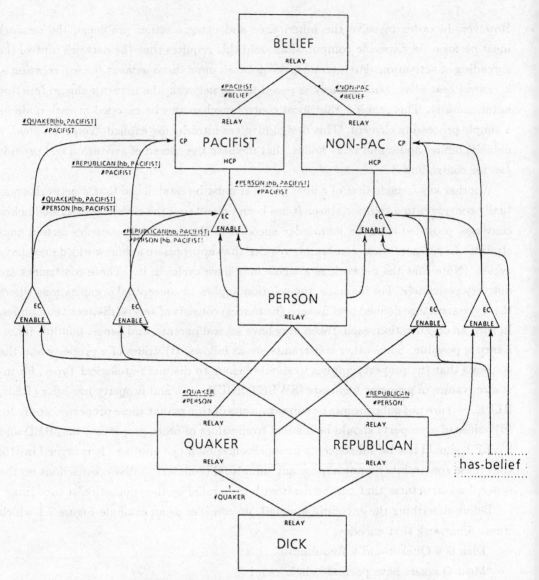

All inputs incident at site ENABLE of δ-node have a weight of 1.0.
Not all sites and weights have been shown.
hb = has-belief

Figure 7.1: An Example Network

has-belief, and BELIEF. The resulting potentials of the nodes PACIFIST and NON-PAC will determine whether Dick is more likely to be a pacifist or or a nonpacifist. It can be shown that the potential of the node PACIFIST equals:

(#QUAKER[has-be, PACIFIST] × #REPUBLICAN[has-bel, PACIFIST]) / (#BE-LIEF × #PERSON[has-be], PACIFIST])

while the potential of the node NON-PAC equals:

(#QUAKER[has-be, NON-PAC] × #REPUBLICAN[has-bel, NON-PAC]) / (#BE-LIEF × #PERSON[has-be], NON-PAC])

Ignoring the common factor (#BELIEF) in the denominator of these expressions, the potential of PACIFIST corresponds to the best estimate of the number of persons that are both quakers and republicans and believe in pacifism, while the potential of NON-PAC corresponds to the best estimate of the number of persons that are both quakers and republicans but subscribe to nonpacifism. Hence, a comparison of the two potentials will give the most likely answer to the question: Is Dick a pacifist or a nonpacifist.

The process of constructing a network given a high level specification of the knowledge to be encoded is fully automated and does not require any fine tuning or ad-hoc setting of weights in the network. Similarly, the high level specification is independent of any implementation level (connectionist) details.

7.3.1   Encoding the Conceptual Structure

The encoding employs five distinct unit types. These are the *concept* nodes (ξ-nodes), *property* nodes (ϕ-nodes), *binder* nodes, *relay* nodes and *enable* nodes. With reference to Figure 7.3, all solid boxes denote ξ-nodes, all triangular nodes denote binder nodes, and the single dashed box denotes a ϕ-node. Relay nodes are used to control directionality of spreading activation along the conceptual hierarchy, while enable nodes are used to specify the type of query (inheritance or categorization). Relay and enable nodes are not shown in Figure 7.1.

Each concept is represented by a ξ-node. These nodes have six sites: **QUERY, RELAY, CP, HCP, PV** and **INV**. With reference to the partial ordering $\ll$, if concept B is a parent of concept A then there is a ↑ (bottom up) link from A to B and a ↓ (top down) link from B to A. The weight on both these links equals #A / #B and the links are incident at the site **RELAY**. Figure 7.2 illustrates this situation. As the ↑ and ↓ links always occur in pairs, they will often be represented by a single undirected arc.

Each property is also encoded as a node. These nodes are called ϕ-nodes, and they have one input site: **QUERY**.

If $\delta(A, P)$ is known, then for every value V_i of P there exists a pair of binder nodes

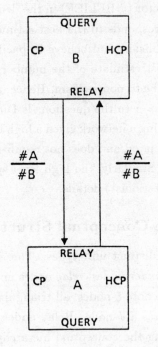

B is a parent of A

Figure 7.2: Parallel Encoding for Inheritance-I

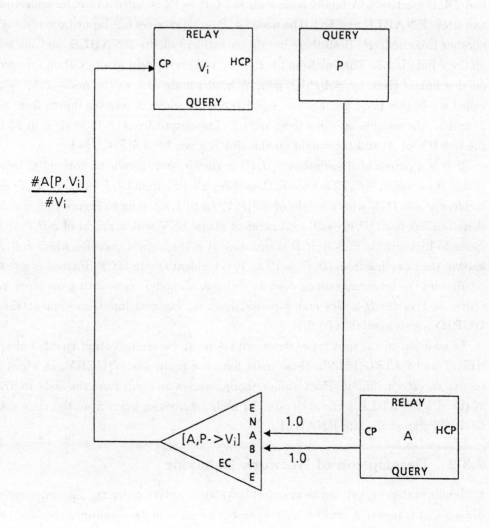

Figure 7.3: Parallel Encoding for Inheritance-II

$[A, P \rightarrow V_i]$ and $[P, V_i \rightarrow A]$ that are connected to A, P and V_i as shown in Figures 7.3 and 7.4, respectively. A binder node such as $[A, P \rightarrow V_i]$ is called a i-binder node and has two sites: **ENABLE** and **EC**. The node $[A, P \rightarrow V_i]$ receives one input from node A and another from node P. Both these inputs are incident at site **ENABLE**, and the weight on these links is 1.0. The link from $[A, P \rightarrow V_i]$ to V_i is incident at site **CP** and the weight on this link is given by $\#A[P, V_i]/\#V_i$. A binder node such as the node $[P, V_i \rightarrow A]$ is called a c-binder node and has one site **ENABLE** where it receives inputs from nodes P and V_i; the weights on these links are 1.0. The output from $[P, V_i \rightarrow A]$ is incident at the site **PV** of A, and the weight on this link is given by $\#A[P, V_i]/\#A$.

If B is a parent of A such that $\delta(B, P)$ is known, and there is no concept C between A and B for which $\delta(C, P)$ is known, then there is a link from $[A, P \rightarrow V_i]$ to $[B, P \rightarrow V_i]$, incident at site **INV** with a weight of $\#A[P, V_i]/\#B[A, V_i]$ (refer to Figure 7.5). Similarly, there is a link from $[P, V_i \rightarrow B]$ to A incident at site **INV** with a weight of $\#B[P, V_i]/\#B$ (refer to Figure 7.8). Finally, if B is such that it is the highest node for which $\delta(B, P)$ is known, then the link from $[B, P \rightarrow V_i]$ to V_i is incident at site **HCP**, instead of site **CP**.

Besides the interconnections described above, all nodes representing concepts, properties, and values (ξ-nodes and ϕ-nodes) have an external input incident at the site **QUERY**, with a weight of 1.0.

In addition to the unit types described above, there are two other enable units: INHERIT and CATEGORIZE. These units have one input site: **QUERY**, at which they receive an external input. Each i-binder node receives an input from the node INHERIT at the site **ENABLE** while each c-binder node receives an input from the node CATEGORIZE also at the site **ENABLE**.

7.3.2   Description of Network Behavior

Each unit in the network can be in one of two states: **active** or **inert**. The quiescent state of each unit is **inert**. A unit switches to an **active** state under conditions specified below, and in this state the unit transmits an output equal to its potential. The computational characteristics of various unit types are described below:

ξ-**nodes:**

>   **State:** A node is in an **active** state if it receives one or more inputs.

>   **Potential:** If there are no inputs at site **HCP** then

>>   potential = the product of inputs at sites **QUERY, RELAY, CP,** and **PV** divided by the product of inputs at site **INV**.

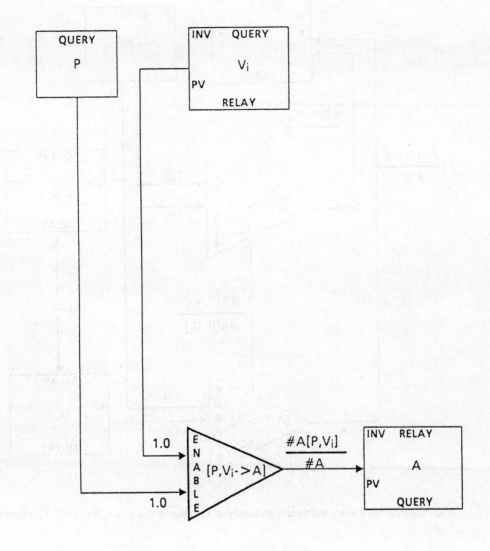

∂(A, P) is known

Figure 7.4: Parallel Encoding for Categorization-I

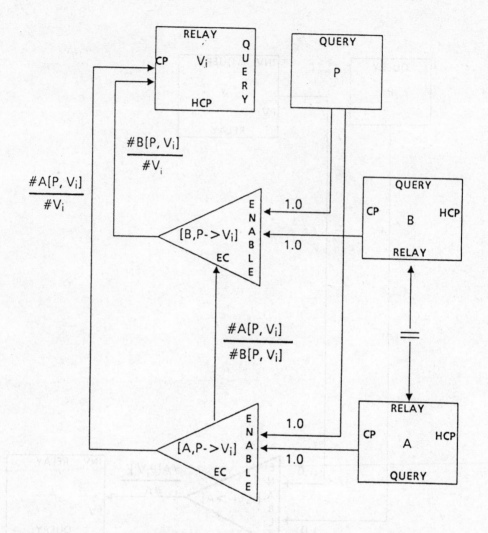

$\partial(A, P)$, $\partial(B, P)$ are known, and there is no concept C such that A $<<$ C $<<$ B and $\partial(C, P)$ is known.

Figure 7.5: Parallel Encoding for Inheritance-III

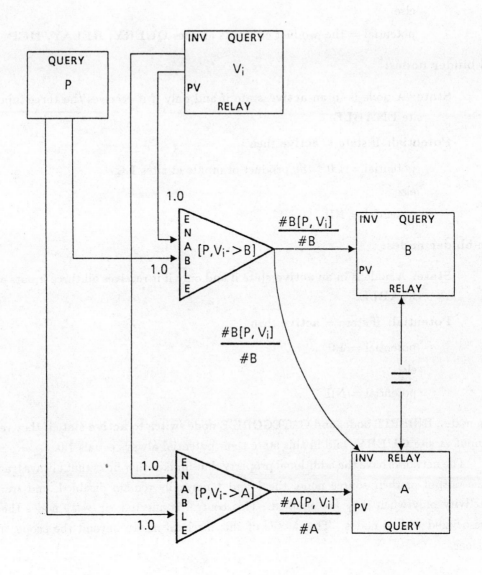

$\partial(A, P)$, $\partial(B, P)$ are known, and there is no concept C such that A $<<$ C $<<$ B and $\partial(C, P)$ is known.

Figure 7.6: Parallel Encoding for Categorization-II

193

else

potential = the product of inputs at sites **QUERY, RELAY, HCP**

i-binder nodes:

State: A node is in an **active** state if and only if it receives the three inputs at
site **ENABLE**.

Potential: If state = **active** then

potential = 1.0 * the product of inputs at sites **EC**

else

potential = NIL

c-binder nodes:

State: A node is in an **active** state if and only if it receives all three inputs at site
ENABLE.

Potential: If state = **active** then

potential = 1.0

else

potential = NIL

ϕ-nodes, INHERIT node, and CATEGORIZE node switch to **active** state if they receive
input at site **QUERY**, and in this state their potential always equals 1.0.

The networks have the additional property that unlike other links that always transmit
the output of their source node, the $\uparrow$ and $\downarrow$ normally remain disabled, and transmit
activity only when they are enabled. This control is affected via *relay* nodes that are
associated with ϕ-nodes. The details of this mechanism are beyond the scope of this
paper.

7.3.3 Posing Queries and Computing Solutions

In the context of the network encoding, inheritance and categorization are posed as
follows:

Inheritance

Given: A concept C and a property P, an explcit enumeration of possible answers, i.e.,
a set $V_{SET} = \{V_1, V_2, \ldots, V_n\}$, and a concept REF where REF is an ancestor of

194

every memebr of V_{SET}. (Typically, REF is a parent of V_i's. For example, if V_i's are RED, GREEN, BLUE, ..., then REF could be COLOR).

Find: $V* \in V_{SET}$ such that relative to the values specified in V_{SET}, $V*$ is the most likely value of property P for concept C.

The inheritance query is posed by setting the external inputs, i.e. the inputs to the site **QUERY**, of nodes C, P and INHERIT to 1.0. If one or more members of V_{SET} reach an **active** state within three time steps, the external input to REF is set to 1.0, and the $\downarrow$ links leaving REF are enabled. If none of the members of V_{SET} receive any activation, the external input to REF is set to 1.0, and the $\downarrow$ links leaving REF as well as the $\uparrow$ links leaving C are enabled. After $d + 3$ time steps—where d is the longest path in the ordering graph defined by $\mathcal{C}$ and $\ll$, the potentials of nodes will be such that for any two nodes V_i and $V_j \in V_{SET}$, the following holds:

$$(potential\ of\ V_i)/(potential\ of\ V_j) = \#C[P, V_i]/\#C[P, V_j]$$

It follows that the node $V* \in V_{SET}$ with the highest potential will correspond to the value that is the solution to the inheritance problem.

Categorization

Given: a set of concepts $C_{SET} = \{C_1, C_2, \ldots, C_n\}$ such that the C_i's are either all Tokens or all Types, a reference concept REF, such that REF is an ancestor of all concepts in C_{SET}, and a description consisting of a set of property value pairs, i.e., a set $DESCR = \{[P_1, V_1], [P_2, V_2], \ldots, [P_m, V_m]\}$

Find: $C* \in C_{SET}$ such that relative to the concepts specified in C_{SET}, $C*$ is the most likely concept described by DESCR.

The solution to the above problem may be computed as follows:

For each $[P_j, V_j] \in DESCR$, set the inputs to the site **QUERY** of nodes P_j and V_j to 1.0. At the same time, set the input to the site **QUERY** of CATEGORIZE and REF to 1.0, and enable the $\downarrow$ links emanating from REF. Wait $d + 3$ time steps, where d is the longest path in the ordering graph defined by $\mathcal{C}$ and $\ll$. At the end of this interval, the potential of the nodes will be such that for any two nodes C_i and $C_j \in C_{SET}$, the following holds:

$(potential\ of\ C_i)/(potential\ of\ C_j) =$

the best estimate of $\#C_i[P_1, V_1][P_2, V_2]\ldots[P_m, V_m]$ divided by the best estimate of $\#C_j[P_1, V_1][P_2, V_2]\ldots[P_m, V_m]$. These estimates are computed on the basis of the result derived in [15]. It follows that the node $C* \in C_{SET}$ with the highest potential corresponds to the solution of the categorization problem.

7.4 Some Examples

In order to explicate the behavior of networks and demonstrate the nature of inferences drawn by them, several examples that are often cited in the knowledge representation literature as being problematic have been simulated. The simulations demonstrate how the evidential approach deals with inheritance and categorization uniformly and solves some classic inheritance problems involving exceptions and conflicting information.

The simulation involves three stages. In the first stage the knowledge to be encoded in the network is stated by specifying i) the set of concepts, ii) the set of properties and their associated values, iii) a list specifying the partial ordering together with the ratios $\#A/\#B$ (for all pairs A and B such that B is a parent of A), and iv) specifying the partial mapping $\delta(C, P)$ in terms of $\#C[P, V]$'s. This information is translated by a compiler (SNAIL) into a set of commands to a general purpose network builder (SPIDER) to create the required ξ-nodes, Φ-nodes, binder-nodes, and relay nodes. Additional commands are also generated to connect these nodes in accordance with the interconnections described in Section 7.3.1. In the second stage, SPIDER constructs the appropriate network, which is then simulated using a connectionist network simulator (CISCON), in the third stage.

The representation language does not involve any network level detail. Furthermore, the construction of the network is fully automated, and does not require any *ad hoc* setting of weights.

The first example is an extension of the "quaker example" discussed in Section 7.3. It demonstrates how the network performs inheritance in the presence of conflicting information arising due to "multiple parents". Figure 7.7 depicts the information to be encoded (not the connectionist network). There are two properties has-bel (has-belief) with values PAC (pacifist) and NON-PAC (nonpacifist), and has-eth-org (ethnic-origin) with values AFRIC (african) and EURO (european). In broad terms, the information encoded is as follows:

Most persons are nonpacifists.
Most quakers are pacifists.
Most republications are nonpacifists.
Most persons are of european descent.

Most republicans are of european descent.

Most persons of african descent are democrats.

As our first example of inheritance, consider the query: "Is Dick a pacifist or a nonpacifist?"

The potentials of PAC and NON-PAC as a result of this query are: 0.00972 and 0.00644 respectively. If the potentials are normalized so that the highest potential equals 1.00, we have PAC = 1.00, NON-PAC = 0.66.

Thus, on the basis of the available information, Dick who is a republican and a quaker, is more likely to be a pacifist. The ratio of the likelihood of his being a pacifist to his being a nonpacifist is about 3.2.

Similar simulations for RICK, PAT, and SUSAN lead to the following results:

Rick who is a mormom republican is more likely to be a nonpacifist. The ratio of pacifist versus nonpacifist for Rick being 0.39 versus 1.00.

Pat who is mormon democrat is more likely to be a nonpacifist, but only marginally so, the ratio being 0.89 versus 1.00.

Finally, Susan who is a quaker democrat is likely to be a pacifist with a very high probability, the ratio being 1.00 versus 0.29.

As an example of categorization, consider the query: "Among Dick, Rick, Susan, and Pat, who is more likely to be a pacifist of african descent?"

The final potentials (shown here after normalization) are SUSAN 1.00, PAT 0.57, DICK 0.11, and RICK 0.05.

As would be expected, Susan who is a democrat and a quaker, best matches the description "person of african descent with pacifist beliefs". The least likely person turns out to be Rick. The letter even seems intuitively correct given that Rick is a republican and a mormon (Rick is neither a democrat who correlates with african origin nor is he a quaker who correlates with pacifism).

The query for finding out the most likely person who is nonpacifist and is of european descent leads to the following normalized potentials: RICK 1.00, DICK 0.50, PAT 0.59, and SUSAN 0.30.

In order to illustrate how exceptions are handled, the following information was encoded in a network (refer to Figure 7.8):

Most Molluscs are shell-bearers.

Cephalopods are Molluscs, but most Cephalopods are not shell-bearers.

Nautili are Cephalopods, and all Nautili are shell-bearers.

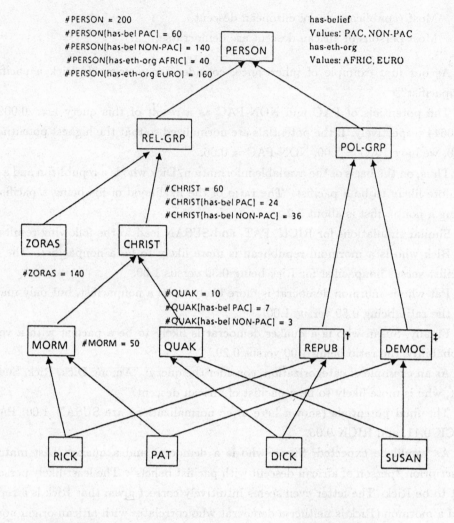

#PERSON = 200
#PERSON[has-bel PAC] = 60
#PERSON[has-bel NON-PAC] = 140
#PERSON[has-eth-org AFRIC] = 40
#PERSON[has-eth-org EURO] = 160

has-belief
Values: PAC, NON-PAC
has-eth-org
Values: AFRIC, EURO

#CHRIST = 60
#CHRIST[has-bel PAC] = 24
#CHRIST[has-bel NON-PAC] = 36

#ZORAS = 140

#QUAK = 10
#QUAK[has-bel PAC] = 7
#QUAK[has-bel NON-PAC] = 3

#MORM = 50

† #REPUB = 80
#REPUB[has-bel PAC] = 16
#REPUB[has-bel NON-PAC] = 64
#REPUB[has-eth-org AFRIC] = 5
#REPUB[has-eth-org EURO] = 75

‡ #DEMOC = 120
#DEMOC[has-bel PAC] = 44
#DEMOC[has-bel NON-PAC] = 76
#DEMOC[has-eth-org AFRIC] = 35
#DEMOC[has-eth-org EURO] = 85

Figure 7.7: The Quaker Example

198

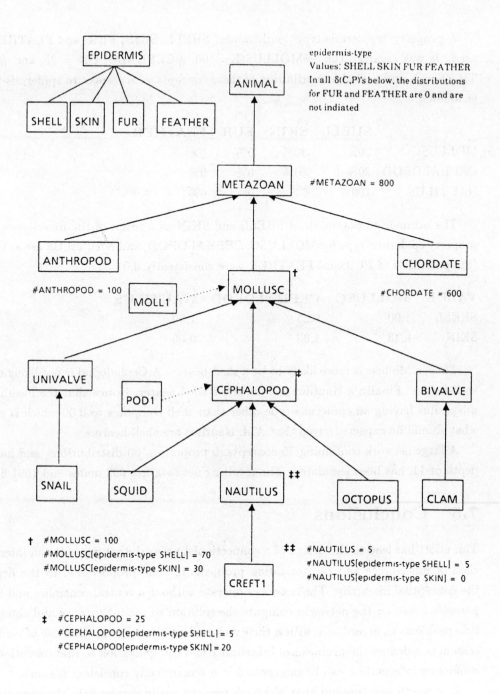

epidermis-type
Values: SHELL SKIN FUR FEATHER
In all δ(C,P)'s below, the distributions
for FUR and FEATHER are 0 and are
not indiated

#METAZOAN = 800

#ANTHROPOD = 100

#CHORDATE = 600

† #MOLLUSC = 100
#MOLLUSC[epidermis-type SHELL] = 70
#MOLLUSC[epidermis-type SKIN] = 30

‡‡ #NAUTILUS = 5
#NAUTILUS[epidermis-type SHELL] = 5
#NAUTILUS[epidermis-type SKIN] = 0

‡ #CEPHALOPOD = 25
#CEPHALOPOD[epidermis-type SHELL] = 5
#CEPHALOPOD[epidermis-type SKIN] = 20

Figure 7.8: The Mollusc Example

199

A property "epidermis-type" with values: SHELL, SKIN, FUR, and FEATHER was used. It was assumed that #MOLLUSC = 100, #CEPHALOPOD = 25, and #NAU-TILUS = 5, and that the distribution of these concepts with respect to epidermis-type is as follows:

	SHELL	SKIN	FUR	FEATHER
MOLLUSC	70%	30%	0%	0%
CEPHALOPOD	20%	80%	0%	0%
NAUTILUS	100%	0%	0%	0%

The normalized potentials of SHELL and SKIN as a result of the inheritance of the property epidermis-type for MOLLUSC, CEPHALOPOD, and NAUTILUS are as follows: (the potentials of FUR and FEATHER were consistently 0.0):

VALUE	MOLLUSC	CEPHALOPOD	NAUTILUS
SHELL	1.00	0.25	1.00
SKIN	0.43	1.00	0.00

Thus, a Mollusc is more likely to be a shell-bearer. A Cephalopod is not likely to be a shell-bearer. Finally, a Nautilus is *definitely* a shell-bearer. Notice that the likelihood of a Nautilus having an epidermis-type other than shell computes to 0.00 which is exactly what should be expected given that ALL Nautilus are shell-bearers.

A large network containing 75 concepts, 5 properties, 30 distributions, and having a depth of 11, has been simulated. The resulting network has 632 nodes and 1591 links.

7.5   Conclusions

This effort has lead to the design of a connectionist network that can solve an interesting class of inheritance and categorization problems in time proportional to the depth of the conceptual hierarchy. The networks operate without a central controller and have a *provable behavior*; the networks compute the solution to the inheritance and categorization problems in accordance with a theory of evidential reasoning. The use of evidential reasoning redefines the problems of inheritance and categorization so that exceptions and conflicting information can be interpreted in a semantically consistent manner.

It is worth pointing out that although one can easily disassociate the connectionist encoding from the evidential treatment, there are distinct advantages in examining this particular encoding. Besides offering a natural way of describing the evidential interactions between pieces of knowledge, the network encoding *suggests* how a physical system, consisting of simple processing elements, may extract from its environment the information required to solve inheritance and categorization problems. Such considerations may eventually lead to a connectionist theory of concept formation.

An examination of the weights on the links reveals that in most cases the weights simply encode the correlation between the activities of the nodes connected by a link. For such links, the weight on the link may be viewed as a measure indicating the ratio:

"how often when the destination node was active, was the source node also active".

The above is directly related to Hebb's interpretation of synaptic weighs in neural nets [9], and suggests the possibility of arriving at a theory of concept formation in massively parallel networks.

Another aspect of the work is that it clearly identifies the sort of information that can be used efficiently. As long as the knowledge about distributions of concepts with respect to property values is in the form of $\#C[P,V]$'s, there exists a way of using it effectively. It can be shown that a limited amount of knowledge outside this form may be incorporated with relative ease. However, the computations soon become too complex. This leads to the following conjecture: if information about correlations between property values of a concept is available, and if this information is significant and relevant, then new concepts are created so that this information may be used effectively. This offers a computational explanation for the creation of new concepts and suggests that the goal of a concept formation (learning) mechanism should be to create concepts so that all the important distributions may be expressed as $\#C[P,V]$'s of existing concepts. For a detailed discussion refer to [15].

Acknowledgements

This research was supported in part by the National Science Foundation under Grants MCS-8209971M IST-8208571, and DCR-8405720. I am grateful to Jerry Feldman for his guidance and support.

References

[1] John R. Anderson, *The Architecture of Cognition*, Harvard University Press, Cambridge, Massachusetts, 1983.

[2] R. J. Brachman, "I lied about the trees," *The AI Magazine*, vol. 6, no. 3, Fall 1985, pp. 80-93.

[3] D. W. Etherington and R. Reiter, "On Inheritance Hierarchies with Exceptions," *Proc. AAAI-83*, Washington D.C., 1983.

[4] A. M. Frish and J. F. Allen, "Knowledge Retrieval as Limited Inference." in D. W. Loveland (Ed.), *Lecture Notes in Computer Science: 6th Conference on Automated Deduction*, Springer-Verlag, New York, 1982.

[5] S. E. Fahlman, *NETL: A System for Representing and Using Real-World Knowledge*, The MIT Press, 1979.

[6] S. E. Fahlman, D. S. Touretzky, and Walter van Roggen, "Cancellation in a Parallel Semantic Network," *Proc. IJCAI-81*, Vancouver, B.C., 1981.

[7] S. E. Fahlman, "Three Flavors of Parallelism," *Proc. CS-CSI-82*, Canada, 1982.

[8] J. A. Feldman and D. H. Ballard, "Connectionist Models and Their Properties," *Cognitive Science*, 1982, vol. 6, pp. 205-254.

[9] D. O. Hebb, *The Organization of Behavior*, Wiley, New York, 1949.

[10] E. T. Jaynes, "Where do we stand on maximum entropy," *The Maximum Entropy Formalism*, R. D. Levine and M. Tribus (Eds.), MIT Press, Cambridge, MA, 1979.

[11] H. J. Levesque, "A Fundamental Tradeoff in Knowledge Representation and Reasoning," *Proc. CS-CSI-84*, London, Ontario, Canada, 1984.

[12] J. Pearl, "Bayesian Networks: A model of self-activated memory for evidential reasoning," *Proc. 7th. Cognitive Science Conference*, Irvine, CA, 1985.

[13] Ross M. Quillian, "Semantic Memory," in M. Minsky (Ed.), *Semantic Information Processing*, The MIT Press, 1968.

[14] L. Shastri and J. A. Feldman, "Evidential Reasoning in Semantic Networks: A Formal Theory," in *Proc. IJCAI-85*, Los Angeles, California, 1985.

[15] L. Shastri, "Evidential Reasoning in Semantic Networks: A Formal Theory and Its Parallel Implementation," Ph.D. Thesis, TR-166, University of Rochester, Rochester, NY, September 1985.

[16] D. Touretzky, *The Mathematics of Inheritance Systems*, Pitman Publishing Ltd., London, 1986.

Lokendra Shastri
Computer and Information Science Department
University of Pennsylvania
Philadelphia, PA 19104

Chapter 8

Semi-Applicative Programming: Examples of Context Free Recognizers

N. S. Sridharan

Abstract

Most current parallel programming languages are designed with a sequential programming language as the base language and have added constructs that allow parallel execution. We are experimenting with an applicative base language that has *implicit* parallelism everywhere, and then we introduce constructs that *inhibit* parallelism. The base language uses pure LISP as a foundation and blends in interesting features of Prolog and FP. Proper utilization of available machine resources is a crucial concern of programmers. We advocate several techniques of controlling the behavior of functional programs without changing their meaning or functionality: program annotation with constructs that have benign side-effects, program transformation and adaptive scheduling. This combination yields us a *semi-applicative* programming language and an interesting programming methodology.

In this paper we deal with context-free parsing as an illustration of semi-applicative programming. Starting with the specification of a context-free recognizer, we have been successful in deriving variants of the recognition algorithm of Cocke-Kasami-Younger. One version is the CKY algorithm in parallel. The second version includes a top-down predictor to limit the work done by the bottom-up recognizer. The third version uses a cost measure over derivations and produces minimal cost parses using a dynamic programming technique. In another line of development, we arrive at a parallel version of the Earley algorithm. All of these algorithms reveal more concurrency than was apparent at first glance.

8.1   Semi-Applicative Programming

Novel parallel machines are being designed and built. Amid the loud applause for the ingenuity of the ideas and implications of their success, we also hear the remark "But how are you going to program such a beast?", thereby implying that the software problem remains once the hardware is designed. Similarly, several attempts are being made at parallel programming language design; one hears the remark "What we really need are ways of thinking and problem solving that incorporate parallelism." This reaction stems from the view that a programming language is merely a notation and new developments in programming methodology are essential for the proper use of the next generation of computers.

We have embarked on a project to explore in tandem programming methodology and programming language design, allowing each to condition and influence the other. Thus, we start with a range of what we consider interesting problems, explore how we would like to express a range of solutions to these, paying attention to the methodology of algorithm development. In the course of doing this we evolve both our language design and our programming methodology. This is in contrast to the more usual approach of making the language reflect the architecture of a given machine and abstracting away selectively from it. Thus our language is rife with functional primitives rather than with machine-oriented primitives. Our aim is to make the tasks of programming and tuning for performance be cognitively simple and error-proof.

Most current parallel programming languages are designed with a sequential programming language as the base language and then constructs are added that allow parallel execution. It is therefore not surprising to see researchers attempting to analyze serial algorithms to discover (or uncover) hidden parallelism. Wisdom has it, and experience proves it, that there is only limited concurrency that can be exposed by examining extant algorithms. One needs to start afresh with the problem and develop parallel algorithms in order to witness greater parallelism.

We are experimenting with a programming language that has an *implicitly* parallel applicative language as the base language, and then we introduce constructs that *inhibit* parallelism. The base language uses pure LISP [14] as a foundation and blends in interesting features of Prolog [26] and FP [22]. *Proper utilization of available machine resources*

204

is a crucial concern of programmers. This is an outstanding problem for both functional programming and logic programming. We introduce several techniques for controlling the behavior of functional programs without changing their meaning or functionality: (i) program annotation with constructs that have benign side-effects; (ii) program transformation; and (iii) adaptive scheduling. This combination yields us a *semi-applicative* programming language and an interesting programming methodology.

Section 8.2 describes the base language SALT and the annotation language PEPPER. The final section 8.3 summarizes our efforts in the area of context-free parsing and discusses the derivation of several recognition algorithms, all related to the recognition method of Cocke-Kasami-Younger [30] and that of Earley [28]. *All of these algorithms reveal more concurrency than was apparent at first glance.*

8.1.1 Motivation

We aim at developing a programming language and programming methodology that allow effective use of medium-scale, medium-grain parallelism; support correct program development; and allow effective, error-free control of program behavior through a variety of means.

As an initial set of problems to study in the project, we are investigating search algorithms (alpha-beta, branch-and-bound, backtrack), constraint propagation and marker propagation algorithms, constraint satisfaction and relaxation algorithms, and natural language parsing algorithms. This paper, however, is concerned solely with recognition algorithms for context-free grammars[1] in Chomsky-Normal-Form.

As an illustration of our programming methodology, we start with the specification of a recognizer for context-free grammars in Chomsky-Normal-Form (CNF) and derive by transformations a variety of different purely applicative parallel recognition algorithms. We then introduce program annotations and display semi-applicative algorithms. In one algorithm we indicate how adaptive scheduling can control the behavior exhibited by the algorithm. Thus we hope the reader observes the use of transformations, annotations and scheduling as means of controlling program behavior.

---

[1]This work was done with the needs of doing Natural Language parsing in mind. For the sake of rigor in algorithm derivation and to illustrate the *semi-applicative programming* methodology in a simple setting we have used the Chomsky-Normal-Form grammars. Andy Haas at BBN has developed and tested a parallel natural language parser using Unification which can be seen as an extension of Algorithm XI.

8.1.2   Experience

The current Butterfly Lisp project [7] is building a parallel Common Lisp for the Butterfly multiprocessor [29] starting with Scheme [24], in cooperation with MIT researchers. This effort represents an important near-term approach to providing parallel computation for AI research. The Butterfly Lisp project at BBN has provided us with an opportunity to gather experience in developing parallel algorithms, coding programs and testing them. We have programmed several algorithms in applicative subsets of both MultiLisp [15] and Scheme [24] and have tested them on the Butterfly multiprocessor and also with simulated parallelism on the VAX-11/780. The range of algorithms with which we have experimented includes:

- Combinatorial search algorithms

  - N-Queens problem; incorporating a variety of modes of parallel computation, e.g., parallel vs. serial evaluation of partial board placements and parallel vs. serial forking of search tree nodes.

  - Dynamic programming for an optimization problem; employing different ways of setting up initial tasks, different dependencies among tasks, different ways of utilizing data flow and caching operations.

- Recursive nonsearch algorithms

  - Parallelism as well as pipelining for elementary recursive functions such as Fibonacci, Ackerman and QuickSort.

This experience has highlighted several key issues that need to be addressed in the development of parallel algorithms. *Generating an appropriate level of concurrency in an algorithm is difficult.* It is possible to generate too little concurrency or too much concurrency in a recursive symbolic program, especially in search algorithms. Moreover, current languages make the programmer indicate explicitly when to spawn new tasks and when to carry out computations serially. The decision to spawn tasks should depend to a great extent on availability of processors, memory availability and other run-time characteristics. Such decisions cannot be made at program composition time, or even at compile time. *Scheduling decisions clearly exceed the capability of the programmer.*

The program development and testing environment should enhance the ability of the programmer to achieve the goal of proper utilization of machine resources. The environment that we envision lays less emphasis on program debugging and encourages correct program development and effective control of program behavior through a variety

206

of methods all of which preserve correctness of the program. Furthermore, it gives the programmer *a simpler computational model* than models prevalent today.

8.2   Detailed Discussion of our Approach

Most efforts at developing a parallel language start with a sequential language (Lisp, Pascal, Algol) and introduce concepts relevant to parallel execution (Fork/Join, Task, Task groups, Critical region, Monitors, Semaphores, Interprocess communication, event-wait/signal, etc.). [See [27] for a survey.] These allow the programmer to state and control parallelism explicitly. In general, they create a very complex model of computation, making the task of the programmer difficult and error prone. Approaches similar to that of Concurrent Prolog [25] present a simpler computational model, but restrict the expressive power of the language by constraining the computational model too much. They are also limited to using only first-order predicates and have unclear techniques for using evaluated functions and for introducing user-defined control structures. Approaches like that of Qlisp [17], MultiLisp [15] and parallel CommonLisp [7] allow sequential code interspersed with parallel constructs. The extent of *residual sequential code* in the program limits the speed-up possible in programs [10], following Amdahl's law[2].

Our approach is based on the use of a side-effect free programming language, which has *implicit* concurrency everywhere. Our annotation language allows the programmer to control concurrency explicitly by adding annotations to the program text. The annotations form a small set, each member of which guarantees that the meaning (clarity and semantics) are unchanged by its introduction. Each annotation can affect the *behavior* of the program, i.e., alter its runtime, space utilization, reuse of computed results, total work, extent of concurrency and extent of intertask communication. *We believe that this approach combining implicit parallelism and explicit control will reduce the risk of introducing bugs in the process of tuning programs for performance*, as well as providing an antidote to Amdahl's law.

---

[2]If S is the fraction of residual sequential code, and N the number of processors available, the maximum speed-up is $N*(1+(N-1)*S)^{-1}$ which is bounded by $1/S$ when N is very large. For example with $N = 1000$ and $S = 0.1, 0.01$ and 0.001 we get the maximum speed-up to be 9.91, 90.99 and 500.25 respectively. Squeezing out the residual sequentiality might, unfortunately, end up being the analog of trying to get the last bug out, i.e., an unending enterprise with each succeeding step consuming disproportionately larger effort on the part of the programmer. Clearly, an alternative approach is called for!

207

8.2.1 Computation Model

The computational model that we advocate to the programmer might be termed <u>unlimited</u> <u>virtual parallelism</u>. The program runs as a large set of concurrent tasks, which may be run in any arbitrary order, subject to certain constraints. Central to the system is a scheduler that maps the unlimited virtual parallelism to the limited physical resources of the machine. Virtual parallelism is analogous to virtual memory systems that allow the programmer a vast amount of virtual space and are aided by a heuristic memory management subsystem. The ordering of task execution is constrained by the three graphs mentioned below. The programmer views control of the computation in terms of three graphs over the set of tasks: the <u>Spawning graph</u> that specifies which tasks are spawned by which other task; the <u>Communication graph</u> that specifies which tasks produce values consumed by which tasks; and the <u>Precedence graph</u> that specifies which tasks can be begun after the termination of which other tasks. A set of program annotations allows flexible control over the behavior of the program, and is conceived in terms of changes to these three graphs.

There are three styles of computation [20] that are quite well understood presently. <u>Control Flow</u>, is viewed in terms of a control token that passes around the program. Only the segment of the program with the control token is in control and thus can be active. For parallel execution, control tokens are copied. When a task terminates, its copy of the control token disappears. In <u>Data flow</u>, all segments of the program are active, pending only the availability of the data they are to consume. In <u>Demand Flow</u>, each (statement or expression) propagates, in parallel, a demand token that activates other statements that can compute the demanded results. In our language we unify these styles of computation allowing the programmer to not only choose a preferred style but also to mix them as s/he sees fit.

8.2.2 Base Language: SALT

SALT is an applicative functional language free of side-effect causing constructions. An initial design document [8] for SALT is available, and it demonstrates the ease with which an interesting range of algorithms may be expressed in SALT. SALT is based on the pure Lambda calculus and adopts a functional syntax. It includes the usual facilities for function definition (using conditionals and recursion), naming, both object and function variables, anonymous functions in the form of Lambda abstractions, and higher-order functionals (like Maps, which provide data-parallelism). Like Scheme, it adopts lexical scoping. From FP, it gets a suitable set of program-forming operators, like the functional Insert, the composition operator (pipelining parallelism) and structured function lists (work-splitting parallelism). We have argued elsewhere [8] that functional programs with parallelism of the kind mentioned above make it simple to arrive at only limited forms of parallelism. Namely, parallel activity where the spawning graph, communication graph and precedence graph all mirror the structure of the function call graph are easy to describe. One has to resort to very complex constructions to describe arbitrary communication between subtasks or arbitrary precedence structures. We have found that introducing the idea of logical variables into the language and allowing these to be shared is a very useful extension which allows us to achieve arbitrary types of parallelism more easily. To this end, from PROLOG we borrow and adapt three important ideas:

1. Functional call semantics is not in terms of <u>binding</u> the values of actual arguments to formal parameters, but in terms of <u>unification</u> of the *values of* actual arguments with formal parameters, thus affording *two way communication* between the caller and the called function;

2. Constructors are used to define compound parameters; they facilitate assembling and disassembling structured arguments and results;

3. Multiple definitions for a single function are allowed; they differ in their parameter structures, allowing the compiler greater freedom in testing/selecting function bodies to execute.

Shared logical variables among tasks are permitted in SALT; their values can be refined in stages by successive unifications. The communication graph is determined by the shared variables as well as by a function-call-return graph. Thus shared logical variables facilitate multi-way communication among tasks without limiting communication to parent/child pairs. These ideas are elaborated in a companion technical report [8]. We do NOT use the backtracking control structure of Prolog. Failure of unification is considered an error condition[3].

For the limited purposes of this paper, that is, to illustrate aspects of semi-applicative programming and to show the derivation of several context-free recognition algorithms, we shall not need many of the properties of SALT. The algorithms in Section 8.3 are exhibited in an informal notation, using fairly standard programming concepts. Some of the notations will be explained as they are introduced. The reader should simply bear in mind that in all cases where "For" loops, "Subset" and "Union" expressions are introduced, they are not serial; all these constructions are parallel forms. A serial "For"

---

[3]We have not explored the issue of error-handling yet.

will be introduced when needed and written "(For <var> in <list> serially ...)".
In the examples in this paper we do not use the unification semantics in any essential
way; but we find the use of structured parameter lists quite convenient for disassembling
and assembling structures, and we find they enhance readability and conciseness.

8.2.3 Resource Control in Applicative Programs

Because we use an applicative language which specifies computations without side-effects,
we gain the advantages of simple clear semantics and generous opportunities for concurrency. Of course, what we lose is direct control over the computational behavior of the
program. *Proper use of parallel resources is a crucial concern of programmers.* This is an
outstanding problem for functional programs and logic programs. We introduce several
methods of altering the *behavior* of programs without altering their correctness or the
functionality of what they compute. Among the techniques we are exploring are:

Program Annotations

Program annotations [18] add resource control features to the source-level algorithm. We
have developed an initial design for an annotation language called PEPPER. Annotations
in PEPPER include precedence control, function call/result caching [19,21], and lazy (or
demand-driven) evaluation. Our initial design document describes PEPPER annotations
and gives several examples of their use. A key feature of PEPPER annotations is that
their introduction will not alter the functional value of a program, and will affect only
its run-time behavior.

Program Transformation

Program transformation [11,34,12] of the source-level algorithms written in SALT is essential. There are two quite different reasons for considering program transformation.
Firstly, given that PEPPER annotations are to be added to the text of a program, it is
evident that *textually different but functionally equivalent programs offer different opportunities for adding annotations*; and hence provide different opportunities for achieving
different behaviors. A programmer can make full use of annotations only in conjunction
with the ability to do program transformations. [An example of this is presented in [8];
see Synchronizing Multiple Streams]. Secondly, *different programs yield different data-
dependency orderings*, thus allowing differing amounts of concurrency. Thus, program
transformation is a technique for controlling the available concurrency in a program.

210

Adaptive Scheduling

Adaptive scheduling can yield improved behavior with repeated runs of the same program. Adaptation requires monitoring and measuring run-time characteristics of SALT+PEPPER programs in order to make scheduling decisions dynamically. In working with virtual parallelism, the program only expresses "available" concurrency without mandating what in fact will execute concurrently with what. The scheduler converts the available concurrency into physical concurrency, making its choices for running tasks by considering available resources, resource requirements and other attributes of tasks. The scheduler typically is a heuristic procedure and does not yield optimal behavior in all cases. Thus, another avenue open to the programmer is to tune some parameters of the scheduler to alter the behavior of the program. We feel this method of control is "indirect", and while that is necessary, it is not likely to be sufficient. It may be useful to construct an adaptive scheduler that tunes its parameters based on empirical measurements.

Consider an example, where a search algorithm has been programmed in terms of a set of tasks that spawn other tasks to span the search space, and a corresponding set of testing and evaluation tasks that examine proposed solutions, but spawn no new tasks. Empirically it may be feasible to identify which tasks terminate without spawning new tasks, and which tasks spawn new tasks but wait for them to finish before they themselves can finish up. A reasonable scheduling strategy is to always give precedence to the evaluation tasks.

8.2.4   Annotation Language: PEPPER

All programs written in SALT permit concurrent evaluation of all subexpressions, generating the possibility of fine-grained parallelism. Pepper annotations are introduced around expressions; they restrict the computational behavior of the expression, but compute correctly the value of the expression. The name PEPPER is chosen to symbolize the idea that functionally correct SALT programs will be sprinkled with PEPPER annotations to derive the desired computational behavior.

The main types of annotations include precedence control and caching. Precedence control annotations introduce conditions that must be met for the triggering of a task, and thus alter the precedence graph for the program. There are three types of precedence control constructs. Control sequencing restricts one task to wait for the completion of one or more other tasks. Data-flow sequencing makes function applications wait for the delivery of (all or some of) their arguments. Suspension annotation causes the evaluation of forms to be postponed till their values are demanded; such suspensions provide one form of lazy evaluation of arguments.

Caching permits expression values to be cached and reused to avoid redundant computation. In several examples we will show an exponential time algorithm reducing to polynomial time, resulting from the proper use of caching. A number of recursive functions can be transformed from the usual top-down version to perform bottom-up computations [19] by means of table build-up. In some cases, the top-down version may cycle endlessly whereas the bottom-up version may efficiently compute and terminate.

We describe here only three caching annotations that will be used in this paper. The remaining annotations are described and illustrated in the companion technical report. Function calls, not merely results, need to be cached in a concurrent environment, to catch all redundant calls. Otherwise, after the first invocation, if a second call is made before the first one completes, a duplicate invocation will be made. *(Cache (f . args))* replaces a normal function call with a cached call. If there is a cache entry and if it contains a result, the result is retrieved and returned as the value of this form. If there is no cache entry, a cache entry is created with no result and the function f is invoked with its arguments. When the function completes the result is posted in the cache entry and the result is also returned to the invoking form. The invoking form waits for the delivery of results. If there is a cache entry which contains no result, this is an indication that computation is in progress concurrently. In this case, the invoking form waits for delivery without calling the function f. This discipline for caching is appropriate for concurrent computation and differs subtly from the standard memo-izing operation which caches only results after they are computed, not the function calls. Another caching construct we use is of the form *(Lookup (f . args))*. This is a straight table lookup without any need to perform checks or waits. The table build-up is either done ahead of time, or there is enough serialization in the algorithm to guarantee that the entry will be ready when the lookup is done. Another caching annotation is mentioned here but is developed more fully in the final example, the Earley parser. *(CacheDefault (f . args) DefaultValue)* is a loop-breaking construct. It behaves like Cache, except that under specified conditions (when a loop is detected), it will not wait for delivery of values, but will return the DefaultValue.

212

8.3 Research Results: Derivation of Recognition Algorithms for CNF Grammars

In this section we demonstrate the derivation of several recognition algorithms for context-free grammars. The initial specification is a standard mathematical definition for what a recognition algorithm should do. In several steps of transformation, we derive a variety of parallel recognizers (see Figure 8.1). In the literature there are two well-known parsing algorithms. Cocke, Younger and Kasami, independently reported on the development of a bottom-up parser, called CKY, that works on a restricted form of grammars called the Chomsky-Normal-Form. Earley published an algorithm that works with unrestricted context-free grammars and parses an input string in a top-down fashion using left-context to limit search. These algorithms are described in this section. Most of us, including the author, have admired the cleverness of such algorithms. One of the things we do in this section is to demonstrate that these algorithms have close affinities to each other and that they can be arrived at systematically. Similar derivations of various SORT algorithms have been previously presented in the literature. All of these have been successful at deriving only a few of the already known sort algorithms; none of these derive any new SORT algorithm. Can one readily adopt these transformational techniques to derive new algorithms? Our attempt hopefully convinces the reader that new parallel algorithms can be derived systematically.

The reader will notice that the transformations used in the derivation are only informally stated, even though the program being derived is precisely written down at each step. Furthermore, the transformations are fairly large, and would take substantial analysis and rewriting capabilities to support in a semi-automated system. We do not hint or suggest at this time that such a derivation sequence can be automated. By using these examples and other examples to be developed in the future, we hope to arrive at a conception of what a programming environment would be that could assist us in the development of semi-applicative parallel algorithms.

8.3.1 Preliminaries: Grammar, Normal Form and Derivation

We start with the standard definition of Chomsky-Normal-Form grammar, Derivation and Recognizer [13].

A *Chomsky Normal Form grammar*, abbreviated CNF, henceforth simply grammar, is identified in terms of

T: a set of terminal symbols,

213

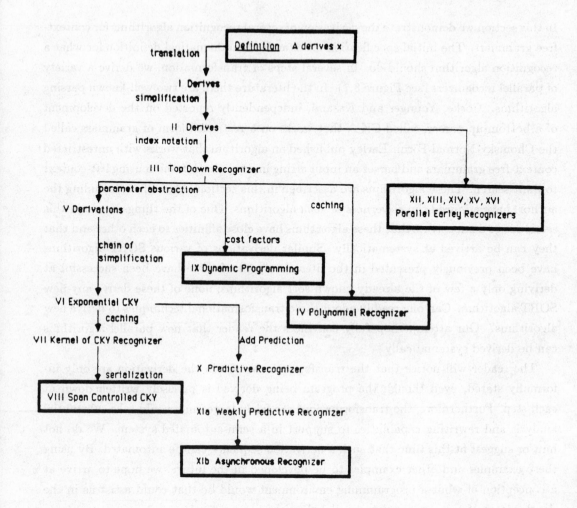

Figure 8.1: Chart showing transformational derivation of different algorithms for context-free recognition using Chomsky Normal Form grammars

N: a set of <u>nonterminal</u> symbols,

V: the set of terminal and nonterminal symbols, T+N,

S: a <u>distinguished</u> nonterminal symbol,

P: a set of <u>productions</u>, comprised of two sets UP and BP.

Each production in UP, a <u>unit</u> production, is of the form

$$A \rightarrow x \text{ where } x \in T, \ A \in N$$

Each production in BP, a <u>binary</u> production, is of the form

$$A \rightarrow BC \text{ where } A, B, C \in N$$

We use the notation

V*: for the set of strings over V,

T*: for the set of strings over T.

A unit production has a single terminal symbol for its right-side and a binary production has a pair of nonterminals. A <u>one step derivation</u> involves starting with a string uAv where $u, v \in V*$ and $A \in N$, and using a unit production $A \rightarrow x$, deriving the string uxv (notation: $uAv \Rightarrow uxv$); or using a binary production $A \rightarrow BC$, deriving the string uBCv (notation: $uAv \Rightarrow uBCv$). A <u>Derivation</u> is a chain of one step derivations (notation: starting-string $\Rightarrow^*$ ending-string). The <u>language</u> generated by the grammar is the set of terminal strings that can be derived starting with the distinguished symbol S.

Any Context-free (CF) grammar can be converted to an equivalent grammar in CNF. From a practical point, however, when a CF grammar is converted to CNF, its size (number of productions) may grow exponentially. Thus, practical algorithms need to work directly with CF grammars. The development of our algorithms is simplified by the use of CNF. However, there is nothing essential in the character of CNF that we depend upon; and thus we believe all the algorithms may be generalized suitably to work with unrestricted context-free grammars. Furthermore, we shall be writing algorithms for "recognizers" which only decide whether the input string is in the language generated by the grammar; they do not return a parse structure. The published algorithms also adopt this route; and they all use a fairly simple technique for reconstructing the parse tree. We shall not elaborate on this any further and confine our attention to the recognition problem, that is, the computation of the predicate "A derives x".

A <u>recognizer</u> is a function (Recognize x) that takes the input string x and returns a boolean value which is the correct answer to the question "Does S derive x?" We start with a more general function, "Does A derive x?" where S, the distinguished start symbol, has been replaced with an arbitrary nonterminal, A. Thus, (Recognize x) = (Derives 'S x).

8.3.2 Derivation of a Parallel Top-Down Recognizer

For any nonterminal $A \in N$ and terminal string $x \in T*$ we define

A <u>derives</u> x

if either there is a $p \in UP$ such that $p = A \rightarrow x$

or there is a $p \in BP$ such that $p = A \rightarrow BC$,

and a partition x=yz, y and z nonempty

and B derives y and C derives z.

Since we have started with a recursive definition of the predicate Derives, it is quite straightforward to turn the specification directly into an effective algorithm (it will always terminate and provide the correct result).

<u>Algorithm I</u> *Top-down recognizer*

```
    Invoke (Derives 'S input)
    Define (Derives A x) =
            (or (member [A --> x] (UP A))
                (For Some [A --> BC] in (BP A)
                    (For Some [y,z] in (split x)
                        (and (Derives B y) (Derives C z)) )))


    with (split x) =
            case |x| < 2   {}
            case |x| = 2   {[(first x), (second x)]}
            case |x| > 2
                (Union {[(first x), (rest x)]}
                    (For [y,z] in (split (rest x))
                        collect [(first x)||y , z]))
```

Notation: We are using square brackets to denote data structuring; curly brackets for sets; || for string concatenation; first and rest functions over strings; $|x|$ denotes length of string x; (UP) for the set of unit productions; (UP A) for the set of unit productions with A as their left-hand-side; (BP) without any arguments to denote all binary productions; (BP A) for all binary productions with A as their left-hand-side. We may introduce a structure, e.g. [y,z] above, where one would normally use a variable. Unification of such a structure produces structure disassembly. Notice that the "For" over the set is a parallel construct. We prefer to use the "For" construct over the "Map" construct for expository convenience.

The above algorithm is guaranteed to terminate since each recursive call to Derives involves strings that are strictly shorter. Thus the depth of recursion is no greater than the length of the input string.

The nondeterminism involved in the use of "Or" is eliminated by introducing a deterministic case analysis. Notice also that the nesting of the two search constructs "For Some" is unnecessary since neither generator depends upon the other. Thus we rewrite Algorithm I to expose greater concurrency. The construct "(For Some [<var1>,<var2>] in <set1> cross <set2> ...)" is used to write unnested loops with var1 taking values in set1 and var2 taking values in set2.

Algorithm II *Exponential top-down recognizer*

```
Define (Derives A x) =
        case |x| = 1 (member [A --> x] (UP A))
        case |x| > 1 (For Some [[A --> BC],[y,z]]
                             in (BP A) cross (split x)
                        (and (Derives B y)
                             (Derives C z) ))
```

Though algorithm II is effective, it can take time exponential in the length of the input. In fact, the following recurrence characterizes the time to recognize a string of length n with p productions:

$$T(n) = constant + p * \sum_{k=1}^{n-1}[T(k) + T(n-k)]$$

Recognizing that much of the effort in this algorithm is wasted in redundant calls to Derives with the same arguments, we introduce caching. Prior to doing that, let us transform the string descriptions (and the Split function) to take advantage of array capabilities of current machines. All of the string arguments given to Derives are substrings of the original input string. Thus substrings can be referenced by a pair of indices marking the beginning and end. Indices range over $(0,n)$ with each index value referring to the space after the ith character and before the $(i+1)^{st}$ character. Thus the entire input string is the pair [0,n]. The unit string involving the ith character is [i,i+1]. Thus all nonempty substrings are referred to by [i,j] with $i < j$.

Algorithm III *Top-down recognizer using indices*

```
Invoke (Derives 'S [0,n])
Define (Derives A [i,j]) =
        case j-i = 1 (member [A --> (input i j)] (UP A))
        case j-i > 1 (For Some [[A --> BC],[[i,k],[k,j]]]
                                in (BP A) cross (split [i,j])
                        (and (Derives B [i,k])
                                (Derives C [k,j])))
with (Split [i,j]) =
        (For k in (i+1 to j-1) collect [[i,k],[k,j]])
```

Notice that "Split" has been converted into an iterative algorithm and string operations have been replaced with index manipulation. The form *(input i j)* refers to the substring of the input string. We now introduce caching of results for "Derives". Since the algorithm has concurrency, caching should be done both for *invocations* of Derives as well as for its *results*. By caching invocations and not merely results, in a concurrent setting we avoid duplicate invocations, as explained before.

Algorithm IV *Polynomial top-down recognizer with caching*

```
Define (Derives A [i,j]) =
        case j-i = 1 (Member [A --> (input i j)] (UP A))
        case j-i > 1 (For Some [[A --> BC],[[i,k][k,j]]]
                                in (BP A) cross (split [i,j])
                        (and (Cache (Derives B [i,k]))
                                (Cache (Derives C [k,j])))))
```

This brings to conclusion one line of development, and gives us a top-down recognizer that uses caching to avoid redundant computations. The entire algorithm is written with no explicit serialization. Various calls to Derives are invoked without explicit synchronization, and if they are looked up before the results are ready, the invoking form will wait for delivery of results. The wait lists so constructed form a data-flow dependency graph and thus provide an implicit form of data-flow scheduling. The algorithm, with data-flow scheduling, exposes more parallelism than the span-controlled recognizer which is usually presented as the CKY algorithm. This span-controlled algorithm is derived further below (see Algorithm VIII). The maximum time taken by Algorithm IV is related the maximum number of distinct calls to Derives. This number can be seen to be the product of the number of distinct first argument values, which is p, the number of productions, and the number of distinct second argument values, which is the number of substrings of the input string of length n, that is, $n * (n + 1)/2$. Each call takes $p * n$ time at most. Thus the worst-case <u>serial</u> timing of the algorithm has been reduced from exponential to $p^2 n^3$. Given unbounded computational resources, this algorithm will run in time linear in n, which is the depth of the data-flow graph. This provides an upper and lower bound for the actual performance for this algorithm on a multiprocessor.

8.3.3   Derivation of a Parallel Bottom-Up Recognizer

We continue a different line of development ending with a parallel version of the Cocke-Kasami-Younger algorithm, which computes bottom-up the set of nonterminals that can derive each substring of its input. It is usually presented in the following sequential form:

```
Algorithm Serial CKY
Declare Procedure CKY(R);
Declare R[0:n,0:n] set of nonterminals; Recognition matrix

    Handle unit characters
for j = 0 to n-1 do
    R[j,j+1] = Set of nonterminals A ∋ A → (input j j+1) ∈ UP;
    Handle binary composition
for l = 2 to n do       l is the span length of substring
    for i = 0 to n-l do  i is the start position of substring
       begin
          j = i+l; j is the end position of substring
          R[i,j] := empty-set;
          for k = i+1 to j-1 do consider all splits into nonempty parts
             for B in R[i,k] do consider all interpretations of [i,k]
                for C in R[k,j] do consider all interpretations of [k,j]
                   begin combine BC to get interpretation A for [i,j]
                      R[i,j] := R[i,j] ∪ Set of nonterminals A ∋ A → BC in BP;
                   end;
       end;
end Procedure CKY;


Declare R[0:n,0:n] initial empty-set;
```

```
Call CKY(R);
Test 'S ∈ R[0,n];
```

When such an algorithm is presented, it needs to be explained and also proved. The
first loop handles unit characters of the input string and applies all unit productions;
entering their interpretations in the corresponding cells R[j,j+1]. The outermost loop
(variable l) in the second section of the program is systematically increasing the span
of the substring considered from 2 to n. The loop variable i ranges over all possible
starting positions for a substring of length l; j is then set to the end position of such
a substring. To arrive at interpretations for the substring [i,j] all possible splits are
considered (loop variable k) and the results combined. The algorithm works bottom-up
arriving at interpretations for substrings of greater length. Since the interpretations for a
substring of length l depends only on substrings that are shorter, we know that the needed
values will already be computed. Despite proper explanation of how it works and the
proof, one is left wondering what the inventive step in the creation of the algorithm was
and how the details were structured to get it correct. For example, are the loop indices
bounded correctly? Is the initialization needed? What steps can be done in parallel?

We fall back to Algorithm III which is still in functional form and propose a series of
transformation steps that culminates in a parallel version of the CKY algorithm.

Algorithm III *Top-down recognizer using indices*

```
Invoke (Derives 'S [0,n])
Define (Derives A [i,j]) =
       case j-i = 1 (member [A --> (input i j)] (UP A))
       case j-i > 1 (For Some [[A --> BC],[[i,k],[k,j]]]
                              in (BP A) cross (split [i,j])
                       (and (Derives B [i,k])
                            (Derives C [k,j])))
with (Split [i,j]) =
       (For k in (i+1 to j-1) collect [[i,k],[k,j]])
```

The first thing to change is that instead of querying (Derives A [i,j]) we would be
querying A ∈ (Derivations [i,j]). In the body of definition of Derives, we have occurrences
of the variable A, whose domain is the set N of nonterminals. Since the variable A is
not going to be a parameter to "Derivations", we surround the expressions for both cases
in Algorithm III by "(subset N (Lambda (A) ...))" where N is the set of nonterminals.
"Subset" takes a set and a predicate, returning the subset with elements for which the

predicate is true.

(Derives A [i,j]) = A ∈ (Derivations [i,j])

<u>Algorithm V</u>

```
Define (Derivations [i,j]) =
      case j-i = 1
          (subset N (Lambda (A) (member [A --> (input i j)] (UP A))))
      case j-i > 1
          (subset N
               (Lambda (A)
                    (For Some [[A --> BC],[[i,k],[k,j]]]
                              in (BP A) cross (split [i,j])
                         (and (member B (Derivations [i,k]))
                              (member C (Derivations [k,j]))))) ))
```

The main point of the algorithm is generating productions paired with splits of the string and testing to see if the production is applicable. We shall focus our attention on the expression involving the second case, j-i¿1, since there is nothing interesting in the transformation for the first case, j-i=1; it merely follows a similar but simpler line of development. We separate the loop over the cross-product set, and create two for-loops, in preparation to eliminate the loop over the productions.

```
(subset N
     (Lambda (A)
          (For Some [A --> BC] in (BP A)
               (For Some [[i,k],[k,j]] in (split [i,j])
                    (and (member B (Derivations [i,k]))
                         (member C (Derivations [k,j]))) ))))
```

Now we use our knowledge of the fact that the outermost loop "subset" ranges over all nonterminals A in N, and that the inner loop ranges over all productions with a given nonterminal A. We combine and collapse the two loops. To do this we eliminate the search through N via the expression (subset N ...), and replace (BP A) with (BP). We get:

```
(Union for [[i,k],[k,j]] in (split [i,j])
     (For [A --> BC] in (BP)
          collect A if (and (member B (Derivations [i,k]))
                            (member C (Derivations [k,j]))) ))
```

221

The above algorithm uses the two membership predicates as tests and the set of productions as the generator. Now we interchange the testing and generating loops in order to isolate a fragment of the algorithm that is dependent only on the grammar and not on the input string. We carry this out by turning the two membership tests into generators and burying the loop over productions in a test.

```
(Union for [[i,k],[k,j]] in (split [i,j])
    (Union for [B,C]
              in (Derivations [i,k]) cross (Derivations [k,j])
        (For [A --> BC] in (BP) collect A))
```

The set of nonterminals A which derive BC written as "(For [A → BC] in (BP) collect A)" is now abstracted as a function "(Binaries B C)".

```
(Union for [[i,k],[k,j]] in (split [i,j])
    (Union for [B,C]
              in (Derivations [i,k]) cross (Derivations [k,j])
        (Binaries B C)))
```

Let us unfold the definition of (split [i,j]) and simplify it to get:

```
(Union for k in (i+1 to j-1)
    (Union for [B,C]
              in (Derivations [i,k]) cross (Derivations [k,j])
        (Binaries B C)))
```

This yields the last step in the development of the CKY algorithm. We have focused our attention on the case where $j - i > 1$. A similar development is done for the case where $j - i = 1$; producing a function "(Units x)" which returns a set of nonterminals which have the production $[A \to x]$ in UP.

Algorithm VI

```
Invoke (member 'S (Derivations [0,n]))
Define (Derivations [i,j]) =
       case j-i = 1 (Units (input i j))
       case j-i > 1 (Union for k in (i+1 to j-1)
                        (Union for [B,C]
                                  in (Derivations [i,k]) cross (Derivations [k,j])
                            (Binaries B C)))
  with (Binaries B C) = (For [A --> BC] in (BP) collect A)
       (Units x) = (For [A --> x] in (UP) collect A)
```

222

We still have to introduce caching. Since the functions "Binaries" and "Units" depend only on the grammar and not on the input string itself, they can be precomputed and set up in a table. They can be queried via a table lookup using (Lookup ...); no testing or waiting is required. We cache "Derivations" to provide us the recognition table. This yields a pure bottom-up recognizer, presented below, with its name changed from Derivations to CKY.

Algorithm VII *The kernel of Cocke-Kasami-Younger algorithm*

```
Invoke (member 'S (CKY [0,n]))
Define (CKY [i,j]) =
       case j-i = 1 (Lookup (Units (input i j)))
       case j-i > 1
          (Union for k in (i+1 to j-1)
             (Union for [B,C]
                    in (Cache (CKY [i,k])) cross (Cache (CKY [k,j]))
                (Lookup (Binaries B C)) ))
```

When we invoke the recognition test (member 'S (CKY [0,n])) it will successfully invoke, in several stages of parallel demand flow, all the entries of the recognition table. Whenever a table entry is not ready the computation will wait for the delivery of values. Thus, the scheduling of parallel activation of all table entries is limited by the demand flow and data flow ordering alone. We get greater concurrency than when the standard control flow version of the CKY algorithm is used.

The standard serial control flow version of the serial CKY algorithm involves no explicit calls for synchronization; the parallel version shown above requires the overhead of checking and waiting. We can proceed to eliminate this by serializing the computation to guarantee that values will be available when looked up. Since each table entry for string [i,j] depends only upon values of table entries of its substrings, ordering the computation by increasing string length is possible. We trade off some of the concurrency available in the data flow version, and we introduce control flow. We eliminate the demand flow and data flow dependency and replace the calls to Cache by calls to Lookup.

Algorithm VIII *Span Control Ordering*

```
Invoke (CKY-span-control n) and (member 'S (CKY [0,n]))
Define (CKY-span-control n) =
       (For span in (1 to n) SERIALLY
            (For i in (0 to n - span)
               do  (CKY [i,i+span])))
```

223

```
with (CKY [i,j]) =
    case j-i = 1 (Lookup (Units (input i j)))
    case j-i > 1
        (Union for k in (i+1 to j-1)
            (Union for [B,C]
                 in (Lookup (CKY [i,k])) cross (Lookup (CKY [k,j]))
                (Lookup (Binaries B C)) ))
```

We have added a serial control flow that systematically increases the span of substrings considered, starting at 1 and ending with n. One can imagine this (as is usually explained in text books) as starting with the main diagonal of the CKY recognition table and filling the next upper diagonal after the one below it is filled in. Notice that the inside For loop in CKY-span-control is a parallel loop. All the n-span+1 calls CKY spawned for each value of span are allowed to execute in parallel and must terminate before the next value of span is executed. This control flow ordering guarantees that whenever CKY does an invocation of the CKY calls contained in its body, the corresponding results it is going to lookup will have been computed and made available. Therefore, we have replaced "Cache" calls with "Lookup" calls which do not require any synchronization waits. All "table build-up" methods cited in [19] rely upon such an ordering to avoid synchronization waits.

The innermost "Union" can be computed in time independent of the string length; the effort it requires is a function of the number of nonterminals, p. The components of the outer "Union" can all be invoked in parallel, as can all the invocations of i for any given span. The time taken by this algorithm, given no bounds on the number of processors, only grows linearly with n corresponding to the serial ordering of the control flow.

8.3.4 Derivation of a Dynamic Programming Technique

By introducing a fixed cost factor with each production in the grammar, and defining the cost of a derivation to be the sum (or maximum) of the productions used in it, we now turn the recognition problem into an optimization problem. In this subsection we display a dynamic programming algorithm that finds the least cost for a derivation (omitting the detailed development of this algorithm). Clearly, if there is any derivation of the input string from S, there must be a least cost one. We merely avoid seeking all possible recognitions.

When a unit production is used, the algorithm should return the cost associated with that production. When a binary production is used, the algorithm should compute the

224

cost of the derivation by adding in the two minimum costs of the sub-derivations to the cost of the binary production. We presume modified functions BP and UP which return a set of pairs, each pair containing a production and also its cost. We also rename Derives to MinCost, to reflect its new meaning.

Algorithm IX *Dynamic Programming for minimum cost parse*

```
Invoke (MinCost 'S input)
Define (MinCost A x) =    ; returns a cost
       case |x| = 1
           (Cache (UnitCost x))
       case |x| > 1
           (For [[[A --> BC],ABCCost],[y,z]]
                   in (BP A) cross (split [i,j])
               min (+ ABCCost (Cache (MinCost B y)) (Cache (MinCost C z))))
   with (UnitCost x) =
       if (member [[A --> x],AxCost]] (UP A))
       then AxCost else +Infinity
```

To retrieve the cost of a production, we are altering the test for membership to include a cost variable. When the test for membership is invoked, the cost variable is uninstantiated and has no value; a successful result not only tests to see if the production is there, but also unifies the cost variable with the stored cost of the production. Thereby, the cost is retrieved. Here is one case where we have stepped outside of the pure functional programming style and have used the capability of SALT to do unifications. Without such a facility this algorithm can still be expressed in a pure applicative style, but it would not be as perspicuous, nor will the relationship between algorithms II and IX stand out clearly. Note that in converting Derives which returns a boolean value, to MinCost which returns a cost, we also introduced the mapping that a false value maps to the cost of $+\infty$. This algorithm runs in time proportional to n^3 in the serial worst case. It runs in time proportional to $n * (\log pn)$ given a sufficient number of processors; n is the depth of the data-flow and spawning graphs, whereas calculating the minimum of pn items could take $(\log pn)$ time.

8.3.5   Derivation of a Predictive Recognizer

The CKY span-control algorithm computes strictly bottom up and enters many values in the recognition table that are eventually useless since they cannot lead to the recognition of S in cell [0,n]. More formally, the requirement on CKY[i,j] is that

$A \in CKY[i,j] \Longleftrightarrow A$ derives (input i j).

There are many ways of introducing some kind of top down prediction. One way is to allow the bottom up method to enter in any cell [i,j] only those nonterminals that "follow" a legitimate parse of (input 0 i). That is, we restrict the entries to obey a second condition:

$A \in CKY\text{-restrict}[i,j] \Longleftrightarrow A$ derives (input i j)

$$\text{and } S \text{ derives } xAy \ni x \text{ is (input 0 i)}.$$

Define A follows x, for any $A \in N, x \in T^*$

$$\Longleftrightarrow S \Rightarrow^* xAy \text{ for some } y \in V^*$$

Using the index notation, we write:

Define A follows i, for any $A \in N, 0 \le i \le n$,

$$\Longleftrightarrow S \Rightarrow^* [0,i]Ay \text{ for some } y \in V^*$$

We would like to turn this definition into a recursive function Follows, which will be used as a filter in a simple fashion. Follows will be used to form an intersection with the already computed cell entries before posting them in the cell.

Algorithm *Schematic version of predictive algorithm*

```
Invoke (member 'S (CKY [0,n]))
Define (CKY [i,j]) =
      case j-i = 1
         (Intersect (Follows i) (Lookup (Units (input i j))))
      case j-i > 1
         (Intersect (Follows i)
            (Union for k in (i+1 to j-1)
               (Union for [B,C]
                     in (Cache (CKY [i,k])) cross (Cache (CKY [k,j]))
               (Lookup (Binaries B C)) )))
```

In the case $j - i > 1$, we can use the distributivity of the Union and Intersect functions to move the Intersect through the two loops, and get:

Algorithm *Schematic version of predictive algorithm*

```
Invoke (member 'S (CKY [0,n]))
Define (CKY [i,j]) =
      case j-i = 1
```

```
            (Intersect (Follows i) (Lookup (Units (input i j))))
    case j-i > 1
            (Union for k in (i+1 to j-1)
                (Union for [B,C]
                        in (Cache (CKY [i,k])) cross (Cache (CKY [k,j]))
                    (Intersect (Follows i) (Lookup (Binaries B C))) ))
```

Now let us focus on converting the definition of the predicate "A follows x" into a recursive function definition. We introduce case analysis into two parts and treat each part separately. The string x is either the empty string or a nonempty string.

When x is the empty string, we need to use as a filter all the leftmost symbols appearing in any sentential form. Let us denote by the form "(left* {'S})", a precomputed set containing all nonterminals A such that $S \Rightarrow^* Az$ for some z in V*. This can be defined in terms of an elementary function

```
(left SetB) = (Union for B in SetB (For [B → AC] in (BP B) collect A)).
```
We will suppress the details of how "left*" is defined in terms of the function "left".

When x is a nonempty terminal string, instead of arbitrary derivations, we can consider only leftmost derivations since in $S \Rightarrow^* xAy$, x is a string of terminals. In a leftmost derivation, A is introduced either by a production of the form $B \rightarrow AC$ or $B \rightarrow CA$. In the first case, using $B \rightarrow AC$, means $S \Rightarrow^* xBz \Rightarrow xACz$, and $y = Cz$. In the second case, using $B \rightarrow CA$, means $S \Rightarrow^* uBy \Rightarrow uCAy$. Eventually C must derive string v such that $x = uv$. That is, $S \Rightarrow^* uBy \Rightarrow uCAy \Rightarrow^* uvAy = xAy$. Thus, we write,

$S \Rightarrow^* xAy$ for nonempty terminal string $x \Longleftrightarrow$
either $S \Rightarrow^* xBz \Rightarrow xACz$ using $B \rightarrow AC \in BP$,
or $S \Rightarrow^* uBy \Rightarrow uCAy \Rightarrow^* uvAy = xAy$ using $B \rightarrow CA \in BP$.

From this we define the predicate <u>follows</u>:

A <u>follows</u> x for nonempty string x $\Longleftrightarrow$
either x=uv, B follows u, and C derives v and $B \rightarrow CA \in BP$,
or B follows x and $B \rightarrow AC \in BP$.

Converting this to a function (Follows x) that returns a set of nonterminals, we get:

```
(Follows x) =
case |x| = 0   (left* {'S})
case |x| > 0
        (Union (Union for [u,v] in (split x)
```

227

```
(Union for B in (Follows u)
            (For [B --> CA] in (BP B)
                collect A if (Derives C v))))
        (Union for B in (Follows x)
            (For [B --> AC] in (BP B) collect A)))
```

Notice that this is not an effective definition, since there is an occurrence of (Follows x) in the definition for (Follows x). However, the function has the following recursive structure: $(F\ x) = (\bigcup(G\ x)(H(F\ x)))$. The fixed point for such a recursive structure can be written as

$$(F\ x) = (\bigcup_{i=0}^{\infty}(H^i(G\ x)))) = (H^*(G\ x)).$$

In other words,

```
(Follows x) =
case |x| = 0  (left* {'S})
case |x| > 0  (H* (G x))
where (G x) = (Union for [u,v] in (split x)
                (Union for B in (Follows u)
                    (For [B --> CA] in (BP B)
                        collect A if (Derives C v) )))
  and (H SetB) = (Union for B in SetB
                    (For [B --> AC] in (BP B) collect A))
```

Both the domain and range of H are finite and hence H^* represents a finitely terminating computation, in view of the fact that H^* will reach its limiting value in a finite number of steps. Typically, in serial computation, a function like $(H^*(G\ x))$ would get expressed as

```
Begin Answer := (G x)
      (Repeat until no new element is produced
      Answer := Answer Union (H Answer))
End
```

The definition of H is in fact the function "(left SetB)" introduced in the last page. Thus, H^* is the same as the function left* that we introduced to handle the case j=0.

```
Define (Follows x) =
        case j = 0 (left* {'S})
```

228

```
case j > 0 (left* (Union for [u,v] in (split x)
                   (Union for B in (Follows u)
                    (For [B --> CA] in (BP B)
                     collect A if (Derives C v)) )))
```

We now repeat the process we followed earlier in introducing the index notation and simplifying by unfolding the definition of split. This gives us the following definition for Follows.

```
Define (Follows j) =
      case j = 0 (left* {'S})
      case j > 0 (left* (Union for i in (1 to j-1)
                         (Union for B in (Follows i)
                          (Union for [B --> CA] in (BP B)
                           collect A if (Derives C [i,j]) ))))
```

Once again, we repeat what by now may be a familiar maneuver, turning the test predicate (Derives C [i,j]) into the loop generator, and using the production as a membership test, in order to isolate a fragment of the algorithm that depends only on the grammar and not on the input string.

```
Define (Follows j) =
      case j = 0 (left* {'S})
      case j > 0 (left* (Union for i in (1 to j-1)
                         (Union for [B,C]
                          in (Follows i) cross (CKY [i,j])
                          (For [B --> CA] in (BP B)
                           collect A))))
```

Now, notice that the expression in the (For ...) is a function of B and C and depends only on the grammar and not on the input string. This can be precomputed, and we denote this by a function (LeadsTo B C). Calling (LeadsTo B C) is done via (Lookup (LeadsTo B C)). We do not carry out this step right now, preparing for further simplifications.

Incorporating this definition into CKY, renaming CKY to CKY-restrict, and introducing the intersection operation as the filter, we obtain the algorithm below.

Algorithm X *A Predictive Recognizer*

```
Define (CKY-restrict [i,j]) =
```

```
        case j-i = 1
          (Intersect (Units (input i j)) (Follows i))
        case j-i > 1
          (Union for k in (i+1 to j-1)
             (Union for [B,C]
                    in (CKY-restrict [i,k]) cross (CKY-restrict [k,j])
                 (Intersect (Binaries B C) (Follows i)) )).
with (Follows j) =
        case j = 0
            (left* {'S})
        case j > 0
            (left* (Union for i in (1 to j-1)
                        (Union for [B,C] in (Follows i) cross (CKY [i,j])
                         (For [B --> CA] in (BP B)
                          collect A))))
```

The use of (Follows i) allows the left-context of a substring [i,j] to restrict the entries that can be posted in a given cell [i,j]. This form of left-context influence is known experimentally to be very useful in parsing natural language texts. The algorithm of Ruzzo presented in [1] also uses left-context to restrict the CKY parser, but generalized to the case of context-free grammars.

Weakening the Predictor

The computation of (Follows j) is quite complex and introduces complex forms of data-flow dependencies. More specifically, notice that (i) (Follows j) requires access to all of the results of (Follows i) for $i < j$, and (ii) (CKY-restrict [i,j] requires access to all of the results of (Follows i). These dependencies effectively serialize the computation and make it move along the index i. How can we get back the concurrency that we have just lost?

One characteristic of using predictive filters is that we can *weaken* the predictor to gain computational and conceptual simplicity, at the cost of making the main algorithm produce some unneeded extra results in the cells. A weak predictor is one that computes a superset of what is computed by the strong predictor; and thus does not filter as strongly as is possible. The weakest predictor is one that admits any nonterminal in any cell; using this is equivalent to the pure bottom-up algorithm. We started with this version and added a strong predictor that lost a great deal of concurrency. Weakening the predictor in this fashion still computes correctly the value for the invocation (member

'S (CKY-restrict [0,n])); it might just store some additional values in various cells of the CKY matrix. We now show an intermediate form of weak predictor, which we will call (Restrictor j).

To arrive at the weakened predictor, called Restrictor, we modify the definition of (Follows i) and replace the occurrence of (Follows i) by the set of nonterminals of the grammar, N.

```
Define (Restrictor j) =
      case j = 0
           (left* {'S})
      case j > 0
           (left* (Union for i in (1 to j-1)
                      (Union for [B,C] in N cross (CKY-restrict [i,j])
                         (For [B --> CA] in (BP B)
                            collect A))))
```

Then we simplify by replacing (BP B) by (BP) and eliminating the loop over N, we get:

```
Define (Restrictor j) =
      case j = 0
           (left* {'S})
      case j > 0
           (left* (Union for i in (1 to j-1)
                      (Union for C in (CKY-restrict [i,j])
                         (For [B --> CA] in (BP)
                            collect A))))
```

Once again, the innermost loop is dependent only on the grammar, not on the input string being parsed, and can be abstracted into a function (Followers C) which can be set up for table look-up.

Algorithm *A Weakened Predictor*

```
Define (Restrictor j) =
      case j = 0 (left* {'S})
      case j > 0 (left* (Union for i in (1 to j-1)
                            (Union for C in (CKY-restrict [i,j])
                               (Lookup (Followers C))
with (Followers C) =
      (For [B --> CA] in (BP) collect A)
```

231

Both occurrences of the call to (Follows i) in Algorithm X are replaced by (Restrictor i) to arrive at Algorithm XI.

Algorithm XI *A Weakly Predictive Recognizer*

```
Define (CKY-restrict [i,j]) =
      case j-i = 1
        (Intersect (Lookup (Units (input i j)))
                   (Cache (Restrictor i)))
      case j-i > 1
        (Union for k in (i+1 to j-1)
           (Union for [B,C] in (Cache (CKY-restrict [i,k]))
                            cross (Cache (CKY-restrict [k,j]))
              (Intersect (Lookup (Binaries B C))
                         (Cache (Restrictor i))) ))
with (Restrictor j) =
      case j = 0 (left* {'S})
      case j > 0 (left* (Union for i in (1 to j-1)
                           (Union for C in (Cache (CKY-restrict [i,j]))
                             (Lookup (Followers C)))))
with (Followers C) =
     (For [B --> CA] in (BP) collect A)
```

The above weakening was done by decoupling the call to (Follows i) within (Follows j). We can also pursue an alternate weakening of the predictor, decoupling the call to (CKY-restrict [i,j] within (Follows j). This would yield a restrictor function that is recursive and depends only on the grammar, hence could be precomputed. Only actual experiments can tell us which of these predictors are practically useful. The second form of Restrictor has the following simplified definition. Within CKY-restrict, the call to Restrictor2 will appear as (Lookup (Restrictor2 i)).

```
Define (Restrictor2 j) =
      case j = 0 (left* 'S)
      case j > 0 (left* (Union for i in (1 to j-1)
                             (Union for B in (Restrictor2 i)
                               (Lookup (Followers2 B)))
with (Followers2 B) =
     (For [B --> CA] in (BP B) collect A)
```

Relaxed Synchronization of Predictor and Recognizer

The data-flow dependencies between Follows/Restrictor and CKY-restrict do not permit the extent of parallelism we witnessed in the CKY-span-control. The synchronization requirement for CKY-restrict moves along successive diagonals of the recognition matrix, whereas that for Follows/Restrictor moves along its columns. The combination of these two destroy a substantial extent of the parallelism available. We can, however, *relax the strict synchronization* to produce an asynchronous parallel algorithm that is nondeterministic. We may allow lax synchronization in the access to CKY-restrict in calculation of Follows/Restrictor and in the access to Follows/Restrictor in the calculation of CKY-restrict. The effect of such a relaxed synchronization is acceptable; *the algorithm is still functionally accurate* [23]. That means that Follows/Restrictor may have not produced its final value and CKY-restrict wants to access it (and vice versa).

We introduce a new form for cache, *(Cache-Initial (f . args) initial-value)*. If the cache cell for (f . args) indicates that it is being computed or has not yet been invoked, the initial-value is used by this call. Otherwise, the stored cache value is used. This caching construct is *nondeterministic* because the value it produces depends on the physical concurrency and scheduling characteristics of the implementation. We replace the cached call to Restrictor from CKY-restrict by a Cache-Initial call; and also the cached call to CKY-restrict from Restrictor by a Cache-Initial call. The cache we use for access to Follows/Restrictor supplies all of the set N if Follows/Restrictor has not produced its final value. Similarly the cache for CKY-restrict will supply all of N to Follows/Restrictor if its final value is not yet available.

Algorithm XI Modified *A Weakly Predictive Asynchronous Recognizer*

```
Define (CKY-restrict [i,j]) =
      case j-i = 1
        (Intersect (Lookup (Units (input i j)))
                  (Cache-Initial (Restrictor i) N))
      case j-i > 1
        (Union for k in (i+1 to j-1)
          (Union for [B,C] in (Cache (CKY-restrict [i,k]))
                        cross (Cache (CKY-restrict [k,j]))
            (Intersect (Lookup (Binaries B C))
                        (Cache-Initial (Restrictor i) N)) ))
with (Restrictor j) =
      case j = 0
```

```
            (left* {'S})
      case j > 0
            (left* (Union for i in (1 to j-1)
                        (Union for C
                              in (Cache-Initial (CKY-restrict [i,j]) N)
                        (Lookup (Followers C)))))
with (Followers C) =
      (For [B --> CA] in (BP) collect A)
```

A variation on the above can be obtained by using the form (Cache-Initial (Restrictor i) (Lookup (Restrictor2 i))) instead of (Cache-Initial (Restrictor i) N). Since Restrictor2 is precomputed it may supply a somewhat filtered set in comparison to using all of N.

Adaptive Scheduling of Tasks

We can also assign priorities to tasks generated by Follows/Restrictor and CKY-restrict, that depend both upon the task type and the parameter values for the invocation. We can control the relative rates of progress for the bottom-up calculation and for the imposing of restrictions. One could experiment with the possibility that this type of priority assignment might be done automatically and adaptively. If the computation of CKY-restrict moves faster than that of Follows/Restrictor, it will have to deal with larger sets and may slow down, allowing Follows/Restrictor to catch up. On the other hand, if Follows/Restrictor moves faster it will slow down waiting for delivery of values from CKY-restrict. Thus, there may be an interesting form of negative feedback governing the functioning of these two functions.

8.3.6   Derivation of a Version of Earley's Algorithm

The algorithm published by Earley [28] is most interesting for its unique character. It works on unrestricted context-free grammars and runs in serial time proportional to n^3 on inputs of length n. What makes it interesting is that when the grammar used is regular, it works in linear time. Earley comments on the fact that this happens automatically and that the user need not identify the grammar to be regular. In fact, the class of grammars for which it runs in linear time is wider than this. Also, in the general case, the algorithm does NOT require any additional conditions such as the absence of nonproducing symbols or empty-productions, as many other algorithms do.

We now outline the serial Earley recognition algorithm, restricted for CNF grammars. Restricting it to CNF grammars gives us continuity to our development and also allows us to conveniently put our algorithm in correspondence with Earley's. We do not foresee any difficulty in giving the same treatment for the more general case of context-free grammars.

Algorithm Serial Earley

This algorithm is modified from Earley's paper to be limited to CNF grammars and uses no lookahead. The productions in the original grammar are numbered in some arbitrary order from 1 to $|UP| + |BP|$. A dummy production numbered 0 is added to get the process started. This dummy production has as its right-hand-side the only symbol 'S. Its left-hand-side is an unused new nonterminal symbol and has no significance.

```
Define (Earley G Input) =
```

The algorithm computes successively a sequence of $n+1$ state-sets, numbered from 0 to n. Each state-set indicates results of parsing the input string up to position i. Each element of a state-set is a 3-tuple $[p, f, j]$,

$[p = $ number identifying the Production,

$f = $ number of symbols of the RHS recognized so far,

$j = $ starting position of the input string].

*A tuple is said to be **final** if all the RHS symbols have been recognized; otherwise, it is **nonfinal**. Thus in the case of CNF grammars, a tuple $[p, f, j]$ is final for a unit production p if f=1; and is final for a binary production p if f=2. Initially, the state-sets are empty sets.*

```
Body Let Sⱼ be empty for 0 ≤ i ≤ n+1
     Add [0,0,0] to S₀.
```

Here the first element of the tuple is production 0, the dummy production. The second element is 0 indicating that no symbol has been recognized so far. The third element is also 0 indicating that the input string is to be scanned from position 0. Since the dummy production has S for its only right hand side, this initialization sets up the state-set to seek to recognize S.

```
     For i from 0 step 1 until n do
     Process the elements of state Sᵢ by performing
          one of the following operations on each tuple [p,f,j].
```

If the next symbol of the production to recognize is a terminal and it matches the input string, advance the pointer into the production.

```
     (1) Scanner: If the tuple is nonfinal and the next symbol
     of p is a terminal (i.e., f=0 and p is in UP), and if the i + 1ᵗʰ
     input character matches the j + 1ᵗʰ symbol of p, then add to Sᵢ₊₁
     the tuple [p,f,j+1].
```

235

If the next symbol is a nonterminal, for each production alternative q for it, enter a new tuple pointing to 0, and scan the input from the same place.

> (2) <u>Predictor:</u> If the tuple is nonfinal and the next symbol
> A of p is a nonterminal (i.e., f=0 or 1 and p is in BP), then
> for each q = [A → BC] or q = [A → x] add to S_i the tuple
> [q,0,i].

If the pointer is at the end of a production, take each tuple that predicted this and advance its pointer.

> (3) <u>Completer:</u> If the tuple is final (i.e., f=1 and p in UP
> or f=2 and p in BP) then for each [q,1,g] in S_j in
> which the next symbol of q (i.e., the $l + 1^{th}$ symbol) is equal to
> the left side of p, add to S_i the tuple [q,l+1,g].

If S_{i+1} is empty, return Rejection.
If i=n and [0,2,0] is in S_{n+1}, then return Acceptance.

The algorithm as presented needs detailed explanation and proof, which is lacking in Earley's paper, but we are told they are available in his thesis. What is the key idea? We attempt to distill this in our own development of Earley's algorithm, one that runs in parallel.

We fall back to Algorithm II and pursue a different line of development that leads us towards Earley's algorithm adapted for CNF grammars.

Algorithm II

```
Define (Derives A x) =
      case |x| = 1 (member [A --> x] (UP A))
      case |x| > 1 (For Some [[A --> BC],[y,z]] in (BP A) cross (split x)
                             (and (Derives B y) (Derives C z) ))
```

We attempt to eliminate the need for (split x) and the corresponding loop over [y,z]. We convert the above definition so that, given A and x, it attempts to derive from A some prefix substring of x, and to return the split in the string corresponding to the prefix. Let us call the new function Absorb. Absorb accepts a nonterminal A and a substring x of the input string, and returns a set of pairs [y,z] meaning that nonterminal A can derive string y, and string z is left over, so that x = yz. To do recognition, we invoke Absorb, passing it 'S and the Input string; we test whether the entire input string is recognized to be 'S by asking whether the pair [Input,""] is a member of the result. Thus if the entire input string is derivable from 'S and the empty string "" is left over, we have a string that is accepted by the grammar.

[y,z] ∈ (Absorb A x) <u>implies</u> (Derives A y)

[x, ""] ∈ (Absorb A x) <u>implies</u> (Derives A x)

In doing the conversion, we have to observe that since Absorb seeks to derive only a prefix of the input string, the case analysis of Algorithm II needs to be modified so that the first case is for $|x| \geq 1$ and the second case is for $|x| > 1$. However, to keep the cases disjoint, we adopt the case break down of $|x| = 1$ and $|x| > 1$, and repeat the treatment of unit productions, UP, so that it appears in both the first and second case.

Algorithm XII

```
Invoke (member [Input,""] (Absorb 'S Input))
Define (Absorb A x) =    ; returns a set of string pairs
      case |x| = 1
        (if (member [A --> (first x)] (UP A))
        then {[(first x),(rest x)]} else {})
      case |x| > 1
        (Union (if (member [A --> (first x)] (UP A))
                then {[(first x) , (rest x)]} else {})
            (Union for [A --> BC] in (BP A)
              (Union for [y,z] in (Absorb B x)
                (For [p,q] in (Absorb C z)
                    collect [y||p , q])))))
```

Once again, we introduce index pairs to denote substrings. Thus, the form of the invocation will be (member [[0,n],[n,n]] (Absorb 'S [0,n])). This yields the following.

Algorithm XIII

```
Invoke (member [[0,n],[n,n]] (Absorb 'S [0,n]))
Define (Absorb A [i,n]) = ; returns a set of pairs of index pairs
      case n-i = 1
        (if (member [A --> (input i i+1)] (UP A))
        then {[[i,i+1],[i+1,n]]} else {})
      case n-i > 1
        (Union (if (member [A --> (input i i+1)] (UP A))
                then {[[i,i+1],[i+1,n]]} else {})
```

237

```
            (Union for [A --> BC] in (BP A)
               (Union for [[i,j],[j,n]] in (Absorb B [i,n])
                  (For [[j,k],[k,n] in (Absorb C [j,n])
                     collect [[i,k],[k,n]])))))
```

The second element of the second argument to Absorb will always be n, since it never changes. We can clearly omit this from the parameter structure and simplify. We then get the following algorithm, renamed Endpositions.

Algorithm XIV

```
Invoke (member n (Endpositions 'S 0))
Define (Endpositions A i) = ; returns a set of end positions
      case n-i = 1
        (if (member [A --> (input i i+1)] (UP A))
        then {i+1} else {})
      case n-i > 1
        (Union (if (member [A --> (input i i+1)] (UP A))
                then {i+1} else {})
            (Union for [A --> BC] in (BP A)
               (Union for j in (Endpositions B i)
                  (Endpositions C j))))
```

Let us abstract the first part of the result to be a function Endpositions1 which will be suitable for caching and then also cache the two calls to Endpositions.

Algorithm XV

```
Invoke (member n (Endpositions 'S 0))
Define (Endpositions A i) = ; returns a set of end positions
      case n-i = 1
        (Cache (Endpositions1 A i))
      case n-i > 1
        (Union (Cache (Endpositions1 A i))
            (Union for [A --> BC] in (BP A)
               (Union for j in (Cache (Endpositions B i))
                  (Cache (Endpositions C j)))))
with (Endpositions1 A i) =
      (if (member [A --> (input i i+1)] (UP A)) then {i+1} else {})
```

A straightforward interpretation of Algorithm XIV will get trapped in a loop if the grammar contains left-recursion, whereas with the use of Cache, Algorithm XV might

238

hang up waiting for cache delivery. A circular cache-request will never deliver. A simple case of this is when a production is of the form $[A \rightarrow AC]$. Scherlis [16] describes a transformation that turns this into a finitely terminating computation, called the "Finite Closure Transformation". Given that the domain of the function is finite, the only way a recursive algorithm can loop forever is because the function is being called with exactly the same arguments. The least-fixed-point semantics of such a function can be arrived at by replacing all redundant calls to the function by the Identity of the operation that combines the results. In our case the results are combined by the Union operation. Thus, trapping redundant calls and making these return {} will give us a finitely terminating computation that determines the least fixed point.

In our situation this transformation is effected simply by using a different caching function, CacheDefault. Its behavior is described simply as follows: (CacheDefault (f x y) DefaultValue) retrieves and returns the result from the cache if (f x y) has been requested and completed. If there is no pending request for it, it will create a request entry and initiate computation of (f x y). In case there is a pending request a more subtle action is required, because of the possibility of concurrent calls. If the request is a circular one, that is, the one who initiated the computation is a spawning ancestor of the current request, then immediately a value of DefaultValue is returned to the current request. Otherwise, the current request is not a circular one, and the current request waits for the other request to complete[4].

Algorithm XVI *A parallel version of Earley algorithm*

```
Invoke (member n (Endpositions 'S 0))
Define (Endpositions A i) =   ; returns a set of end positions
       case n-i = 1
           (Cache (Endpositions1 A i))
       case n-i > 1
           (Union (Cache (Endpositions1 A i))
               (Union for [A --> BC] in (BP A)
                   (Union for j in (CacheDefault (Endpositions B i) {})
                       (CacheDefault (Endpositions C j) {}))))
with (Endpositions1 A i) =
```

---

[4]The implementation of CacheDefault is quite intricate; we have to be careful to distinguish between the two kinds of returns in addition to the two kinds of pending requests. One kind of cache return is the return from a circular call with the default value; the other kind of return is a normal return. One kind of cache request is a circular request; the other is not. There are many issues involved in the design of Cache memory. Specifically, we have not yet addressed the issue of cache retention period, and thus the issue of when to clear the cache.

```
(if (member [A --> (input i i+1)] (UP A)) then {i+1} else {})
```

To see the correspondence to the Earley algorithm we must explain the three operations that Earley uses: Scanner, Completer and Predictor; and also explain the differences in the way we express the control structure and the way he does it. Earley structured his computation to be based on producing a sequence of n+1 state-sets numbered from S_0 to S_n, each state set containing a tuple[5]. A tuple [p,f,i] entered in state set S_j means that the production p has been partially recognized, starting at the substring of the input beginning at i and ending at j, where f (the pointer) indicates the number of symbols in the production's right side which have been successfully recognized. In a CNF grammar, f can be 0, 1 or 2 if p is in BP and f can be 0 or 1 if p is in UP.

```
Case p is in UP and f=0:
        Apply scanner
Case p is in UP and f=1:
        Apply completer
Case p is in BP and f=0 or 1:
        Apply predictor
Case p is in BP and f=2:
        Apply completer
```

The function Endpositions1 and the expression (if ... then ... else ...) defining it constitutes the Scanner. It reads one terminal symbol in the input string and moves the pointer past the nonterminal that needed to be recognized. The part of the program that translates a call to (Endpositions A i) to (Endpositions B i) for some production [A → BC] is the Predictor. The continuation which would then call (Endpositions C j) based on the value of j returned by (Endpositions B i) is also part of the Predictor. The return of a function call continues the computation that was in effect before the function call; this operation corresponds to the Completer operation of Earley.

I trust that with moderate effort the reader is able to see how the above algorithm applies the proper operators to the proper cases. Since the Unions can all be invoked in parallel, the only necessary serialization is the data-flow dependency that requires the arrival of values j from the calls to (Endpositions B i). This is, again, more concurrency than the "obvious" concurrency one might have captured in directly translating the Earley algorithm into a parallel form[6].

---

[5]We are simplifying the Earley algorithm by omitting the look-ahead feature; the tuple in the original algorithm contains a fourth element, which is the look-ahead string. The original algorithm takes an additional parameter which indicates the size of the look-ahead string to be computed; our algorithm corresponds to zero length look-ahead. The algorithm complexity is unaffected by variations in this parameter.

[6]There is a possible trap in anyone's first attempt in parallelizing Earley's algorithm. One would be

8.4 Conclusion

We have illustrated the systematic derivation of parallel algorithms for context-free recognition. We have derived versions of the two most well-known general context-free recognition algorithms *in addition to deriving several new ones.* Similar treatments of sorting and other algorithms have been previously presented in the literature [36,35,33]. Our work is distinguished in two respects: We have attempted a somewhat more complex problem than sorting algorithms and we have derived several new algorithms in addition to reproducing known ones. Deak [32] has presented a derivation of the CKY algorithm; we invite the reader to compare the level of perspicuity in the derivations that Deak gives with the ones presented here. We suspect that the complexity of Deak's derivation stems from the introduction of side-effect causing construction very early in the development; and also, specifically, the choice of assignment to a variable (rather than caching as is in our case) further complicates matters. Amarel [31] has given a general formulation of the problem of syntactic analysis as a theorem-proving problem in a reduction system. He shows sets of reduction rules that do bottom-up, top-down, left-right as well as right-left derivations. He shows that by altering the attention focusing method systematically, that is varying the priorities on rule application, his formulation spans a wide range of possible algorithms. Included in his formulation are some new as well as old algorithms. However, we were not able to detect in his range of algorithms the equivalent of the Earley algorithm; this algorithm requires a specific type of abstraction (abstraction over one of the parameters, thus producing the function Absorb) that is not included in the formulation given by Amarel. Since Earley published his results two years after Amarel's report was made available, this is perhaps not surprising. *Our paper makes a contribution in the area of parsing by showing the close affinity between the CKY and Earley algorithms as well as by displaying a new mixed top-down and bottom-up algorithm and a dynamic programming algorithm.*

The major thrust of the paper, however, is the demonstration of *semi-applicative programming*, that is, using an applicative programming language combined with program transformations, program annotation (precedence control and caching) and adaptive scheduling. Context-free parsing is just one area of study; we are in the process of dealing with a wider range of common problems that arise in Artificial Intelligence programming. We hope we have given the reader a sample of semi-applicative programming by focusing on one specific case. The use of precedence control and the several forms of

---

tempted to process each tuple in the state-set S_i in parallel, retaining the serial processing of the sets S_0 through S_n. However, this cannot be done so readily, since the action of the predictor in state S_i is to add more tuples to the same state-set S_i.

caching in combination with program transformations are useful ways of controlling the behavior of applicative programs. At a high level, *tuning for performance need not be a machine-oriented activity; and it can be done in a safe and reliable manner preserving the functionality of the program.* This might be considered a contribution to programming methodology.

Postscript

I am indebted to Douglas Smith of Kestrel Institute, who read an earlier draft of this paper and brought to my attention two papers by H. Partsch [2,3]. Partsch has demonstrated transformational developments for both the CKY and the Earley algorithms executable on parallel machines. Indirectly, I have learned that there is also related work by Scherlis [4] and Jones [5] but strictly for the serial case. The development of the predictive top-down recognizer and its weakened and asynchronous versions, the dynamic programming solution appear, in any case, to be novel results for this paper.

The SALT and PEPPER interpreters are under development and were not available for experiments at the time of this writing. To partially validate the approach and the research results of this report, several algorithms derived here were converted to a parallel implementation of Scheme [7] on the BBN Butterfly multiprocessor with 16 processors. The algorithms were encoded mostly in a side-effect free manner using the Future construct to indicate parallel tasking. The caching constructs were implemented using data structures and side-effecting them. Test results were encouraging. The algorithms ran at first-try producing correct results on sample grammars. The version of the Scheme we used was an early release and lacked a compiler and various simple optimizations anticipated for later releases; thus, we did not witness interesting speedup for any of the algorithms. (Speedup was not a goal of this work anyhow). The queue of pending concurrent tasks built up to 500 to 10,000 units, indicating generous concurrency in all of the algorithms. We hope to present, in the future, not only empirical results on this set of algorithms but also derivations of new algorithms for typical search problems.

Acknowledgements

It is my pleasure to thank Andy Haas for the help he has offered always with enthusiasm. I also thank my several colleagues at BBN Laboratories who have provided me their generous help and support. One of the referees gave this paper a thorough reading; his/her comments have improved the presentation in addition to removing a technical flaw in the exposition.

This research was sponsored by the Advanced Research Projects Agency of the Department of Defense and was monitored by ONR under Contract No. N00014-85-C-0079. The views and conclusions contained in this document are those of the author and should not be interpreted as necessarily representing the official policies, either expressed or implied, of the Defense Advanced Research Projects Agency or the U.S. Government. The work reported here was performed while the author was with BBN Laboratories Inc., 10 Moulton Street, Cambridge, MA 02238.

References

[1] S. L. Graham, M. Harrison, W. L. Ruzzo, "An Improved Context-Free Recognizer," *ACM Transactions on Programming Languages and Systems*, vol. 2, no. 3, July 1980, pp. 415-462.

[2] H. Partsch, "Structuring Transformational Developments: A case study based on Earley's recognizer," *Science of Computer Programming*, vol. 4, April 1984, pp. 17-44.

[3] H. Partsch, "Transformational Derivation of Parsing Algorithms Executable on Parallel Architectures," in *Programmiersprachen und Programm-Entwicklung*, ed. U. Ammann, Informatik-Fachberichte 77, Springer-Verlag, 1984, pp. 47-57.

[4] W. L. Scherlis, "Expression procedures and program derivation," TR STAN-CS-80-818, Stanford University, 1980.

[5] C. B. Jones, *Software Development: A rigorous approach*, Prentice-Hall, Englewood Cliffs, NJ, 1980.

[6] N. S. Sridharan, "Semi-Applicative Programming: Examples of context-free recognizers," TR 6135, BBN Laboratories Inc., November 1985.

[7] D. Allen and staff, "A Lisp for the Butterfly parallel processor," (in progress), BBN Laboratories Inc.

[8] N. S. Sridharan, "A semi-applicative language for artificial intelligence programming," TR 6134, BBN Laboratories Inc., November 1984.

[9] A. L. Wasserman et al., "Software Engineering: The turning point," *IEEE Computer*, September 1978, pp. 30-41.

[10] D. F. Kibler and J. Conery, "Parallelism in AI Programs," *Proc. 9th IJCAI*, Morgan Kaufman Publishers, 1985, pp. 53-56.

[11] R. Balzer, "A 15 year perspective on automatic programming," *IEEE Transactions on Software Engineering*, vol. SE-11, no. 11, November 1985, pp. 1257-68.

[12] H. Partsch and R. Steinbruggen, "Program transformation systems," *Computing Surveys*, vol. 15, no. 3, 1983, pp. 199-236.

[13] J. E. Hopcroft and J. D. Ullman, *Introduction to Automata Theory, Languages and Computation*, Addison-Wesley, Reading, MA, 1979, (See Chapter 4).

[14] J. McCarthy et al., *LISP 1.5 Programmer's Manual*, MIT Press, Cambridge, MA, 1963.

[15] R. Halstead Jr., "Multilisp: A language for concurrent symbolic computation," *ACM Transactions on Programming Languages*, October 1985.

243

[16] J. Reif and W. Scherlis, "Deriving efficient graph algorithms," CMU-TR, Carnegie-Mellon University, Pittsburgh, PA, 1982.

[17] R. P. Gabriel and J. McCarthy, "Queue based multi-processing Lisp," STAN-CS-84-1007, Stanford University, June 1984.

[18] F. W. Burton, "Annotations to control parallelism and reduction order in the distributed evaluation of functional programs," *ACM Transactions on Programming Languages and Systems*, vol. 6, no. 2, April 1984, pp. 159-174.

[19] R. S. Bird, "Tabulation techniques for recursive programs," *Computing Surveys*, vol. 12, no. 4, December 1980, pp. 403-417.

[20] P. C. Treleaven, D. R. Brownbridge and R. P. Hopkins, "Data-Driven and demand-driven computing architecture," *Computing Surveys*, vol. 14 no. 1, March 1982, pp. 93-143.

[21] R. M. Keller and M. Ronan Sleep, "Applicative caching," *Proceedings of the 1981 ACM Conference on Functional Programming Languages and Computer Architecture*, October 1981, pp. 131-140.

[22] J. Backus, "Can programming be liberated from the Von Neumann style?" *Communications of the ACM*, vol. 21 no. 8, July 1982, pp. 613-641.

[23] V. R. Lesser and D. D. Corkill, "Functionally accurate cooperative distributed systems," *Proc. IEEE 1st Int'l Conference on Cybernetics and Society*, October 1979, pp. 346-353.

[24] H. Abelson et al., "The revised report on Scheme or An uncommon Lisp," MIT AI Memo 848, August 1985.

[25] E. Shapiro, "A subset of Concurrent Prolog and its interpreter," TR-003, ICOT - Institute for New Generation Computing, Tokyo, Japan, February 1983.

[26] R. Kowalski, *Logic for Problem Solving*, Elsevier North-Holland, New York, 1979.

[27] G. R. Andrews and F. B. Schneider, "Concepts and notations for concurrent programming," TR 82-520, Cornell University, New York, September 1982.

[28] J. Earley, "An efficient context-free parsing algorithm," *Communications of the ACM*, vol. 13, no. 2, February 1970, pp. 94-102.

[29] BBN Staff, "Butterfly parallel processor overview," BBN Laboratories Inc., Cambridge MA, June 1985.

[30] T. Kasami and K. Torii, "A syntax-analysis procedure for unambiguous context-free grammars," *Journal of the ACM*, vol. 16, no. 3, July 1969, pp. 423-431.

[31] S. Amarel, "Problem-solving procedures for efficient syntactic analysis," Scientific Report 1, RCA Laboratories, Princeton NJ, May 1968.

[32] E. Deak, "A transformational derivation of a parsing algorithm in a high level language," *IEEE Trans. on Software Engineering*, vol. SE-7, no. 1, January 1981, pp. 23-31.

[33] D. R. Smith, "Top-down synthesis of divide-and-conquer algorithms," *Artificial Intelligence*, vol. 27, no. 1, September 1985, pp. 43-96.

[34] W. Bibel, "Syntax-directed semantics-supported program synthesis," *Artificial Intelligence*, vol. 14, 1980, pp. 243-261.

[35] J. Darlington, "A synthesis of several sort programs," *Acta Informatica*, vol. 11, no. 1, 1978, pp. 1-30.

[36] D. R. Barstow, *Knowledge-Based Program Construction*, Elsevier North-Holland, New York, 1979.

N. S. Sridharan
FMC Corporation
Central Engineering Labs
1205 Coleman Avenue
Santa Clara, CA 95052

Part III

Applications and Examples

Chapter 9

DAI for Document Retrieval: The MINDS Project

Michael N. Huhns, Uttam Mukhopadhyay, Larry M. Stephens and Ronald D. Bonnell

Abstract

MINDS (Multiple Intelligent Node Document Servers) is a distributed collection of knowledge-based systems for efficiently managing and retrieving documents in an office environment of networked workstations. The knowledge-based system located at each workstation is an expert in the domain of "documents". The systems share both knowledge and tasks to cooperate in retrieving documents for users. They are able to customize these document retrievals for each user by learning document distribution patterns, as well as user interests and preferences, during operation. Because of this ability to learn, they are also self-initializing.

The knowledge base used by the query engine is learned with the help of heuristics for assigning credit and recommending adjustments; these heuristics are manually refined at the upper level in a simulator with two-level learning.

9.1 Introduction

9.1.1 Problem Description

Computers are often used for the storage of information, such as data, electronic mail, letters, reports, graphics, spreadsheets, and records. A convenient form for a unit of this information is a document. However, the information stored in documents in a multiple-user environment is difficult to utilize for the following reasons:

1. the name given to a document is typically short and not completely descriptive

2. the name given to a document is sometimes not unique

3. a document name can mean different things to different users

4. users are neither fully aware of the information stored by each other, nor do they know where documents are stored, the form of the stored documents, or the organization for the storage

5. the document distribution patterns change with time.

These problems are exacerbated in an environment where the users are located on physically separate workstations. Some method is needed to help users manage, utilize, and share information. The goal of the MINDS project has been to develop a distributed system of document servers which utilize knowledge-based systems for document management and query processing [1,2].

Our approach in the MINDS project has been to utilize concepts from office automation [3,4,5,6], distributed artificial intelligence [7,8,9], and machine learning [10,11]. Concepts from office automation can be applied to provide a structure for organizing the documents in a distributed multiple-user office environment: this requires an analysis of office information requirements and a development of data models which allow the access of both structured and unstructured data. Principles of distributed artificial intelligence can be used to develop an intelligent, distributed, query-processing system, which efficiently retrieves information located somewhere in a large network and customizes this retrieval for individual users with the help of metaknowledge acquired during system usage. Machine learning can be used to determine the best set of heuristics for the automated acquisition and updating of this metaknowledge. This chapter addresses these concepts and reports on a system which incorporates them.

9.1.2 Background

A review of the literature in office automation reveals the inadequacy of current database systems for handling the diverse types of data and applications found in offices. Also, they are unsuitable for an environment of distributed workstations which are becoming pervasive in both structured and unstructured offices. (A structured office usually deals with a high volume of standardized transactions, whereas an unstructured office deals with policy and professional functions in which the focus is on the selection and meeting of goals. Typical activities in the structured office include typing and records management. Unstructured offices typically use decision-support and problem-solving aids such as spreadsheets and business graphics.)

Traditionally, offices have maintained information systems by using file cabinets to store paper copies of important information. The information is organized by either an alphabetic, geographic, numeric, subject, or chronologic method [12]. Sharing this information within a large corporation is often difficult because different departments may use different filing methods.

Computer filing systems need to accommodate both structured and unstructured document types. Structured documents include forms, tables, computer-generated reports, and other traditional data processing files; unstructured documents include text files, spreadsheets, software, electronic mail messages, graphics, images, and audio/voice storage-and-forward messages. In addition, there are external documents whose description rather than their content are entered into the computer. The phrase *multimedia document* is meant to include all of these.

A number of systems have been designed to process multimedia documents. These have been developed around the database paradigm and/or the file-cabinet paradigm. Among these are IBM's Office-By-Example and DISOSS [13,14], INGRES [15], the Xerox Star Office System [16], and the Visi On operating environment [17].

The key problem to be faced in the retrieval of multimedia documents is the selection of a data model which can provide a unified approach to the access of both structured and unstructured data. Current research has focused on three models: surrogation, hypertext, and the inverted file. The inverted file data model offers the most capability, but it imposes very high storage requirements and file maintenance overhead [18]. Hypertext provides links for the internal structure of documents, as well as links to other documents. Retrieval in hypertext is then the result of traversing these links. A problem is how to maintain and update the links within a distributed environment [6].

A surrogate is an encrypted representation of a document that serves as an index to the original. Because searches are conducted on the surrogated indices rather than on the documents themselves, searches take less time [18]. Because the surrogates can be copied and distributed throughout a network, this is the model that has been chosen for the MINDS project.

In addition to the studies on data models, a great deal of work has been devoted to the construction of sophisticated mechanisms for retrieval. These mechanisms are based on pattern recognition as well as on decision theoretic considerations [19,20]. However, they cannot be easily extended to distributed environments, and we feel that this is where distributed artificial intelligence can be successfully applied.

Distributed artificial intelligence systems are characterized according to the methods of control and cooperation used to organize their operation. These methods can be described in terms of their approaches to task sharing and result sharing. Davis and Smith [21] developed the basic methodology for each of these, using negotiation and a contract-net formalism for task sharing.

The concept of distributed problem solving by cooperating expert systems was first considered by Lesser and Erman during their development of the Hearsay-II speech understanding system [22,23]. This system introduced the idea of multiple knowledge sources (KS's) interacting through the sharing of results and hypotheses. This interaction utilized a *blackboard* data structure, a multilevel structure which contained tentative results available to all KS's and which each KS could modify, create, or delete. Each level in the blackboard specified a different representation of the problem space. The elements at each level were hypotheses with fixed attributes about aspects of that level. The attributes were the mechanisms for implementing the goal-directed scheduling of the KS's and their data-directed execution. More recently, a formal characterization of blackboards for the control of intelligent systems has been developed [24].

Work by Fox [25] has shown the similarity between organizational theories and the design of complex knowledge-based AI systems. Also, it is expected that as computer workstations for individuals are introduced into office and engineering environments [26], they will be integrated into the particular structure extant, which is often hierarchical. Tenney and Sandell [27,28] have provided a means for constructing and analyzing these structures in a decision-making environment. This work has been extended to the description of complex processes for their instantiation on distributed computing systems [29].

The performance of many knowledge-based systems is attributable to the large bodies of domain-specific heuristics that they employ. Heuristics are informal, judgmental rules-of thumb that arise through specialization, generalization, and analogy and that are learned from past observations [32]. In the context of searching, they suggest promising alternatives at a node and point out unproductive ones. The automated acquisition of this knowledge has long been a goal of AI researchers [33,34].

The spectrum of machine learning extends from rote learning at the lower end to inductive learning at the higher [10]. Lenat's AM and EURISKO programs were experiments in learning by discovery, an inductive learning paradigm, embodying principles of empirical theory formation [30,31]. The discovery of theories was guided by a set of heuristics.

The worth of individual heuristics for searching has been studied at length [35]. However, the problem of combining the knowledge from several heuristics has not been studied in detail. A body of heuristics, when applied to a problem-solving task such as document retrieval, should ideally perform better than any of its subsets.

9.2 Document Knowledge and Metaknowledge

9.2.1 Organization of Documents

The presumed environment for MINDS consists of a network of single-user workstations, each identified by a name. Documents, the basic units of information for the network, are distributed among the workstations. A document is not permanently located but may migrate to other workstations. Different versions of a document are allowed at the same workstation, but two copies with the same name are not. Since a document and its copies all have the same name, the concatenation of a document name with a workstation name is necessary to identify the document uniquely within the network. The documents in the system are dynamic because new documents are created or copied from other users, and sometimes existing documents are deleted or moved to other locations.

9.2.2 Document Directory

A document directory, located at every workstation, contains object-level knowledge about the logical and physical structures of documents and metaknowledge about document contents and locations. This directory is organized into three units: document surrogates, a keyword dictionary, and document metaknowledge.

Document Surrogates

Each document is represented within the document directory by a surrogate containing its attributes. The surrogate is constructed from information supplied by the operating system, by the user, and by defaults. The document and its surrogate are subsequently updated or deleted as dictated by system usage. Surrogates occupy only a fraction of the storage space needed by the documents, but usually contain enough information for users to determine whether a document is useful. This information consists of the following attributes: name, version, location, authors, creation date, type, access privileges, and keywords.

The keywords represent document contents; each document may be associated with several keywords and each keyword may be associated with many documents. A user may issue content-based queries about his own locally-stored documents or about those stored at other workstations. Automatic text-understanding systems could conceivably process these queries by reading the documents, but would be expensive to develop and use. The names of documents provide clues to their contents, but names are not descriptive enough for reliable processing of content-based queries. However, augmenting the names by a set of keywords achieves a more precise description of document contents: the retrieval of documents can then be predicated on these keywords, as well as on other document attributes. Conjunctions or disjunctions of predicates on these attributes can also be used.

The relevance of a keyword to a particular document is assumed to be either zero or one, in accordance with traditional (Boolean) indexing. Further, query-term weights are also assumed to be either zero or one. (See Bartschi [36] or Kraft and Buell [37] for a survey of fuzzy and generalized information retrieval techniques.)

Keyword Dictionary

When a document is created (updated), its author is asked to create (update) keywords that represent its contents. Content-based retrieval relies on the accuracy of the keywords, so it is essential to find a uniform representation of keywords for all users. This is simplified by mapping the set of all keywords to one of its proper subsets, *primary* keywords. The mapping is accomplished in two ways: 1) synonyms or closely related keywords are mapped to one of the synonymous keywords, and 2) keywords that are instances of a category are mapped to the category name. For example, the keyword dictionary would map the synonomous keywords "auto", "automobile", and "car" to the primary keyword "car". As an example of the second type of mapping, "apples", "oranges", and "bananas" are all instances of "fruit", so the dictionary would map all four keywords to the primary keyword "fruit".

This mapping is application dependent. The keyword dictionary is tailored to an application by 1) splitting some categories to make them more specific, 2) merging categories to form more general categories, and 3) adding new keywords and categories which are not initially available.

Metaknowledge

In typical document-management systems, document retrieval consists of matching predicates for retrieval with document attributes stored in a directory. The documents for which the match is successful are then retrieved from the indicated storage addresses. In *distributed* document-management systems, the directories may be either centralized or distributed, with or without redundancy [38]. However, the directory information is consistent throughout the system; information is stored redundantly only to reduce directory access time. Because of this consistency, the response to a query is independent of the identity of the query originator.

However, the documents relevant to one user may be quite different from those relevant to another. This is a problem that at first appears to originate from a lack of specificity in formulating the query: a more judicious choice of predicates should cause all the documents that are irrelevant to the query originator to be rejected. However, this would require a sophisticated query language, rich enough to allow the expression of a user's goals, plans, and interests. A comprehensive representation for documents would also be required. The increased power of the system would be offset by the additional effort needed to formulate queries.

Assume that the response to a query is a set of retrieved documents, R. In general, R will be an approximation to the set of most relevant documents, R^*. An ideal document retrieval is one for which $R = R^*$ for all queries. A realistic design goal is to maximize

- the fraction of relevant documents that are retrieved, given by

$$RECALL = \frac{|R \cap R^*|}{|R^*|}$$

- and the fraction of retrieved documents that are relevant, given by

$$PRECISION = \frac{|R \cap R^*|}{|R|}$$

The ideal response to a query would depend on the model of the user issuing the query. Assume that R_i^* is the ideal response for $user_i$. The ideal reponse for a system without any models of its users is

$$R^* = \bigcup_{i=1}^{N} R_i^*$$

The precision from the viewpoint of $user_j$, assuming a 100% selection and a 100% RECALL is then

$$\frac{|R_j^*|}{|\bigcup_{i=1}^{N} R_i^*|}$$

Thus, in the absence of any information about a user, whether explicitly stated in a query or embedded in the system's knowledge base, the best possible response would be the union of the sets of relevant documents described by the query from the perspective of each user. In a large multiple-user environment, a response would then contain a large number of irrelevant documents. A better response could be obtained only if the system maintained models of its users.

MINDS obtains more precise responses by storing document metaknowledge at each workstation. This metaknowledge provides models of both the current system state and the local user's document preferences. These models are dynamic, i.e., they are self-initializing and develop as the system is used, so that the system improves its performance with usage. The metaknowledge allows the system to scan the document bases of all users in a best-first fashion from the viewpoint of the query originator.

Each metaknowledge element is a four-tuple with fields for two users, a keyword, and a certainty factor in the closed interval [0,1]. The metaknowledge element, (Smith, Jones, compiler, 0.8), represents the following:

> Smith's past experience suggests that the possibility of finding relevant documents on compilers among those owned by Jones is high (8 on a scale of 10).

Formally, given U, the set of all users, and K, the set of all primary keywords, the metaknowledge function, M, is the mapping

$$M : U \times U \times K \rightarrow [0, 1].$$

The metaknowledge is partitioned among the workstations such that if U_i is the subset of users at workstation i, then only the metaknowledge for $U_i \times U \times K$ is stored at that workstation.

The certainty factor [39] provides a basis for ordering the search for documents. It reflects 1) the breadth of information at a workstation pertaining to a specific keyword, 2) how useful documents concerning this keyword have proven to be in the past, and 3) how recently the workstation has acquired its information. The metaknowledge is first initialized with default values of certainty factors. A set of heuristic learning rules, described in a subsequent section, defines the techniques for modifying these values during system usage.

If a user had metaknowledge for each document rather than for each user of the system, the knowledge would be precise. However, the disadvantages of this approach are 1) for an average of n documents per user, the metaknowledge overhead would be n times as

256

much, and 2) for new documents, no prediction of relevance could be made. On the other hand, by storing metaknowledge as a relation between two users, new documents will be assigned the value of relevance from this relation. There are positive correlations among the attributes of a user's documents, and it is reasonable that his new documents would have similar attributes.

9.3 System Architecture

9.3.1 Query Processing

The MINDS system operates on a network of workstations. The workstations share tasks, knowledge, and metaknowledge to cooperate in processing queries involving the retrieval of documents. This retrieval is primarily a search problem. The strategy for this search is to satisfy the query while minimizing

- the total processing taking place,
- the communications between the workstations, and
- the time needed to complete the search.

The difficulties are that

- the query represents a fuzzy goal which might not be satisfied exactly, and
- the search should cease at all workstations as soon as the query is either satisfied or found to be unsatisfiable.

In the MINDS system, the metaknowledge is used to guide the search, which is not exhaustive, proceeds according to a best-first strategy, improves in efficiency as the system is used, and occurs in parallel.

A complex query is processed by first decomposing it into subqueries, using locally-stored metaknowledge, so that the search space for a subquery is limited to the documents owned by one user. Subqueries are then transmitted to the respective workstations where they are processed. Responses are transmitted to the workstation that initiated the subqueries, where they are combined and ranked in decreasing order of relevance, as estimated by the metaknowledge. For example, assume that the following query is issued:

$$(QueryID, Source, Destination, Description) =$$
$$(query1, user1, all, ``find\ all\ documents\ on\ compilers")$$

and assume that user1's metaknowledge on "compilers" is

$$(user1, user1, compiler, 0.6)$$
$$(user1, user3, compiler, 0.3)$$
$$(user1, user7, compiler, 0.8)$$

This query is then decomposed into the following three queries:

$$(query1a, user1, user1, ``find\ all\ documents\ on\ compilers")$$
$$(query1b, user1, user3, ``find\ all\ documents\ on\ compilers")$$
$$(query1c, user1, user7, ``find\ all\ documents\ on\ compilers")$$

The results of these three queries would be returned to $user1$ where they would be ordered by certainty factor as

$$\{result1c, result1a, result1b\}$$

If the subquery is content-based, relevant metaknowledge is also sent to the query originator along with the documents and surrogates constituting the response to the subquery. The transmitted metaknowledge is used for updating the metaknowledge of the receiver in accordance with a learning strategy to be described. For example, assume that $user1$ tries to retrieve documents from $user2$ based on the keyword "compilers". $user1$ is given not only the documents from $user2$ associated with the keyword "compilers" but also the list of other users that $user2$ is aware of with associations to the keyword (along with their certainty factors). $user1$'s scheduler uses these certainty factors, along with $user1$'s certainty factor associating $user2$ with "compilers", to enable it to place these other users in the appropriate positions in the ordered list of sources for information about "compilers". $user1$'s metaknowledge is also updated so it can be used for planning subsequent searches.

When a local document server detects a new user in the network, it assigns by default a certainty factor associating the new user with each keyword it has stored. The only keywords a new user starts with are those that are associated with its own documents. Additional keywords may appear in the knowledge base as a side effect of processing queries. For example, if $user1$ tries to retrieve documents with the keyword "compilers" from $user2$ and $user2$ has no associations between $user1$ and this keyword, then a new association is created by $user2$ associating $user1$ with this keyword with a default value for its certainty factor. The rationale for this is that $user1$ will shortly be knowledgeable in the area of keyword "compilers." $user1$ also learns from this interaction by reducing the certainty factor associating the keyword "compiler" with $user2$.

Other activities, such as creating, deleting, and copying documents, require cooperation among the workstations. Metaknowledge is modified as a side-effect of these activities also.

258

9.3.2   Dynamic Allocation of Documents

There is also a trade-off involving the location of documents. The parameters of this trade-off are storage requirements, access time, update time and difficulty, document integrity, document security, and document reliability. For example, one copy of each document implies 1) guaranteed integrity, 2) slow acess, and 3) minimum storage. Allowing multiple copies of each document implies 1) increased storage, 2) faster access, 3) increased reliability, 4) slower updates, and 5) possible loss of integrity.

The MINDS system dynamically allocates documents, involving the placement, copying, and migration of documents among the network of workstations. The allocation problem is

Given:

- the number of retrievals and updates from each workstation to each document, and

- the network topology, communication link capacities, communication costs, node capacities, and node costs

Find:

- an assignment of documents to workstations which minimizes total cost and does not exceed any capacity constraints, and

- an assignment of metaknowledge to workstations which minimizes the sum of the query processing costs and the metaknowledge updating costs.

It is assumed that all queries can be decomposed into subqueries about single documents, so that the placement of each document may be optimized independently. Although this reduces the complexity of the problem, it has been shown to be NP-complete [40]. Heuristics have been used to manage this complexity [41,42], yielding solutions which are nearly optimal. The heuristics which we have employed are based on the relevances of documents to users.

9.4   Updating Metaknowledge

9.4.1   System Dynamics

MINDS is being developed for operation in a wide range of office environments. The state of an environment at any instant of time is given by the content and configuration of the metaknowledge and document bases of the system. Commands issued by users comprise the system inputs, and retrieved documents and surrogates constitute the outputs. The state of the system changes as a result of executing a command [43]. These system dynamics are shown in Figure 9.1.

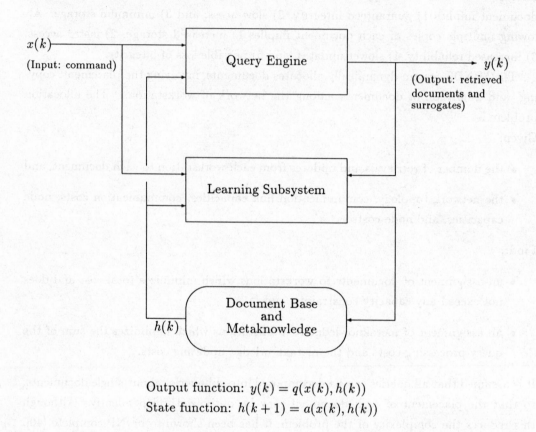

Output function: $y(k) = q(x(k), h(k))$
State function: $h(k + 1) = a(x(k), h(k))$

Figure 9.1: Block diagram of the system dynamics.

9.4.2 Heuristics for Updating Metaknowledge

The heuristics for updating metaknowledge are based on the paradigm of an intelligent office-worker who conducts an ordered search for documents based on past experiences in the office environment. When Smith asks Jones for documents on compilers and Jones provides one or more documents that are relevant to him, Smith learns that Jones' document base is likely to continue having useful documents on compilers. If Jones has no documents on compilers, or if none of the documents on compilers are relevant to him, Smith will learn that this may not be a good place to search for documents on compilers in the future. In either case, Jones may assume that Smith will continue searching other locations and acquire documents on compilers from some other user. Consequently, Jones will increase his belief in Smith's ability to provide documents on compilers in the future. This increase in belief will be modest since Smith's newly acquired knowledge on compilers may not be of the type relevant to Jones.

The set of heuristics used for the initial experiments do not include metaknowledge sharing. The metaknowledge of a user is updated only with the evidence that is directly obtained while processing commands, and the experience of other users is not leveraged. Also, some of the heuristics have parameters that may be tuned. The results shown in Figures 9.6 and 9.7 were generated by the following parameterized heuristics:

```
Heuristic 1.  (also applicable for the DELETE part of MOVE)
    IF   a document is deleted
    THEN no metaknowledge is changed
```

```
Heuristic 2.
    IF   a document is created by user1
    THEN metaknowledge of user1 about user1
         regarding each keyword of the document
         is increased to 1.0 (the maximum
         relevance).
```

```
Heuristic 3.
    IF   a retrieve command predicated on keyword1
         is issued by user1
    AND  at least one user2 surrogate contains
         keyword1
    THEN (a) user1 metaknowledge about user2 regarding
         keyword1 is increased (weight 0.1)
         (b) user2 metaknowledge about user1 regarding
         keyword1 is increased (weight 0.1)
```

Heuristic 4.

    IF   a retrieve command predicated on keyword1
        is issued by user1

    AND no user2 surrogate contains keyword1

    THEN (a) user1 metaknowledge about user2 regarding
        keyword1 is decreased to zero
        (b) user2 metaknowledge about user1 regarding
        keyword1 is increased (weight 0.1)

Heuristic 5.

    IF   a read command predicated on keyword1 is
        issued by user1

    AND no user2 document contains keyword1

    THEN (a) user1 metaknowledge about user2 regarding
        keyword1 is decreased to zero
        (b) user2 metaknowledge about user1 regarding
        keyword1 is increased (weight 0.1)

Heuristic 6.

    IF   a read command predicated on keyword1 is
        issued by user1

    AND at least one user2 document contains keyword1

    THEN (a) user1 metaknowledge about user2 regarding
        keyword1 is changed, based on the highest relevance
        of all user2 documents regarding keyword1.
        (b) user2 metaknowledge about user1 regarding
        keyword1 is increased (weight 0.1)

Heuristic 7.

    IF   a read command predicated on keyword1 is
        issued by user1

    AND document1 owned by user2 contains keyword1

    AND the relevance of document1 to user1 by way

```
          of keyword1 exceeds the move_copy threshold
AND  user1 does not have document1
THEN (a) user1 copies document1 from user2
     (b) metaknowledge of user1 about user1 regarding
         keyword1 of the document is increased to 1.0
```

```
Heuristic 8.
     IF   a read command predicated on keyword1 is
          issued by user1
     AND  user1 has copied document1 from user2
     AND  the maximum relevance of document1 to
          user2 by way of any keyword is less
          than the delete_threshold
     THEN document1 is deleted from the document
          base of user2
```

9.4.3   Assimilation of Evidence

The learning heuristics shown above enable the metaknowledge to be changed on the basis of new evidence, which typically consists of the relevance rating of a document, the observation of a document being copied, etc. The metaknowledge updating scheme should be able to take into account

1. temporal precedence: the system is dynamic and therefore recently acquired evidence is more indicative of the current state of the system than evidence acquired earlier. If f_1 is the mapping function for a downward revision of the certainty factor (contradiction) and f_2 is the mapping function for an upward revision (confirmation), then

$$f_2(f_1(x)) \geq f_1(f_2(x)), \quad 0 \leq x \leq 1.$$

This is illustrated in the bottom graph of Figure 9.2 for linear functions of f_1 and f_2. The choice of linear functions is arbitrary; any monotonically increasing function which maps a given certainty factor into one having a greater (smaller) value can be used for confirmation (contradiction).

2. reliability of evidence: some types of evidence are more reliable than others. If a surrogate with a desired keyword is successfully retrieved by Jones from Smith, this action by itself does not completely support the proposition that Smith's documents

on compilers are going to prove relevant to Jones in the future, since the relevance of this document to Jones is not known. However, if this document is read by Jones, then the relevance value assigned by him constitutes reliable evidence. The reliability of the source is also important for evaluating the metaknowledge sent by a user. When Smith offers metaknowledge to Jones about documents on compilers, Jones will pay heed to it only if he has found Smith to be a reliable source of documents on compilers in the past.

3. degree of support: the degree of support for a proposition may vary. When a user is asked if the document he has read is relevant to him, his answer does not have to be limited to "yes" or "no" but may be a value in the interval [0,1].

4. saturation characteristics: when the initial certainty factor for a metaknowledge element is high, additional confirmatory evidence will not change (increase) it substantially. However, if the evidence were to be contradictory, the change (decrease) in certainty factor would be large. The situation is exactly reversed when the initial certainty factor is low.

The metaknowledge updating scheme presented here has all these features and is based on two linear functions that map the current certainty factor to a new one (Figure 9.2). The choice of linear functions is arbitrary as discussed previously. The first function deals with confirmatory evidence that causes upward revision while the second one deals with contradictory evidence that causes downward revision. When a surrogate with a keyword is retrieved successfully, the revised certainty factor is given by $(1-r)f_1(x)+rf_2(x)$, where f_1 and f_2 are the functions dealing with downward and upward revision, x is the original certainty factor, and r is the reliability of this type of information (typically 0.1). For example, if the evidence supports a proposition to a degree of $r = 0.7$, the mapping function is the weighted average of the two original functions (see Figure 9.3).

9.5   Heuristic Refinement Testbed

9.5.1   Simulator Design

A simulator has been implemented to develop a body of robust learning heuristics for MINDS. A strategy for this development is based on simulating the performance of different versions of MINDS, each implemented with a different set of learning heuristics. Each simulation is run on a representation of a specific office environment, consisting of an initial database of documents and their locations, the initial metaknowledge of the

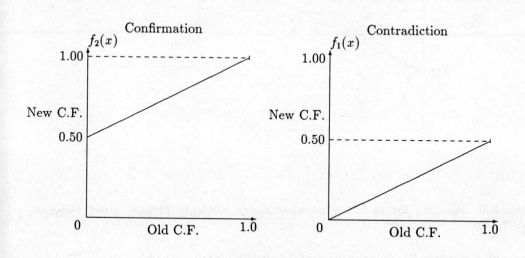

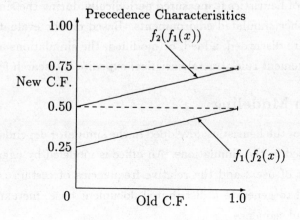

Figure 9.2: Update functions for metaknowledge certainty factor and temporal precedence characteristics.

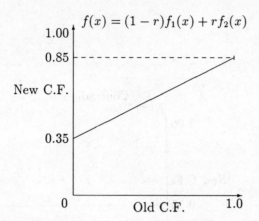

$$f(x) = (1-r)f_1(x) + rf_2(x)$$

New C.F.

1.00
0.85
0.35
0
Old C.F.
1.0

Figure 9.3: Function for updating metaknowledge certainty factors, given relevance $r = 0.7$.

users, and a command sequence representing plausible document transactions. The performance of the set of heuristics is measured periodically during the simulation. This set is then tested on other simulated environments. Based on the evaluations of each simulation, heuristics are discarded, added, or modified; the simulations are then repeated. Good heuristic refinement rules (metaheuristics) expedite the search for an optimal set.

9.5.2 Domain Modeling

The practical value of the heuristics developed in the simulator depends on the validity of the office models used in the simulations. An office is modeled by aggregate descriptors such as the number of users and the relative frequencies of certain commands. These descriptors are used to generate a distributed document base, metaknowledge for each user, and a command sequence.

Although document retrievals may be based on several types of predicates such as authorship and location, only content-based (keyword) retrievals are considered in the simulations since other types of retrievals do not modify the metaknowledge. Commands which do not affect the system state, and thus are not important for learning, are also not simulated.

Each document is given a name and several descriptive keywords. A READ operation with a keyword-based predicate is a retrieval that culminates in the reading of one or more documents from the set returned. In an actual system, a user would then provide a relevance factor on a [0,1] scale for each document read. If the documents were to be retrieved and read by another user, the relevance factors would probably be different. They would also be different if the same user evaluated the same documents in terms of some other keyword. In the simulations, the contents of each document are not stored, only the relevance factor it would be accorded by each user in terms of each descriptive keyword.

If documents are distributed uniformly such that there is no preferred sequence of workstations to search, the metaknowledge will not prove helpful. However, instead of employing an exhaustive search strategy, people in offices (computerized or otherwise) always seem to rely on past experiences to order their searches in a best-first fashion. This suggests that the distribution of knowledge in offices is not uniform.

The correlation among the documents owned by a particular user is modeled in the simulator by biasing the relevance factors associated with the documents. For example, if Jones' documents on compilers are biased from Smith's viewpoint by 0.2, then the relevance factors associating Smith with compilers in documents owned by Jones will have a uniform distribution between 0.2 and 1.0. A bias of −0.4 would cause a distribution between 0 and 0.6. The bias is mutual in that

$$BIAS(Smith,\ Jones,\ compiler)\ =\ BIAS(Jones,\ Smith,\ compiler).$$

A typical document base is shown in Figure 9.4.

```
((user1
  (doc27 (key13 (ob-user1 .0)(ob-user2 .1)(ob-user3 .3))
         (key7  (ob-user1 .7)(ob-user2 .2)(ob-user3 .5))
         (key5  (ob-user1 .7)(ob-user2 .9)(ob-user3 .4)))
  (doc28 (key0  (ob-user1 .1)(ob-user2 .4)(ob-user3 .3))
         (key11 (ob-user1 .2)(ob-user2 .1)(ob-user3 .0))))
   .
   .
   .

 (user3
  (doc37 (key10 (ob-user1 .6)(ob-user2 .5)(ob-user3 .7))
         (key14 (ob-user1 .6)(ob-user2 .3)(ob-user3 .4)))))
```

Figure 9.4: Document base representation in the simulator.

Metaknowledge is stored as shown in the example of Figure 9.5. Each user has metaknowledge which captures his personal view of the dispersion of relevant documents and consists of certainty factors for all combinations of users and keywords, including his view of his own documents. A system of n users and m keywords would result in $n \times m$ certainty factors in each of the n metaknowledge sets.

```
((user1 (key0 (ob-user1 .4) (ob-user2 .4) (ob-user3 .4))
        (key1 (ob-user1 .9) (ob-user2 .7) (ob-user3 .7))
          .
          .
          .
        (key9 (ob-user1 .2) (ob-user2 .2) (ob-user3 .5)))
  .
  .
  .
 (user3 (key0 (ob-user1 .1) (ob-user2 .6) (ob-user3 .4))
          .
          .
        (key9 (ob-user1 .9) (ob-user2 .0) (ob-user3 .4))))
```

Figure 9.5: Metaknowledge representation in the simulator.

Two choices were considered for initializing the metaknowledge at the start of the experiment. The first, an unbiased assignment of certainty factors (say 0.5), would result in ties for determining the best locations to search; if the conflict-resolution strategy is to choose the first location to appear in the list, then the system would tend to learn about users placed at the top of the list earlier than those placed near the end. The second initialization strategy would be to randomly allocate certainty factors, possibly with a uniform distribution, to ensure that the learning progresses in an unbiased fashion. The second strategy was adopted for the simulations reported in this chapter.

9.5.3 Evaluation of the Heuristics

A heuristic function is used to compute how much the current metaknowledge differs from the ideal metaknowledge for a particular system state. The actual search sequence adopted by a user for a keyword-based search would depend on his metaknowledge; individual document bases would be scanned in decreasing order of certainty factors. These sequences are computed from the current metaknowledge base for all search-pairs (user, keyword).

The ideal search sequences, on the other hand, are obtained from the current document base. For reasons explained earlier, documents in the simulated environment are augmented with the relevance factor assignments they would have elicited from users reading them. The best sequences for conducting keyword-based searches are obtained from this information.

The two sets of search sequences are now compared. If the two search sequences for a given search-pair are similar, the distance between them is small. One measure of disorder in a list is the number of exchanges between adjacent list elements required by a bubble-sort procedure to derive an ordered list. In this case the initial list is an actual search sequence derived from the metaknowledge, and the final ordered list is the ideal search sequence obtained from the document base. The measure of disorder of all the search-pairs are added together in order to obtain the heuristic distance between the current and ideal metaknowledge patterns.

This heuristic distance is measured at the beginning of each simulation and after each measurement cycle of ten transactions. For the simulation results shown in Figures 9.6 and 9.7, 450 transactions (commands) were executed and a total of 46 measurements were made. Although the learning heuristics for these simulations were not changed, different office models and usage patterns were employed. The graph of the distance measurements as a function of the number of transactions produces the learning curve for one office environment and one set of learning heuristics. These particular graphs show an improvement in performance obtained by lowering the "move-threshold" to allow documents to migrate more easily to where they are needed. Properties of these graphs, such as time-constants and steady-state values, are used to evaluate the performance of the heuristics in order to derive an optimum set. The resultant heuristics are then used in the MINDS prototype, resulting in a system that learns efficiently.

9.6   Implementation

The MINDS system has been implemented in three forms, consisting of

1. a simulation which executed as a single process written in Franz Lisp. This simulation, described in Section 9.5, was used to design and evaluate the heuristics needed for updating the metaknowledge in the system.

2. a simulation which executed under the VAX/VMS operating system as multiple, communicating Franz Lisp processes. This simulation was used to test the real-

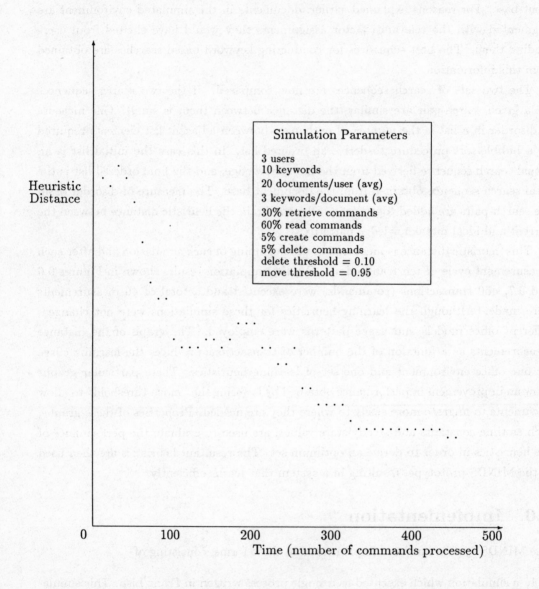

Heuristic Distance

Simulation Parameters

3 users
10 keywords
20 documents/user (avg)
3 keywords/document (avg)
30% retrieve commands
60% read commands
5% create commands
5% delete commands
delete threshold = 0.10
move threshold = 0.95

0   100   200   300   400   500

Time (number of commands processed)

Figure 9.6: Learning (decrease in heuristic distance) as metaknowledge is accumulated while processing document commands.

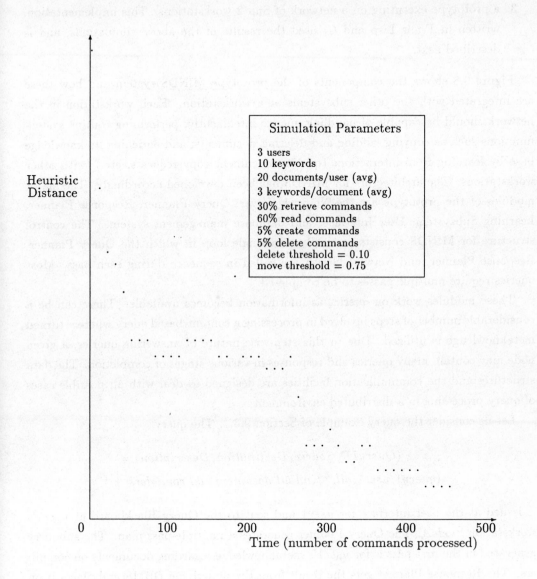

Figure 9.7: Learning (decrease in heuristic distance) as metaknowledge is accumulated while processing document commands.

time interactions of multiple users and insure that the system was not subject to deadlock.

3. a prototype executing on a network of Sun-2 workstations. This implementation, written in Franz Lisp and C, used the results of the above simulations, and is described next.

Figure 9.8 shows the components of the prototype MINDS system and how these are integrated with the other subsystems at a workstation. Each workstation in the network should be capable of handling queries intelligently; performing routine system functions such as copying, adding and deleting documents; and enriching its knowledge base by learning from interactions (queries, document copy requests, etc.) with other workstations. The architecture for MINDS has been developed accordingly. The major modules of the prototype are the Network Server, Query Planner, Response Planner, Learning Subsystem, User Interface, and database management system. The control structure for MINDS consists primarily of a single loop in which the Query Planner, Response Planner, and Network Server are called in sequence during each pass. Most queries require multiple passes to be completed.

These modules work on queries as information becomes available. There can be a considerable number of steps involved in processing a content-based query where returned metaknowledge is utilized. Due to this step-wise nature of answering queries, a given node may contain many queries and responses in various stages of completion. The data structures and the communication facilities are designed to deal with all possible cases of query processing in a distributed environment.

Let us consider the query example of Section 9.3.1. The query

$$(QueryID, Source, Destination, Description) =$$
$$(query1, user1, all, ``find\ all\ documents\ on\ compilers")$$

is issued at the user interface for $user1$ and sent to the Query Blackboard at $user1$'s workstation, $nodeA$. The Query Planner generates a multiple-pass plan. The subquery generated in the first pass is for $user1$'s metaknowledge regarding documents on compilers. The Response Planner gets the result from the underlying DBMS and places it on the Response Blackboard. Assume that $user1$'s metaknowledge on "compilers" is

$$(user1, user1, compiler, 0.6)$$
$$(user1, user3, compiler, 0.3)$$
$$(user1, user7, compiler, 0.8)$$

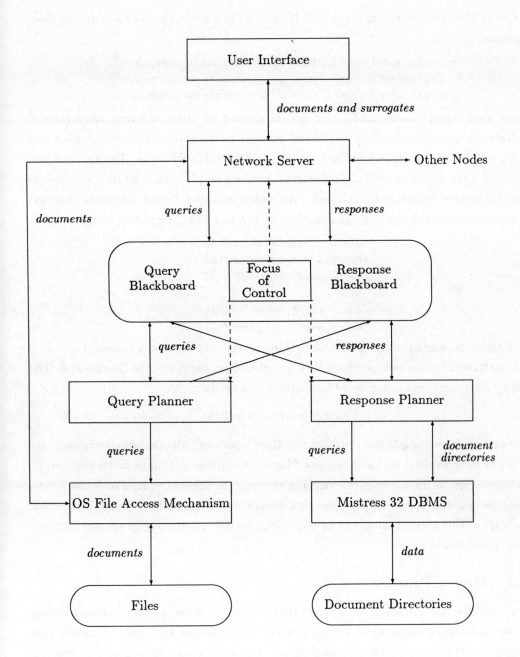

Figure 9.8: The architecture of MINDS at one workstation.

The Query Planner now expands the plan for $query1$ in a second pass by generating three subqueries:

$$(query1a, user1, user1, \text{``}find\ all\ documents\ on\ compilers\text{''})$$
$$(query1b, user1, user3, \text{``}find\ all\ documents\ on\ compilers\text{''})$$
$$(query1c, user1, user7, \text{``}find\ all\ documents\ on\ compilers\text{''})$$

Assume that $user1$, $user3$ and $user7$ are supported by three different workstations. The Network Server transmits $query1b$ and $query1c$ to the respective nodes, $nodeB$ and $nodeC$, where they are placed on their respective Query Blackboards. The Query Planners at all three nodes process the subqueries locally and place the resulting documents on the respective Response Blackboards. At $nodeB$ and $nodeC$, the Response Planners also retrieve the metaknowledge possessed by $user3$ and $user7$ regarding compilers:

$$(user3, user1, compiler, 0.4)$$
$$(user3, user3, compiler, 0.8)$$
$$(user3, user5, compiler, 0.2)$$

and

$$(user7, user1, compiler, 0.4)$$
$$(user7, user7, compiler, 0.5)$$

The Network Servers at $nodeB$ and $nodeC$ transmit the responses, comprising documents and metaknowledge, to $nodeA$ where they are placed on the Response Blackboard. The resulting document sets are ordered by certainty factor as

$$\{result1c, result1a, result1b\}$$

The Network Server sends the result to the User Interface. Metaknowledge from $user3$ and $user7$ may be used by the Response Planner to update certainty factors in $user1$'s metaknowledge, as dictated by the learning strategy. In this example, $user3$ has knowledge about a new user, $user5$. The metaknowledge of $user1$ may be expanded to include knowledge of this user. A subquery to $user5$ is generated recursively in yet another pass of the Query Planner.

9.6.1   Query Planner

The Query Planner is the essence of the MINDS system. When a query is received from the user interface, a sequence of actions is generated to satisfy the query. This sequence typically involves the retrieval of information from the databases of document surrogates and metaknowledge, the accessing of files via the Unix file-management system, the communication of messages through the Network Server, the processing of errors, and the generation of responses to the user interface. This sequence, or plan, is constructed for each allowable input from the user interface.

Structure of the Query Blackboard

All queries, whether from the local User Interface, the remote nodes, or the Response Planner, are queued on the Query Blackboard. There are five queues on this blackboard. The first, Query-buffer-1, stores the initial queries from both local and remote nodes. Query-buffer-2 stores a list of new users to be accessed for multipass planning. This queue is updated by the Response Planner.

Query-buffer-3 stores pointers to documents which are to be copied from other users. For example, the command "Copy all documents where keyword = compilers" would first cause the creation of a set of queries for pointers to documents about "compilers." Responses to these queries would consist of a query identifier and a list of document pointers. These would be stored in this queue by the Response Planner. During a subsequent pass, copy commands would be generated for all items in the queue.

Query-buffer-4 stores the modifications to be made to the metaknowledge records. Query-buffer-5 stores surrogate records to be updated.

Query Planning

A query is first parsed to set up a control block for it. The control block keeps track of the status of each query. A query identifier that is unique for the entire network is generated for each query, and this identifier is the key to the control block. Each query may have single or multiple destinations. Also, some queries may be processed in a single pass, while for others, metaknowledge returned from previous passes is used to locate new users, who are then queried in a subsequent pass.

Queries to the local database are queued for processing by the underlying DBMS (Mistress 32). A response from the DBMS is then queued on the Response Blackboard for processing by the Response Planner. Queries to remote nodes are queued for transmission by the network server. The use of the syntax in Figure 9.9 ensures that commands received by the Query Planner are in the proper format.

9.6.2 Response Planner

The Response Planner is responsible for merging partial responses to queries into a final response which is transmitted to the user interface. It must keep track of which nodes are being queried and which have responded. Metaknowledge received from other nodes in the network is used by the response planner to update the metaknowledge tables. The Response Planner also cooperates with the Query Planner by informing it of other nodes to query. This is accomplished by comparing the certainty factor of its local

```
<query> ::= '(' '(' 'query-id'      <query ID>  ')'
                '(' 'originator'     <user-name> ')'
                '(' 'destinations' <user-name> ')'
                '(' 'message'        <message>   ')' ')';

<message> ::= {'(' <command> {<argument>} ')'} | <copy-file>;

<command> ::= 'select' | 'from' | 'where' | 'update' |
              'set' | 'insert into' | 'values' | 'delete' |
              'create table' | 'drop table' | 'empty table';

<argument> ::= <table-name> | <attribute> {,<attribute>} |
               <requirement> | <value list>| <empty>;

<copy-file> ::= '(' '(copy)' '(' 'from' <pathname list> ')'
                            '(' 'to' <new file name> ')'
                            '(' 'where' <requirement> ')';
```

Figure 9.9: BNF syntax for queries.

metaknowledge to a threshold value used to determine when queries should be generated.

Structure of the Response Blackboard

The format of the Response Blackboard is as follows:

```
Response Blackboard ::= ({<response>})

<response> ::= (('query-id' <query ID>)
                ('users-to-respond' ({<user-name>}))
                ('originator' <user-name>)
                ('status' <complete | nil>)
                ('metaknowledge' ({<reduced-metaknowledge>}))
                ('result' ({<user-name> <result>})))
```

where the users-to-respond field contains a list of users who have not responded to the query, the reduced-metaknowledge is metaknowledge grouped by user, and the results are grouped in descending order of the certainty factor of each respondent.

Response Planner Operation

The response planner performs the following functions:

1. Given a query from the Query Planner, the Response Planner creates a corresponding slot on the Response Blackboard. At the same time, if any local metaknowledge and document surrogates are obtained from the Query Planner, they are placed in the slot. If the response is to a query from a remote node, the status is set to "complete."

2. Based on the metaknowledge, the Response Planner creates a list of users to query. A user is selected if the certainty factor associating him with a given keyword is higher than the specified threshold. This list provides the information needed to update the list of users to be accessed. This list is then placed in a slot on the Response Blackboard.

3. The list of users to be accessed is used to keep track of the users that have not responded to the query. For each response that the Network Server appends to the Response Blackboard, the corresponding respondent is deleted from this list. If the list of users to be accessed is empty, then responses have been returned from all the queried users.

4. For each response slot, the Response Planner determines if all responses are in. If yes, it then synthesizes the results and calculates the updated metaknowledge. If no, the slot is skipped.

5. After the metaknowledge has been recalculated, any user that has a certainty factor higher than the specified threshold is queried.

6. These new users that are to be queried are added to the list of users to be accessed.

7. The new metaknowledge is placed in Query-buffer-4 by the Response Planner. The Query Planner retrieves the metaknowledge from this buffer and updates the metaknowledge table of the database.

8. When the list of users to be accessed is empty and no other users are to be queried, the results are synthesized and the status of the response slot is marked with value "complete." This informs the Network Server that the response is ready to be sent to the originator.

9. After each response slot on the Response Blackboard is examined and processed, control is returned to the Focus of Control module.

Learning Subsystem

When metaknowledge is sent from other nodes in response to a query, the Learning Subsystem updates the local metaknowledge as described in Section 9.4. It first determines its own certainty in the knowledge of the sender in the subject area of concern and uses it to weight the influence this new piece of knowledge will have. It also updates its metaknowledge from user reactions to query responses. It allows other heuristics to be incrementally added to the system as desired.

9.6.3 Network Server

The network server is responsible for establishing network connections among the MINDS systems at different workstations, and for organizing queries and their responses into the proper messaging format. It is used for internode communications as well as user-node interactions. In addition, it maintains information on the status of the other nodes in the network in order to facilitate communications. These communications are conducted according to a formal query language. Its goal is to make all communications outside of a given node transparent to the other modules. Thus, it is the only module which knows about physical device names: the other modules can refer to nodes by just their logical names, such as *user1*.

The Network Server handles both queries and responses. If a received message is a query, then it is placed on the Query Blackboard, whether its source is local or remote. If the message is a response, then the Response Blackboard is updated. Responses, consisting of both results and metaknowledge, will come only from remote nodes, since the user will not issue a response and local responses (from the underlying DBMS) are placed directly on the Response Blackboard by the Query Planner.

The Network Server also transmits completed responses and remote queries. The Query Planner places all queries which should be transmitted into a buffer on the Query Blackboard. The Network Server checks this buffer and transmits the queries until the buffer is empty. The Network Server next checks the Response Blackboard to see if any of the responses are complete. The Network Server then sends the response to the query originator, which could be a local user or a remote node, and cleans the Response Blackboard.

9.6.4 Focus of Control Module

Blackboards store all initial, intermediate and final data and thus provide information about the state of query processing at a node. This state information enables the Focus of

Control module to decide which subsystems to invoke next. These subsystems operate on the blackboard data to produce new data. Some of these operations may be performed concurrently, but others must be executed sequentially. The problem of handling the flow of control among the subsystems in an organized and efficient manner is especially compounded when several queries are active at a single node. The Focus of Control module draws on a body of largely heuristic knowledge to enable the system to function efficiently. Some of the heuristics are geared towards pipelining the queries to avoid synchronization and deadlock problems.

9.6.5 User Interface

The User Interface supports the maintenance of documents and document directories, and consists of a natural language interface and a document handler. This document handler reads, creates, copies, and updates documents and their surrogates. When a new document is created by a user, its surrogate is created by the document handler. Some slots of the surrogate model are filled by default, some are filled from the knowledge the system has about the user, and the rest are filled by the user interactively. When keywords are provided by the user, the document handler maps these into primary keywords using the keyword dictionary and stores the resultant pairs of keywords in the document surrogate.

9.7 Summary

This chapter has described a distributed artificial intelligence system for the organization and retrieval of documents. The system allows queries based on Boolean relations of document attributes, including content, to be processed in parallel by multiple workstations. Each workstation contains an expert query processor and a database management system which interact through a blackboard (containing partial results) and a document directory (containing metaknowledge). The key features are that

- the system uses both knowledge and metaknowledge about the contents and locations of documents—these are acquired dynamically.

- the system uses certainty factors to control the system-wide processing of queries. These certainty factors, each indicating the likelihood that one user will supply relevant information to another, are maintained at each workstation by the DBMS. By using certainty factors, the query processor decides how to schedule the documents from different workstations for inspection by a user.

- a view of the system is maintained at each workstation.

- a model for each user is maintained at each workstation.

These models are implicit in the metaknowledge which is stored at each workstation. The metaknowledge is in the form of associations among workstations, keywords, and documents. This metaknowledge is initialized with default values and changed as the workstation learns about its neighbors through interaction.

The method for learning, i.e., updating the metaknowledge, is embodied in a set of heuristics. These heuristics have been developed with the aid of a simulator, which models users at distributed workstations exchanging information. The simulations yield learning curves which are then used to identify improved heuristics.

Because of the system's ability to update its metaknowledge, it

- is self-initializing, i.e., a new workstation can join the network and accumulate the metaknowledge it needs to efficiently access the resources of the network, without off-line training

- improves its performance as a result of processing queries

- allows cooperation among the workstations, enabling queries to be processed best-first and in parallel.

References

[1] R. D. Bonnell, M. N. Huhns, L. M. Stephens, and U. Mukhopadhyay, "MINDS: Multiple Intelligent Node Document Servers," *Proceedings IEEE First International Conference on Office Automation*, December 1984, pp. 125-136.

[2] _____, "A Distributed Expert System Approach to the Intelligent Filing System," *USCMI Technical Report 84-17*, Department of Electrical and Computer Engineering, University of South Carolina, Columbia, SC, November 1984.

[3] K. J. King and F. J. Maryanski, "Information Management Trends in Office Automation," *Proceedings of the IEEE*, Vol. 71, No. 4, April 1983, pp. 519-528.

[4] R. H. Anderson and J. J. Gillogly, "The RAND Intelligent Terminal Agent (RITA) as a Network Access Aid," *AFIPS Conference Proceedings*, Vol. 45, 1976, pp 501-509.

[5] F. H. Lochovsky, "A Knowledge-Based Approach to Supporting Office Work," *IEEE Database Engineering Bulletin*, Vol. 6, No. 3, September 1983, pp. 43-51.

[6] Y. Vassiliou, M. Jarke, and J. Clifford, "Expert Systems for Business Applications," *IEEE Database Engineering Bulletin*, Vol. 6, No. 4, December 1983, pp. 50-55.

[7] J. D. Yang, M. N. Huhns, and L. M. Stephens, "An Architecture for Control and Communications in Distributed Artificial Intelligence Systems," *IEEE Transactions on Systems, Man, and Cybernetics*, Vol. SMC-15, No. 3, March 1984, pp. 316-326.

[8] M. N. Huhns, L. M. Stephens, and J. D. Yang, "Dynamic Planning for the Control of Distributed Problem Solving," USCMI Technical Report 83-10, University of South Carolina, June 1983.

[9] M. N. Huhns, L. M. Stephens, and R. D. Bonnell, "Control and Cooperation in Distributed Expert Systems," *Proceedings of IEEE Southeastcon*, Orlando, FL, April 1983, pp. 241-245.

[10] R. S. Michalski, J. G. Carbonell, and T. M. Mitchell, eds., *Machine Learning, An Artificial Intelligence Approach, Vol. I*, Tioga Press, Palo Alto, CA, 1983.

[11] R. S. Michalski, J. G. Carbonell, and T. M. Mitchell, eds., *Machine Learning, An Artificial Intelligence Approach, Vol. II*, Morgan Kaufman, Los Altos, CA, 1986.

[12] M. M. Johnson and N. F. Kallus, *Records Management*, Third Edition, South-Western Publishing Company, Cincinnati, Ohio, 1982.

[13] M. M. Zloof, "Clarifying Some Issues in Office Automation," *IEEE Database Engineering Bulletin*, Vol. 6, No. 3, September 1983, pp. 4-11.

[14] M. M. Zloof, "QBE/OBE: A Language for Office and Business Automation," *Computer*, Vol. 14, No. 5, May 1981, pp. 13-22.

[15] M. Stonebraker et al., "Document Processing in a Relational Database System," *ACM Transactions on Office Information Systems*, Vol. 1, No. 2, April 1983, pp. 143-158.

[16] G. A. Curry, "An Overview of the Architectures of the Xerox Star Office System," *IEEE Database Engineering Bulletin*, Vol. 6, No. 3, September 1983, pp. 12-20.

[17] W. T. Coleman, III, "The Visi On Operating Environment," *IEEE Database Engineering Bulletin*, Vol. 6, No. 3, September 1983, pp. 21-30.

[18] J. Slonim, L. J. MacRae, W. E. Mennie, and N. Diamond, "NDX-100: An Electronic Filing Machine for the Office of the Future," *Computer*, Vol. 14, No. 5, May 1981, pp. 24-35.

[19] D. C. Oppen and Y. K. Dalai, "The Clearinghouse: A Decentralized Agent for Locating Objects in a Distributed Environment," *ACM Transactions on Office Information Systems*, Vol. 1, No. 3, July 1983, pp. 230-253.

[20] G. Salton, "Automatic Information Retrieval," *Computer*, Vol. 13, No. 9, September 1981, pp. 41-55.

[21] R. G. Smith and R. Davis, "Frameworks for Cooperation in Distributed Problem Solving," *IEEE Transactions on Systems, Man, and Cybernetics*, Vol. SMC-11, No. 1, January 1981, pp. 61-69.

[22] L. D. Erman and V. R. Lesser, "A Multi-Level Organization for Problem Solving Using Many, Diverse, Cooperating Sources of Knowledge," *Proceedings of the 4th International Joint Conference on Artificial Intelligence*, USSR, September 1975, pp. 483-490.

[23] V. R. Lesser and L. D. Erman, "A Retrospective View of the Hearsay-II Architecture," *Proceedings of the 5th International Joint Conference on Artificial Intelligence*, Cambridge, MA, August 1977, pp. 790-800.

[24] B. Hayes-Roth, "A Blackboard Architecture for Control," *Artificial Intelligence*, Vol. 26, No. 3, July 1985, pp. 251-321.

[25] M. S. Fox, "An Organizational View of Distributed Systems," *IEEE Transactions on Systems, Man and Cybernetics*, Vol. SMC-11, No. 1, January 1981, pp. 70-80.

[26] R. E. Cullingford and M. W. Krueger, "Automated Explanations as a Component of a CAD System," *Proceedings International Conference on Cybernetics and Society*, Cambridge, MA, 1980.

[27] R. R. Tenny and N. R. Sandell, Jr., "Structures for Distributed Decisionmaking," *IEEE Transactions on Systems, Man and Cybernetics*, Vol. SMC-11, No. 8, August 1981, pp. 517-527.

[28] ___, "Strategies for Distributed Decisionmaking," *IEEE Transactions on Systems, Man and Cybernetics*, Vol. SMC-11, No. 8, August 1981, pp. 527-538.

[29] H. E. Pattison, D. D. Corkill, and V. R. Lesser, "Instantiating Descriptions of Organizational Structures," *COINS Technical Report 85-45*, Department of Computer and Information Sciences, University of Massachusetts, Amherst, MA, November 1985.

[30] D. B. Lenat, "Theory Formation by Heuristic Search," *Artificial Intelligence*, Vol. 21, Nos. 1,2, March 1983, pp. 31-59.

[31] D. B. Lenat, "EURISKO: A Program That Learns New Heuristics and Domain Concepts," *Artificial Intelligence*, Vol. 21, Nos. 1,2, March 1983, pp. 61-98.

[32] D. B. Lenat, "The Nature of Heuristics," *Artificial Intelligence*, Vol. 19, No. 2, October 1982, pp. 189-249.

[33] L. A. Rendell, "Conceptual Knowledge Acquisition in Search," *Knowledge Based Learning Systems*, L. Bolc, ed., Springer-Verlag, New York, to appear.

[34] T. G. Dietterich and R. S. Michalski, "Learning and Generalization of Characteristic Descriptions: Evaluation Criteria and Comparative Review of Selected Methods," *Proceedings Sixth International Joint Conference on Artificial Intelligence*, 1979, pp. 223-231.

[35] J. Gaschnig, "Exactly How Good Are Heuristics?: Toward a Realistic Predictive Theory of Best-first Search," *Proceedings Fifth International Joint Conference on Artificial Intelligence*, Cambridge, MA, 1977, pp. 434-441.

[36] M. Bartschi, "An Overview of Information Retrieval Subjects," *IEEE Computer*, Vol. 18, No. 5, 1985, pp. 67-84.

[37] D. H. Kraft and D. A. Buell, "Fuzzy Sets and Generalized Boolean Retrieval Systems," *International Journal of Man-Machine Studies*, Vol. 19, 1983, pp. 45-56.

[38] J. B. Rothnie, N. Goodman, "A Survey of Research and Development in Distributed Database Management," *Proceedings IEEE Third International Conference on Very Large Data Bases*, 1977, pp. 30-44.

[39] B. G. Buchanan, E. H. Shortliffe, "Reasoning Under Uncertainty," *Rule-Based Expert Systems*, Addison-Wesley Publishing Co., Reading, MA, 1984.

[40] K. P. Eswaran, "Placement of Records in a File and File Allocation in a Computer Network," *Information Processing 74*, IFIPS, North Holland Publishing Co., 1974.

[41] M. E. S. Loomis and G. J. Popek, "A Model for Data Base Distribution," *IEEE Symposium on Trends and Applications*, 1976, pp. 162-169.

[42] S. Mahmoud and J. S. Riordan, "Optimal Allocation of Resources in Distributed Information Networks," *ACM Transactions on Data Bases*, Vol. 1, No. 1, March 1976, pp. 66-78.

[43] D. B. Lenat, F. Hayes-Roth, and P. Klahr, "Cognitive Economy In a Fluid Task Environment," in R. S. Michalski, ed., *Proceedings of the International Machine Learning Workshop*, Urbana, IL, 1983.

Michael N. Huhns
Microelectronics and Computer Technology Corporation
3500 West Balcones Center Drive
Austin, TX 78759

Uttam Mukhopadhyay
General Motors Research Labs
Warren, MI 48090-9057

Larry M. Stephens and Ronald D. Bonnell
Center for Machine Intelligence
University of South Carolina
Columbia, SC 29208

Chapter 10

Manufacturing Experience with the Contract Net

H. Van Dyke Parunak

Abstract

We are implementing a control system for a discrete manufacturing environment that partitions tasks using a negotiation protocol like the contract net described by Smith and Davis [24,25,26,3]. The application domain differs in interesting ways from those to which contract nets have previously been applied.

This report outlines our architecture, summarizes some differences between the factory floor and other problem domains, and discusses how we accommodate these distinctive features.

10.1 A Contract Net for Manufacturing Control

To set the rest of the discussion in context, we summarize briefly

- the contract net model,

- some previous applications of the model, and

- our architecture for a factory control system that uses this model.

10.1.1 Review of the Contract Net Model

The contract net models transfer of control in a distributed system with the metaphor of negotiation among autonomous intelligent beings. The net consists of a set of *nodes* that

285

negotiate with one another through a set of *messages*. *Nodes* represent the distributed computing resources to be managed. In any given transaction, three classes of nodes may be identified.

- The *Manager* is the node that identifies a task to be done, and assigns it to other nodes for execution.

- The *Bidders* are nodes that offer to perform a task.

- The *Contractor* is a successful bidder, one whose bid has been accepted by the manager.

Nodes communicate by means of different classes of *Messages*:

- A manager issues a *Task announcement* describing the task to be done and the criteria for bids.

- Bidders send *Bids* to announce their willingness and ability to perform a task.

- The *Award* message from the manager to the successful bidder establishes that bidder as the contractor for the task.

- The contractor sends an *Acknowledgment* of the award, either accepting or rejecting it.

- The contractor sends *Reports* to the manager announcing status or termination of a task.

- The manager may send a *Termination* to a contractor to interrupt its performance of a contract prematurely.

- Idle nodes may broadcast their availability with a *Node Availability Announcement*.

10.1.2 Some Examples of the Contract Net

Several previous applications of negotiation for control offer helpful comparisons for our architecture. These include

- vehicle tracking in a distributed sensor system, and

- allocating tasks in a network of CPU's.

286

The Distributed Sensor System

Much of the original work with the contract net is defined in the context of a Distributed Sensor System (DSS), such as one might use in air traffic control. Individual nodes are able to carry out one or more specific tasks. Signal collectors invite bids from sensors, and evaluate them on sensory capabilities as well as geographical location. A node responsible for monitoring a local area solicits bids from nodes that can integrate information from sensors, and evaluates bids on the basis of the geographical location of the bidders. An area manager, confronted with sensory information, invites bids from vehicle managers to find which one is best suited to manage the sensed object. For a detailed description see [3].

Several features of the DSS are important for comparison in this paper.

- The system interfaces with the real world through nodes that have sensory capabilities. These "bottom level" nodes are distinct from the other nodes in the system, since only the sensory nodes can directly "see" the real world.

- Both the negotiation process and the tasks being allocated are computational in nature.

- Because of the diversity of tasks to be performed, the parameters on which bids are selected differ depending on the task, and are specified by the manager when announcing a task.

Multiprocessor Task Allocation

Negotiation has been extensively studied as a means for distributing tasks among the members of a distributed system of CPU's [20,27,28]. Each node accepts only those tasks whose execution it can guarantee by a specified deadline. If it discovers tasks that it cannot guarantee, it uses either direct negotiation or information retained from previous negotiations to find another node that can guarantee their execution.

- In this application, the real world is identical with the computational world, and there is no distinguished class of bottom level nodes to interface with it.

- Both negotiation and execution are computational.

- The criteria for assigning a task to a node do not vary from node to node. They are the size and estimated run-time of the task, its due date, and the current load of nodes under consideration. Thus bids can be more stereotyped than in a DSS.

287

- The consistency of bidding criteria also allows general classes of information to be spread throughout the system before a task appears, so that some tasks can be assigned without bidding.

- The system attempts to meet real-time constraints by guaranteeing tasks as they arrive. It uses heuristics to avoid combinatorial explosion in deciding whether each successive task can be guaranteed, given the set of tasks that have already been guaranteed.

10.1.3 Factory Control with the Contract Net

YAMS (Yet Another Manufacturing System) is a prototype factory control system that apportions tasks by negotiation. Parunak *et al.* [16,18] contain a more detailed description. For our purposes, we can summarize

- some constraints that the system is designed to satisfy,

- its overall architecture and general functioning, and

- details of its present implementation.

Design Constraints

Several domain constraints lead to the use of distributed AI in general, and the contract net in particular. YAMS can control, not just a single localized set of operations, but several factories widely separated from one another. Many operations on the factory floor must be controlled in real time, faster than a wide-area network can respond, so each plant (and in most cases, each machine) needs its own CPU. The system must also coordinate the actions of each machine and factory, so these CPU's need to talk with one another. Thus YAMS is *distributed*.

The problem of factory control can be formulated as a search through a space whose dimensions include the equipment available at a site, the products to be manufactured, and available resources such as time, inventory, and storage space. Traditional factory software is written with the knowledge of these parameters, and many decisions among them can be built into the code, drastically reducing the search space. The resulting code is tailored to one factory and one product line, and modification is expensive. In YAMS, the same software runs at each site. The individual characteristics of each factory are recorded, not in the control logic, but in local databases. As a result, the control code must cope with the full complexity of the problem space, yet still make decisions in real time. The British Museum algorithm and traditional optimization techniques are too slow. YAMS uses techniques of *artificial intelligence* to cut the combinatorial knot.

The factory floor is a stochastic environment. There is often considerable variance in the time required for individual operations. The resources required for an operation at a workstation may depend in a complex way on the current load of that workstation. Machines may fail completely, and their tasks may have to be taken over by other machines less well suited to the work. As a result, static models of the capabilities of individual workstations are unreliable. We need to monitor the status of resources continually, so as to adapt to changes. Yet we want to hide as much of the local state of each resource as possible, to reduce pathological coupling between components of the system. *Negotiation* allows a node to disclose as much of its state as needed for a particular decision, without making its complete state continually visible to the rest of the system.

The YAMS Architecture

YAMS models a manufacturing enterprise as a hierarchy of workcells, or functional groups of machinery. This model corresponds closely to the traditional manufacturing view of a corporation as a hierarchical system of plants, flexible manufacturing systems (FMS's), and machines. Exhibit 10.1 shows a possible instance of YAMS.

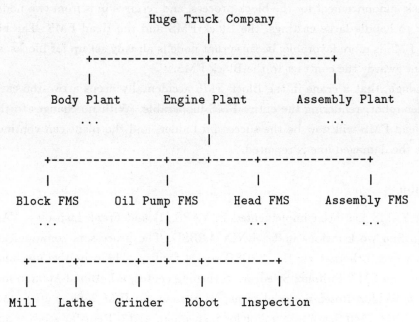

```
                  Huge Truck Company
                         |
       +-----------------+-----------------+
       |                 |                 |
   Body Plant       Engine Plant     Assembly Plant
      ...                |                ...
                         |
       +-----------------+-----+-------+---------------+
       |                 |             |               |
   Block FMS        Oil Pump FMS    Head FMS       Assembly FMS
      ...                |             ...             ...
                         |
    +------+--------+---+----+-----------+
    |      |        |        |           |
  Mill   Lathe   Grinder   Robot     Inspection
```

Exhibit 10.1

289

Each *node* in this diagram corresponds to a node in a contract net, and to a *workcell* of a manufacturing company. Workcells at the bottom of the hierarchy are also called *workstations*.

This hierarchy records composition, not control. Each node is a component of its parent, and is in turn composed of its children. YAMS views each node as a negotiating entity that can communicate not only with its parent and children, but also with its siblings. (On the need for lateral communications within a composition hierarchy, see [22,23].)

Each node has a library of process plans describing the processes it knows how to perform. These process plans refer in turn to other processes, processes that often are not known to the node hosting the main process. Nodes use negotiation to find other nodes to execute processes that they cannot handle themselves.

The existence of process plans means that the problem decomposition phase of distributed problem solving is trivial. The process plan constitutes an *a priori* division of the problem, available to the entire system at the outset.

For example, assume that the Engine Plant is a contractor to execute a "make-engine" process. Consulting its process library, it finds that the first step in making an engine is the process "make-block," and that it does not know how to perform this operation. It broadcasts a task announcement for the block process, and receives bids from two nodes that know how to handle large castings, the Block FMS and the Head FMS. The bid from the Block FMS is more favorable, because that node is already set up for blocks, so the Engine Plant awards the contract to the Block FMS.

Suppose, though, that a crane in the Block FMS accidentally drops a two-ton casting on a transfer robot, rendering the entire FMS inoperable. With no changes to the software, the Head FMS will now be the successful bidder, and the plant can continue operating while the damaged line is repaired.

Implementation

A prototype of YAMS has been implemented in YAPS [1] and Franz Lisp on a VAX 11/785 and two Sun workstations under UNIX 4.2BSD. The processors communicate with one another over Ethernet via the 4.2BSD socket facility. The primitive machines controlled include an SMT-Pullmax Swedturn 6 turning center, a LeBlond-Makino machining center, a Weldun-Bosch material transport system, an IBM 7565 gantry robot for assembly, an IBM 7540 Scara arm robot for inspection, and a Remstar storage and retrieval system with a custom-built transfer robot. The machines are interconnected with a network described in [11], which is being upgraded incrementally to an IEEE

802.4 broadband network supporting MAP (Manufacturing Automation Protocol) [9]. These machines are under the immediate supervision of a variety of machine controllers, which are microprocessors specially configured to manipulate machinery. The floor-level microprocessors in our laboratory include a VME-1000, a Remstar MP3000, a Fanuc 11, and an Allen-Bradley GA and Programmable Logic Controllers (PLC 3, PLC 2/15) communicating over a Data Highway.

10.2 Analyzing the Factory Problem

Factory control differs from many other problem domains. In this section, we examine three areas of difference.

- *Volatility* measures how likely the system being controlled is to change during operation.

- *Specialization* measures the extent to which the nodes of the system are tailored for special tasks, to the exclusion of others.

- *Medium* is more qualitative than volatility and specialization. It describes the ontological realm being manipulated by the system.

10.2.1 System Volatility

Real-life systems are subject to change. Nodes may be added or deleted; the capacity of a single node may change; a node's load may vary, affecting its availability for other work. The more distributed a system is, the less individual nodes know about the state of their colleagues. Negotiation offers a mechanism for making decisions in the face of such lack of knowledge.

For example, in a Distributed Sensing System, the vehicles being tracked move from one area to another in ways that the DSS cannot predict. With negotiation, a node can take responsibility for those vehicles that it can see most clearly, and the assignment of nodes to vehicles can change as vehicles move about.

Assume that a system changes very slowly. If we know that the system is stable, negotiation is an inefficient way to manage it. Davis and Smith [3] point out one example of this inefficiency by showing how reliance only on local knowledge can yield suboptimal performance. It is worth our while to learn about the overall state of a stable system, so that this global knowledge can help guide its performance.

If a system changes very rapidly, there is no point to gathering global knowledge, for it will be obsolete before we have a chance to use it. Only local knowledge is current, and negotiation offers a reasonable way to use that local knowledge in achieving reasonable performance.

The choice between these two strategies depends on whether the system is changing "slowly" or "rapidly." A reasonable time scale in each case is some measure of location (such as mean, median, or mode) of the distribution of transaction times in the system. If a typical subtask takes on the order of minutes to perform, then a system that is stable for days at a time probably merits global analysis, while one that changes every few minutes can profit from negotiation.

To allow a more quantitative discussion, we distinguish between *tasks* and *task classes*.

- A *task class* is defined intensionally as a process plan, or extensionally as the set of all tasks that require the same series of steps for their performance. One task class might be "Make a widget," while another might be "Make a gizmo." A task class is not bound to a specific time of performance or specific pieces of inventory.

- A *task* is an instance of a task class, for example, "Make widget #24857" or "Make the gizmo that Joe Green ordered on May 23, 1985." Each step in the execution of a task begins at a specific time, and the task consumes and produces particular, identifiable units of inventory.

The concept of a task class is useful in discussing the abstract performance of a node. Let

d_{ij} = the median duration of task class i on node j;

c_{ij} = the median time between changes of node j that affect task class i.

Then we define the *volatility* of a node with respect to task class i: $v_{ij} = d_{ij}/c_{ij}$

Systems with high volatility invite a bidding strategy. Low volatility suggests the distribution of global knowledge. The factory falls in the middle.

- Certain aspects of the factory have extremely low volatility:

  - Arrangement of machinery on the floor;

  - General capabilities of a particular machine tool;

  - The costs of basic resources (such as power and labor).

- Others have very high volatility, particularly in a flexible manufacturing environment:

  - Load on a particular machine;

- Available inventory space for work in process and finished goods;
- Workstation tooling and fixturing;
- Product mix.

- A third category of change is relatively infrequent, but when it does occur, the system must respond rapidly to avoid loss of productivity. A particular machine tool may fail infrequently, but when it does fail, the system must continue to operate.

10.2.2 Specialization

Much of the motivation for the contract net comes from the need to make efficient use of multiprocessing systems, whose nodes are logically similar to one another. Their different abilities arise from differences in their states. The net provides a way to exploit differences in this state more efficiently than a global state reporting scheme would.

For example, in a DSS, many nodes control sensors. These nodes are computationally identical, and differ only in their geographical location and in the response characteristics of the sensors that they monitor. There may be a hundred different nodes all capable of tracking a jeep. Similarly, in a multiprocessor resource, any task can run on any CPU, provided the processor's load is consistent with the task's requirements and deadline. In both cases, negotiation allows the system to compare the state of a candidate node with the requirements of a task.

In the factory, nodes commonly differ in mechanical structure as well as in their state. Certain task classes may be physically restricted to certain nodes, and this information is typically available independently of any run of the system. Negotiation is useful in partitioning tasks among nodes with similar capabilities. There is no point, though, in using it to offer tasks to nodes that can never run them.

Let

N = total # of nodes in the system;
n_i = # of nodes able to perform task class i.

For later discussion, it is useful to characterize the *system specialization* for a given task class i: $s_i = (N - n_i)/n_i$. In general, the higher the specialization of a node for a task class, the less important is bidding as a strategy for assigning tasks to that node. The lower the specialization of a node, the more need there is for it to compete with other nodes for a task in order to allocate resources effectively.

There is an ironic exception to these generalizations. Ramamritham and Stankovic [20] observe from simulations that if nodes are too similar to one another in capability and

293

in task load, bidding is not effective in meeting real time constraints, because a task that cannot be guaranteed on one node will find approximately the same conditions on other nodes. This insight suggests that negotiation is especially useful in systems whose nodes have overlapping but not identical capabilities. The nature of machine tool specialization in discrete manufacturing industries tends to meet this criterion. Even two machines of the same make and model are often not identical in their capabilities. They may differ in their fixturing and tooling, as well as in their maintenance schedule and the actual degree of accuracy they can hold. Our simple model of node specialization does not reflect these nuances, but our bidding scheme does allow managers to specify precisely the categories of information required in a bid, so that such differences can be taken into account. A more rigid characterization of node capability, such as that proposed by Shaw and Whinston [21], is likely to model many nodes as effectively identical to one another, leaving the system unable to select the best contractor from the available information.

10.2.3   Medium

Applications of contract nets such as DSS or task allocation on a multiprocessor work almost entirely in the domain of information management. The net is not only the control medium, but also the performance medium. The reports issued by a contractor not only synchronize the negotiation mechanism, but also often furnish the information that the contract was established to provide. We call such a system *homogeneous*.

In a *heterogeneous* system, such as a factory control system, the control and performance media are decoupled. The net serves only for control and status monitoring. The goal of the system, producing parts, takes place in a world of machine tools and material transport systems known to the net only by way of abstractions and models.

There are three noteworthy differences between the control and performance media in the factory.

1. The control medium is *faster* than the performance medium. The time scale for negotiation is marked in fractions of a second, while most transportation and processing operations require minutes or hours.

2. The control medium is *more reliable* than the performance medium. Mechanical components are more prone to failure than are electronic ones, and repair is more complex, since machine tools are too expensive to be swapped out as one can do with a defective board of digital logic.

3. The control medium is *disjoint* from the performance medium. Interactions among machines in the performance medium are invisible to the control medium unless

294

they are explicitly modeled there. In a homogeneous system, this mismatch is less likely to occur.

10.3 Tailoring the Contract Net for the Factory Floor

The factory floor differs from contract net domains such as DSS in volatility, specialization, and medium. This section discusses some adjustments that an implementation must make to deal with these differences. In particular, we consider

- the impact of volatility and specialization on when to bid and when not to bid,

- the impact of volatility on the usefulness of global knowledge, and the coordination of local knowledge (obtained by negotiation) and global knowledge in scheduling, and

- some effects of heterogeneity between the control and performance media.

10.3.1 To Bid or Not To Bid

Negotiation serves well for systems with high volatility, while fixed task assignments are efficient for systems with low volatility. Factory control lies between these extremes, and invites a hybrid of these strategies that we call *audience restriction*. In this section we

- outline the need for audience restriction,

- identify two requirements that it imposes on the contract net protocol,

- analyze the impact of the strategy on communications overhead, and

- compare audience restriction with focused addressing, another scheme for reducing the need for negotiation.

The Need for Audience Restriction

An early implementation of YAMS relied entirely on broadcast task announcements and negotiation to find contractors for tasks in the factory. Because the floor configuration has low volatility, this approach wastes communication bandwidth. In later systems, each node broadcasts task announcements for tasks it has not previously put out for bids, and remembers who responds as a function of the requested task. It maintains a set called the *audience* for each task class that it has announced, recording the nodes that have responded to bids on tasks of that class. Later announcements for similar tasks go

295

only to nodes in the audience. The audience is redefined after each round of bidding to include only those nodes that participate in that round. We call this strategy "audience restriction."

In extreme cases, only one node may respond to announcements of a certain task class. When the manager learns this, it issues directed contracts to the node for future tasks of that class, reducing communications overhead further. When it receives a node availability announcement, it resumes negotiation, to take advantage of possible new resources.

Requirements of Audience Restriction

Audience restriction requires two conventions among participating nodes.

1. Smith [24] provides for the system to be driven by task announcements when the net is lightly loaded, and by node availability announcements when the net is heavily loaded. Audience restriction requires that nodes issue node availability announcements not only when they perceive the net to be heavily loaded, but also when they join the system, or when their capacity increases. When one node receives a node availability announcement from another, it adds that other node to all the audiences that it is maintaining. Thus later task announcements will give the new or enhanced node a chance to compete.

2. A node may be too loaded to bid for a task that it is otherwise qualified to process. Yet if it does not bid, audience restriction will shut it out from learning about future tasks of the same sort. Nodes must agree on some mechanism for nodes to stay on the audience list without offering to work. In our implementation, a special form of bid message, the *null bid*, means "I don't want to do this task, but I would like to learn of future tasks of the same class." Another approach [20] provides a separate *status* message that the manager can use to query silent nodes about their capacity without asking them to make a commitment. Null bids have the advantage of letting potential contractors, who know their own capabilities best, decide whether or not to continue subscribing to bids.

Performance Analysis

Both of these conventions save on task announcements at the expense of other messages (node availability announcements and null bids). We can show that for systems with the characteristics of a factory, audience restriction is worthwhile. Let

d_{ij} = median duration of task class i on node j;

c_{ij} = median time between changes of node j that affect task class i;

v_{ij} = volatility of node j with respect to task class i

$\quad = d_{ij}/c_{ij}$;

N = total # of nodes in the system;

n_i = # of nodes able to perform task class i;

s_i = specialization of task class i

$\quad = (N - n_i)/n_i$;

f_i = frequency with which task class i is required in the system

$\quad$ = rate at which task announcements for task class i are broadcast.

To keep the problem tractable, we make several assumptions and simplifications.

- All nodes that can do a given task class i require the same amount of time d_i to do it: $\forall j.d_{ij} = d_i$.

- Similarly, the median time between changes that affect a given task class i is the same c_i for all nodes: $\forall j.c_{ij} = c_i$.

- Thus volatility is a function only of task class, not of node, v_i.

These three simplifications have the effect of removing all node subscripts from the notation. Further, we will focus our attention on a single task class, thus eliminating the need for task class subscripts as well.

There are further useful assumptions.

- We are considering a task class for which an audience set has been established. That is, we are looking at the steady-state behavior of the system, not its start-up characteristics.

- In reality, a node might bid for more business than it can handle, reasoning that other nodes will probably win some of that business. Our nodes do not overbid in this way, but offer bids only for as much work as they can handle.

- There are more task announcements than any single node can handle by itself, so that there is some null bidding.

- Each node can do only one task at a time. Exceptions to this assumption exist in real life, but the simplification makes analytical description of the system simpler.

297

With these parameters, we can compare the communications traffic saved through using audience restriction, with the overhead of null bids and node availability announcements that it generates.

Audience restriction saves traffic by addressing task announcements only to nodes that can potentially service them, rather than to all nodes: $Savings = f(N - n)$.

Audience restriction introduces two costs:

1. $CostNAA$ is the number of extra node availability announcements required.

2. $CostNB$ is the number of null bids required.

We wish to examine the behavior of the ratio

$$CostRatio = \frac{CostNAA + CostNB}{Savings}$$

$CostNAA$ is just the number of nodes capable of performing a task class, times the rate of change of such a node. This rate in turn is the inverse of c, so $CostNAA = n/c$.

To determine $CostNB$, we note that a node can issue new bids at the rate $1/d$ (under our assumption that a node does only one task at a time). Since task announcements are coming at a rate f, the node must issue refusals at the rate $f - (1/d)$. Thus we can compute

$$CostRatio = \frac{(n/c) + (f - (1/d))}{f(N - n)}$$

It is instructive to simplify this in two cases.

First, assume that the system is fully loaded. Then the rate of bidding times the number of bidding nodes is just equal to the rate of task announcement, yielding the identities

$$f = (n/d)$$

$$cf = (cn/d) = (n/v)$$

Substituting and simplifying, we have

$$CostRatio = \frac{1}{ns}(v + 1 - \frac{1}{n})$$

This result shows that the cost of audience restriction decreases as volatility decreases and specialization increases. For reasonable factory-like situations, the ratio is strongly in favor of audience restriction. For example, in a factory with twenty nodes, five of which can perform a function, if the volatility is 1/24 (reflecting a task duration of one hour and failure once a day), the cost ratio is less than 0.06.

Now we turn to the case where the factory is not fully loaded. In other words, some of the nodes capable of performing a task are not needed. Let x be the number of extra nodes for the task class in question. Then we have the identities

$$f = ((n - x)/d)$$
$$cf = ((n - x)/v)$$

Substituting and simplifying yields

$$CostRatio = \frac{1}{ns}(\frac{nv - 1}{n - x} + 1))$$

In our hypothetical factory, assume that only two of the five nodes are really needed to keep up with demand. Then the cost ratio is less than 0.04. The decrease in cost ratio reflects the drop in null bids due to excess factory capacity. That is, since each node is underloaded most of the time, it rarely needs to issue null bids.

A similar argument shows that if the factory is overloaded, the cost ratio goes up because of the increase in null bids.

Audience Restriction and Focused Addressing

Ramamritham and Stankovic [20] propose a technique called *Focused Addressing* to reduce communications overhead in negotiation for task allocation in a distributed multiprocessor computing environment. When nodes submit bids, they provide not only information relevant to the task for which they are competing, but also general information on their surplus capacity. Managers use this information to assign other tasks to these nodes without going through the negotiation process.

Focused addressing is a feasible strategy for allocating CPU tasks because the criteria for matching a task to a processor are stereotyped. Once a manager knows a node's surplus CPU time, it can reach reasonable conclusions about what other tasks the node can handle. At very little expense, a node can include a measure of its surplus CPU capacity on every bid.

In a factory control system, the criteria for assigning tasks to nodes are more complex and vary with the task. There is no single measure of capacity that nodes can routinely report to their managers as a basis for focused addressing. Audience restriction identifies favored nodes on the basis, not of a single capacity measure, but of their previous interest in tasks of a given type. Focused addressing effectively indexes from new tasks to nodes on the basis of node loading. Audience restriction indexes on the basis of task type.

Shaw and Whinston [21] propose to control a flexible manufacturing system with bidding over a fixed set of criteria:

- distance between two successive cells in the manufacturing sequence,

- estimated processing time, and

- loading of the bidders.

Focused addressing could be used in such a system, but we have already mentioned reasons to suspect that using a fixed set of criteria may render the bidding process ineffective.

10.3.2 Local vs. Global Scheduling

As Davis and Smith [3] point out, negotiation allows locally optimal use of nodes, but does not guarantee overall optimality. When problem decomposition and task load are not known ahead of time, one is happy to have a system that runs at all, and optimality is not a central issue.

The volatile aspects of the factory lead us to value negotiation, and tolerate the locality of its solutions. Other aspects, though, are relatively stable. For instance, problem decomposition is known very well, and overall factory layout does not change unexpectedly. A factory control system should be able to exploit this knowledge for global advantage, while retaining the flexibility in the face of change that negotiation offers.

A volatile environment requires local scheduling through negotiation, while a stable environment allows global scheduling and the probability of better optimization. In this section, we

- define the notion of a schedule,

- review some scheduling anomalies that can result from the absence of global knowledge, and

- discuss various strategies for merging elements of a predetermined global schedule with a real-time local scheduling mechanism like the contract net.

What is a Schedule?

Scheduling in a manufacturing environment is the process of determining what happens when and where. More precisely, it selects a subset of the Cartesian product of three sets.

- There is a set of tasks (**What**) that need to be done. These are not mutually exclusive. They include global tasks ("Make widget 3295") and primitive tasks from which the global tasks are constructed ("Order more screws"). **What** is a set of tasks, not of task classes.

- There is a set of times (**When**), usually the non-negative real numbers, where 0 represents some reference origin (say, the opening of the plant) and the other values represent displacements after that origin in a standard unit of time (say, seconds).

- There is a set of locations (**Where**), intuitively, workstations in the factory. For our purposes, we lump in the "how" with **Where**. That is, we treat a machine that performs two distinct processes as two virtual machines. Inventory is also a subset of **Where**, since parts and subassemblies are resources consumed in performing tasks.

A schedule is a subset of **What** × **When** × **Where**. Intuitively, it specifies the resources that each task needs and when it needs them.

The selection of a schedule implies the existence of a cost function mapping schedules to the real numbers, thus inducing a total order on the set of all schedules and allowing us to prefer one schedule to another. Scheduling seeks to find a schedule for which the cost function is minimal.

It seems reasonable to conjecture that a factory is formally equivalent to a Turing machine [17], so that in the general case no more efficient way exists to determine the result of its "execution" than to run it (or simulate it). Nevertheless, technologies like MRP [13], finite resource planning (*e.g.*, OPT, discussed by Jacobs [10]), or constraint-directed scheduling [6] offer heuristics to aid in selecting a schedule.

Problems with Local Scheduling

Davis and Smith [3] identify two types of scheduling anomalies that can arise in a contract net, because decisions are made with only local knowledge. In terms of our model of scheduling, these reflect three kinds of ignorance.

- *Temporal ignorance* is limited knowledge of the **What** × **When** relation implicit in the schedule.

- *Spatial ignorance* is limited knowledge of the **What** × **Where** relation.

- *Loading ignorance* is limited knowledge of the **Where** × **When** relation.

One of the anomalies discussed by Davis and Smith [3] arises from *temporal ignorance*. Nodes can only see task announcements and bids that have already arrived, not those that are about to arrive. A node may bid on a task for which it is marginally suited and thus commit resources to the extent that it cannot later bid on a task for which it is much better suited. Or a manager may accept a bid moments before a much more attractive one appears.

The second anomaly concerns two nodes (X, Y) bidding on contracts offered by two managers (A, B). Imagine that the resulting bids have these values:

	A	B
X	0.9	0.8
Y	0.8	0.2

In a simple contract net, X would receive both tasks, and Y would be left idle. Yet, if Y is lightly loaded and X is relatively busy, we might prefer to give A's task to Y and let X concentrate on B's task. Because the solution involves compromising local preferences for a global advantage, we call this anomaly the "compromise anomaly." It can be viewed as resulting either from spatial ignorance or from loading ignorance, with differing implications for its solution.

Spatial ignorance arises because nodes have knowledge only of contracts to which they are party, and cannot take advantage of the details of other contracts in making their own decisions. Y wants to keep busy, and very much prefers A's task to B's. If Y knows that X is a competitor for A's task, its preference for A will lead it to bid more aggressively for that task. Of course, X will also know of Y's competition. But in the compromise anomaly, X does not have a strong preference between the two tasks, so it will not be as aggressive as Y in bidding on A's task. In the presence of more knowledge about **What × Where**, the resulting bids might come out more like this, so that each node receives one contract:

	A	B
X	0.8	0.8
Y	0.9	0.2

Loading ignorance arises because nodes do not know how busy other nodes are. Distributing knowledge about **Where × When** can help solve the compromise anomaly in two ways.

1. If X knows that Y is idle, or Y knows that X is busy, the tendency of Y to bid more aggressively than X will be strengthened, increasing the likelihood that each contractor will outbid the other on exactly one contract.

2. Managers can also use loading knowledge to resolve the compromise anomaly. When two bids are close together (as are the bids of X and Y for A's task), a manager can factor knowledge of the contractors' respective loads into the award decision.

The nature of the contract net requires a broadcast capability for distributing task announcements, and many implementations use a bus for all traffic, including bids and awards. In such a system, nodes can reduce their ignorance of one another by eavesdropping on the net. By monitoring bids, a node can learn who its competitors are for various task classes, and by monitoring awards, it can track their loading. The possible politics of such a system quickly become fascinating, and very complex. One can imagine two competing nodes, each waiting until the last possible moment to submit its bid in the hopes of peeking at the other's bid first, together jeopardizing the timely performance of the entire system. There is room for much research into the effective management and engineering of negotiating systems. Until we understand eavesdropping and its side effects better, the disciplined use of global information is probably a preferable strategy for building real-life systems with effects on property and human safety.

Merging Local and Global Schedules

For a domain like the factory floor with reasonably low volatility and relatively high specialization, some of the scheduling anomalies introduced by the contract net can be avoided or made less damaging by relieving the three kinds of ignorance (temporal, spatial, and loading) that arise in the most general applications. We can relieve this ignorance by distributing throughout the net copies of a global schedule produced by a technology such as MRP or OPT. Nodes can then use this information in the ways outlined in the last section to offer more intelligent bids and issue more intelligent awards.

The problem with this approach is the stochasticity that leads to the need for the contract net in the first place. Changes in resource availability not only introduce the need for negotiation, but render previous global schedules invalid. In fact, it is proverbial among shop foremen that the schedules produced by the front office are out of date the moment they hit the floor. If a global schedule contains wrong information, nodes are in fact still in ignorance, though they think they are not.

Two insights can let nodes make use of global schedules, in spite of uncertainty about their accuracy.

1. The entire system can adopt a policy of *turnpike scheduling*, which tends to restore the validity of a global schedule whenever the system strays from it.

2. Some *subsets* of the information in a global schedule are more likely to become wrong than others. Nodes can rely on those aspects that are least likely to change.

Turnpike scheduling is the recognition that under some circumstances, the best way to cope with a scheduling disturbance is to return as quickly as possible to a previously

303

planned schedule, rather than rescheduling the entire course from present location to destination. The name comes from the analogy of a highway system. If a driver en route from Chicago to Los Angeles somehow wanders off the interstate highway, the best correction may be not to plan a new route from the present location to the destination, but to get back on the interstate as quickly as possible. In scheduling problems, the global schedule is the turnpike.

The conditions under which return to the turnpike is at least as good as rescheduling are discussed in [2]. The same theory in another domain is available in [12], among other places. Even if return to the turnpike is not optimal, it still may be better than not having a global schedule at all. Global schedules are expensive to formulate. (If they were free, they could be recomputed after every change in the system, and there would be no need for negotiation.) The benefits gained from having some distributed knowledge may outweigh the disadvantages of following what has become a suboptimal schedule. The tradeoffs are the subject of continuing research.

The *subset* approach recognizes that some information from a global schedule is useful even if the schedule as a whole becomes obsolete. For example, the precise times in **What** × **When** may be in error, but the ordering of events reflected in the schedule is much less variable, depending on the physical realities of the product being manufactured. (That is, rough machining of a surface must always precede finish grinding, whether it starts when scheduled or two hours late.)

One could implement the subset strategy by computing a full global schedule, then observing it become obsolete, reasoning about the information that is still valid, and using that information. It is simpler to compute only a very coarse schedule at the global level, embodying constraints that are general enough not to become obsolete. As nodes closer to the factory floor begin to execute, they take advantage of their more detailed knowledge of the factory state to refine the global schedule. This strategy, which has been described as "opportunistic scheduling" [4,5,14], uses the principle of least commitment to play the complexity and uncertainty of the environment off against one another. It is one basis of the hierarchical constraint-directed scheduling provided by ISIS [6]. Parunak *et al.* [17] gives more detail on the approach.

10.3.3   Heterogeneous Media and Factory Control

The control and performance media in a factory control system are heterogeneous. Both provide communications among nodes, but because they are disjoint, they are likely to conflict with one another unless care is taken to coordinate them. In this section, we

- outline a simple model of communications,

304

- use this model to characterize the various systems we have discussed, and

- indicate problems, solutions, and opportunities that arise from heterogeneity.

A Communications Model for the Contract Net

It is analytically useful to model a contract net with a formalism for concurrent processing such as CSP [8].

- Each node is a state machine communicating with other nodes over unidirectional *channels*, each connecting exactly two nodes. (The channel is a modeling tool, not an implementation specification. The model represents the net as having point to point connections, even though most implementations will use a bus-like organization.)

- Each channel has an *alphabet*, consisting of the repertoire of messages that can travel over it.

- The alphabet of a node is the union of the alphabets of all channels over which it communicates.

This formalism allows us to characterize the nodes in a contract net by the set of messages in their alphabets. The alphabet of the entire system includes the set of messages outlined in Section 10.1.1 above. Those messages are of two types: those sent by the manager of a task (Task Announcements, Awards, and Terminations), and those sent by the contractor for a task (Node Availability Announcements, Bids, Acknowledgments, and Reports). We can distinguish three types of nodes: manager specialists, contractor specialists, and generalists.

1. A *generalist* can initiate or receive any of the messages in Section 10.1.1 above.

2. A *manager specialist* can manage tasks but not perform them. The alphabet of its output channels includes the manager messages but not the contractor messages, while the alphabet of its input channels includes the contractor messages but not the manager messages.

3. A *contractor specialist* can perform tasks but not manage them. The alphabet of its input channels includes the manager messages but not the contractor messages, while the alphabet of its output channels includes the contractor messages but not the manager messages.

305

For ease of discussion, we will label the alphabets of generalist, manager specialist, and contractor specialist nodes as αG, αM, and αC, respectively, and the alphabet of the canonical contract net (Section 10.1.1) as αN.

Characterizing Contract Nets

The typology of nodes developed in the last section suggests that a generalist can communicate directly with any node in the system. A manager specialist can communicate with anyone except another manager specialist, and a contractor specialist can communicate with anyone except another contractor specialist. This generalization is guaranteed only as long as the system alphabet is restricted to αN. In a homogeneous system, these messages support both control and performance. In a heterogeneous system, though, the performance medium acts as a separate set of channels with an alphabet disjoint from that of the control medium, and the communications topology of the system changes.

We have considered three applications of the contract net: a Distributed Sensing System, task allocation for multiple CPU's, and the YAMS architecture for factory control. From the point of view of communications, each of these is distinctive.

In the task allocation problem, all nodes are generalists. There is no "bottom level" to the system (or, from another point of view, every node is at the bottom level, since every node can perform the services for which negotiation allocates resources). The world outside of the computer is neither sensed nor changed. Unless a particular application restricts the topology in some way, any node can communicate with any other node, and all nodes have the same alphabet: $\alpha G = \alpha N$.

The DSS consists of manager specialists (the top level of the system), contractor specialists (the nodes that manage individual sensors), and generalists (all the other nodes in between). Contractor specialists form a clearly identifiable bottom level. The system can sense the outside world, but (apart from quantum effects and details of information entropy) cannot modify it. Thus the outside world does not provide a secondary communications channel among nodes. Every node's alphabet is a subset of αN, so the generalization about who can communicate with whom is valid. In particular, $\alpha C \cap \alpha M = \emptyset$; $\alpha C \subset \alpha G$; and $\alpha M \subset \alpha G$.

Like the DSS, YAMS has all three kinds of nodes, with workstations as contractor specialists at the bottom layer. These workstations not only sense the external world but also change it as they process parts. Because one workstation often senses the changes made in a part by another workstation, the performance medium acts as a separate communications channel with an alphabet disjoint from the set of contract net messages. We label the alphabet of the performance medium as αP. This new channel invalidates our generalization about communications paths, for contractor specialists can now communicate directly with each other through the performance medium. Now $\alpha P \cap \alpha C \neq \emptyset$ and $\alpha G \cap \alpha P = \alpha M \cap \alpha P = \emptyset$, so $\alpha C \neq \alpha C \cap \alpha G \neq \alpha G$.

Managing Heterogeneous Systems

The distinctive features of heterogeneous systems present special problems that invite new techniques for their solution. These techniques, in turn, offer opportunities for new capabilities. Lack of coordination between the control and performance media leads to new problems of system design.

- Because of the additional communications paths available through the performance medium, a heterogeneous system has opportunities for deadlock not possible in a pure contract net. (The occurrence of such a deadlock in an early prototype of YAMS motivated much of this analysis!)

- Error correcting protocols for communication in the performance medium are not nearly as well developed as their analogs in the control medium. Recovery from the manual removal of a pallet from the transport system, for instance, is much more difficult than recovery from a lost packet over a LAN. Yet, once we realize that the pallet is as much a message as is the packet, the importance of developing robust protocols for the performance medium becomes clear.

These problems arise because the couplings between the two media are usually designed myopically, ignoring the communications function of the performance medium. The problems can be solved by coordinating the two media more closely.

- A simple step for error management in material transportation is a label on each pallet that is checked at every intersection in the material transport system. The use of bar codes for pallet tracking is commonplace in advanced manufacturing facilities.

- Some vendors are giving substance to the "pallet as message" metaphor by offering smart pallet labels containing RAM that workstations can read and write. These systems allow the performance medium to carry information that would ordinarily have to travel over the control medium. By increasing the overlap between the two media, they make coordination easier.

- Once we recognize the performance medium as an important part of the system, we can engineer it to make it more tractable. The Kanban system for controlling material flow through a factory [7] can be viewed as a way of structuring the performance medium to allow better control of its interaction with workstations and the control medium. The transportation component of YAMS uses CASCADE, a superset of the Kanban technique, to strengthen the cooperation between the two media [17].

These solutions, in turn, enlarge the set of techniques available for intelligent factory control. The information conveyed by parts over the performance medium can reduce the three classes of ignorance discussed above, and help overcome scheduling anomalies. Parts can also serve as control tokens to coordinate workstations, much as Ramamritham [19] uses software tokens.

10.4   Summary

The contract net is a useful architecture for the distributed adaptive control of a factory. The use of negotiation accommodates the stochasticity inherent in manufacturing. The factory floor differs from some other domains to which the architecture has been applied, and offers both problems and opportunities relative to those domains.

We have identified three dimensions in which to compare the factory with other domains. It is 1) less *volatile* than other domains, 2) more *specialized*, and 3) distinguishes the *control medium* from the *performance medium*. We have discussed three implications of these differences for using the contract net model in the domain of factory control:

1. the addressing strategy of *audience restriction*,

2. ways to combine information from a *global scheduling* process with the local adaptability provided by negotiation, and

3. modifications to the *communications model* to accommodate the differences between control and performance media.

Acknowledgements

YAMS is a product of the Distributed Factory Software Group in the Communications and Network Laboratory of the Industrial Technology Institute. Bruce Irish, Jim Kindrick, and Pete Lozo did much of the design and implementation, following some early ideas of Gus Teschke. The ideas in this paper profited greatly from discussions with other participants at the 1985 Workshop on Distributed Artificial Intelligence, in particular Vic Lesser and Peter Green. This work was financed by grants from the Kellogg, Dow, and Mott foundations and the State of Michigan.

References

[1] E. M. Allen, "YAPS: Yet Another Production System," University of Maryland Dept. of Computer Science TR-1146, 1983.

[2] J. C. Bean and J. R. Birge, "Match-Up Real-Time Scheduling," Technical Report 85-22, Dept. of Industrial and Operations Engineering, University of Michigan, 1985.

[3] R. Davis and R. G. Smith, "Negotiation as a Metaphor for Distributed Problem Solving," *Artificial Intelligence*, vol. 20, pp. 63-109, 1983.

[4] B. R. Fox and K. G. Kempf, "Opportunistic Scheduling for Robotic Assembly," *Proceedings of the IEEE International Conference on Automation and Robotics*, St. Louis, pp. 880-889, 1985.

[5] B. R. Fox and K. G. Kempf, "Complexity, Uncertainty, and Opportunistic Scheduling," *Proceedings of the Second IEEE Conference on Artificial Intelligence Applications*, Miami, pp. 487-492, 1985.

[6] M. Fox, "Constraint-Directed Search: A Case Study of Job-Shop Scheduling," Carnegie-Mellon University: Robotics Institute CMU-RI-TR-83-22; Computer Science Department CMU-CS-83-161, 1983.

[7] R. W. Hall, *Driving the Productivity Machine: Production Planning and Control in Japan*, American Production and Inventory Control Society, 1981.

[8] C. A. R. Hoare, *Communicating Sequential Processes*, Englewood Cliffs: Prentice-Hall International, 1985.

[9] ITI, *Gateway: The Map Reporter*, vol. 1.1, P.O. Box 1485, Ann Arbor, MI 48106, January-February 1985.

[10] Jacobs, "OPT Uncovered," *Industrial Engineering* vol. 16, October 1984.

[11] P. W. Lozo, "A Network Architecture for Unix Processes," Industrial Technology Institute: DFSG Memo 85-36, 1985.

[12] L. W. McKenzie, "Turnpike Theory," *Econometrica*, vol. 44, no. 5, pp. 841-865, 1976.

[13] R. I. Millard, "MRP Is None Of the Above," *Production and Inventory Management*, vol. Q1, pp. 22-30, 1985.

[14] P. A. Newman and K. G. Kempf, "Opportunistic Scheduling for Robotic Machine Tending," *Proceedings of the Second IEEE Conference on Artificial Intelligence Applications*, Miami, pp. 168-175, 1985.

[15] H. V. D. Parunak, "The Theory and Practice of Scheduling," Industrial Technology Institute: DFSG 85-26, 1985.

[16] H. V. D. Parunak, B. W. Irish, J. Kindrick, and P. W. Lozo, "Fractal Actors for Distributed Manufacturing Control," *Proceedings of the Second IEEE Conference on AI Applications*, Miami, p. 653, 1985.

[17] H. V. D. Parunak, P. W. Lozo, R. Judd, B. W. Irish, and J. Kindrick, "A Distributed Heuristic Strategy for Material Transportation," *Proceedings of the Conference on Intelligent Systems and Machines*, Oakland University, 1986.

[18] H. V. D. Parunak, J. F. White, P. W. Lozo, R. Judd, B. W. Irish, and J. Kindrick, "An Architecture for Heuristic Factory Control," *Proceedings of the American Control Conference*, Seattle, 1986.

[19] K. Ramamritham, "Enabling Local Actions by Global Consensus," *Information Systems* vol. 10,:3, pp. 319-324, 1985.

[20] K. Ramamritham and J. A. Stankovic, "Dynamic Task Scheduling in Hard Real-Time Distributed Systems," *IEEE Software*, July 1984, pp. 65-75.

[21] M. J. Shaw and A. B. Whinston, "Task Bidding and Distributed Planning in Flexible Manufacturing," *Proceedings of the Second IEEE Conference on Artificial Intelligence Applications*, Miami, pp. 184-189, 1985.

[22] K. G. Shin and M. E. Epstein, "Communication Primitives for a Distributed Multi-Robot System," *Proceedings of the IEEE International Conference on Robotics and Automation*, 1985.

[23] K. G. Shin, M. E. Epstein and R. A. Volz, "A Module Architecture for an Integrated Multi-Robot System," *Proceedings of the 18th Annual Hawaii International Conference on System Sciences*, pp. 120-129, 1985.

[24] R. G. Smith, "A Framework for Problem Solving in a Distributed Processing Environment," Stanford University: Heuristic Programming Project Memo HPP-78-28, Computer Science Department Report STAN-CS-78-700, 1978.

[25] R. G. Smith, "The Contract Net Protocol: High-Level Communication and Control in a Distributed Problem Solver," *IEEE Transactions on Computers* C-29:12 (December), pp. 1104-1113, 1980.

[26] R. G. Smith and R. Davis, "Frameworks for Cooperation in Distributed Problem Solving," *IEEE Transactions on Systems, Man, and Cybernetics*, vol. SMC-11, no. 1, January 1981, pp. 61-70.

[27] J. A. Stankovic and I. S. Sidhu, "An Adaptive Bidding Algorithm For Processes, Clusters and Distributed Groups," *Proceedings of the Fourth International Conference on Distributed Computing Systems*, San Francisco, pp. 49-59, 1984.

[28] W. Zhao, K. Ramamritham, and J. A. Stankovic, "Scheduling Tasks with Resource Requirements in Hard Real-Time Systems," Unpublished Manuscript, Dept. of Computer and Information Science, University of Massachusetts at Amherst, 1985.

H. Van Dyke Parunak
Industrial Technology Institute
P.O. Box 1485
Ann Arbor, MI 48106

Chapter 11

Participant Systems for Cooperative Work

Ernest Chang

Abstract

A *Participant System* is a computer system that facilitates the simultaneous interaction
of several persons or intelligent agents working together, possibly over several physical
locations, on a shared complex task. To do so, it must support communications, multiple
views, and common data, action and cognitive spaces. Such a system must coordinate access to a common problem representation, and contain sufficient knowledge and expertise
in the problem domain to integrate the activity of the users, and even to participate as
one of the experts. This represents a new paradigm for computing, a departure from the
traditional one-person-to-one-virtual machine model, to one that more directly reflects
the nature of human problem solving in a group situation.

This paper presents some essential concepts relating to group cooperation drawn from
the social sciences, and a few proposals for implementing them in the computer-based
participant environment. A general structure for participant systems is then considered,
and a number of current projects are discussed.

11.1   Introduction

Participant Systems are computer systems that support the collaboration of persons or
intelligent agents working together on a common intellectual problem. For instance,
an architect, engineer and client may design a building using a computer system that
supports shared visual space, action space and cognitive space, through the use of a

common problem representation, while the participants may be physically distributed over several locations. The system would contain one or more knowledge-based modules, such as an expert system in the structural use of materials, another in the interpretation of the building code, another in design methodology, and so on.

The idea of Participant Systems represents a radical departure from the usual way in which computers are used as single-person tools, applied to what may be called *personalizable* problems. Inherent in human social systems are another set of problems, which require the coordinated efforts of people, and are among the most difficult to handle. Examples of these are found in the treatment of patients by a medical team, the management of organizations, the design and implementation of large software systems, etc. These problems can be characterized as *collaborative*, and are the ones addressed by Participant Systems.

Distributed Artificial Intelligence (DAI) is an emerging research area dealing with intelligent agents solving problems in distributed environments, through planning, cooperative or competitive paradigms. There are three important ways in which distributed artificial intelligence is related to Participant Systems. First, intelligent agents refer as much to humans as to machines. Second, the paradigms for interactions between intelligent agents generally derive from human models of behavior. Third, intelligent machine agents will need to deal with humans, and therefore must use protocols to which humans can relate. Participant Systems therefore reflect the same concerns as DAI, but emphasize human-human cooperation, and how the traditional protocols that humans use might be implemented in computer-based systems.

In this paper, we will examine some of the fundamental attributes of human group communication and behavior (in problem solving) that need to be considered in the design and implementation of Participant Systems. We will then propose a taxonomy of Participant Systems, based on a structural model reflecting the desired functional characteristics. Two examples of Participant Systems currently being constructed are described, and discussed in terms of related work in distributed graphics, computer conferencing, and distributed artificial intelligence.

11.2 Background

Human beings associate in groups for a multiplicity of reasons, only some of which are relevant to this paper: we aggregate by chance while attending events or travelling; we deliberately group together to engage in recreation and social exchange; we work cooperatively to communicate information, solve specific problems, and perform tasks requiring more than one agent. The last three classes of group activities are particularly goal-oriented, and it is to these that we address Participant Systems, tools for enhancing the efficiency and effectiveness of group interactions. In general, activities of this type involve groups of a few rather than a large number of people, and we now turn to a consideration of the behavior of small groups in communication and problem-solving.

11.2.1 Communication in Small Groups

Shimanoff [31] has identified seven rules for structuring communications in small groups, that serve to coordinate interaction among their members. These relate to

1. Who speaks

2. What is said (specific topic, general)

3. To whom (the chair, the group, etc.)

4. When (turn-taking)

5. With what duration and frequency

6. Through what medium (paper, speech)

7. By what decision procedure

Rules may be explicit, implicit, decreed or evolved, and serve above all to maintain the cohesiveness of a group in the accomplishment of its objectives, by regulating and restricting the behavior of its members. However, even if the operative rules of a group are understood by all its members, procedures must still exist for their implementation, so that each person knows when a particular rule is to be applied. Many of these procedures are effected through paraverbal and nonverbal modes of communication [2,1]. Over and above what is being communicated on the level of explicit goals, paraverbal mechanisms such as delivery style, intensity, phraseology and interpretive expression convey other messages. Nonverbal communications are based on oculesics (eye movement, eye contact, pupil dilation), kinesics (body movement, facial expressions, gestures), haptics (interpersonal touch for reassurance, insult, etc.), proxemics (interpersonal distance), and chronemics (time sense). These are involved in the acquisition of turns, the expression of approval or disapproval, and in general, in the coordination of group communication. For example, making eye-contact with the chairman indicates a desire to speak; lowering one's voice and moving the body back indicates giving up one's turn. These mechanisms are important for group communications, and must be taken into account in implementing computer-based systems that are to facilitate group interactions.

11.2.2 Problem Solving

Two important aspects of human problem solving are considered below. The first is: what methodology is the most useful, and the second is: how do members of a group interact in solving a problem?

Problem Solving Methodologies

Newell [25] has identified the central debate of problem solving as being one of specificity versus generality: are most solutions specific to particular problems, or are there general techniques which can be extended from one domain to another? From this debate arises a spectrum of methods for problem solving, ranging from *strong* methods, based on selecting the best from a set of highly specific procedures, to *weak* methods. These have general applicability, and are based on strategies such as: generate-and-test, hill climbing, heuristic search, means-ends analysis, subgoal decomposition, planning, etc. If weak methods are applicable, then techniques to map the current problem into a known one [27], such as arrangement, inducing structure and transformation, are essential parts of the methodology of problem solving.

Group Approach to Problem Solving

A group of individuals is not necessarily better than a good expert at solving some kinds of problems, as pointed out by Maier [24]. Tasks that have a single best answer or a high component of technical expertise, which we have identified as *personalizable* problems, are often best done by one person. However, there are other kinds of tasks: those that require group consensus and commitment, such as a management board establishing a course for the coming year; those that simply involve information and opinion exchange, such as a conference; and those that require multiple knowledge sources, such as the design of a marketing strategy for a new product; those that require the balancing of conflicting interests, such as the allocation of research grants from a fixed pool. These collaborative problems necessarily involve group interaction as the method of choice.

There appears to be a trade-off between the social aspects of group interaction and the effectiveness of the group in problem solving [10]. In general, a certain level of social cohesiveness is necessary for a group to be productive, but as it achieves extremely high cohesiveness, it decreases in productivity. This is related to the observation that the imposition of structure is conducive to task performance. Consider, for example, the Nominal Group technique of Van de Ven, discussed by Hiltz in [14]. A leader states the problem, and the group then writes their ideas down in silence. A round robin discussion then takes place, followed by voting. This strict procedure is in contrast to that of an unstructured group, which might first have to reach consensus on a strategy for decision-making.

This is not to imply that structure can be imposed only by stipulating rules of communication explicitly. There are many tasks which lend inherent structure to the group by the implicit assignment of specific roles to individuals. For example, the interaction between a physician, nurse and patient is usually quite effective, as each person has an implicit understanding of the role he or she is to take, and therefore they know and follow a common set of rules for communication and behavior.

Of course, group activities that do not contain a high degree of inherent structuring in the form of distinct roles, may need explicit mechanisms. It is interesting, in this light, to compare the social chat with the typical executive meeting of a special interest group. The first has neither specific objectives other than information and opinion exchange, nor a specific allocation of roles, nor explicit rules for communication. The second, in contrast, has a specific agenda representing its set of objectives, an explicit allocation of roles, and usually adopts a rigid set of communication rules, such as Robert's Rules of Order. There is a striking relationship in evidence between the need of a group to accomplish a set of goals, and the structure it imposes on itself, either implicitly, in the roles inherent to the task, or explicitly, in the communication rules used.

It follows from the observations above that the effectiveness of a computer system supporting group activity is related to both the nature of the task and to the communication rules that have been implemented. It is instructive to look at computer conferencing in this perspective.

11.2.3 Computer Conferencing

Three technologies have been developed to support the requirements of people at different locations who need to interact with each other [19]. These are: audio teleconferencing, in which the spoken word is shared on a common channel, video teleconferencing, in which voice and images are transmitted on TV-based systems, and computer conferencing, which is a print-based communications medium based on computer networks and terminals.

Characteristics of Computer Conferencing

The typical computer conference system such as PLANET [Lipinski 1974], CONFER [6], MINT [21], and EIES [15], provides an environment in which "users type their messages to other conference participants on standard computer terminals, usually linked by telephone to a computer network. They receive printed messages at their terminals each time they join a computer 'activity'. Such activities typically involve 3 to 25 people ... participants can come in at their own convenience, see what has happened ... and leave" [19].

A distinctive aspect of this kind of interaction is its *asynchronous* nature: users come and go; they compose messages in their entirety, and see new ones at their leisure, so that the totality of messages in the conference can be thought of as a virtual bulletin-board. Systems such as EIES have other features as well, such as private messages, notebooks and voting.

The Utility of Computer Conferencing

The two outstanding features of these systems are the asynchronous nature of the communications, and the virtual bulletin-board character of the messages. The first is a double-edged virtue: on the one hand, it is not necessary to bring all persons together at the same time in order to hold a conference; persons can take as long as they like to respond and reply; they can deal with many subjects and subconferences in one session. On the other hand, Umpleby [34] reports that many users are frustrated by the slow replies to their messages and comments, while those who use the system infrequently are swamped by the massive numbers of unread messages waiting for them when they do rejoin the conference. Bregenzer [4] reported that of the large numbers who expressed interest in joining a conference, many did not participate at all, many others were relatively inactive, and very little discussion went into depth. Most of the messages did not provoke more than one or two levels of responses. Hiltz [15] found that the voting mechanism was perceived as the least useful feature of EIES, a vivid illustration that decision making was not a strong feature of this medium.

On the other hand, the availability of information in bulletin-board form has been shown to be an attractive means of disseminating timely and important news and relevant opinions. A number of network information services have come into being in the last few years, such as the Source, Compuserve, and net.news on the Unix Newsnet; furthermore, it is now common for user groups to exchange information this way, as seen in the various news bulletin services for the PC, Macintosh and Amiga.

Relationship to Group Problem Solving

Computer conferencing systems appear to serve two functions, with different degrees of success: the first is that of information exchange, and the second is that of group decision-making. It is clear that as a bulletin-board medium, computer conferencing is a great success; as a medium for problem solving, its usefulness is more qualified. Let us examine the comunication rules used in the computer conference environment, and the nature of the tasks involved.

With respect to Shimanoff's paradigm, computer conferencing permits anyone to "speak," on a specific topic, to one or more persons, whenever they choose, for as long as they like, through a sequential character-based medium. The absence of turn taking is implied in "whenever they choose," and this, combined with the sequential bulletin-board nature of the medium, implies that an unpredictable amount of time can elapse between issuing a message and getting a response. If the task of the group is information exchange, and there is indeed information to send or receive, then each member can accomplish, upon rejoining the conference, the common goal of the group: information exchange.

Consider, however, the task of problem solving in a computer conference environment. We have seen, from Fisher [10], that a minimum amount of social cohesiveness is necessary to the effective performance of a task. This cohesiveness is usually obtained through the regulation and coordination that occurs in the process of communication. The unpredictable time occurring between message sending and response makes this cohesiveness difficult to achieve. This absence of *time coherence* among its users is a major flaw of the computer conferencing environment.

It therefore comes as no surprise that other researchers such as Johansen and Vallee [19] observed that it is not sufficient just to hook people together electronically to get effective communication, because people take their old, unconscious rules for a meeting from their familiar cultural surroundings into a new medium. They pointed out, in addition, that electronic meetings such as computer conferences do not deal well with other aspects of group interaction such as the use of physical space, a shared understanding of time, social structures that can integrate divergent views and initiatives, nonverbal messages, and the control of group interactions. Although some systems such as EIES can support conference moderators, and are able to impose a number of structures for interaction, it is not clear what interaction protocols are most effective. According to Johansen, the strictly sequential round-robin exchange is the least effective way of arriving at consensus decisions; Hiltz [14] pointed out that the Nominal Group technique (see 11.2.2 above) generates more ideas, and produces a more balanced focus, than unstructured discussion. The problem is a complex one: a specific communication medium constrains, through attributes like bandwidth and display capability, the kind of interaction rules that are feasible, which in turn permit a specific balance to be achieved between social cohesiveness and structure in the group interaction. The relationships that exist between these dimensions of computer-based communications have yet to be fully understood.

11.3 Participant Systems

This section describes the functional characteristics of Participant Systems in the context of group communications as discussed above, and proposes a structural model of Participant Systems that provides a taxonomy reflecting variations in functionality and implementation.

11.3.1 Functional Characteristics

A distinction can be made between a *weak* and *strong* notion of Participant Systems. In the first one, users interact with a system in the performance of shared tasks without essential communication between them. An example of this is an airline reservation system. A strong notion of a Participant System is one in which an individual task is seen as being only part of a mutual task involving a number of interacting participants. Although this distinction is relative rather than absolute, it is this latter class of Participant Systems which will be considered from this point onward.

We require a Participant System to support a possibly distributed set of persons who interact to accomplish a specific common task. We have seen that in the group setting, this requires both social cohesiveness and a shared understanding of time, which are ususaly provided by rules of communication that include paraverbal and nonverbal messages. To provide these elements, we will require Participant Systems to operate in real-time, so that actions and responses can be observed by all participants within a temporal window in the order of a few seconds in duration. In addition, there should be at least two levels of communication, one at the level of the task, and the other at a *metatask* level, so that the participants can exchange messages in lieu of paravebal and nonverbal signals that usually regulate and coordinate a group's interactions. In other words, Participant Systems must permit communication of task-specific messages, such as an architect moving the position of a doorway using graphical icons, as well as metatask messages, which are about the task and the interaction of the group in the execution of the task.

We have previously observed that problems containing implicit group structures tend to be more effectively solved than problems which do not have this property. They have preassigned roles for the participants, who bring different sets of knowledge to the task; this is evident in the roles taken by an architect, an engineer, a contractor and a client in the problem of designing a house. A Participant System supports a plurality of roles in two ways: on the one hand, it provides a shared approach to the problem, in terms of a common action space, visual space, and cognitive space. On the other hand, it must also take into account the different requirements of the users, so that it can provide several different views of a common problem representation to one or more participants, and give access to actions specific to the capabilities of those involved.

In summary, a Participant System is a computer system that supports a possibly distributed set of users who interact in real-time to accomplish a common task, communicating at two distinct and separate task and metatask levels. It supports a common problem representation, providing shared action, visual and cognitive spaces, while giving specific views and actions where required to particular users. It is therefore capable of being an intermediary, an advisor, and even a participant, to the human users of the system.

11.3.2   A Diversity of Participant Systems

The extent to which a Participant System implements the functional characteristics described in the previous section forms a spectrum ranging in complexity from simple communication channels to multiperson design systems. A few examples will serve to illustrate this diversity.

Consider a chess game played by two persons at different physical locations. At the simplest level, a computer might present each player with the same board, with white players at the bottom of the screen, and black above. Pieces would be represented by name, and a move would cause a piece to relocate from one square to another, without checking for legality or capture, so that a captured piece has to be removed explicitly. This program can be enhanced by the domain-dependent knowledge of legal moves and captures, and by presenting each player with their natural view of the chessboard, perhaps in 3-D shaded graphics, with perspective added. A further improvement in the expertise provided by the system might be an advisory component, based on book-moves or some other chess algorithms. This example shows a Participant System with a common data representation, multiple views, domain knowledge, distributed access, and shared cognitive and visual space. Note that the players do not share action space, for neither is permitted to move the other's pieces, and furthermore that this task is so highly structured that there is no place for metatask communications. Metatasks might involve who plays white, what is the time limit for moves, how many games might be played, etc.

319

A second example is that of a Participant System for architectural design, involving a client, contractor, engineer and architect. The engineer may be designing the mechanical layout, the contractor working on the wiring, while the architect and client are viewing a different part of the building. A change made by any one of them is immediately reflected in the views they are seeing. The architect might then communicate directly with the engineer, both referring to the same graphical image, and each of them may then engage in design activity and discussion, using both task and metatask communications, as if they were sitting together. This Participant System introduces shared action space within common data space, in an environment where multiple views of the same problem representation are a necessary feature.

A further example is that of a medical expert system, extended to be a Participant System in which a family physician, a medical laboratory database, a patient and a nurse might interact. The system supports the collection of case information from the patient, doctor and nurse, each of whom has a particular view of the data and contributes that to the composite picture. The physician may be the principal actor in the system, and direct questions to the patient and the nurse. However, interactions between nurse and patient may also produce useful data, which are then accesssible, as are the information in the laboratory database. The expert system acts as consultant to the group, but each of them may see a different view of the conclusions: the physician in technical terms, the nurse receiving a set of orders, and the patient getting a clear and understandable explanation. This complex example illustrates a Participant System with multiple agents and data sources, complex domain knowledge, simultaneous distributed access, and a common problem representation giving a shared data space with multiple views.

11.3.3   A Structural Model of Participant Systems

There are a number of software components readily identifiable from the examples given above. There is a *domain* related component, in which the knowledge about the problem area is captured, and a *database* component, dealing with the representation of multiple views and shared access to a single problem domain, over possibly many physical sites. There is a *communication* component, which handles the exchange of messages between a set of distributed users and machines. A *user interface* component deals with the exchange of information between the system and its users, involving text, graphics, voice and so on. A *protocol* component is concerned with the integration of activity between users, implementing a metatask channel to provide the coordination usually obtained through paraverbal and nonverbal mechanisms. It may be necessary for metatask channels to communicate more than text in order to provide complex functions like initiative and topic continuity.

The structural model of Participant Systems proposed below distributes these components among a few simple modules, and suggests implementation strategies which in turn give rise to a taxonomy of Participant Systems. We consider every Participant System to consist of a small number of interacting abstract modules, any of which may be implemented in distributed or centralized form. Depending on the complexity of the modules, and the extent of their distribution, a range of Participant Systems with different operational characteristics can be created. The modules are called: the **Expert**, the **Display Coordinator**, the **Action Synchronizer**, and the **Registrar**. They are related to one another as shown in Figure 11.1. The Registrar keeps track of the identities of the participants and their characteristics, like the actions permitted each, and their display privileges (the views specific to each). The Action Synchronizer sequences requests for actions from the participants, and passes them to the Registrar. Legal actions are given by the Registrar to the Expert, which takes the appropriate action. The Display Coordinator is notified by the Registrar if any changes occur to the problem representation, and it then updates the view specific to each participant.

It follows that the Expert module maintains the domain knowledge and database representation components, and that actions that change the problem representation are effected by the Expert. The communication and user interface components are best seen as software layers implementing the Display Coordinator, Action Synchronizer and Registrar. The protocol component is an additional part of the Registrar, since that is the module that receives all action requests and instructs the Display Coordinator to update displays.

11.3.4 A Taxonomy of Participant Systems

Participant Systems have an intrinsic potential for distributed implementations, since they concern problems involving interacting agents. The extent to which the modules of a Participant System are distributed gives rise to a variety of systems with different characteristics. Based on the distributed or centralized implementation of each of the four modules, we can theoretically have 16 different flavors of Participant Systems. However, it is useful to consider just the following three classes:

Class 1 Totally Centralized

Class 2 Mixed

Class 3 Totally Distributed

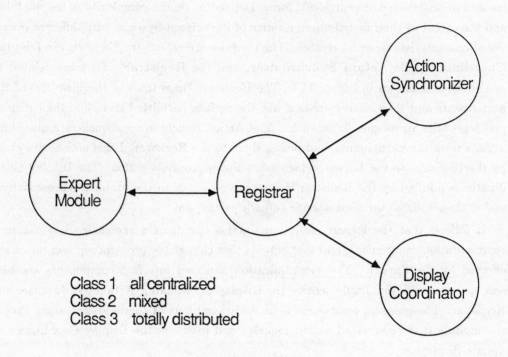

Class 1   all centralized
Class 2   mixed
Class 3   totally distributed

Figure 11.1: A Taxonomy of Participant Systems

If the entire system is centralized, all modules are implemented in a single machine, and the users may be connected through communciation lines such that each may have a display and input device(s), or may even share a single display unit. An example of this kind of Participant System might be a war-game simulator for a large room, with a single NORAD-type floor-to-ceiling display, and participants having input devices only.

If the system is totally decentralized in all its modules, each participant has a distributed version of the Registrar, the Display Coordinator, the Action Synchronizer, and the Expert. The Cantata real-time dialogue system (see below) is an example of this class of Participant System. The Registrar at each node keeps track of the same list of participants; the Action Synchronizer at each node deals with actions specific to the user, and the Registrar and Display Coordinator permit a participant to set up local screen configurations. The Expert maintains, at each node, the database of dialogues that have taken place, and allows the user to access any portion of a participant's previous messages.

Class 2 (Mixed) Participant Systems are of special interest, because they include Participant Systems based on expert systems used collaboratively by a number of users at separate workstations, possibly having different views of the same problem. It would be useful to develop techniques for building this class of Participant Systems by taking existing expert systems and extending them, with the addition of modules, to be Participant Systems, as this would be a practical and effective method of construction.

Assume therefore that the Expert module in a Class 2 Participant System is implemented centrally. It follows that the Action module should also be central, since its function is to synchronize requests from distributed participants. The Registrar, which keeps track of the privileges specific to each user, therefore should also be central: it can be told directly by the Expert what parts of the problem representation have changed, and then send the relevant updates to the affected participants. To permit participants to have different views, the Display module should be distributed, so that each node can maintain its own screen image. In summary, a typical Class 2 system has a central Expert, Action and Registrar module, communicating with distributed Display modules.

Note that the Class 1 and 2 Participant Systems assume a single problem representation, possibly with multiple views and user actions for affecting change. However, Class 3 Participant Systems, which are totally distributed, can support a distributed Expert module in which each user has a slightly different problem representation, and only the union of all the views and representations will give the totality of the problem. The Participant Construct System (see below) being implemented at the Alberta Research Council is such a system.

11.3.5 Participant Systems in Progress

In this section, we consider two Class 3 Participant Systems that have been designed and in part or in whole constructed. One of them is called Cantata, a real-time computer system for human dialogue, and the other, Participant Construct System (PCS), deals with knowledge acquisition from a group of persons.

Cantata: A Simple Real-Time Dialogue System

Implemented originally at the University of Victoria on IBM-XTs and Ethernet, Cantata is a distributed computer system that supports real-time text exchange between its users, such that each person's messages (called a *monologue*) are broadcast to all the other participants, and displayed in text windows on each user's screen. The windows are sizable, movable, scrollable, visible (or not) and support word wrap-around. Text that comes to a particular node from a participant whose window is not presently visible causes a status message to appear on that screen, and the local user can bring that window into visibility.

This is a Participant System that supports a number of persons interacting in the common task of exchanging text messages in real-time. The implementation of Cantata addresses the provision of real-time message exchange in the following way: messages are received in real-time, as they are generated. Clearly this is not possible where there are more than two persons in a bulletin-board model of message space, for arbitrary inter-leaving of text fragments would result. Therefore, Cantata provides a window for each user at every screen and received text fragments are displayed at the visible windows. In Cantata, there are no explicit rules for communication, since everyone can address everyone else at the same time for as long as each likes with no specific topicality. Concepts like turn-taking, topic switching, and decision-making must be dealt with through structures that evolve from the participants themselves. In its simultaneity and presentation, Cantata is different from most computer conferencing systems, which by contrast, support asynchronous communications and a bulletin-board model. Systems like **write** in UNIX require strict turn-taking, while the UNIX **talk** command supports only two conversants in a split-screen conversation.

Cantata users face an enigmatic situation. On the one hand, they are able to receive messages as they are constructed and can respond to one or more messages before the sender(s) complete them. The ability of the eye to read much faster than the hand can type means that recipients can understand and act upon several input streams in parallel while messages are being constructed. This is therefore a medium that has no analogue in the normal world of personal interaction: you can interrupt without interrupting, and listen to three people at the same time in Cantata. On the other hand, the absence of structure in the communications between participants causes some confusion. It is difficult to get away from the cultural expectation that only one person in a conversation has the floor, that there are leadership or consensus methods for changing or maintaining topics, and that feedback is expected as one speaks. It is difficult, at present, to know whether the advantages of this kind of medium can be better exploited by building structuring mechanisms into the system or by more metaconversational exchanges, so that participants can create rules for using Cantata dynamically and follow them voluntarily. Cantata has been built as a vehicle for exploring Participant Systems, in part as a structure for building other Class 3 systems with task capabilities, and in part to understand more about human-human interaction in the computer-based medium.

Cantata has now been implemented on an Apple Macintosh network at the Alberta Research Council. Figure 11.2 illustrates the way the Macintosh window system supports communications in Cantata. A "Free Thought" area has been added, which permits a user to create text in advance of transmission, and then send it to all at once. The system has been in use for a period of time, but a formal study has not yet been conducted.

Strategies for implementing behavioral analogues of human interpersonal mechanisms are being actively pursued. The most important of these deal with focus of attention and topic continuity. The model that would be used to support focus of attention is to relate the speed at which text appears in a window to the attention that a user wishes to give it. This, combined with a finite amount of attention, means that the more attention is given to one window the less is available to the others. Feedback from attention distributions at other workstations would make possible a display of the total amount of group attention given to each participant, updated dynamically at each person's screen. This mechanism would be supported simply by a slider or dial effector for giving attention at each window, and a display for how much group attention that window has over the whole network. This technique provides a mechanism for flexible self-regulation of behavior: the more attention is given by the group to one individual, the more encouragement to continue; conversely, if no one is paying attention, a person is more likely to stop for a time. This model needs to be tested in real situations, of course, to determine its effectiveness.

A method of providing topic continuity versus new topic introductions or topic shifts is to explicitly indicate the topic to which a comment is addressed. This can be done in the workstation environment by using a mouse, for example, to highlight a few words in a particular window prior to entering a message: at the other stations, the reference might be made explicitly, through lines drawn from the message to the referenced window.

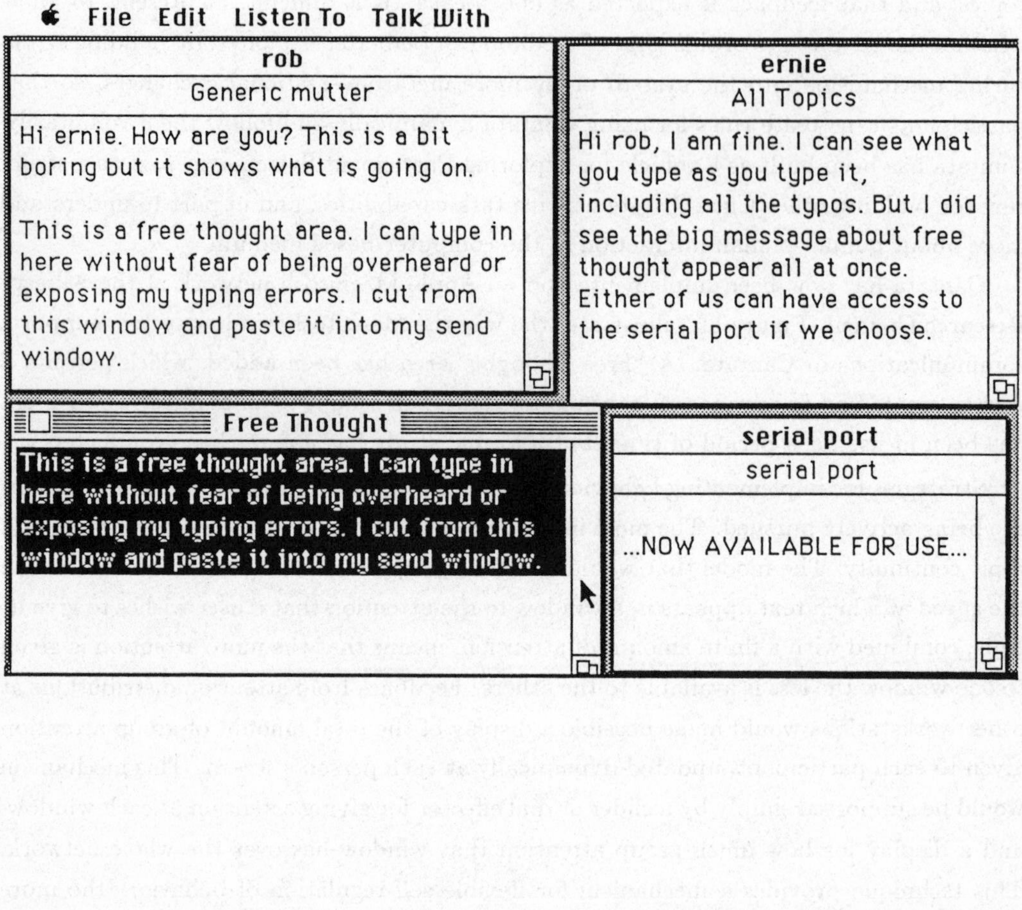

```
┌─────────────────────────────────────┐ ┌─────────────────────────────────────┐
│               rob                   │ │              ernie                  │
│          Generic mutter             │ │           All Topics                │
├─────────────────────────────────────┤ ├─────────────────────────────────────┤
│ Hi ernie. How are you? This is a bit│ │ Hi rob, I am fine. I can see what   │
│ boring but it shows what is going on.│ │ you type as you type it,            │
│                                     │ │ including all the typos. But I did  │
│ This is a free thought area. I can  │ │ see the big message about free      │
│ type in here without fear of being  │ │ thought appear all at once.         │
│ overheard or exposing my typing     │ │ Either of us can have access to     │
│ errors. I cut from this window and  │ │ the serial port if we choose.       │
│ paste it into my send window.       │ │                                     │
└─────────────────────────────────────┘ └─────────────────────────────────────┘
┌─────────────────────────────────────┐ ┌─────────────────────────────────────┐
│            Free Thought             │ │            serial port              │
├─────────────────────────────────────┤ │            serial port              │
│ This is a free thought area. I can  │ ├─────────────────────────────────────┤
│ type in here without fear of being  │ │                                     │
│ overheard or exposing my typing     │ │ ...NOW AVAILABLE FOR USE...         │
│ errors. I cut from this window and  │ │                                     │
│ paste it into my send window.       │ │                                     │
└─────────────────────────────────────┘ └─────────────────────────────────────┘
```

Figure 11.2: Cantata2+ with Free Thought and Serial Port Windows

Another way to generate the reference is to create appropriate text for it, by naming the owner and quoting the referenced text passage as a prologue to the actual message. These mechanisms are being considered for implementation.

A Class 2 variant of Cantata has been developed, called Cantata2+. This system permits any Macintosh serial port to connect to an external computer program, which is then brought into the network as a special participant, with its own display window, broadcast to all users. Each person can request access to enter input to the program, in a sequential FCFS manner. In this way, an expert system can be shared by several persons remotely, while they discuss the findings on their text windows. Although the external program can only be supported with a text-based interface at the moment, it is desirable to support full graphics and pointer-based interactions in the future. Several such programs can be invoked, one from each Macintosh station. The interaction between persons and computer resources creates an interesting new environment for group productivity. Figure 11.3 illustrates an expert system on medical diagnosis being used by two persons. In this case, the use of the expert system represents task level interaction, while the commentary in text windows represents metatask activity.

PCS: Participant Construct System

One interesting and well-studied approach to knowledge elicitation is based on Kelly's Personal Construct theory [22]. Essentially, a person ranks elements of a particular problem domain along dimensions considered by that person to be important in relating these elements one to another. In this way, the system of beliefs and values of that person are brought out in spite of the cognitive defenses that may be present. Shaw [30] has constructed computer programs for enhancing this process, and the Participant Construct System is intended to be an extension to this work. Since constructs can deal with procedural acts as well as beliefs, this is potentially a powerful method of automated knowledge acquisition for expert systems, especially since Boose [3] and Gaines and Shaw [11] have constructed computer-based methods for converting construct relationships into IF-THEN rules.

The approach to the Participant Construct System is that persons who work together, or who are specialists in the same area, hold some but not all of their constructs in common, and it would be useful to elicit them interactively from the group as a whole. Three benefits would accrue: the first is that a person may create constructs better reflecting their own values by observing the constructs that other people have, in the same domain; the second is that a person may understand another person better by trying to create constructs in their place, and observing the actual differences; finally,

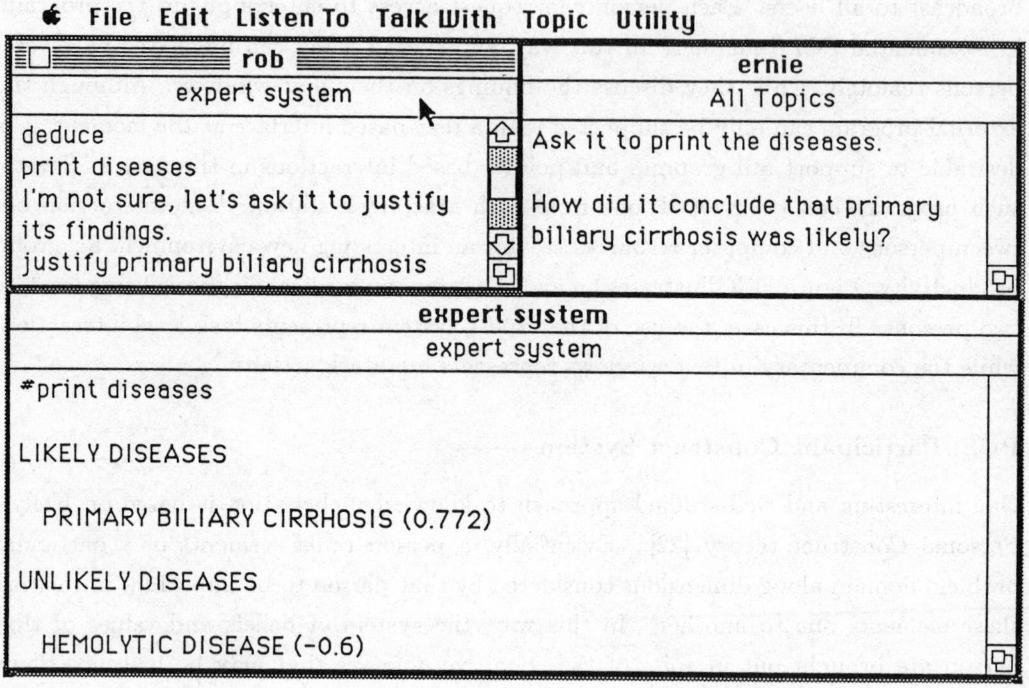

** File   Edit   Listen To   Talk With   Topic   Utility**

rob	ernie
expert system	All Topics
deduce	Ask it to print the diseases.
print diseases	
I'm not sure, let's ask it to justify	How did it conclude that primary
its findings.	biliary cirrhosis was likely?
justify primary biliary cirrhosis	

expert system

expert system

#print diseases

LIKELY DISEASES

  PRIMARY BILIARY CIRRHOSIS (0.772)

UNLIKELY DISEASES

  HEMOLYTIC DISEASE (-0.6)

Figure 11.3: Cantata2+ Showing Shared Use of Expert System

this participant technique is a method of eliciting a consenus, by identifying the constructs for which specific agreement and disagreement exist.

The Participant Construct System is being created on the Macintosh Appletalk network environment, and will permit a person to elicit personal constructs locally, and also to observe the constructs that others are generating in the network, possibly anonymously. Figure 11.4 shows a list of elements that a user has entered in the knowledge elicitation of distinctions between various computers. Figure 11.5 illustrates one way in which the poles of a construct are elicited, and Figure 11.6 shows the construct [Single-User Machine || Multi-User Machine] being generated, using a five point rating scale. Figure 11.7 is a screen image of how one may view the elements that other persons are using and copy them, and Figure 11.8 shows a comparison of constructs with Tony. This method of eliciting and exchanging information is anticipated to be useful not only in obtaining explicit consensus and points of disagreement, but also in assisting persons to have a better understanding of each other's points of view.

As a Participant System, this is a Class 3 distributed implementation, in which each node has its own Expert, Registrar, Display Coordinator and Action Synchronizer modules. It has already been pointed out that the problem representation at each node (the database of constructs) may not be the same, and therefore there is no single world representation except in the distributed sense. It is a system in which interaction between persons is highly structured, as compared to Cantata. Hence there is no metatask activity, since communication between individuals is limited to the exchange of constructs and elements. Nevertheless, it is a participant system in that persons cooperate to achieve a common goal, that of establishing a common set of constructs with measurable degrees of agreement and disagreement. It is possible to imbed PCS within Cantata, so that persons can exercise more metatask freedom, in being able to hold discussions while constructs are being created. This work is being considered.

11.4 Related Work

Sarin and Greif [29] have implemented two real-time conference systems. One of them, RTCAL, uses a shared calendar-window in association with a private window to permit the interactive scheduling of meetings under the auspices of a chairperson. The other, MBlink, is a shared bit-map graphics system centered on a DEC VAX connected to Xerox workstations, with multiple cursors representing users. The authors discuss problems of common reference points where multiple views are permitted, but do not consider in any depth the relationship between communication structures and effectiveness. They do,

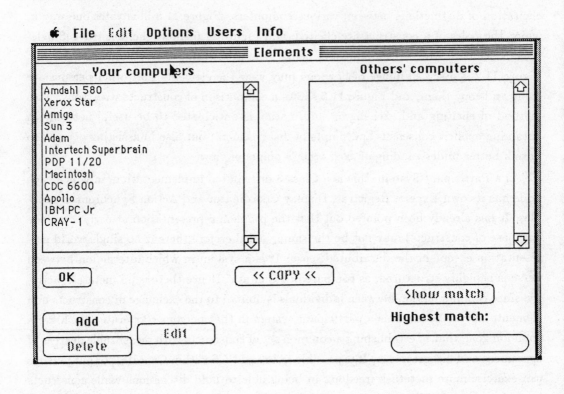

Figure 11.4: List of Computers as Elements in PCS

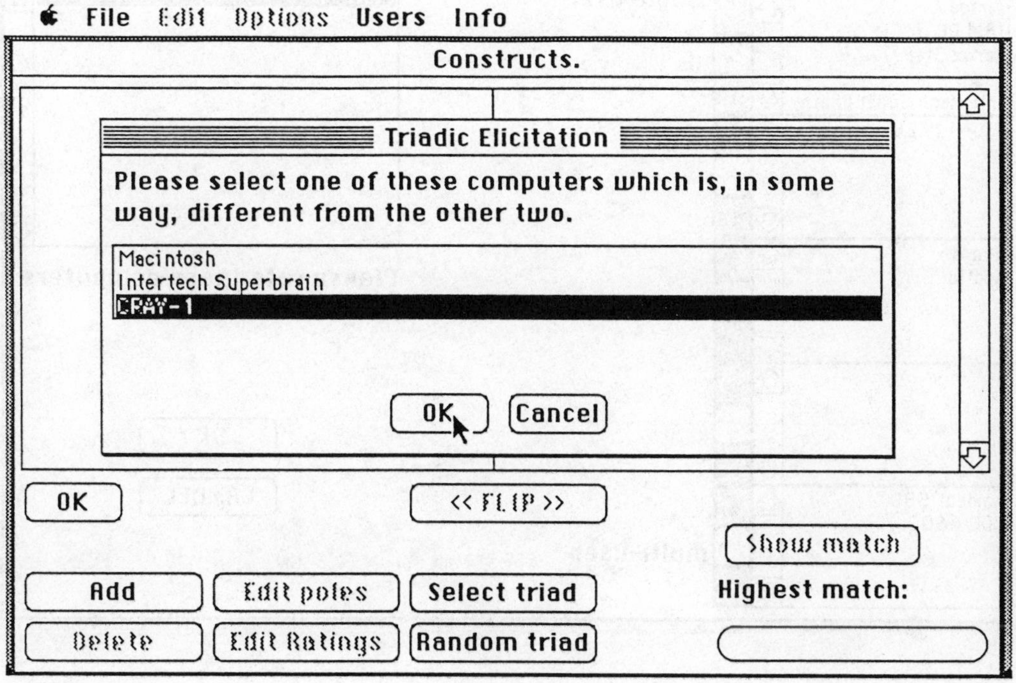

File Edit Options Users Info

Constructs.

═══ **Triadic Elicitation** ═══

Please select one of these computers which is, in some way, different from the other two.

Macintosh
Intertech Superbrain
CRAY-1

[**OK**] [Cancel]

[OK]   [<< FLIP >>]

[Show match]

[Add]   [Edit poles]   [Select triad]   **Highest match:**

[Delete]   [Edit Ratings]   [Random triad]   (   )

Figure 11.5: Using Random Triadic Elicitation to Derive Constructs

331

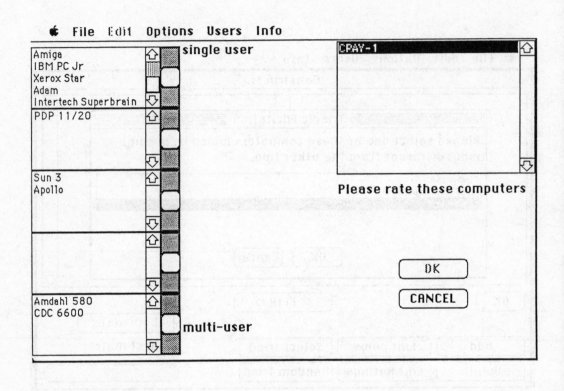

Figure 11.6: Creating the Single vs. Multiuser Construct

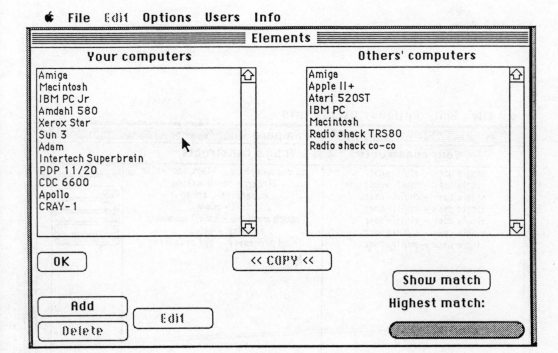

Figure 11.7: Viewing and Copying Others' Data in PCS

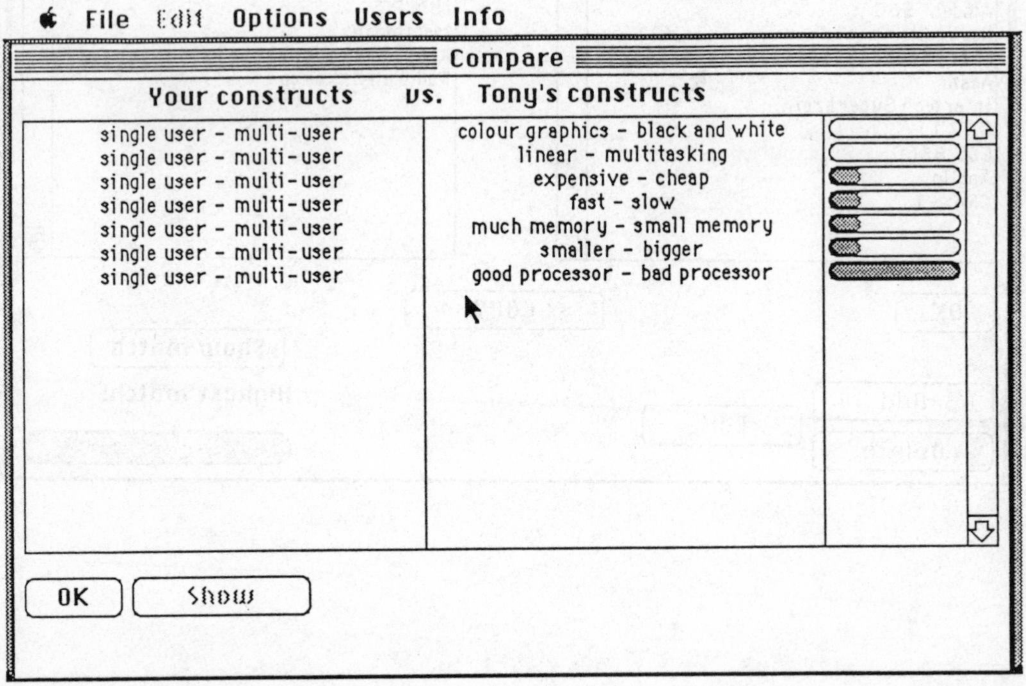

Compare

Your constructs	vs.	Tony's constructs	
single user – multi-user		colour graphics – black and white	
single user – multi-user		linear – multitasking	
single user – multi-user		expensive – cheap	
single user – multi-user		fast – slow	
single user – multi-user		much memory – small memory	
single user – multi-user		smaller – bigger	
single user – multi-user		good processor – bad processor	

OK   Show

Figure 11.8: A Comparison of Constructs with Tony in PCS

however, propose two strategies of creating such systems: one starting from an existing application, and the other by constructing entirely new systems.

The limitations in their methodology of using virtual terminal controllers, rather than Registrar, Action and Display modules, is that the functionality of their overall system is limited to that of the application. In our design, the functionality is based on specifications given to the Registrar, while the application program (the Expert module) is simply a tool used by the Registrar to accomplish the given task. A point made both by Sarin and Greif [29], and by Lantz [23] is that in a distributed environment, the sharing of graphical images is best done by sending object descriptors rather than display lists to the nodes, permitting each to generate the required images locally. This is the most reasonable method for supporting a distributed graphics system and one that forms a sound implementation base for Participant Systems.

The Colab project [33] at Xerox PARC is close in spirit to a Participant System, using the computer to augment face-to-face meetings. A number of software tools are used to support collaboration, brainstorming, evaluation and linkage between meetings. In contrast, Participant Systems do not assume personal presence, so that the facilitation of interactive protocols must be supported by the communication medium. Other shared activity systems have been constructed, notably NLS [8], which supports a shared screen mode for collaborative authoring of structured documents, and TOPES from Bell Labs [26], which has a graphics teleconferencing mode for designing the layout of buildings. Hybrid systems using a communication link for both voice and phone have also been created, such as the Tango Interactive Word Processor from Teneron Corporation [see [29]], which allows two PCs to be switched between voice and data communications. The term often used for a task-specific computer conference system has been *computer-mediated communication*, which is indeed an example of a Participant System. Hiltz [16] has, in this context, proposed systems that support multiperson games such as bridge and Monopoly, and Johansen [20] has certainly pointed out that a participant might be an AI-oriented program or an expert system. However, this term lends too much emphasis to the aspect of communication and not enough to the task-oriented nature of collaborative work, which is the domain that Participant Systems address in particular. Another contribution of this paper is to point out the need to explicitly address characteristics of Participant Systems founded in the psychology of small group behavior and to provide mechanisms for implementing them in computer-based systems supporting human collaboration.

There is a growing literature in the area of distributed artificial intelligence, contributed by researchers like Smith, Rosenschein, Genesereth, Corkill, Lesser, Ensor, Cam-

335

marata, Georgeff and Hewitt [32,28,7,9,5,12,17,18]. The general orientation is on how intelligent agents actually solve problems in distributed environments, through planning, cooperative or competitive paradigms. In Participant Systems, we have addressed the characteristics of human group behavior conducive to problem solving, without stating what the actual group processes of problem solving are. In order for Participant Systems to support human collaboration, we have emphasized the need to provide mechanisms conducive to establishing social cohesiveness. It is anticipated that the research in Participant Systems will be very relevant to the design of hybrid systems that feature symbiotic relationships between intelligent human and cybernetic agents in the task of cooperative problem solving. After all, if humans collaborate with machines, we can only do so within our cultural framework, which finds expression in terms of elements like cohesiveness and paraverbal messages.

11.5 Conclusion

In summary, this paper has presented Participant Systems as computer systems that support collaborative intellectual tasks among a number of persons, possibly distributed in different locations. Based on observations of the psychology of small groups, we have noted the balance that needs to be maintained between social cohesiveness and structural rigidity, and the requirement that a shared understanding of communication rules is present. This extends to paraverbal mechanisms such as chronemics, dealing with a person's view of time, and we proposed that effective Participant Systems should implement time coherence by providing messages in real-time and deal with the subclass of problems that inherently lend structure to the group. Furthermore, we suggested that it is desirable to provide verbal and paraverbal analogues in Participant Systems in the form of task and metatask levels of communication.

We then proposed a software structure for implementing Participant Systems, based on a few simple modules that implemented operational components such as user interfaces, data bases, graphics, and computer communications. The implementation of this structure in a mix of distributed and centralized paradigms gave rise to a taxonomy of Participant Systems, which describe a range of systems that vary in implementation strategy and behavior. Cantata and PCS are two Participant Systems whose design reflect some of the considerations stated above.

It is the convergence of a number of technologies like distributed control, bit-mapped workstations, expert systems, and computer networks that make the creation of Participant Systems feasible. There are many human problems that require collaboration, and it is to these that Participant Systems are addressed. Successful implementations of Participant Systems can only be beneficial, for collaboration is a human activity that is sometimes painful, sometimes rewarding, often difficult, but indelible from the face of human society.

Acknowledgements

This chapter is based on "Participant Systems", which appears in *Future Computing Systems*, vol. 1(3), 1986, with the permission of the editors.

References

[1] P. A. Andersen, "Nonverbal Communication in the Small Group," in *Small Group Communication*, ed. R. S. Cathcart and L. A. Samovar, Wm. C. Brown, Dubuque, Iowa, 1984.

[2] J. E. Baird Jr. and S. B. Weinberg, "Elements of Group Communication," in *Small Group Communication*, ed. R. S. Cathcart and L. A. Samovar, Wm. C. Brown, Dubuque, Iowa, 1984.

[3] J. H. Boose, "A knowledge acquisition program for expert systems based on personal construct psychology," *International Journal of Man-Machine Studies*, vol. 23, no. 5, pp. 495-526, November 1985.

[4] J. Bregenzer and J. P. Martino, "Future Research Group Experience with Computerized Conferencing," in *Electronic Communication: Technology and Impacts*, ed. M. M. Henderson and M. J. MacNaughton, AAAS Selected Symposium 52, Westview Press, Boulder, CO, 1980.

[5] S. Cammarata, D. McArthur, and R. Steeb, "Strategies of Cooperation in Distributed Problem Solving," *Proceedings IJCAI-83*, 1983.

[6] G. Carter, "CONFER - A Preliminary Design Concept," *Proc. IEEE International Conference on Systems, Man and Cybernetics*, Dallas, 1974.

[7] D. D. Corkill and V. R. Lesser, "The Use of Meta-Level Control for Coordination in a Distributed Problem Solving Network," *Proceedings IJCAI-83*, 1983.

[8] D. C. Englebert and W. K. English, "A Research Center for Augmenting Human Intellect," *Proc. Fall Joint Computer Conference*, Thompson Book, Washington, DC, 1968.

[9] J. R. Ensor and J. D. Gabbe, "Transactional Blackboards," *Proceedings IJCAI-85*, Los Angeles, CA, 1985.

[10] B. A. Fisher, *Small Group Decision Making*, McGraw-Hill, 1974.

[11] B. R. Gaines and M. L. Shaw, "Induction of inference rules for expert systems, Fuzzy Sets and Systems," (to appear), 1985.

[12] M. Georgeff, "Communication and Interaction in Multi-Agent Planning," *Proceedings AAAI-83*, 1983.

[13] S. R. Hiltz and M. Turoff, "Structuring Computer-Mediated Communications Systems to Avoid Information Overload," *Communications of the ACM*, vol. 28, no. 7, pp. 680-689, July 1985.

[14] S. R. Hiltz, *On-line Communities*, Ablex Publ., Norwood, NJ, 1984.

[15] S. R. Hiltz and M. Turoff, "The Evolution of User Behavior in a Computerized Conferencing System," *Communications of the ACM*, vol. 24, no. 1, pp. 739-751, November 1981.

[16] S. R. Hiltz and M. Turoff, *The Network Nation*, Addison Wesley, 1978.

[17] C. Hewitt and P. De Jong, "Analyzing the Roles of Descriptions and Actions in Open Systems," *Proceedings AAAI-83*, 1983.

[18] C. Hewitt and P. De Jong, "Open Systems," Report AIM-691, Artificial Intelligence Laboratory, Massachussetts Institute of Technology, Cambridge, MA, 1982.

[19] R. Johansen, J. Vallee, and K. Springer, *Electronic Meetings: Technical Alternatives and Social Choices*, Addison Wesley, 1979.

[20] R. Johansen, *Teleconferencing and Beyond*, McGraw-Hill, 1984.

[21] I. N. Jilson, "Final Evaluation Report: Nonmedical Use of Drugs," *Computer Engineering Conferenceing System Pilot Phase*, Non-Medical Use of Drugs Directorate, 365 Laurier St., Ottawa, 1975.

[22] G. A. Kelly, *The Psychology of Personal Constructs*, W. W. Norton, New York, 1955.

[23] K. A. Lantz and W. I. Nowicki, "Structured Graphics for Distributed Systems," *ACM Transactions on Graphics*, vol. 3, no. 1, pp. 23-53, January 1984.

[24] R. F. Maier, *Proble Solving Discussions and Conference*, McGraw-Hill, NY, 1963.

[25] A. Newell, "One Final Word," in *Problem Solving and Education*, ed. Tumci and Reif, Lawrence Erlbaum Assoc., Hillsdale, NJ, 1980.

[26] W. Pferd, L. A. Peralta, et al., "Interactive Graphics Teleconferencing," *IEEE Computer*, November 1979.

[27] S. K. Reed, *Cognition: Theory and Applications*, Brooks/Cole Pub., Monterey, California, 1982.

[28] J. S. Rosenschein and M. R. Genesereth, "Deals Among Rational Agents," *Proceedings IJCAI-85*, Los Angeles, CA, 1985.

[29] S. Sarin and I. Greif, "Computer Based Real-Time Conferencing Systems," *IEEE Computer*, October 1985.

[30] M. L. Shaw, "Conversational heuristics for eliciting shared understanding," *International Journal of Man-Machine Studies*, vol. 1, no. 1, pp. 621-634, 1979.

[31] S. B. Shimanoff, "Coordinating Group Interaction Via Communication Rules," in *Small Group Communications*, ed. R. S. Cathcart, L. A. Samovar, Wm. C. Brown, Dubuque, Iowa, 1984.

[32] R. G. Smith, "Negotiation as a Metaphor for Distributed Problem Solving," *Artificial Intelligence*, vol. 20, no. 1, pp. 63-109, 1983.

[33] M. Stefik, "The Next Knowledge Medium," *The AI Magazine*, vol. VII, no. 1, Spring 1986.

[34] S. A. Umpleby, "Computer Conference on General Systems Theory: One Year's Experience," in *Electronic Communication: Technology and Impacts*, ed. M. M. Henderson and M. J. MacNaughton, AAAS Selected Symposium 52, Westview Press, Boulder, CO, 1980.

Ernest Chang[1]
Advanced Technologies
Alberta Research Council
Calgary, Alberta

---

[1]On leave from Department of Computer Science, University of Victoria, Victoria, B.C.

Chapter 12

Distributed Artificial Intelligence: An Annotated Bibliography

V. Jagannathan and Rajendra Dodhiawala

Abstract

Distributed Artificial Intelligence (DAI) refers to the subarea of AI concerned with the problem of using multiple processors to solve AI problems. The question is how does one harness the advances in the hardware technology in a meaningful manner? This has spurred research in a variety of theoretical and practical issues. On the theoretical side, there has been considerable interest on the issue of modeling human cooperation. On the practical side, for instance, the blackboard model has been proposed as a vehicle to implement such cooperation. Considerable effort has been spent on identifying the intrinsic parallelism in AI problems which can then be exploited using multiple processors. This has resulted in an ongoing debate on the granularity of the parallelism, an area that needs further study. On the one hand, we have the concept of a knowledge source that basically defines a unit of knowledge, as well as the granularity level. On the other, we have the logic programming group that envisions granularity at the individual clause level. This annotated bibliography is an effort to compile the various perspectives which are relevant to the area of DAI. The annotations have been organized on the basis of the institutions with which the first author is/was associated when the research was done. This approach was selected to allow the reader to identify those institutions which are sponsoring work in this field.

Advanced Information and Decision Systems
Mountain View, CA

J. M. Abram, C. Y. Chang, V. G. Rutenburg, E. Tse, and R. P. Wishner, "Distributed Decision Making Environment," Interim Report, Report RADC-TR-82-310, Advanced Information and Decision Systems, December 1982.

> The authors present an extensive survey of different areas which have bearing on distributed problem solving. These include decision theory and decision analysis, optimization theory, distributed dynamic programming, decentralized stochastic control, distributed AI, etc. The rationale for examining these widely varying areas is to come up with a unified environment for distributed decision making.

C. Y. Chang, S. Mori, E. Tse, and R. P. Wishner, "A General Theory for Bayesian Multitarget Tracking and Classification—Generalized Tracker/Classifier (GTC)," Technical Report, ARPA Order 4272, Contract MDA 903-81-C-0333, Advanced Information and Decision Systems, December 1982.

> The authors discuss a theoretical approach for situation assessment for multiple target identification. The approach is centralized; however implications for a more distributed decision making are pursued in the related paper by Abram et al. (1982).

M. Fehling and L. Erman, "Report on the the Third Annual Workshop on Distributed Artificial Intelligence," *SIGART Newsletter*, no. 84, Spring 1983.

> Contains abstracts of papers presented in this workshop and a summary of the informal discussions. The themes in the informal discussions were: the value of DAI in promoting modular design, communication/computation tradeoffs, representation of knowledge sources, control issues, coherence and focusing in control, can individually dumb agents collectively be intelligent? and, finally, a realization that most conventional AI issues remain relevant in a distributed setting.

342

AT&T Bell Laboratories
Short Hills, NJ

J. R. Ensor and J. D. Gabbe, "Transactional Blackboard," *Proceedings of the Ninth IJCAI*, August 1985, pp. 340-344.

> The authors have extended the database concepts of locking records to enable concurrent access to the implementation of a blackboard system.

N. A. Khan and R. Jain, "Explaining Uncertainty in a Completely Distributed Expert System," *Proceedings of the Workshop on Coupling Symbolic and Numerical Computing in Expert Systems*, Bellevue, WA, August 1985.

> Here complete distribution is taken to mean the following: In a hierarchically structured set of knowledge sources, there is cooperation at any given level as well as between levels, accomplished with the help of a blackboard. The problem domain is recognition of an object.

Boeing Advanced Technology Center for Computer Sciences
Seattle, WA

M. Benda, V. Jagannathan, and R. Dodhiawala, "On Optimal Cooperation of Knowledge Sources," Boeing Artificial Intelligence Center, Boeing Computer Services, Technical Report BCS-G2010-28, August 1985.

> This paper describes the experiments performed to measure how organization of knowledge sources influences the performance of a system within a blackboard framework. Basic organizations are described from which more complex ones can be derived. The scenario chosen for experimentation is one where multiple agents are required to corner an adversary. Cooperation between knowledge sources was dependent on the organization, and measures for the degree of effectiveness are proposed for some of the organizations experimented. Results are discussed based on the proposed measures.

K. M. Chalfan, "A Knowledge System that Integrates Heterogeneous Software for a Design Application," *AI Magazine*, Summer 1986, pp. 80-84.

Discussion of an expert executive system which analyses data dependencies in large numerical programs and executes them in the proper sequence. The individual programs may be distributed in heterogeneous hardware/software environments. The system is built in MRS.

R. Dodhiawala, V. Jagannathan, and L. Baum, "Integrating architecture for complex system design," *Proceedings of ROBEXS-86*, Houston, Texas, June 4-6, 1986.

This paper presents considerations that go into building a complex system such as the safety advisor within the space station environment. The paper explains a prototype system that was built, using a blackboard framework, to investigate the issues of cooperation within the subsystems of the space station.

V. Jagannathan, L. Baum, and R. Dodhiawala, "Constraint satisfaction and reasoning using the Boeing Blackboard System," Boeing Technical Report, March 1986.

This paper investigates the representation and reasoning with constraints in a blackboard environment. Some of the issues in constraint satisfaction are raised, and a comparison is made of similar work using AI techniques for handling constraints.

T. L. Skillman, Jr., "Distributed Cooperating Processes in a Mobile Robot Control System," Workshop on Blackboard Systems for Robot Perception and Control, June 1986.

Discussion of a blackboard based system for a "flying eye" robot. The flying eye embodies the concept of an autonomous robot with a camera useful for inspection of the outside of the space shuttle. The system described involves the simulation of the robot movement based on actual voice commands. Voice commands are interpreted by the listner/speaker knowledge source. The command interpreter knowledge source interprets commands posted to the blackboard. The path planner knowledge source provides routing information to move the flying eye. The motion control knowledge source translates this information to actual fine grained movement. And there are other knowledge sources to control the camera angle, and maintaining the graphic simulation. All of the knowledge sources are independent processes running on diverse hardware/software environments. The hardware environments are Apollo DN660, Symbolics, Interstate VRT200 and DEC DECTALK. The software include Franz Lisp, Zetalisp and C.

Carnegie-Mellon University
Pittsburg, PA

L. D. Erman and V. R. Lesser, "A Multi-Level Organization for Problem Solving Using Many, Diverse Cooperating Sources of Knowledge," *Proceedings of IJCAI*, Tbilisi, USSR, 1975, pp. 483-490.

This paper presents the implementation details of HEARSAY-II. It mainly stresses the hypothesize-and-test paradigm for cooperative problem solving by diverse and independent KSs. Details of the KS structure and mechanism, and the blackboard have been described along with the notions of goal directed scheduling and data directed KS activation. It also includes an in-depth explanation of the approach to cooperative problem solving.

L. D. Erman, R. D. Fennell, V. L. Lesser, and D. R. Reddy, "System Organizations for Speech Understanding: Implications of Network and Multiprocessor Computer Architectures for AI," *IEEE Transactions on Computers*, vol. C-25, no. 4, April 1976, pp. 414-421.

This paper explains the considerations that led to the development of the HEARSAY speech understanding system. The problem lent itself well to the concept of multiple knowledge sources cooperating to solve a single problem. Each knowledge source represents a process in a multiprogramming environment, each independent and capable of removal without affecting the others. However, there needs to be some interaction amongst the processes so as to achieve the system goals. This conflict in requirements led to the design of a uniform global data structure (later to be known as the blackboard) through which the processes would communicate and interface. The paper further explores the organizations of closely coupled processor systems to exploit the parallelism that is evident in speech understanding type of problems. The newer issues raised by these architectures are further discussed. Also evaluated is the loosely coupled network architecture where each set of processes has

345

its own processor, and communication is by sharing physical address spaces. There is no shared data and efficient control schemes are now needed. It is this network organization that seems very promising to the authors, and requires more attention for solving a large class of AI problems.

L. D. Erman, F. Hayes-Roth, V. Lesser, and R. Reddy, "The HEARSAY-II Speech Understanding System: Integrating Knowledge to Resolve Uncertainty," *Computing Surveys*, vol. 12, no. 2, 1980, pp. 213-253.

HEARSAY-II, a speech understanding system, handles a limited vocabulary of about 1000 words. The HEARSAY-II system introduced the concept of a global database called the Blackboard, with diverse knowledge sources controlled by an opportunistic scheduler. The task of speech understanding as implemented in HEARSAY-II requires cooperation among the knowledge sources which operate in a layered space of hypotheses. These hypothesis levels are acoustic parameters, acoustic segment, syllable classes, word control, word sequence, and parsing phrases. There is a continuous interaction with a database to generate plausible hypotheses between appropriate levels. HEARSAY-II did reasonably well to address the problems of large search spaces, possible inconsistencies in input speech signal, and time constraints. It does both top-down and bottom-up processing.

L. D. Erman, P. E. London, and S. F. Fickas, "The Design and an Example Use of HEARSAY-III," *Proceedings of IJCAI*, August 1981, pp. 409- 405.

This paper describes the implementation of the domain independent HEARSAY-III expert system building tool. The blackboard is divided into domain and control blackboards, and the whole system is built on top of a relational database called AP3. It introduces "context" mechanism, "choice sets" of alternate hypotheses, "poisoning" of contexts and choice sets. AP3 provides strong typing in database access, and all facilities of AP3 are also available to the user. Objects on the blackboards are called "units," and are connected by relations called "roles." Knowledge sources have triggering information, immediate code, and action parts. The scheduler is built in two layers, with flexible encoding facilities for sophisticated scheduling. An example is included.

R. D. Fennel and V. R. Lesser, "Parallelism in Artificial Intelligence Problem Solving: A Case Study of HEARSAY-II," *IEEE Computer*, vol. C26, no. 2, February 1977, pp. 98-111.

This is an analysis of HEARSAY-II with respect to parallelism and multiprocessor implementation of the system. It discusses the "hypothesize and test" paradigm, "data integrity" mechanism to implement the concept of critical sections, and the "local context" concept to segment the knowledge base and to provide for personalized operating environments for the knowledge sources. Simulation experiments include tests on overhead of multiprocessing, and parallelism and processor utilization, interprocess communication, and different system organizations. These performance results help gain an insight and provide a guidance in the development of blackboard architecture systems.

C. L. Forgy, "A Production System Monitor for Parallel Computers," AFOSR-TR-77-0795, Carnegie-Mellon University, Dept. of Computer Science, April 1977.

This paper presents an implementation of a monitor for a small production system, based on OPS. The need for parallel execution of the LHS and RHS of rules is necessitated by the fact that large production systems tend to be slow. Besides, the capability of parallel computers can be used advantageously as is done using monitors in operating systems. The issues of context and structural similarities will help make matching relatively easier in a large parallel production system. However, the monitors are hard to implement.

M. S. Fox, "An Organizational View of Distributed Systems," *IEEE Transactions on Systems, Man, and Cybernetics*, vol. SMC-11, no. 1, January 1981, pp. 70-80,

Distributed computer systems and human organizations are compared. Organization theoretic concepts are introduced and these ideas are compared to the concept behind the HEARSAY-II system. It further elaborates the organizational structure and control, starting from single-person, to group, to a hierarchy, to a multidivision hierarchy, to a pricing system. These evolve with the complexity of the task and are explained with reference to the HEARSAY structure for speech understanding. It also elucidates factors which influence the choice of a particular organization, with emphasis on the complexity and uncertainty reduction techniques.

C. H. Howard and D. R. Rehak, "Knowledge-Based Database Management for Expert Systems," *SIGART Newsletter*, no. 92, April 1985, pp. 95-97.

CAD system design, integrating concepts from distributed database design and distributed AI, is discussed. The idea here is that each of the distributed databases is fitted with an AI frontend. Queries are transmitted back and forth based on the idea of cooperation on a blackboard. KADBASE, the system under implementation, is built using Common Lisp and SRL and interfaces to INGRES and RIMS over an Ethernet.

D. R. Rehak, "An Integrated Knowledge-Based Systems Architecture for CAE," *SIGART Newsletter*, no. 92, April 1985, pp. 53-55.

See comments on Howard and Rehak (immediately above).

M. D. Rychener, R. Banares-Alcantara, and E. Subrahamanian, "A Rule-Based Blackboard Kernel System: Some Principles in Design," *Proceedings of IEEE Workshop on Principles of Knowledge-Based Systems*, December 1984, pp. 59-64.

Discussions are provided of some applications implemented based on the blackboard model.

S. N. Talukdar, A. Elfes, E. Cardozo, R. Joobbani, M. Rychener, and R. Benares, "Some Blackboard Schemes for Linking Parallel Processes," *Proceedings of the Workshop on Coupling Symbolics and Numerical Computing in Expert Systems*, August 1985.

The authors discuss a blackboard-based architecture for mobile robot control.

Columbia University
New York, NY

S. J. Stolfo and D. E. Shaw, "DADO: A Tree Structured Machine Architecture for Production Systems," pp. 242-246.

The paper explains the DADO machine being built at Columbia University to help improve performance of large production systems. It is a binary tree structured machine having the capability of parallel execution of commutative and multiple independent production systems.

Defense Research Establishment
Dartmouth, Canada

R. G. Smith and R. Davis, "Frameworks for Cooperation in Distributed Problem Solving," *IEEE Transactions on Systems, Man, and Cybernetics*, vol. SMC-11, no. 1, January 1981, pp. 61-70.

This paper explores two important elements of distributed problem solving, namely task-sharing and result-sharing. It begins by giving the differences between traditional distributed processing and distributed problem solving. It then explains the task-sharing paradigm with reference to the contract-net protocol and gives the major features of this form of cooperation. Result-sharing is explained with reference to examples from the blocks world and distributed interpretation in HEARSAY-II. Then, these two approaches are compared and some ideas are presented on problem domains where each could be applicable.

Harvard University
Cambridge, MA

Yu-chi Ho, "Team Decision Theory and Information Structures," *Proceedings of the IEEE*, vol. 68, no. 6, June 1980, pp. 644-654.

This paper presents methodologies for decentralized statistical decision making in an uncertain environment. Examples of the concepts are given. It also explores the value of information in such situations and asserts that there could be a relation to organizational theory because the organizational structure is designed to achieve information efficiency.

IBM Research Laboratory
San Jose, CA

J. Y. Halpern and Y. Moses, "Knowledge and Common Knowledge in a Distributed Environment," *Journal of the Association for Computing Machinery*, January 1984, pp. 50-61.

An understanding of distributed protocols is possible by understanding how messages change the state of knowledge of the system. Knowledge is presented as a hierarchy and the communication that would be required to move up the hierarchy. Common knowledge is the highest in this structure and is essential for reaching agreements and proper coordination. However, it is shown that common knowledge is not attainable in real world systems. Alternatives to common knowledge are presented which make a compromise as to the knowledge that really would be attainable. This knowledge perspective approach to distributed processing gives a broader understanding of the distributed communication and distributed consensus protocols.

IBM Zurich Research Laboratory
Ruschlikon, Switzerland

D. Brand and P. Zafiropulo, "On Communicating Finite-State Machines," *Journal of the Association for Computing Machinery*, vol. 30, no. 2, April 83, pp. 323-342.

This paper explains the use of finite-state theory in designing communication protocols in a distributed computing and networked environment. It presents a lot of results and definitions, and discusses theoretical issues of this form of protocol design.

Information Sciences Division, Electrotechnical Laboratory
Toyko, Japan

M. Suwa, K. Furukawa, A. Makinouchi, T. Mizoguchi, F. Mizoguchi, and H. Yamasaki, *Fifth Generation Computer Systems*, ed. T. Motooka, 1982, pp. 139-145.

This paper gives some of the goals of the Fifth Generation project with regard to knowledge base mechanisms. It addresses issues of knowledge acquisition, knowledge representation, distributed knowledge-bases and distributed problem solving. The plan is to build a Fifth Generation Knowledge Representation Language (FGKRL) which would attempt to solve these issues in three phases of the project. It addresses the importance of cooperative, distributed problem solving as an ultimate project objective.

INRIA Sophia-Antipolis
Valbonne, France

P. Haren, B. Neveu, J. P. Giacometti, M. Montalban, and O. Corby, "SMECI: Cooperating Expert Systems for Civil Engineering Design," *SIGART Newsletter*, no. 92, April 1985, pp. 67-69.

A discussion is provided of a CAD system for ocean harbor design based on cooperating expert systems on a blackboard.

Institute for Co-ordination of Computer Techniques
Budapest, Hungary

I. Futo and J. Szeredi, "System Simulation and Cooperative Problem-Solving on a Prolog Basis," *Implementations of Prolog*, ed. Campbell, J. A., John Wiley & Sons, 1984, pp. 163-174.

The authors developed a T-Prolog system for simulation capable of recognizing failures in a system simulation, and backtracking from the situation to try new alternatives. Thus, a whole class of possible models can be specified in a simulation of a problem, and the system will automatically investigate these by careful selection. T-Prolog incorporates problem solving by cooperative processes, communication by messages, and modeling time duration. Scheduling and control components for the problem solving task are also included.

Institute for New Generation Computer Technology
Tokyo, Japan

N. Ito, H. Shimizu, M. Kishi, E. Kuno, and K. Rokusawa, "Data-Flow Based Execution Mechanisms of Parallel and Concurrent Prolog," *New Generation Computing*, vol. 3, 1985, pp. 15-41.

> This is a discussion of how AND and OR parallelism can be implemented in a data-flow machine using either Parallel or Concurrent Prolog. Though parallelism and concurrency more or less refer to the same thing, in Prolog it refers to two different languages. The former exploits AND/OR parallelism and the latter implements an object-oriented paradigm.

K. Murakami, T. Kakuta, R. Onai, and N. Ito, "Research on Parallel Machine Architecture for Fifth-Generation Computer Systems," *Computer*, June 1985, pp. 76-92.

> This article includes reviews of different methods for developing a parallel inference machine-reduction mechanism, which is based on exploiting the AND/OR parallelism for Prolog programs and the data flow mechanism. Architectures based on these models are presented. An architecture based on a database machine is also reviewed.

Laboratoire d'Autamatique
Toulouse, France

P. Azema, G. Juanole, E. Sanchis, and M. Montbernard, "Specification and Verification of Distributed Systems Using Prolog-Interpreted Petri-Nets," *Proceedings of the IEEE Software Engineering Conference*, 1984, pp. 510-518.

> This paper describes the use of petri nets as a modeling tool and prolog as a programming environment for predicate-transition nets. Also described is a technique for interfacing concurrent processes in such a distributed system.

Louisiana State University
Baton Rouge, LA

G. R. Cross, "Design of a Knowledge-Based Multi-Sensor Information Integration System," Private Communication, July 1983.

> This paper describes the use of distributed problem solving techniques to detect and track enemy ships using sonar, ESM, ISAR, and radar data. The design is based on the HEARSAY-II system, incorporating a blackboard and knowledge sources for generating hypotheses on the blackboard. This approach is selected after reviewing work by Davis and Smith on Contract Net, Hewitt on Actors and message passing, and Wesson's work on Network Structures. A Sensor Representation Language is proposed which would include features of object- oriented programming.

R. T. Dodhiawala and G. R. Cross, "A Distributed Problem-Solving Approach to Point-Pattern Matching," *Proceedings of Winter 85 Machine Vision Conference*, Lake Tahoe, Nevada, March 1985.

> This paper describes an expert system built using HEARSAY-III to analyze cosmic ray data. It uses point-pattern matching algorithms to track the linear movement of cosmic particles in three-dimensional space. The methodology incorporates the techniques of distributed problem solving and image processing.

Massachusetts Institute of Technology
Cambridge, MA

R. Davis, "Meta-Rules: Reasoning About Rules," *Artificial Intelligence Journal*, vol. 15, no. 3, December 1980, pp. 179-222.

> This paper describes the concept of meta-rules, specifically as applied in the control of problem solving tasks. In the presence of a large number of knowledge sources that can be invoked at any point in the problem solving task, it becomes necessary to reduce/reorder the KSs so as to improve the result of KSs' invocation. Any problem solver has to retrieve, refine, and execute the KSs to achieve its goal. Use of knowledge about knowledge, especially in the refinement stage helps make the system more flexible in its approach to problem solving. This paper describes the shortcomings of a system without meta-rules, and further explores the advantages of introducing meta-rules.

R. Davis, "Content Reference: Reasoning About Rules," *Artificial Intelligence Journal*, vol. 15, no. 3, December 1980, pp. 223-239.

This paper is a follow-up of the previous paper. It deals with the engineering issue related to the implementation of meta-rules in a knowledge-based system. It discusses ways to deal with saturation at KS selection and asserts that the content reference mechanism is most advantageous in giving the system the ability to reason about its content of knowledge.

R. Davis, "Report on the Workshop on Distributed AI," *SIGART Newsletter*, no. 73, October 1980, pp. 42-52.

This report on the first workshop to be conducted in this area discusses differences between distributed AI and distributed processing. A breadth of ideas are presented and include: organizational issues, planning and multiagent planning, contract-net systems, message passing systems, and some applications of DAI.

R. Davis and R. D. Smith, "Negotiation as a Metaphor for Distributed Problem Solving," *Artificial Intelligence*, vol. 20, no. 1, January 1983, pp. 63-109.

Similar to the other contract-net paper (Smith et al.), this one contains a comparison between distributed processing and distributed problem solving.

C. Hewitt, "Viewing Control Structures as Patterns of Passing Messages," *Artificial Intelligence*, August 1977, vol. 8, pp. 323-364.

This paper introduces the concept of actors and message passing, and how this metaphor can be used in problem solving. This theory lends itself well to communication and parallelism in a general problem solving environment. An actor language called PLASMA is given in the appendix.

C. Hewitt and P. de Jong, "Analyzing the Roles of Descriptions and Actions in Open Systems," *Proceedings of AAAI*, 1983, pp. 162- 167.

This paper describes the concept of actors as related to large-scale open-ended, geographically distributed, concurrent systems. It further explains the distinction between description and action in such systems. It is similar to stating that something exists or that a goal needs to be achieved. But these concepts are different from actually taking the actions needed to accomplish anything. Actors seem to provide the required conceptual interface between hardware and software for parallel computer systems. It is claimed that the actor definition is based on sound mathematical theories, and is logically independent of all other programming languages and hardware architectures. Descriptive languages based on first order logic and/or the lambda calculus have been designed to express properties, but are incapable of taking actions. On the other hand, procedural languages have been designed to take action, but lack descriptive features. ACT2 developed at MIT is designed to combine these two features.

W. A. Kornfeld and C. E. Hewitt, "The Scientific Community Metaphor," *IEEE Transactions on Systems, Man, and Cybernetics*, vol. SMC-11, no. 1, January 1981, pp. 24-33.

This paper discusses modeling distributed problem solving on the scientific community, specifically the idea of resource constraints modeled after proposals and sponsors. Knowledge sources (agents) are called sprites and are triggered when certain fact(s) are asserted on a global data base (not called blackboard). It follows work on ACT1 and precedes ACT2 system design.

Reid G. Smith, "The Contract Net Protocol: High-Level Communication and Control in a Distributed Problem Solver," *IEEE Transactions on Systems, Man, and Cybernetics*, vol. C-29, no. 12, December 1980.

This protocol is basically modeled after government contract awarding setup. It generates considerable communication overhead.

R. R. Tenney and N. R. Sandell, "Structures for Distributed Decisionmaking," *IEEE Transactions in Systems, Man, and Cybernetics*, vol. SMC-11, no. 8, August 1981, pp. 517-527.

This paper presents a framework for structuring decision makers in a real-time, complex, distributed, environment. The framework is based on the assumption that each decision maker has incomplete, and possibly inconsistent, information about the system. Thus, this agent needs to communicate with other such agents in the system so as to reach a plausible solution to the problem. Each agent has no knowledge of the effects of its processing on the rest of the system. Decentralized control in decision makers and coordination of the planning activities is highly dependent on the communication facilities available to them. Each individual agent and its state is called a "domule", which has the dynamic structure of the subsystem in which it is an "expert." The coordination process may be achieved by first selecting interactions between system components, and then solving local, decoupled optimization problems. A companion paper discusses cooperation strategies. (See next item.)

R. R. Tenney and N. R. Sandell, "Strategies for Distributed Decisionmaking," *IEEE Transactions on Systems, Man, and Cybernetics*, vol. SMC-11, no. 8, August 1981, pp. 527-538.

This paper explains and provides measures to compare different strategies of decentralized control in distributed decision making. Centralized control does not seem to produce acceptable decisions and fails to exhibit anticipated behaviors. Decentralized control makes use of knowledge local only to an agent, use of uncertainty, and opportunistic problem solving strategies. This permits reduction of information inconsistency from other agents about future capabilities, use of high-level abstraction of the complete system, and analysis of system topologies as appropriate. The coordination strategies discussed and compared using different system structures are static–no communication, prediction, finite horizon, abstraction, and hybrid. Finally, it is suggested that most of these could be implemented more efficiently depending on the problem being solved.

A. Yonezawa and C. Hewitt, "Modeling Distributed Systems," AI MEMO-428, Massachusetts Institute of Technology, Artificial Intelligence Laboratory, Cambridge, MA., June 1977.

A description is presented of multiprocessing, distributed problem solving based on the concept of "actors". Communication and cooperation between actors is by message passing with flexible control structures. This model of computation has been implemented as a programming language called PLASMA. The concept is further explained by an example of an airline reservation system. It seems that this approach to problem solving would have limited capability and could be integrated with other techniques for problem solving. The concept of actors and messages is a forerunner to object-oriented programming.

NASA Langley Research Center
Hampton, VA

N. E. Orlando, "An Intelligent Robotics Control Scheme," *IEEE American Control Conference—Control and Automation in the Information Age*, 1984, pp. 204-209.

This material discusses a hierarchical robot control scheme that distinguishes between two levels of control termed tactical and strategical. Here tactical corresponds to the emulation of the involuntary control of muscles in humans and strategical corresponds to the voluntary (explicit planning) control. Distributed processing is explored so as to achieve parallelism and real-time performance. Implementation of DAISIE incorporates AI techniques and provides a testbed for experimentation into the concepts proposed in this paper.

Naval Air Development Center
Warminster, PA

J. Goodson, W. Zachary, J. Deimler, J. Stokes, and W. Weiland, "Distributed Intelligence Systems: AI Approaches to Cooperative Man-Machine Problem Solving in C3I," *Proceedings of the AIAA Computers in Aerospace IV Conference*, Hartford, Connecticut, October 1983, pp. 1-8.

The authors discuss an application drawn from the domain of antisubmarine warfare that illustrates the concept of distributed AI as well as cooperation between man and machine.

Naval Oceans Systems Center
San Diego, CA

S. Y. Harmon, W. A. Aviles, and D. W. Gage, "A technique for coordinating autonomous robots," *IEEE International Conference on Robotics and Automation*, San Fransisco, CA, April 7-10, 1986, pp. 2029-2034.

This paper describes a distributed blackboard environment for information exchange and structuring in a single robot and also in a collection of co-operating robots. Since communication bandwidth is a significant limiting factor compared to the processing capabilities, a distributed black-board system offers a variety of features which deal with the inherent complexity of sophisticated robot systems. The papers describes some of these features and the implementation of single robot and multiple robot systems. It also gives the advantages of the blackboard paradigm in the applications the authors have built.

Northwestern University
Evanston, IL

S. S. Yau and S. M. Shatz, "On Communication in the Design of Software Components of Distributed Computer Systems," *Proceedings of the Distributed Computing Systems Conference*, August 1982, pp. 280-287.

Petri-net formalism is used to design specifications of message passing in distributed computer systems. An overview of distributed communications network is given, and a formal definition of communication modules is presented, accompanied by identification of the more useful ones. Communication by message passing can be accomplished by asynchronous, synchronous, or remote invocation. These must be considered in the design of any module. A communication module should consist of input message ports, output message ports, input test ports to verify destination buffer status, output test ports, and behavior that specifies the kind of communication the module supports. Construction guidelines for communication modules is established and the dining philosopher's problem is explained in the formalisms presented in the paper.

D. C. Brown and B. Chandrasekaran, "An Approach to Expert Systems for Mechanical Design," *IEEE Computer Society Trends and Applications Conference*, Gaithersburg, MD, May 1983.

Refer to description of next paper.

D. C. Brown and B. Chandrasekaran, "Expert Systems for a Class of Mechanical Design Activity," *Proceedings of IFIP WG5.2 Working Conference on Knowledge Engineering in Computer Aided Design*, Budapest, Hungary, September 1984.

The authors discuss how to approach a class 3 design problem. Design in general can be considered as a planning activity and class 3 design is the routine form of design (or low-level design undertaken in most organizations). The approach is to use a hierarchical set of specialists. Each specialist at each level works on one abstract level of the design. An attempt is made to mimic human design process by first attempting a rough design and then cycling through the entire hierarchy of specialists to do a more refined design. Communication between specialists is in the form of messages. When a particular specialist fails, it puts forth a set of suggestions to remedy the situation. These suggestions are examined by the specialists at higher levels to invoke other specialists for redesign. Basically, this is their mechanism to implement dependency directed backtracking.

T. Bylander, S. Mittal, and B. Chandrasekaran, "CSRL: A Language for Expert Systems for Diagnosis," *Proceedings of IJCAI*, 1983.

This paper proposes a Conceptual Structures Representation Language (CSRL) based on the concept of cooperating diagnostics specialists. The domain knowledge is composed of specialists, each of which specializes in a concept of the domain. The diagnostic task is divided into a hierarchy of hypotheses, with nodes at the higher level being more general than those at the lower levels. Each node in the hierarchy is associated with a specialist who evaluates the hypothesis at its node depending on the case at hand, and, if established, will be refined by its subspecialists. CSRL is used to represent the specialists of the diagnostics hierarchy and for encoding the knowledge within them at different levels of abstraction. Message procedures describe the behavior of specialists upon receiving messages from other specialists. Knowledge groups define focus of attention for specialists, and contain rule-like knowledge. The paper then gives examples of the implementation of CSRL, and its use in building a few systems.

B. Chandrasekaran, F. Gomez, S. Mittal, and J. Smith, "An Approach to Medical Diagnosis Based on Conceptual Structures," *Proceedings of IJCAI*, Tokyo, Japan, August 1979.

Knowledge representation should reflect the underlying conceptual structures of the problem domain so that the control problem can be approached to model that used by the domain experts. This paper proposes the knowledge representation scheme called conceptual structures which is a hierarchy of concepts. Each node on this hierarchy knows about its subnode's speciality, so that the concepts it establishes can be refined. Each concept has associated with it a set of rules and control information which helps guide the problem solving. Effective cooperation between nodes is an essential part of the problem solver. The example chosen to illustrate these ideas is taken from the field of medicine–to diagnose a liver syndrome called Cholestasis. This work is compared to MYCIN, INTERNIST, and CASNET.

B. Chandrasekaran, "Natural and Social System Metaphors for Distributed Problem Solving: Introduction to the Issue," *IEEE Transactions on Systems, Man, and Cybernetics*, vol. SMC-11, no. 1, January 1981, pp. 1-5.

This paper presents some naturally occurring metaphors for distributed problem solving. It seems to be prevalent in most problems, and how these are approached by human problem solvers is very much dependent on the complexity of these tasks. Most approaches work towards organizing the problem solving activity so as to reduce the complexity. This usually gives rise to cooperation between subproblem solvers, and thus the communication required to achieve the goals reflects on the decomposition. The notion of a society of

360

specialists is presented. It also introduces other articles on this special issue on distributed problem solving.

B. Chandrasekaran, "Decomposition of Domain Knowledge into Knowledge Sources: The MDX Approach," *4th National Conference of Canadian Society for Computational Studies of Intelligence*, Saskatchewan, Canada, May 1982.

> This paper is in the series of the work on specialists. Each concept of a particular problem solving domain is represented in a hierarchy of specialists, with those at the top being more general than those at the lower levels. Thus, all knowledge of the system is distributed in such problem solvers. There is no distinction between knowledge bases and problem solvers. Implementation of these ideas is in MDX (a system for medical diagnosis), PATREC (for patient record database), and RADEX (a radiology consultant). It is emphasized that the kind of problem decomposition as suggested by the specialist concept results in a more natural control of the system. Detailed examples of the diagnostician are presented.

B. Chandrasekaran and S. Mittal, "Conceptual Representation of Medical Knowledge for Diagnosis by a Computer: MDX and Related Systems," *Advances in Computers*, Academic Press, New York, 1983, pp. 217-293.

> This paper describes in detail the MDX system and the underlying concepts. MDX is based on a hierarchy of specialists which with the help of a patient database (PATREC) and radiology data (RADEX) help to diagnose diseases. Several cases are explained. The knowledge representation and semantics of the procedural part of the system are explained. Further, the paper elaborates the use of a blackboard to introduce parallelism in the problem solving. This is a detailed paper on the approach to distributed problem solving techniques as applied to the medical domain.

B. Chandrasekaran, "Distributed Knowledge-Base Systems for Diagnosis and Information Retrieval," Annual Report, Air Force Grant No. AFOSR-82-0255, Ohio State University, August 1984.

> Basically, this paper discusses the use of a hierarchical set of specialists. The language developed to aid this process is CSRL, conceptual structures representation language. Applications developed as part of the funding were RED,

a red cell antibody identification system, and some diagnostic applications and design applications.

F. Gomez and B. Chandrasekaran, "Knowledge Organization and Distribution for Medical Diagnosis," *IEEE Transactions on Systems, Man and Cybernetics*, vol. SMC- 11, no. 1, January 1981, pp. 34- 42.

This paper basically explains the organization of knowledge into a hierarchy of knowledge sources (specialists) who cooperate on a blackboard to solve a diagnostic task.

F. Gomez and B. Chandrasekaran, "Knowledge Organization and Distribution for Medical Diagnosis," *IEEE Transactions on Systems, Man, and Cybernetics*, vol. SMC-11, no. 1, January 1981, pp. 34-42.

An extension of the blackboard architecture to a medical diagnosis problem domain is presented in this report . However, the knowledge representation is unique and revolves around "concepts" and "specialists." The authors also discuss how distributed problem solving techniques are incorporated into their approach.

V. S. Moorthy and B. Chandrasekaran, "A Representation for the Functioning of Devices That Support Compilation of Expert Problem Solving Structures—An Extended Summary," *Proceedings of Medcomp*, IEEE Computer Society, 1983.

Refer to the description of the next paper.

V. S. Moorthy and B. Chandrasekaran, "Functional Representation of Devices and Compilation of Diagnostic Problem Solving Systems," AI Group, Department of Computer and Information Sciences, Ohio State University, August 1984.

Both this paper, and the previously listed one, draw on the concept of abstraction. Each level of a causal relationship is represented with a functional orientation. Each level consists of 1) structure, 2) function, 3) behavior, 4) generic knowledge, and 5) assumptions. It discusses de Kleer's idea of assumption-based reasoning: If assumption1 is true then $x \Rightarrow y$, because behavior1 is represented as

362

```
function :   y (state)
             IF x (state) is true
             PROVIDED assumption1 holds
             BY behavior1
```

It also discusses a hierarchy of specialists, but does not consider how the control issue is tackled. A contrast is drawn between this functional approach and de Kleer's more behavioral approach. Knowledge represented in the above form is then compiled to obtain production rules for a diagnostician.

M. C. Tanner and T. Bylander, "Application of the CSRL Language to the Design of Expert Diagnosis Systems: The Auto-Mech Experience," Report, Department of Computer and Information Science, Ohio State University, November 1983.

This paper discusses an application of the specialist concept.

Rand Corporation
Santa Monica, CA

S. Cammarata, D. McArthur, and R. Steeb, "Strategies of Cooperation in Distributed Problem Solving," *Proceedings of IJCAI*, 1983, pp. 767-770.

The authors discuss four different ways distributed problem solving in a particular application can be applied. The application is distributed air traffic control. Some of the features described are: 1) one agent arbitrarily selected to replan its activity to avoid conflict with others, 2) the least constrained agent selected, 3) the most knowledgeable one selected, and 4) most knowledgeable agent replans other agents for global coherence. Measurements are taken that show the behavioral properties of complex cooperative strategies under different organizations.

B. Hayes-Roth, F. Hayes-Roth, S. Rosenschein, and S. Cammarata, "Modeling Planning as an Incremental, Opportunistic Process," *Proceedings of IJCAI*, 1979, pp. 375-383.

This paper is a forerunner to the BB1 system. It focuses on the planning of tasks using the blackboard model of computation. It takes the example of an errand task to explain the planning process as computationally feasible and psychologically reasonable. The planning blackboard incorporates the independent and asynchronous activity of several specialists (KSs), each making tentative decision on the tentative plans that focus towards the achievement of the final plan. The blackboard is hierarchically structured into five planes, each containing several levels of abstraction. This complete scheme is also available in the BB1 system.

B. Hayes-Roth and F. Hayes-Roth, "A Cognitive Model of Planning," *Cognitive Science*, vol. 3, no. 3, 1979, pp. 275-310.

This paper gives the concepts of planning that led to the implementation in BB1. The paper describes an opportunistic model of planning, and the use of the blackboard as a means for the realization of the theory.

F. Hayes-Roth and V. R. Lesser, "Focus of Attention in the HEARSAY-II Speech Understanding System," *Proceedings of IJCAI*, August 1977, pp. 27-35.

First, the paper establishes some measures to be considered in the selection and execution of KSs so as to focus the attention of the problem solver in the direction of the goal. The five measures are: 1)competition principle: best of several alternatives should be performed first, 2) validity principle: KSs operating on the most valid data must be executed first, 3) significance principle: KSs whose response frames are most important should be executed first, 4) efficiency principle: KSs which perform most reliably and inexpensively must be executed first, and 5) goal satisfaction principle: execute those KSs whose response are most likely to satisfy the goals of the system. Then, the paper describes how the focuser can direct the attention of the system towards the goals. The requirements of the focuser, and its capabilities are discussed. Results of some experiments that give the characteristics of the focuser are presented.

D. McArthur, R. Steeb, and S. Cammarata, "A Framework for Distributed Problem Solving," *Proceedings of the National Conference on Artificial Intelligence*, Pittsburg, PA, 1982, pp. 181-184.

The authors discuss briefly an application to illustrate their distributed AI problem solving approach. The application domain is air traffic control. Each plane is represented as an independent agent that cooperates to determine what its individual flying path should be. Each agent at any point has a set of instantiated tasks to perform. Tasks are scheduled to be executed based on some general scheduling rules available to each agent. Tasks are allocated some resources, namely time quantas. The stated use of this mechanism is when a suspended task is resumed (when a task runs out of its time slice), all the preconditions for the execution of the task are reexamined. The task is resumed only if it is determined that the task is still relevant. Synchronization problems are presumably taken care of by the time slice mechanism. Each task is basically a function call and the preconditions are represented as if-then rules.

S. Randall, S. Cammarata, F. A. Hayes-Roth, P. W. Thorndyke, and R. B. Wesson, "Distributed Intelligence for Air Fleet Control," R-2728-ARPA, Rand Corporation, October 1981.

Discussions are presented of various architectures for distributed processing and their relevance to air fleet control. The architectures proposed are: 1) object centered autonomous architecture where each agent independently and in parallel plans without communication e.g.. drivers of cars who manage to avoid collision with other cars, 2) object centered cooperative architecture, essentially same as above but with cooperation based on communicating plans, 3) space centered architecture based on the concept of a control tower communicating with individual air crafts and other control towers to avoid conflicts in plans, 4) function centered with respect to AFC, where one processor monitors a particular function say, takeoff and another monitors another function such as cruising at a given altitude and so on, 5) plan centered based on searching in parallel the efficacy of different plans, and 6) hierarchical architecture.

H. A. Sowizral, "Experiences With Distributed Heuristic Agents in ROSIE," *Proceedings of the International Conference on Systems, Man and Cybernetics*, Bombay-New Delhi, India, December 83-January 84, pp. 355-358.

Two approaches to model problem solving using distributed agents using ROSIE are discussed. In one, the agents talk to each other over what are termed ports. Complex string messages are constructed and sent over these ports. In the other technique, a shared database (which can be viewed as a blackboard) is used. The second approach is more flexible and supports many of the necessary (interagent) interactions.

R. Wesson, F. Hayes-Roth, J. W. Burge, C. Stasz, and C. A. Sunshine, "Network Structures for Distributed Situation Assessment," *IEEE Transactions on Systems, Man, and Cybernetics*, vol. SMC-11, no. 1, pp. 5-23, January 1981.

The authors compare and contrast committee organization with that of a hierarchical one, in the context of situation assessment tasks. Experiments were conducted first involving human subjects trying to solve a dynamic, crossword-like message puzzle task. They note that the 'anarchic' human committee organization performed much better than the hierarchical organization. The yard stick was an omniscient single expert. Machine version of the experiments involved a blackboard to model the anarchic committee. In order to minimize communication, they note that the individual KS (expert) should have knowledge about what other experts know.

Schlumberger-Doll Research
Ridgefield, CT

R. G. Smith, "Report on the 1984 Distributed Artificial Intelligence Workshop," *The AI Magazine*, Fall, 1985, pp. 234-243.

This is a collection of 10 or so abstracts on work in DAI. It contains a figure which places DAI in perspective of ongoing research in AI, and which has evolved from informal discussion at DAI workshops over the past few years.

SRI International
Menlo Park, CA

D. E. Appelt, "A Planner for Reasoning About Knowledge and Action," *Proceedings of the First Annual National Conference on Artificial Intelligence*, Stanford, CA, August 1980.

A planning system that deals with multiple agents is discussed. The KAMP (Knowledge and Modalities Planner) system extends NOAH concepts to represent knowledge of agent's beliefs.

M. Georgeff, "Communication and Interaction in Multi-Agent Planning," *Proceedings of AAAI*, August 1983, pp. 125-129.

A method is presented for decomposing single agent plans into multiagent plans by introducing communication acts in the single agent plans. Each plan is considered to be a sequence of states, and interaction and safety analysis between these is developed avoiding combinatorial explosion. This kind of planning can be used in areas like factory automation and cooperative assembly tasks.

M. P. Georgeff, "A Theory of Process," *Proceedings of the Distributed AI Workshop*, pp. 109-133, November 1985.

Georgeff presents a formal model for processes well-suited to the representation of multiple agents working concurrently. This is a highly technical paper requiring careful reading.

K. Konolige, "A First-Order Formalism of Knowledge and Action for Multi-Agent Planning," *Machine Intelligence*, vol. 10, pp. 41-73.

This paper presents a formalism (and theory) for knowledge and action. An agent must be able to intelligently perform cooperative tasks involving other agents like itself, in a complex world. Planning of actions would be a key concern of each agent and it must incorporate plans of other agents in its own plans. It uses the syntactic (versus the possible world) approach to describe the agent's beliefs of the world. First order logic is used. The paper goes into extensive detail to explain the concept, and gives several examples of planning and inference.

K. Konolige and N. J. Nilsson, "Multiple-Agent Planning Systems," *Proceedings of the First National Conference on Artificial Intelligence*, August 1980, pp. 138-142.

Refer to the above paper by the first author.

N. J. Nilsson, "Distributed Artificial Intelligence," Report, SRI International, March 25, 1981.

This author defines DAI as a network of loosely coupled AI systems. Most (complex) problems have inherent spatial distribution and can be best approached by distributing the computational resources available to solve the problem. Examples of such problems are given. Technical issues in the design of such systems are presented. The particular approach suggested to attempt these problems is based on the model of belief of an agent of the world around it, including its belief of other agents' worlds. Agents plan for themselves and effective use of this knowledge should contribute to the overall solution. The need to research these issues more thoroughly is addressed. Planning is also of interest, as it is an important part of most DAI systems. The approach to DAI presented differs from that used in HEARSAY-like systems.

R. Reboh, "Extracting Useful Advice from Conflicting Expertise," *Proceedings of the IJCAI*, 1983, pp. 144-150.

A system is described that helps users select from conflicting advice given by multiple experts. Basically, this approach allows examination of explanation of all experts and users confidence on those explanations.

S. Rosenschein, "Research on Distributed Artificial Intelligence," SRI Project Report 1350, SRI International, August 1982.

This is a collection of three papers on DAI from Rand by Rosenschein, Konolige, and Appelt.

E. D. Sacerdoti, "Planning in a Hierarchy of Abstraction Spaces," *Artificial Intelligence Journal*, vol. 5, 1974, pp. 115-135.

This paper describes the ABSTRIPS system for robot task planning. The problem domain is presented as an abstraction of spaces which has successive layers of detail of varying granularity. The system augments the power of a heuristic search process by first searching the abstraction planes before going into the detail of the search space. Examples of robot planning tasks are given.

D. E. Wilkins, Parallelism in planning and problem solving: Reasoning about resources, Technical note 258, SRI Project 8871, January 1982.

> The basic theme of this writing is that knowledge of resource contention can be used to detect parallelism in plans. The language "SIPE" briefly discussed allows declaration of objects (e.g., blocks) to be declared as resources for a particular planning activity.

Stanford University
Stanford, CA

N. Aiello and H. P. Nii, "BOWL: A Beginner's Program Using AGE," Heuristic Programming Project Report HPP-81-26, 1981.

> An example use is shown of the AGE program, the blackboard system developed at Stanford.

N. Aiello and H. P. Nii, "AGEPUFF: A Simple Event-Driven Program," Heuristic Programming Project Report HPP-81-26, 1981.

> This paper discusses another example of the use of the AGE program.

N. Aiello, "A Comparative Study of Relative Strategies for Expert Systems: AGE Implementation of Three Variations of PUFF," Heuristic Programming Project, June 1983.

> The relative effectiveness of the three problem solving strategies of AGE is explained using the PUFF expert system (diagnosis of pulmonary disease). The event-driven strategy is data driven. The model-driven strategy is based on expectations. The goal driven strategy uses back-chaining. These strategies are compared with respect to speed, accuracy, and naturalness to the expert of the results. The model driven strategy seemed to be the best and the reasons for this are summarized.

N. Aiello, "User-Directed Control of Parallelism; The CAGE System Solving," *Proceedings of Expert Systems Workshop*, Sponsored by DARPA, Pacific Grove, CA, April 16-18, 1986.

CAGE or Concurrent AGE is a blackboard based system which provides a series of switches to exploit parallelism at different levels in the specification of a knowledge source. The system is implemented using Flavors in Zetalisp. The KSs are defined as flavors and the individual rules in a KS as methods. The switches for parallelism include executing KSs in parallel, with and without synchronization, rules in parallel with/without synchronization, clauses in parallel. Evaluation of the benefits of CAGE will start with the reimplementation of CAGE on CARE, a simulation environment for multiprocessor hardware architecture.

R. Anderson, "The Complexity of Parallel Algorithms," Ph.D. Thesis, Report No. STAN-CS-86-1092, Stanford University, Stanford, CA, November 1985.

A theoretical thesis on the complexity of parallel algorithms. The author examines the class of (graph-related) problems called NC, which have fast parallel solution. Also looks at another class of algorithms termed P-Complete, which are inherently sequential and not amenable to parallel implementation. The thesis presents a variety of parallel algorithms and insight into the sequential nature of some problems. Approximation techniques for P-Complete algorithms (after the idea of approximations for NP-Complete algorithms) are also presented.

M. R. Genesereth, M. L. Ginsberg, and J. S. Rosenschein, "Solving the Prisoner's Dilemma," Heuristic Programming Project Report HPP 84-41, November 1984.

This paper presents the solution to the prisoner's dilemma problem using the metaphor of game theory. It contains a great deal of mathematical detail, and elaborates on concepts given in a previous paper (listed above).

M. R. Genesereth, M. L. Ginsberg, and J. S. Rosenschein, "Cooperation Without Communication," *Proceedings of AAAI*, Pittsburg, PA, August 1986, pp. 51-57.

This paper describes a metaphor for communication which is different from those proposed by Lesser and Corkill, and Davis and Smith. It is based on game theory. Each agent in a distributed environment works for its own selfish ends, and tries to produce better results than those of other agents working on the same problem. Interactions are minimal, and conflict is predominant. Each agent in a multiagent environment has a distinct set of goals to pursue. An example of the prisoner's dilemma is given in this context.

B. Hayes-Roth, "The Blackboard Architecture: A general framework for problem solving?," Heuristic Programming Project Report HPP-83-30, May 1983.

This paper explores the usefulness of the blackboard model. Further discussion appears in the following paper.

B. Hayes-Roth, "BB1: An Architecture for Blackboard Systems that Control, Explain, and Learn About their Own Behavior," Heuristic Programming Project, Report HPP 84-16, Stanford University, December, 1984.

BB1 is a blackboard system that has all the features of previous blackboard systems, and also explicitly incorporates, the treatment of control problem solving. The wide range of control behavior includes execution of predefined control procedures; dynamic creation and modification of complex control procedures; explanation capability; and learning new control heuristics from experience, applying them to the current problem solving session, and using them for future problem solving strategies. These capabilities are illustrated using the PROTEAN system which, given a test protein, elucidates the structure by reasoning at multiple levels of abstraction about relative locations of structures within the given constraints. In comparison to HEARSAY-III and AGE, this model is superior in its problem solving, learning, and explanation capabilities.

B. Hayes-Roth and M. Hewett, "Learning Control Heuristics in BB1," Heuristic Programming Project, Report 85-2, January 1985.

Using PROTEAN as an example domain, this paper presents learning within the BB1 blackboard framework. Built into this system is a knowledge source that learns control heuristics during the problem solving process, and later with minimal user interaction, generates a knowledge source from the learned heuristic. Thus, it claims to eliminate the important bottleneck of knowledge acquisition in expert systems.

371

B. Hayes-Roth, "A Blackboard Model of Control," *Artificial Intelligence Journal*, vol. 26, no. 3, pp 251-321, July 1985.

> This paper proposes seven behavioral goals that need to be achieved by any AI system in order to solve the control problem. Then, using a multiple-task planning example, it shows how a blackboard system achieves the behavioral goals set forth. The paper further elaborates this blackboard model of control. The blackboard is partitioned into a domain blackboard which contains domain specific information and KSs, while the control blackboard maintains the problem solving strategy using control KSs. Solution intervals and domain independent levels of abstraction which define the decision making on the domain blackboard are specified on the control blackboard. The control blackboard also contains the three basic control knowledge sources required for the problem solving activity. This work is compared to other blackboard models, namely the sophisticated scheduler, solution-based focusing, and metalevel reasoning, and is found to be better on the achievement of the behavioral goals. As with the other models, the weakness of the blackboard model of control is in the high overhead of storage and computational costs.

D. B. Lenat, "BEINGS: Knowledge as Interacting Experts," *Proceedings of the IJCAI*, September 1975, pp. 126-133.

> The author explores automatic programming in the context of distributing knowledge among a group of experts specialized in their respective domains, and interact to reach plausible solutions. Each of these experts is called a BEING. Each BEING has a uniform structure and is composed of facts and strategies designed for its speciality task, recognizes its relevance, sets up and modifies structures, and interacts effectively. An experimental system called PUP6 was developed, and is explained in this paper.

H. P. Nii and E. A. Feigenbaum, "Rule Based Understanding of Signals," *Building Expert Systems*, Waterman & Hayes-Roth, ed., Academic Press, 1978, pp. 483-501.

> This paper describes the application of a blackboard model of problem solving to build two expert systems: one for understanding continuous signals like

372

sonar (sensory) data, and the other to interpret protein x-ray crystallographic data. It incorporates data-driven and model-driven hypothesis generation. Metalevel control is available for the problem solving process.

H. P. Nii and N. Aeillo, "AGE (Attempt to Generalize): A Knowledge-Based Program for Building Knowledge-Based Programs," *Proceedings of the IJCAI*, 1979, pp. 645-655.

This paper explains the AGE system in complete detail, giving an example of an application of translating cryptograms. The implementation concepts and the use of the system are described.

H. P. Nii, E. A. Feigenbaum, J. J. Anton, and A. J. Rockmore, "Signal-to-Symbol Transformation: HASP/SIAP Case Study," *AI Magazine*, Spring 1982, pp. 23-36.

This is a later version of the above paper. SU/X and SU/P are now called HASP and SIAP, respectively.

H. P. Nii, "CAGE and POLIGON: Two frameworks for Blackboard-based Concurrent Problem Solving," *Proceedings of Expert Systems Workshop*, Sponsored by DARPA, Pacific Grove, CA, April 16-18, 1986.

Discussion on the underlying philosophical considerations for the two completely different systems being built in Stanford's knowledge systems laboratory. CAGE is a conventional blackboard system which supports parallelism at the knowledge source (KS) level. The KSs can be executed in parallel, the rules in KS can be executed in parallel or the clauses in a rule can be executed in parallel. The hardware architecture assumed by CAGE is a shared memory multiprocessor system—the number of processors in the tens to hundreds range. The POLIGON system assumes a hardware architecture which has distributed memory, multi-processor systems having thousands of processing nodes. The parallelism in POLIGON is derived from an almost dataflow like architecture where the KS are bound to the blackboard nodes and if triggered just execute; there is no explicit control through the scheduler.

H. P. Nii, "Blackboard Systems: The Blackboard Model of Problem-Solving and the Evolution of Blackboard Architectures," *AI Magazine*, vol 7, no. 2, Summer 1986. pp 39-53.

This paper traces the history of blackboard systems, and the early applications which evolved the blackboard framework to its current state. It describes briefly the HEARSAY-II and the HASP systems which pioneered the use of the blackboard paradigm of problem-solving.

H. P. Nii, "Blackboard Systems: Blackboard Application Systems, Blackboard Systems from a Knowledge Engineering Perspective," *AI Magazine*, vol 7, no. 3, Conference 1986, pp 82-106.

This paper is a continuation of the above paper. It describes some of the black-board systems like HEARSAY-II, HASP/SIAP, Crysalis, TRICERO, OPM, and ACAP. These systems are described and compared with respect to the task, the blackboard structure, the knowledge source structure, control issues, and other application and system characteristics. Also described is the knowledge engineering perspective: use of blackboard as a problem formulation tool, system development tool, and as a research tool.

J. S. Rosenschein, "Synchronization of Multi-Agent Plans," *Proceedings of the AAAI*, Pittsburg, PA, August 1982, pp. 115-119.

Smith's metaphor of negotiation is used as a means of planning for activities at local and remote nodes and achieving synchrony to accomplish these plans. The paper describes primitives of this type of communication, and the kind of knowledge needed for forming the plan (in the form of an agent's beliefs and goals, and their capabilities). An example is given.

J. S. Rosenschein and M. R. Genesereth, "Communication and Cooperation," Heuristic Programming Project, Report HPP-84-5, October 1984.

The authors discuss ways in which cooperation and communication can occur under four different sets of assumptions: 1) Under monotonic assumptions: The agents are assumed to possess correct (but possibly a subset) of the global knowledge and also some knowledge (meta) about each others knowledge. The monotonicity assumption here is that the plans derivable from whatever knowledge the agent possesses are also valid if new information becomes available. That is, new information does not invalidate any already derived plans. 2) Under nonmonotonic assumptions: Basically, the strategy for cooperation indicated is to somehow make a union of all facts which all agents possess. 3) If agents have incorrect information: Here the strategy is to identify, and then resolve, a core set of facts with which the agents disagree, 4) Utility of lying: In some cases, to minimize communication costs it may be desirable for agents to communicate information inconsistent with their database (that is, to lie) in order to achieve concurrence on a plan.

J. S. Rosenschein and V. Singh, "The Utility of Meta-Level Effort," Heuristic Programming Project, Report HPP-83-20, March 1983.

An examination is made of the metalevel cost for task allocation to multiple processors, using probabilistic derivations.

E. Schoen, "The CAOS System," *Proceedings of Expert Systems Workshop*, Sponsored by DARPA, Pacific Grove, CA, April 16-18, 1986.

CAOS is a part of an experiment at Stanford to achieve highly parallel architectures for expert systems. It is an operating system, which relies on a simulated multiprocessor hardware called CARE. The primary responsibility of CAOS is to create, control, and execute independent computing tasks, and is based on the object oriented paradigm. An application built on top of CAOS would essentially consist of a collection of communicating agents, each of which has a set of messages to which it can respond. The CAOS architecture favors course-grained problem decomposition, with minimal synchronization between processors. Unlike the blackboard paradigm, the "triggering" of agent activity is achieved only by explicit message passing. CAOS supports course-grained parallelism; fine-grained parallelism can be supported by the implementation language. Concurrency is achieved by "pipelining" and "replication". The paper describes CARE, the CAOS programming environment, runtime structure of CAOS, and an example application called ELINT.

V. Singh and M. R. Genesereth, "A Variable Supply Model for Distributing Deductions," Heuristic Programming Project Report HPP-84-14, May 1984.

The authors discuss protocols for distributing the workload for deductions in a fashion which takes into account the communication costs involved. The idea is that if the communication bandwidth is high, then a supply-driven strategy is invoked. As soon as some task is found that needs to be done, the task is broadcast to all processors and any processor that has the resources to carry out the task can grab the task. If the communication bandwidth is low, then the task is put on the network, only when some processor requests it, a strategy that is demand driven. The authors indicate that they can combine the strategies to maximize processor utilization and to minimize communication costs. The limitation is that only OR parallelism is considered.

M. Stefik, "Planning with Constraints," *Artificial Intelligence Journal*, vol. 16, 1981, pp. 111-140.

This paper describes an approach to hierarchical planning using constraints. Constraints are used for eliminating solution space, describing partial solutions, and as the communication medium between subproblems and their interactions. Constraint posting is used for hierarchical planning. Constraint operations include formulating constraints to add information, propagation of constraints to spread information, and satisfaction of constraints to instantiate variables. The main effectiveness of using constraints lies in timely formulation and propagation, so as to eliminate interfering solutions and thus to increase the efficiency of the system. All these concepts have been implemented in MOLGEN.

M. Stefik, "Planning and Meta-Planning," *Artificial Intelligence Journal*, vol. 16, 1981 pp. 141-170.

This paper describes the MOLGEN experiment as a case study of metaplanning. The problem has been structured into a hierarchy of spaces, representing different levels of problem solving. It has been emphasized that this approach to problem solving in knowledge-based systems seems to be particularly attractive, because the systems now have the capability to reason about their own reasoning processes. The implementation of meta-planning and planning in MOLGEN is described. Also, work in related concept areas like HEARSAY-II, SU-X and SU-P, Hayes-Roths' model of planning, TEIRESIAS, and GPS is compared.

SUNY at Stony Brook
Stony Brook, NY

D. S. Warren, M. Ahamad, S. K. Debray, and L. V. Kale, "Executing Distributed Prolog Programs on a Broadcast Network," *Logic Programming*, 1984, pp. 12-21.

> This paper proposes an algorithm to execute distributed Prolog programs that query distributed databases. The communication is done over a broadcast network. It exploits the OR parallelism inherent in Prolog programs. The properties of the algorithm are explained by using an example query.

System Development Corporation
Paoli, PA

B. G. McDaniel, "Issues in Distributed Artificial Intelligence," *Proceedings of the IEEE First International Conference on Data Engineering*, 1984, pp. 293-297.

> This is a brief paper presenting some DAI issues, accompanied by an example involving two hospitals cooperating (and competing) to provide patient care.

Teknowledge Inc.
Palo Alto, CA

L. D. Erman, J. S. Lark, and F. Hayes-Roth, "Engineering Intelligent Systems: Progress Report on ABE," *Proceedings of Expert Systems Workshop*, Sponsored by DARPA, pp. 89-100, Pacific Grove, CA, April 16-18, 1986.

> This report describes the new object oriented environment developed by Teknowledge to address integration issues. The environment supports among other things a blackboard model for problem solving, a dataflow model, black boxes (procedures), MRS interface, PROLOG interface, KRS interface (KNOBS system), and has some specific planning shells on top of which applications can be mounted. The paper briefly discusses a mission planning application.

377

Universidade Nova de Lisboa
Lisbon, Portugal

L. Monteiro, "A Proposal for Distributed Programming in Logic," *Implementations of Prolog*, ed. Campbell, J. A., John Wiley & Sons, 1984, pp. 329- 340.

> Prolog, or Horn Clause Logic, is extended to include the concept of parallel processing and co-routine executions. Interprocess communication is based on ' interface predicates' which is introduced in 'events' and 'traces' (sequence of events). The declarative and operational semantics of the language for distributed logic are introduced. The concept of events can be extended to write programs or modules which, in turn, contain submodules that can be executed in parallel on distinct machines.

University of California
Irvine, CA

J. S. Conery and D. F. Kibler, "AND Parallelism in Logic Programs," *Proceedings of the IJCAI*, 1983, pp. 539-543.

> Refer to the paper by the same authors, listed under University of Oregon.

D. F. Kibler and J. Conery, "Parallelism in AI Programs," *Proceedings of the Ninth IJCAI*, Los Angeles, CA, August 1985, pp. 53-56.

> The authors here argue that, contrary to the pervasive pessimistic attitude currently prevalent, the use of parallel processing would provide significant increases in AI program processing.

University of California
Los Alamos National Laboratory, NM

J. H. Fasel, R. J. Douglass, R. Michelsen, and P. Hudak, "A Distributed Implementation of Functional Program Evaluation," *Proceedings of the First Annual AI and Advanced Computer Technology Conference*, Long Beach, CA, May 1985, pp. 306-315.

> The authors discuss a functional model called Distributed Applicative Processing Systems (DAPS). This is a graph reduction approach to exploiting parallelism. They define a 'serial combinator' as a block of code that has no inherent parallelism in it and is also not a subset of any other serial combinator. For this approach to be feasible, the granularity of programs distributed on different processors should be at the level of a serial combinator in order to minimize communication overhead.

University of California
Los Angeles, CA

J. J. Helly, Jr., W. V. Bates, M. Cutler, and S. Kelem, "A Representational Basis for the Development of a Distributed Expert System for Space Shuttle Flight Control," NASA Technical Memorandum 58258, May 1984.

> A Boolean representation for specifying production rules for a system that controls Space Shuttle Flight is presented. The motivation behind the representation is that it easily lends itself to hardware realization. An implication that the representation has on a distributed expert system design is briefly presented in the end.

J. Pearl, "Reverend Bayes on Inference Engines: A Distributed Hierarchical Approach," *Proceedings of National Conference on AI*, August 1982, pp. 133-136.

> This paper presents a method of asynchronously propagating certainty factors up and down a hierarchical structure.

University of Florida
Gainsville, FL

S. Chen, "On intelligent CAD systems for VLSI design", *IEEE International Conference on Computer Design: VLSI in Computers*, 1983, pp. 405-408.

> This brief paper proposes that a distributed expert system approach may be useful in building a CAD system for VLSI design.

University of Houston
TX

S. N. Rajaram, "Design of Intelligent Systems with Cooperating Knowledge Based Components," *IEEE Computer Society Proceedings of Trends and Applications*, 1983 pp. 135-141.

> The author discusses some motivations for building cooperating expert systems, with each expert component working on a subproblem of a larger problem. This paper describes two design scenarios: one for analysis of satellite data, and the other for intelligent robot control using sensory feedback with model registration.

University of Illinois
Chicago, IL

S. M. Shatz, "Communication Mechanisms for Programming Distributed Systems," *IEEE Computer*, June 1984, pp. 21-28.

> A survey is presented of communication protocols for distributed computing. The paper gives pros and cons of asynchronous and synchronous communication. Examples using ADA are included.

University of Illinois
Urbana, IL

J. S. Greenstein and W. B. Rouse, "A Model of Human Decisionmaking in Multiple Process Monitoring Situations," *IEEE Transactions on Systems, Man, and Cybernetics*, vol. SMC-12, no. 2, March/April 1982, pp. 182-193.

> This paper presents a model of human decision-making in a multiprocess environment. It shows how a monitoring task can be automated, especially when actions are to be performed during the monitoring. It contains some experimental results and analysis of these with reference to the proposed model.

University of Kansas
Lawrence, KA

G. Veach, "An annotated bibliography of systems and theory for distributed artificial intelligence," University of Kansas Technical Report No. TR-86-16, Computer Science Department.

> This report is a DAI bibliography similar to this one. However, it is not quite extensive as this one. It does have a few entries we have not included in this bibliography.

University of Maryland
College Park, MD

S. Kasif, M. Kohli, and J. Minker, "Prism: A Parallel Inference System for Problem Solving," *Proceedings of IJCAI*, 1983, pp. 544-546.

> A discussion is given of a system that can exploit the AND/OR parallelism in logic programs. The strategy is to provide additional control information on the order in which clauses can be resolved, in parallel or not.

B. A. Lambird, D. Lavine, and L. N. Kanal, "Distributed Architecture and Parallel Non-Directional Search for Knowledge-Based Cartographic Feature Extraction Systems," *International Journal of Man-Machine Studies*, vol. 20, 1984, pp. 107-120.

381

This paper describes how the problem of understanding cartographic images obtained through a variety of sensors can be approached using a distributed expert system standpoint. It draws on the hierarchy of specialists theme proposed by Chandrasekaran et al. and work done at the University of Maryland on theoretical parallel algorithms for branch-and-bound search.

C. Rieger and S. Small, "Towards a Theory of Distributed Word Expert Natural Language Parsing," *IEEE Transactions on Systems, Man, and Cybernetics*, vol. SMC- 11, no. 1, January 1981, pp. 43-51.

The concept of cooperating word experts in understanding natural language is presented. This paper is related to the one by Small and Rieger, discussed below.

S. Small and C. Rieger, "Parsing and Comprehending with Word Experts (A Theory and its Realization)," *Strategies for Natural Language Processing*, edited by Lehnert, W. G., and Ringle, M. H, Hillsdale, NJ, 1982, pp. 89-147.

The authors discuss a radically different view for implementing natural language processing, at least from the linguistic point of view. The work, however, bears some resemblance to the HEARSAY-II approach. The language comprehension problem is attacked with the approach of each word in the language being an individual knowledge source or expert, which cooperates with other word experts to determine the meaning of a given sentence. There is the notion of active, inactive, and reactible experts as parsing of the sentence is executed. Communication is by the use of messages.

University of Massachusetts
Amherst, MA

N. F. Carver, V. R. Lesser, and D. L. McCue, "Focusing in Plan Recognition," *Proceedings of the AAAI*, 1984, pp. 42-48.

Presents a plan recognition architecture (blackboard based) which uses application-specific heuristics to focus on a small set of plans from a possibly large set of competing and cooperating interpretations. It also features explanation. The heuristics which constrain the search deal with the relative likelihood of alternative plans, the likelihood that plan steps are shared, and the likelihood of continuing an existing plan versus starting a new one. This system is a part of POISE, an intelligent user interface system.

D. D. Corkill, "Hierarchical Planning in a Distributed Environment," *Proceedings of IJCAI*, Tokyo, Japan, August 1979, pp. 168-175.

Distributed planning control using NOAH [Sacerdoti] as a framework to formulate the problem is described . The paper gives examples of planning from the blocks world domain. The main thrust in this paper is on decentralized planning in a distributed environment, mainly because of high communication costs and localized information (available to each processor).

D. D. Corkill, V. R. Lesser, and E. Hudlicka, "Unifying Data-Directed and Goal-Directed Control: An Example and Experiments," *Proceedings of the AAAI*, Pittsburg, PA, August 1982, pp. 143-147.

This paper describes how data-directed and goal directed control can be used to develop a wide range of scheduling and planning strategies for KS activities in a blackboard based system. Multilevel KS cooperation is increased by adding an additional goal blackboard to the HEARSAY-II domain blackboard. The HEARSAY-II system has a distinct disadvantage in that scheduling is instantaneous and the system has no capability to look beyond the immediate state of the database. The goal blackboard is used to focus on such activities. Events on the blackboard get related to the goals of the problem solver which, in turn, will cause appropriate KS execution to achieve these goals. Thus, a planning component is also added that can respond to the development of plans to achieve the goals. Thus, sophisticated scheduling is possible. A distributed vehicle monitoring experiment is described, which is built around these concepts.

D. D. Corkill and V. R. Lesser, "The Use of Meta-Level Control for Coordination in a Distributed Problem Solving Network," *Proceedings of the IJCAI*, 1983, pp. 748-756.

This paper presents a distributed problem solving methodology in a networked environment using meta-level control for the coordination of problem solving strategy, and thus achieve coherence amongst the nodes. Each node makes local (decentralized) decisions about its activity, influenced by the activities of the other nodes. This concept is presented using the paradigm of network organizational structure that specifies in some way the control of information and relationships between nodes. The major emphasis is on more local activity and minimal communication between nodes so as to reduce system overhead, and control misallocation of activities. Also significant is the degradation of the system in the presence of faults. To obtain a balance between the problem solving activity and coordination, the network organizational structure is used to guide the experimentation of the distributed vehicle monitoring testbed. Results of several experiments using different system configuration are given.

D. D. Corkill, K. Q. Gallagher and K. E. Murray, "GBB: A Generic Blackboard Development System," *Proceedings of AAAI*, Pittsburg, PA, August 1986, pp 1008-1014.

Drawn from experiences with blackboard systems, this paper describes a system for developing efficient blackboard database kernel with primitives for inserting and retrieving blackboard objects, and a control shell to generate a complete application system. The emphasis in GBB is on performance and flexibility because most real blackboard applications deal with thousands of blackboard objects. The paper discusses the blackboard database support and pattern matching capabilities of GBB.

E. H. Durfee and V. R. Lesser, "Incremental Planning to Control a Blackboard Based Problem Solver," *Proceedings of AAAI*, Pittsburg, PA, August 1986, pp 58-64.

This paper discusses the effect of control on the problem-solver's actions within the distributed vehicle monitoring system. The planner which is capable of recognizing the current state if the problem solving should choose goals which would best meet the system objectives. The planner plans sequences of actions which would help resolve uncertainty about possible solutions, and plan incrementally by monitoring and correcting current plans. Results of experiments are presented. Some benefits of these mechanisms are ability of problem-solver to work under real-time constraints, and enhance the cooperation in a network of problem-solvers.

A. R. Hanson and E. M. Riseman, "VISIONS: A computer system for interpreting scenes," University of Massachusetts, Report.

This paper uses the HEARSAY-II model of blackboard and knowledge sources for the scene interpretation problem. The complexity of the system is comparable to the speech understanding system attempted by HEARSAY-II. Scene interpretation is done by model building. The four major components to model building are representation at multiple levels of abstraction for image specific short term memory and long term general knowledge, processes of knowledge sources which work at these different levels, control strategies to guide the problem-solver, and a model search space. KS instantiations generate hypotheses, which may be bottom-up or top-down.

V. R. Lesser and L. D. Erman, "An Experiment in Distributed Interpretation," *Proceedings of the First International Conference on Distributed Computing Systems*, Huntsville, Alabama, October 1979, pp. 553-571.

The HEARSAY-II system is decomposed to test distributed problem solving techniques. Although it was originally developed as a speech understanding system, HEARSAY-II embodies a structure that lends itself well to such experimentation. The requirements for an effective operation within a distributed environment include sufficiency of knowledge so as to unable generation of plausible solution(s); sufficiency of credibility evaluation to weigh the partial solutions according to their impact on the problem solving task; and sufficiency of control strategy to direct maximum resources that lead to desired solution(s). The issues that are considered in a distributed environment relate to information on the blackboard, processing capabilities of KSs, and control. Various strategies for each of these aspects are discussed. Also analyzed are the various distributed strategies of the HEARSAY-II system like intranode, network, and internode communication. Of these, the last one seemed most attractive to the authors, and a simulation using a three-node HEARSAY-II system was performed. Each node has its own (blackboard) information which implicitly defines its area of interest, with transmission of its hypotheses to a local subset of nodes. Each node has a subset of KSs, which are activated only by the events on the local blackboard. Thus, control is also decentralized, and each node does its own scheduling depending on its

local information. The very encouraging results of the network versus centralized approach are discussed, the details of the simulation and implications
to various issues in distributed problem solving are presented well.

V. R. Lesser and L. D. Erman, "Distributed Interpretation: A Model and Experiment,"
IEEE Transactions on Computers, vol. C-29, no. 1, December, 1980, pp. 1144-1163.

The previously discussed paper is an expanded version of this one.

V. R. Lesser, S. Reed, and J. Pavlin, "Quantifying and Simulating the Behavior of
Knowledge-Based Interpretation Systems," *Proceedings of the AAAI*, 1980, pp.   111-
115.

This paper attempts to provide a methodology to measure behavior of HEARSAY-
like systems where the solution to a problem is built up incrementally, with
opportunistic problem solving. It proposes that the belief in a higher-level
hypothesis depends upon the belief and consistency of the lower-level supporting hypothesis. A measure of system reliability comes from the certainty
and accuracy of the system knowledge base during the process of problem
solving, that, in turn, depends upon the "goodness" of the knowledge sources
at that time in the problem solving cycle. The paper explains simulations
done for measuring the accuracy and reliability of KSs and scheduler.

V. R. Lesser and D. D. Corkill, "Functionally Accurate, Cooperative Distributed Systems," *IEEE Transactions on Systems, Man, and Cybernetics*, vol. SMC-11, no.   1,
1981, pp. 81-96.

Due to the increased demand for distributed problem solving capability in AI
systems, this paper proposes the concept of functionally accurate, cooperative
distributed systems (FA/C). It distinguishes these from the traditional distributed systems in that each node is capable of producing some results, even
in in the presence of incomplete and possibly inconsistent information towards
a single system goal. Some of these results may be incomplete, inconsistent,
and even incorrect. Cooperation between nodes is critical in the synthesis of
intermediate solutions. Hence, these systems have the inherent capability to
deal with uncertainty. The processor nodes are loosely coupled in that more

386

time is spent on computation than on communication. Experiments are presented in FA/C systems including HEARSAY-II type of hypothesis and test systems, distributed planning systems, and iterative refinement control systems. This work is compared with organizational theory and relevant issues in distributed problem solving are discussed.

V. R. Lesser and D. D. Corkill, "The Distributed Vehicle Monitoring Testbed: A Tool for Investigating Distributed Problem Solving Networks," *AI Magazine*, Fall 1983, pp. 15-33.

This paper describes the experimentation of distributed problem solving techniques using the vehicle-monitoring task with information collected by a geographically distributed network of sensor nodes. This paper details the concept of distributed processing versus distributed problem solving, other work in the domain of distributed problem solving, its uses, and a pilot experiment to further illustrate the features and potential of such techniques to AI research in general.

J. Pavlin, "Predicting the Performance of Distributed Knowledge Based Systems: A Modeling Approach," Computer and Information Science Dept., University of Amherst, December 1984.

In order to control complex knowledge based systems, it is important to analyze the relation between its environment, system structure and the performance. The paper describes a model of a distributed knowledge based system, with interactions among knowledge sources and the relationship between nodes. A petri-net representation is used to model the basic concepts which include activities, domains and data units. As an example, the paper uses the communication strategies used in the Distributed Vehicle Monitoring Testbed.

University of New South Wales
Kensington, Australia

M. J. Wise, "Epilog: Re-Interpreting and Extending Prolog for a Multiprocessor Environment," *Implementations of Prolog*, Ellis Horwood Ltd, pp. 341-351.

This discussion of Epilog, a parallel form of Prolog, includes example constructs, i.e., p :- a → [b, c] → d which is interpreted as execute 'a' and if it succeeds, execute in parallel 'b' and 'c'; and, if they both return true, then execute 'd'. This construct called 'CAND' allows one to exploit 'AND' parallelism. The symbol '→' works more or less like the following Prolog statements:

```
        p :- q ! r
        p :- ...
```
can be represented as:
```
        p :- p1 || p2
        p1 :- q -> r
        p2 :- ...
```

University of Oregon
Eugene, OR

J. S. Conery and D. F. Kibler, "AND Parallelism and Nondeterminism in Logic Programs," *New Generation Computing*, no. 3, 1985, pp. 43-70.

A methodology to exploit AND parallelism in logic programs is discussed. The basic idea is that if a clause such as $p(X) \uparrow q(Y) \uparrow r(Z)$ needs to be solved, and there are, say, two ground clauses C1 and C2 which match X, then the two values for X can be pursued in parallel. The authors explore different scenarios in which the variables are shared, thus forcing some sequential execution. The mechanism adopted is to identify those clauses that act as generators of values for variables (that is, after their execution, the variables get instantiated) and those that act as consumers of the instantiated variables. A dataflow graph of the variables being generated and consumed is used to drive the parallel execution and backtracking when necessary. All processes can be in a blocked, pending, or solved state. State transitions are effected on message- based communication.

University of South Carolina

Columbia, SC

M. N. Huhns, L. M. Stephens, and R. D. Bonnell, "Control and Cooperation in Distributed Expert Systems," *Proceedings of IEEE Southeastcon*, April 1983, pp. 241-245.

This paper explains a methodology for communication between multiple experts using meta level control primitives. Each node in the distributed problem solving environment has a blackboard which has metaknowledge about the questions and answers broadcasted over the network in the form of values for question difficulty, question importance, and answer confidence. This is a brief paper.

Vanderbilt University

Nashville, TN

J. Sztipanovits and J. Bourne, "Design of Intelligent Instrumentation," *First Conference on Artificial Intelligence Applications*, December 1984, pp. 490-495.

The authors discuss architectural requirements in building a real-time instrumentation system. The approach proposed consists of an architecture of four layers : 1) knowledge-base, 2) module, 3) system, and 4) physical. The knowledge-base layer involves a cooperating system of experts who communicate over a real-time blackboard. This layer is to be built using LISP. The module layer, is based on a data-flow machine architecture. The idea is that in order to get real time performance, parallelism should be exploited in the knowledge-base layer (possibly using concurrent LISP) and in the lower-level layers (using data-flow machines).

Weizmann Institute of Science

Israel

E. Shapiro and A. Takeuchi, "Object Oriented Programming in Concurrent Prolog," *New Generation of Computing*, vol. 1, 1983, pp. 25-48.

389

This paper is an attempt to provide the functionality of object-oriented programming in a Concurrent Prolog environment. In a Prolog construct of the form A :- B1,...,Bn is interpreted in a variety of fashions: 1) A is true if B1 and ... are true; 2) procedural interpretation; and 3) process interpretation (here the form can be thought of as objects). Communication to objects is via the instantiation of shared variables. Some variables are declared as read-only variables. If read-only variables cannot be instantiated, the process suspends itself. The authors define several primitives to facilitate the object-oriented programming. These include guard clauses (acts somewhat like triggers in frames), of objects, and a mechanism to deal with 'incomplete messages'. An incomplete message is one in which there are uninstantiated variables.

Xerox Palo Alto Research Center
Palo Alto, CA

J. de Kleer, "An Assumption-Based TMS," *Artificial Intelligence Journal*, vol. 28, no. 2, March 1986, pp. 127-162.

This paper presents a new approach to truth-maintenance systems. Besides manipulating justifications, the system also manages assumption sets. The author gives the limitations of the traditional TMS and identifies what needs to be incorporated to extend it. The concept of contexts is introduced within this framework to assist in nonmonotonic reasoning. Three important properties of an Assumption-based TMS (ATMS) are relevancy, no-irrelevancy, and parsimony. The reasons for their importance are given. The paper also includes a discussion of the mathematical background behind the ATMS, and explains the important considerations, accompanied by examples. A language for ATMS is presented, and gives implementation details. This work is compared to similar work by Doyle, McDermott, and others.

V. Jagannathan and Rajendra Dodhiawala
Boeing Advanced Technology Center for Computer Sciences
Seattle, WA

390